The Sounds of Place

Advisor in music to Northeastern University Press
GUNTHER SCHULLER

THE SOUNDS
OF PLACE

*Music and the American
Cultural Landscape*

DENISE VON GLAHN

Northeastern University Press
BOSTON

Northeastern University Press

Library of Congress Cataloging-in-Publication Data
Von Glahn, Denise, [date]
The sounds of place : music and the American cultural landscape /
Denise Von Glahn.
p. cm.
Includes bibliographical references (p.   ) and index.
ISBN 1-55553-583-6 (alk. paper)
1. Music and geography—United States. 2. Music—United States—20th
century—History and criticism. 3. Composers—United States. 4. Nature
in music. I. Title.
ML200.5.V65 2003
780′ .92′273—dc21   2003010690

Designed by Dean Bornstein

Composed in Adobe Garamond by Coghill Composition, Richmond, Virginia. Printed and bound by Sheridan Books, Ann Arbor, Michigan. The paper is House Natural, an acid-free stock.

MANUFACTURED IN THE UNITED STATES OF AMERICA
07   06   05   04   03   5   4   3   2   1

for
my sons

Haynes and Evan

ACKNOWLEDGMENTS

As all scholars appreciate, little work is accomplished without the help of family, friends, colleagues, and one's home institution, and I am no different. In the earliest stages of this project, The Florida State University awarded me a First Year Faculty Summer Research Grant. This support allowed me to carry out essential background research. Additionally, the School of Music granted me a semester's research leave. I am grateful to Dean Jon Piersol for his understanding that without time completely free of university responsibilities, it is unlikely the book would have come to fruition when it did. My colleagues in the Musicology Division are nurturing and sustaining. I am indebted to Charles Brewer, Andrew Killick, Douglass Seaton, and most especially Jeffery Kite-Powell, who regularly provides a model of what a division chair can be. My graduate assistants Amy Keyser, Deborah Olander, Lincoln Ballard, and Patrick Nolan chased down details and citations, and in the process saved me months of work. Doctoral students Laura Moore Pruett and Sarah Meredith regularly shared my excitement over a new discovery, and Akihiro Taniguchi created digitized recordings of music for me to consult where none had previously existed. In direct and indirect ways my students have energized this work.

Librarians, both at my home institution and across the nation, provided essential help in locating and consulting materials. At Florida State I am grateful to the head music librarian, Dan Clark, as well as to Mark Frohlich, Gary Markham, Don Fortner, and Sarah Hess Cohen, all of whom, at some point or other, made my project their own. Jeffrey Barr, curator of rare books at Smathers Library, University of Florida, provided essential help in locating graphics. At the New York Public Library, I, like so many other scholars of American music history, am indebted to George Boziwick; at the Library of Congress to Wayne Shirley; at Yale University to Ken Crilly and Suzanne Eggleston; and at the Free Library of Philadelphia to Kile Smith. Kevin Kelly of the University of Georgia's music library shared ideas regarding pieces that focus on the city place. Joyce Henri Robinson, curator at the Palmer Museum of The Pennsylvania State University, was generous with her time and expertise, as were numerous librarians at that university. Individual faculty at Penn State also offered assistance; in particular, Stanley Weintraub directed me to sources, both literary and personal, that altered the course of my research. Among them was the Hudson River School collector Elliot Vesell, who shared his expertise, enthusiasm, and collection, and put me in touch with other resources.

I am indebted to the engraving expertise of Tom Brodhead and Peter Pohorence, neither of whom lost patience with my many inquiries. At Northeastern University Press, William Frohlich, recently retired director and editor in chief, showed faith in this project when others might have been less believing, and Ann Twombly invested a degree of care in its production that most writers only dream of. I sincerely appreciate all their efforts.

Over the past few years a host of musical Americanists have taken the time to discuss ideas of music and place with me, and many have read through individual chapters. I am grateful for the insights, suggestions, and encouragement of Jonathan Bernard, J. Peter Burkholder, James Farrington, Stuart Feder, Wiley Hitchcock, Wiley Housewright, William Kennedy, Tammy Kernodle, Beth Levy, Vivian Perlis, Howard Pollack, Catherine Parsons Smith, Larry Starr, and Judith Tick.

Many of the composers treated in this study agreed to be interviewed. I appreciate the afternoon I spent with Robert Starer, the hours of meetings and numerous e-mail exchanges with Dana Paul Perna, an ongoing series of conversations with Ellen Taaffe Zwilich, and a phone interview with Steve Reich that he sandwiched between rehearsals of his latest work. His energy and passion for what he does were palpable even over fiber-optic cable. Judith Anne Still spoke with me at length multiple times about her father and his music, and she provided essential resources.

On more than one occasion, I have benefited from the generosity of complete strangers. In an attempt to ascertain whether Edgard Varèse would have had the opportunity to hear modern fire sirens in 1918 New York, Kevin O'Connell, a California collector of sirens and author of books on emergency vehicles, spent several hours explaining the history of emergency signals and sirens. Another gentleman, Dr. Robert Blake, having heard of this project secondhand from a family member, sent me a newspaper article that discussed Dana Paul Perna and *Three Places on Long Island.* Blake's completely unexpected mailing led to an interview with the composer and a discussion of his works in this book.

Given the enthusiasm expressed by so many colleagues for this project, it is with sadness and frustration that I ultimately had to delete numerous musical examples from the text. Multiple attempts to secure permission to reproduce brief excerpts of music by Edgard Varèse, Ferde Grofé, and Roy Harris went unanswered. Beyond wasting months of time and delaying production, the greater frustration is the realization of the power that publishers and rights holders have to determine what gets studied and, in a very real sense, how histories get written. I regret the omission of works that readers should have been able to consult.

Throughout the entire process, I have been bolstered by friends and family. Sherry Williams and Kathy Strickland have cheered me from the sidelines for as long as I have known them. Regardless of my endeavors, they have always been confident, even when I have not been. The value of their friendship cannot be measured. My parents, William and Lorraine Von Glahn, and my sisters, Carol and Janet, are my very own pep squad. Not understanding fully why I would choose to pursue such a project, they never questioned my commitment or its worth. My cousin Gary Roth, a former curator of President Theodore Roosevelt's summer White House, Sagamore Hill, shared his insights into the meaning of this once-famous retreat. My aunt and uncle, Ellie and George Smith, regularly took me to operas, ballets, and concerts when I was young. They filled my world with music of all kinds. It was with them that I first heard Ella Fitzgerald, Van Cliburn, and Joan Sutherland. It is my good fortune to have been born into this family.

Final thanks go to those who have lived with this project in an ongoing, immediate, and personal way. My husband, Michael Broyles, is my friend, collaborator, anchor, and steady source of emotional and intellectual support. Over the course of this project he has commented upon numerous drafts, and he never balked when I needed to talk through an idea one more time. He provided expert technical support, accompanied me as I tracked down sources and composers, encouraged me when I was overwhelmed with the task I had taken on, and through it all kept me laughing. He has the remarkable gift of hearing me even when I don't speak. In every sense of the word, he is my best reader. And lastly, my sons, Haynes and Evan, deserve a special kind of thanks. As young boys they opened my eyes and mind to new ways of seeing and thinking; their candor and curiosity were an endless source of surprise and inspiration. As adults they are thoughtful, caring, creative human beings; their love has been a source of sustenance and amazement. By simply being themselves, they have taught me so much. As children do for lucky parents everywhere, my children have helped me find my place. This book is for them.

CONTENTS

ILLUSTRATIONS

Introduction: A Place to Start

But it is in and by places that the most lasting and ramified connections, including personal connections, are to be made.
— EDWARD S. CASEY, *The Fate of Place: A Philosophical History*

Inspiration for books comes from myriad sources. In my own case, something more than intellectual curiosity and professional advancement excited the project; in a very personal way, *The Sounds of Place* became the book I had to write. Driving west on state route 34 after a week of research at Yale University's Beinecke Library, I headed toward Danbury, Connecticut. Having just combed through folders and boxes of Charles Ives's scores, papers and memorabilia, I wanted to see the environs that had nurtured the composer, the house where he had lived, the village green where his father's bands had marched. But as the Housatonic River emerged first on the left and then on the right side of the road, a curious sensation overtook me. I had spent years reading about Danbury's favorite son, yet no amount of study could explain the sensation of familiarity that I experienced. Without any recollection of having been here before, I recognized a particular white frame house that I passed, and a rock wall that hugged the road. I knew that view of the water. It was comforting, exhilarating, and unnerving.

Not until a phone conversation weeks later did I understand the significance of what had occurred. I learned that during the summers between my first and fourth years, my family had vacationed in just that part of Connecticut. We'd stayed in the area at a boardinghouse owned by a distant relative, and I had played in the Housatonic. The house I'd passed, the river, and the rock wall were familiar to me because I had been there and traveled that road, and unconsciously soaked up the place. Although I had been born in the city, I was also a child of the Connecticut countryside. The place had imprinted itself on my four-year-old's memory. How much more powerful must have been Ives's connections to the place where he had spent his entire youth: his orchestral set *Three Places in New England,* which I had been researching that same week, took on new meaning. The seeds of a book that explored the connections between places and music were firmly planted. What started as an exploration of Ives's music and its relation to American places grew to a study of fourteen composers and how their American "place pieces" reflected a changing nation. At a more basic level, it became a study of finding one's own place.

My observations regarding the power of place were, of course, not unique. The idea has gripped the imaginations of thinkers since the beginning of recorded time. Plato, Aristotle, Descartes, Locke, Newton, Kant, Whitehead, and Foucault have all pondered the meaning and significance of place. Place is one way we organize our experiences and order our memories. A sense of place, along with a sense of time, helps form our identity; together they are fundamental to a healthy mental life.[1] This is true of individuals, groups of people, and nations. In addition to locating us in the cosmos, place tells us who we are. In the case of nations, the ways in which people view their places says much about their shared values—the evanescent ones and the enduring ones. What do musical commemorations of place tell us? This book assumes that the title of a piece, when chosen by a composer, is part of the composer's work and the listener's experience. In including the name of a place in the title, the composer encourages an association. This may vary from documentary-like correspondences of place and sound to the most impressionistic of relationships. *Sounds of Place* is premised upon the belief that places can inspire art, and that musical responses can, at some level, evoke those places.

Place weaves itself into our lives in the most intimate ways; it determines the food we eat, the clothes we wear, our occupations, diversions, sleep habits, mobility, sense of history, awareness of nature, tolerance for noise and distractions, feelings of security and identification. In a very real sense, place creates us. Place also acts as the backdrop for our most treasured stories about ourselves. It is a part of every experience. While place has affected all peoples and cultures throughout history, in modern times it has played an especially significant role in shaping America's development, values, and identity. The impact of place in this country might not be unique, but it has enjoyed a central position in discussions of American character since the beginning of the union. Whether New World settlers sought religious freedom, commercial advancement, escape, or adventure, America promised a vast place in which to realize dreams.

Writers and artists have responded to their environs for centuries and, in the process, communicated essential values of their cultures. As Robert Hughes demonstrated in his book *American Visions: The Epic History of Art in America,* three hundred years of painted, photographed, sculpted, built, and drawn images create persuasive narratives.[2] But powerful artistic responses to one's place are not confined to what can be seen on the canvas or read on the page. Music captures places as well. Where painters remember a landscape for its light and shade, the ways in which colors and shapes animate images, composers hear the rhythms and timbres of a place and recall it in sound. Although sonic images may be more fleeting than painted or sculpted ones, and less specific than prose descriptions, they are no less eloquent or evocative; their commentary is no less poignant. Some might even argue that their lack of material form imbues them with greater profundity.

But music in the United States of America developed differently from its artistic cousins. By the 1820s Washington Irving (1783–1859) and James Fenimore Cooper (1789–1851) had secured the attention of the European literati for America and given the nation its first mythical heroes. A generation later, Ralph Waldo Emerson (1803–82), Edgar Allan Poe (1809–49), and then Henry David Thoreau (1817–62), Walt Whitman (1819–92), and Herman Melville (1819–91) spoke with a recognizably American accent. American literature had a native voice that was acknowledged at home and abroad. And American artists benefited from their close ties with literary colleagues. Cooper was close to the painter Thomas Cole (1801–48), who was also a personal friend of the poet and editor William Cullen Bryant (1794–1878). Both writers championed the efforts of their artistic ally. Another painter celebrated the unanimity of the literary and visual arts: Asher B. Durand (1796–1886), a student of Thomas Cole, captured his teacher and Bryant in 1849 in one of his most famous works, *Kindred Spirits.* Here the two men are pictured standing on a rocky ledge overlooking a pristine wilderness. Protected by an arching tree, the friends look out on mountains, water, and sky. The message is clear: such a setting not only brings man closer to nature (and God as revealed in nature), but also brings man closer to his fellow man. Nature is a source of consensus. America's vastness could unite its citizens with each other and with a higher being.

While nineteenth-century literary, visual, and musical arts all endured comparisons with their better-established European counterparts, American music benefited neither from a critical mass of practitioners—nowhere equal to the number of artists who were eventually crowded under the banner of the Hudson River School, or of thinkers who collectively identified with Transcendentalism—nor from a set of compositional conventions equivalent to the Claudian ones that had guided both painters and viewers in the most general of ways.[3] Although Hudson River School artists displayed relatively individual styles and painted a vast range of scenes—including vistas in Maine, New York, Pennsylvania, the Far West, Mexico, and South America—they shared a common understanding of the natural place and its importance to America, which was nurtured and buoyed by their own intense communalism.

Artistic communalism was aided in no small way by the Tenth Street Studio Building, which provided professional space for artists in New York City beginning in the middle of the nineteenth century.[4] Annette Blaugrund compared the camaraderie and "contagious communal . . . spirit" found at the Tenth Street Building with other more formalized utopian communities found in America in the first half of the nineteenth century.[5] The Studio Building opened in January 1858 and provided working and personal space for twenty-three of the most active artists and writers of the day.[6] It became a destination for painters and patrons alike.

Beyond the support of proximate colleagues, artists enjoyed the encouragement and endorsement of influential scientists, philosophers, religious thinkers, and writers who actively promoted romantic renderings of the American landscape, another kind of nurture not given to American musicians. A few writers also occupied studios in the Tenth Street Building, Henry T. Tuckerman and Theodore Winthrop among them. Winthrop's lofty prose mirrored the elevating vistas of the Hudson River School painters. The writers became willing partners in the marketing of an American school of art that presented a relatively unified vision of the value of America and its places.[7] As Blaugrund concluded: "For the United States, a country intent on elevating its cultural standards and advancing its economic status in the world at this time, an altruistic communal spirit was a means of creating a national school of art and developing a class of art patrons."[8]

American composers, however, enjoyed no such affirming Greek chorus. Composers were few in number, those consciously seeking to develop a representative, national voice even fewer, and their champions nearly nonexistent.[9] In the early years of the nation, there was little spirit of communalism to nurture American music. There was no physical environment dedicated to the needs of American composers comparable to the Tenth Street Studio Building, although performance venues were available and increasing in number. Mid-nineteenth-century painters were lionized by eager patrons who attended receptions and bought hundreds of paintings. They also enjoyed numerous opportunities for employment with the government and railroad, mining, and agricultural industries alike to record and advertise the burgeoning nation. Their creations had real and tangible commercial value to large numbers of people. There were no similar opportunities for musicians to create music associated with grand, national projects; there were no incentives to record the sounds of the American place.[10] What opportunities existed were often tied to small businesses that wanted catchy songs to advertise particular products or to celebrate the opening of a new bank. There was no single goal motivating all composers to develop an American high-art music, no overarching philosophy or point of view to unite their efforts.

It would appear that for the first three quarters of the nineteenth century, music was generally regarded as a less effective tool than the visual or literary arts for *national* expression and promotion, although this opinion was not necessarily held by composers themselves, as the first chapter of this book will demonstrate. One could read music's separation in the most positive of lights and conclude that American composers enjoyed a degree of freedom and autonomy that was denied to their literary and visual artist colleagues, who were beholden to patrons, employers, and readers for their livelihood. And on a very practical level, musicians also avoided the physically dangerous situations that accompanied many artists' and photographers' work.[11] Dangling over promontories or climbing down steep inclines to a rocky ledge to capture just the right angle or view were legitimately life-threatening activities that composers avoided.[12] But there was a significant downside to the absence of numbers and conventions for the first American composers. In the nineteenth century, America's composers were on their own, fighting to have their music taken seriously both at home and abroad. If the nation confidently exported political philosophy, literature, and art to an eager, receptive, and respectful world, it imported its musical culture—both music and musicians—and continued to do so for generations. It would take until the early decades of the twentieth century for American composers to organize themselves and be perceived as possessing a distinctive national voice.

The early nineteenth century was, perhaps, not an auspicious moment for a nascent American music that celebrated place. In 1818 John Rowe Parker (1777–1844), an amateur musician and founder of the *Euterpeiad,* the first serious music journal in the United States, bemoaned the conditions under which American arts labored. A champion of the morally uplifting potential of instrumental music, he observed that "the state of society in our country furnishes little aid to the progress of the fine arts, and scarcely admits of their successful cultivation."[13] And such was the case with music even while the National Academy of the Arts, founded in 1825, promoted the visual arts and provided systematic instruction to students. Clearly the visual arts were aggressively involved in such cultivation. Decades after Parker, America's most read music critic, John Sullivan Dwight (1813–93), discounted the desirability of a distinctly American music or, worse yet, a descriptively American music. He touted the newly canonized European tradition (especially as it was commuted by Beethoven) as something elevated, sacred, abstract, and apart, beyond the need for programmatic association or description. Here was music worth aspiring toward; here was "Art." His specific criticisms of America's first symphonist, Anthony Philip Heinrich, especially as regarded the composer's preference for musical depictions of "scenes and histories," will be discussed in the first chapter.[14]

One can understand that the idea of associating "Art" with something as mundane as a place or a landscape, or of finding elevating virtue in American wilderness stories, would have been anathema to Dwight, who preached the spiritual value of music that was abstract, absolute, and universal. The same critic heard American music as decidedly inferior—too concerned with entertainment and amusement and not "much consciousness . . . of the higher meaning of music," and he did not hesitate to say so even though the comparisons he made were often between dissimilar musics.[15] It did not help Dwight's cause that even his physical being struck one as overly refined. In recounting Dwight's attendance at a performance of Mozart's *Don Giovanni,* a contemporary observer found him to be "one of the most genial, dainty, and philosophic musical critics of the country. If he could once break through the shell of his library and mingle a little with the world, he would become a glorious fellow—yet after all, perhaps, not so *precious* as now."[16] Although in many ways Dwight was more responsible than any other nineteenth-century American for establishing some kind of high-art musical culture in the United States, the timing of his narrow pronouncements couldn't have been worse for encouraging a distinct native musical voice, one that might have provided a musical analog for other artistic celebrations of America's places.

A curious parallel emerges, however, between the Hudson River School painters' perceptions of the American landscape as infused with spiritual significance, and J. S. Dwight's perception of music as commuting a religious experience. In both cases art and music are portrayed as conduits to God, as manifestations of a revealed religion. But the parallels have different ramifications. The Hudson River School painters found their God-infused landscape in America and identified it as such: God had touched the American landscape in unique ways. This was all part of Manifest Destiny thinking.[17] Dwight found his God-infused music in the classical tradition of Europe, in the music of Beethoven especially, and worked throughout his life to assure that Americans would be educated to appreciate the same. Consequently, where the Hudson River School painters saw their commitment to landscape as a high and holy calling serving both the nation and the divinity simultaneously, and so aimed their activities at developing a style that showcased America's uniqueness, Dwight's efforts to conflate music and spiritual significance discouraged distinctiveness—national or otherwise. His intentions may have been noble, but the results of his public espousal of such beliefs severely crippled the development of a distinctly American high-art music or a music that focused on America. It took Herculean efforts by a few nineteenth-century composers to unleash America's musical voice and join with other artists and writers in celebrating that which was most distinctive about the New Found Land.

The Sounds of Place: Music and the American Cultural Landscape looks at one recurring idea that has helped shape our nation's history and identity, an idea that has helped define the United States as a unique political entity: the idea of place. But rather than simply revisit this well-rehearsed theme in a general way, the book focuses specifically on a single venue of its manifestation: music of the high-art tradition written by American composers. It considers what their American "place pieces" tell us about the nation's search for its own voice, and about its always-morphing sense of self.[18]

In the past, cultural geographers interested in music have trained their focus on the vernacular tradition—country, folk, and popular songs and pieces—that refer to the American place in a variety of ways. The same, however, has not been done for music of the cultivated tradition. While numerous anecdotal remarks relating specific places to individual composers and works are scattered throughout music scholarship, there has been no systematic exploration connecting this repertoire with the idea of place. *Sounds of Place* is the first study of its kind.

Reality is sloppy. No single reading of events explains a complex entity. Perry Miller spoke directly to this issue in an address he delivered in 1954 at Wellesley College: "He who endeavors to fix the personality of America in one eternal, unchangeable pattern not only understands nothing of how a personality is created, but comprehends little of how this nation has come along thus far. He who seeks repose in a unitary conception in effect abandons personality."[19]

I have no desire to confine an image of the United States to that which resides in a few select places or the musical pieces they inspired, although I do want to listen to what they tell us. Occasionally, given time and distance, patterns emerge; we detect recurring ideas and behaviors that illuminate the thinking that has prevailed and the choices that have been made. The high-art music tradition offers one perspective from which to view this cultural landscape. While not the equivalent of a Rosetta stone, these patterns help explain an object or system that might otherwise be too fragmented and complicated to be understood at all. It is here that the idea of place provides an entrée, not only into the works of some of America's most respected composers, but also into their perception of America itself.

It was not simply an alliterative title that caught the ear and eye of intellectual historians when Perry Miller's posthumous book *Nature's Nation* ap-

peared in 1967.[20] The two words summed up what had indeed been one of
the recurring themes of pre-twentieth-century American thought: the United
States was a nation blessed with abundant, varied, and verdant land; a nation
closer to nature than any other in the modern Western world. And Miller
argued it was the way Americans interacted with and interpreted nature that
played a large role in shaping the nation that emerged.[21]

Over two hundred years of nationhood, America's natural places have been
declared proof of God's special promise for America, and cited as an uncon-
taminated laboratory for the study of natural science and the source of our
industrial might. The natural American place provided James Fenimore Cooper with the substance of his Leatherstocking tales' main character, Natty
Bumppo, and Ralph Waldo Emerson with the symbol for an entire philosophical movement. The principles of Transcendentalism were anchored in the
promise of the New World's unique nature, and articulated in Emerson's
pivotal utterance "Nature."[22] Almost 160 years later, the cachet of America's
nature was still vital. As President Bill Clinton awarded Senator Gaylord Nel-
son the Presidential Medal of Freedom in 1995, he credited the founder of
Earth Day with "inspir[ing] us to remember that the stewardship of our natural resources is the stewardship of the American Dream."[23] At some level, at
the close of the twentieth century the promise of America was still tied to its
nature, to its place.

A study of American music inspired by place could include thousands of
pieces from a range of genres. Why not "Hurrah! For Buffalo," a simple piano
solo written in honor of the city that hosted the Pan American Exposition of
1901; the 1954 song "I Left My Heart in San Francisco," with lyrics by Douglass Cross and music by George Cory, forever associated with the singer Tony
Bennet; or West Side Story, the Sondheim-Bernstein musical set in New York
City; or "Knoxville, Summer of 1915," Samuel Barber's voice and orchestra
setting of James Agee's Tennessee-inspired poem? Frederick Delius wrote a
"Florida Suite," and Frederick Shepherd Converse composed a tone poem to
"California." Elie Siegmeister paid homage to a New York borough in his
one-act opera Sunday in Brooklyn, and John Cage commemorated all of the
city in his 1977 "Forty-Nine Waltzes for the Five Boroughs," which he contributed to The Waltz Project album in 1981. The list goes on and on. Why
not Virgil Thomson's Plough That Broke the Plain or Henry F. Gilbert's Dance
in Place Congo, two pieces that I seriously considered and then did not include
for different reasons. An explanation of the thinking behind their exclusion is
illustrative of the numerous issues at stake.

Thomson's piece was originally written to accompany a 1936 film by Pare
Lorentz, entitled The Plough That Broke the Plain. Six years later, Thomson

revisited his score and arranged it as an orchestral suite. The six movements contain evocations of "tom-tom" rhythms, a rendering of "Old Hundredth," a medley of cowboy songs including "Houlihan," "Laredo," and "Git Along, Little Dogies," and the plucking sound of a banjo. There is much to recommend the work. In selecting a piece to represent the idea of the West, I chose Roy Harris's *Cimarron* as the more resonant symbol, although one is free to take issue with the comparative quality of the works. Both Thomson and Harris had links to the places about which they wrote. Thomson was born in 1896 in Kansas City, Missouri, and Harris in 1898 in Oklahoma, but Harris, with his well-known associations with musical Americanism and prevailing myths about the West (which he helped to create and then perpetuate), seemed the more powerful choice. Discussing Harris also allowed me to get at a number of issues that would not have emerged with Thomson, such as the tie-ins with Edna Ferber's novel and the Hollywood film both named *Cimarron,* themselves important artistic statements about the importance of the West. Comparisons between Harris and William Grant Still were more vivid as well; they suffered similar fates in part because of their close associations with musical Americanism. Virgil Thomson did not, perhaps because of his remarkably successful career as a music critic for the *Herald Tribune.*

Henry F. Gilbert and *The Dance in Place Congo* presented a different set of issues. I sought out pieces written by composers who had personal investments in the place(s) they wrote about, whenever that was possible. Gilbert was born, educated, and died in New England. Like MacDowell, his teacher, he spent much time in Europe, and at some level he responded to Antonin Dvořák's call for American composers to use indigenous musical materials. He had transcribed Native American songs as part of the work he'd done with Edward Curtis, and so he knew that music with an unusual level of depth. *The Dance in Place Congo* (1908) was one of many pieces he wrote to answer Dvořák's charge, but it is in no way representative of an insider's view of the place. Gilbert's work takes its title and borrows a tune from the first of a pair of articles that George Washington Cable wrote in 1886 for *Century Magazine.* To my knowledge Gilbert never ventured south and had no personal experience with black culture, that of New Orleans or elsewhere. I consciously chose not to interpret the significance of a place associated with African slaves and Creole culture through the eyes of a distant white observer whose piece was based upon the work of a second white observer, even if Cable was originally from New Orleans. The ideal spokesperson for New Orleans might have been Louis Moreau Gottschalk, a true product of the city's unique ethnic culture, but unfortunately he wrote no pieces whose titles refer to specific American places, and this was a basic requirement for inclusion in this study. Surely pieces that deserve attention have been left out; there are books' worth on the clipping room floor. I cannot hope to be inclusive, only representative and fair.

A more pressing question for readers might be the preponderance of north-eastern locales. If they seem to dominate the discussion, the bias reflects trends apparent in high-art place pieces themselves more than a conscious effort on my part to focus on the East. The predisposition itself, however, reveals much about American cultural history and deserves a word of explanation. One must separate nineteenth- and twentieth-century perspectives.

Even though many mid-to-late nineteenth-century artists and photographers traveled to the West to capture nature there, the focus of seventeenth-, eighteenth-, and early nineteenth-century American artists remained, to a large extent, confined to the East Coast. This is reflected, most prominently, in the works of the first truly indigenous group of artists, the Hudson River School painters. Additionally, dioramas and panoramas that circulated widely in this country and abroad focused upon the East Coast's natural scenes. This was so even when they were created by Canadians or artists from the Midwest. No native composers established themselves in the West until the twentieth century, and thus musical depictions of place, like the majority of artworks that celebrated place, were dominated by renderings of what artists and composers knew, and most knew the East Coast.

The most enduring national icons of the United States throughout the nineteenth century remained natural ones found in the East: the Hudson River, the Berkshires, and above all Niagara Falls. These were places that artists and musicians were likely to know from firsthand experiences or from circulated popular renderings. When, toward the middle of the nineteenth century, commercialism threatened to overtake the iconic value of Niagara Falls, Frederic E. Church's phenomenally famous painting of 1857, *Niagara,* resuscitated interest in the waterfall. Its fame strengthened the power of the cataract and hence perpetuated the domination of the East Coast as home to America's most iconic place.

San Francisco was the one city that might have provided a West Coast perspective on American artistic culture in the middle of the nineteenth century. Its thriving operatic scene, directly attributable to the presence of a large population of prospectors, did not, however, produce or inspire any known works by native composers that celebrated the locale. Throughout most of the nineteenth century, American composers were confined to, and confined their perspectives to, the East and Southeast.

In all disciplines, America's nineteenth-century cultural tastemakers were themselves easterners. In the cases of William Billings, Lowell Mason, John

Sullivan Dwight, William Henry Fry, Richard Storrs Willis, and others whose ideas regularly shaped musical opinions, their perspectives were oriented toward the East Coast (and Europe), not the West. In attempting to establish America's musical identity, they sought comparison with what lay across the ocean, not across the plains.

The only "artistic" medium in the nineteenth century that regularly (and even dominantly) celebrated the West was dime novels. Within these short booklets, the struggles of pioneers, outlaws, cowboys, and young damsels against both untamed nature and indigenous peoples provided source material for a thriving literary genre. But their popularity and obvious mixture of truth and fantasy made them suspect among those intent on establishing a high-art culture for America. While the importance of the West in American consciousness would continue to grow throughout the second half of the nineteenth century and into the twentieth, and would blossom into a central theme in Hollywood, the realities of national expansion would always be accompanied by and oftentimes overshadowed by the myths that grew around it.

Coincident with large numbers of settlers moving out West, the nation also experienced a change in its self-perception. While natural icons sufficed for a nation short on established institutions or world power, by the end of the nineteenth century the United States had evolved from a rural outpost to a major international player. In the twentieth century, industrial might and technical know-how identified the nation as much as Niagara had earlier. Urban images replaced natural ones as symbols of the nation. While Oklahoma was experiencing the last of its land rushes and Washington was enjoying its first years of statehood, while tales of westward expansion established a firm foothold in the national imagination, visualizations of America became urban, and music followed. East Coast visualizations prevailed.

Large instrumental works celebrating the West emerged simultaneously with trained composers moving there and becoming aware of the unique features of the area, and with Hollywood popularizing the place. Three of the composers considered in this study, Ferde Grofé, William Grant Still, and Roy Harris, wrote place pieces with a decidedly western focus, and all spent significant portions of their lives there. Grofé and Still also wrote for Hollywood. Partly for the same reason that Gilbert was not included, these composers and works were selected: because of the authority rendered by personal experience. While it might be argued that no one knows the extent of Heinrich, Fry, or Bristow's experience with Niagara, the ubiquity of the symbol and dissemination of information about Niagara made most Americans insiders with the Falls. My reason for including four Niagara pieces is precisely because of the importance of the Falls as a symbol, which I try to demonstrate, and which the existence of four different pieces over a wide span of time confirms. Along the same lines, I was initially hesitant to include Ellen Zwilich's Symphony No. 4, *The Gardens,* until I learned in numerous personal interviews of her transformative experience at the Michigan State University gardens. She resides in New York and Florida, but she went to the gardens and spent time there. Similarly, Steve Reich, although associated with New York City, lived for a time near the missile range in the desert of New Mexico. *The Desert Music* is energized by real knowledge of the place. An insider's perspective was important to me.

Beginning and ending with pieces that focus on the Northeast provides a useful perspective on both the music and the larger idea of national identity. After discussing *Kaintuck', American Scenes, Cimarron, Mississippi Suite, Grand Canyon Suite,* Symphony No. 4, *The Gardens,* and *The Desert Music,* it is instructive to come back to the Northeast. Because the book looks at how attitudes toward place can reflect changing national perceptions, a return to the region where it all started allows for comparisons between the original natural focus and the later urban one, between a celebration of nature and a concentration on the human presence. Again, this was not preordained, but emerged.

Confining the discussion to dominantly instrumental works of the high-art tradition was the single most limiting factor in selecting music, but it was a necessary one to make the project manageable. Hence, all the pieces studied are either purely instrumental works or ones that include a limited vocal presence; all aspire to the concert tradition. Additionally, only pieces that made reference to an American place in their titles, whose composers intended to commemorate a place (as closely as that could be determined), and that were written by native U.S. or naturalized citizens were considered.[24] These criteria make the study controllable without stripping it of all integrity and value. Alternatives are of course possible, and one hopes that this volume will inspire such studies. *The Sounds of Place: Music and the American Cultural Landscape* joins a growing body of literature on place, and focuses on the unique ways in which music of the cultivated tradition expresses, defines, and celebrates places. In so doing, it articulates one way the nation has expressed, defined, and celebrated itself.

As restrictions were placed on the repertoire—performing force; consideration of the title; and the intentions, perspective, and citizenship of the composer—three basic groups of questions were asked of the composers and works discussed: (1) What was the purpose of the memorialization of this place? Was it a commissioned work intended to celebrate or document a place, or a piece the composer felt compelled to write without outside encouragement? (2) How did the composer relate to the place? (3) What compositional techniques did the composer employ to capture the place? Were there tunes or styles of music associated with the specific place, or evocative sounds of a more generic type suggesting a soundscape?

These questions beg a final and most important one: What vision of the place and hence of the United States do each of these pieces convey? *Sounds of Place* does not primarily track correspondences between topographical details of places and individual musical gestures, although such comparisons are suggested from time to time. Of the composers interviewed, all eschewed such associations; there is no narrow comparison between place and piece. Rather, the book looks at musical works that were inspired by places and considers what these works tell us about the responses of fourteen composers, about the issues that compelled a broad, interdisciplinary artistic response, and about the larger mood of the nation. Though the book is organized chronologically, it is best read as a series of studies, something akin to a collection of postcards related by topic, rather than as a single, linear narrative through a subject.

The study starts with a little known Bohemian immigrant named Anthony Philip Heinrich, and considers his calculated uses of American places in the titles of his pieces to earn identification with his adopted land. His work *The War of the Elements and the Thundering of Niagara* ties him to two other nineteenth-century composers who also recognized the symbolic value of the world-famous cataract. William Henry Fry and George Frederick Bristow each wrote his own paean to the Falls.

Collectively these three early American symphonists reflected a much broader national artistic emphasis. Nineteenth-century pride in Niagara resulted in thousands of artworks, commercial images, poems, essays, sermons, and musical offerings. As the nation pinned its uniqueness on its natural environment, the Falls symbolized the purest and most powerful of America's natural images, and composers intent on establishing an American musical tradition sought the dignity that the premiere symbol afforded. A fourth symphonic work, one written by Ferde Grofé in 1961 to celebrate the opening of the Robert Moses Power Plant at Niagara, provides a very different perspective on the natural wonder and its meaning to a twentieth-century American sensibility.

As the United States redefined itself as a locus of modern industrial strength, musical celebrations of rural phenomena declined. Writers, artists, and composers looked elsewhere for symbols of the American place, specifically the city. At the turn of the century, Charles Ives remembered the power of nature in his tone poem *The Housatonic at Stockbridge*. But even he, perhaps most famous for his nostalgic embrace of the past, turned to the city as the new signifier of America. Ives's work *From Hanover Square North, at the End of a Tragic Day, the Voice of the People Again Arose* depicts an elevated train station in lower Manhattan on the day the *Lusitania* sank. Ives painted the sounds of the city, the crowds, the train, the heterogeneous mix of humanity that distinguished the modern American urban environment. It would seem that Ives, always reluctant to express his affection for the city, nonetheless recognized its centrality to American identity. When he looked for a uniquely American response to this world-changing event, he looked to Manhattan.

Other works reflect this shift to the urban scene as the one identifying the United States in the twentieth century. Aaron Copland's *Quiet City* suggests a different city experience, a deeply introspective and personal one. Drawing upon his own insights as the son of Jewish immigrants, and working with music he had composed for a Group Theatre production of the same name, Copland offers a soulful meditation on city life, one that speaks of the con- flicted emotions borne by thousands who flee their homelands. Although Copland's portraits of western landscapes are more well known, this piece offers perhaps the most chiseled and personal portrait that Copland ever cre- ated. Edgard Varèse's *Amériques* is the wide-eyed, wide-eared work of an en- thusiastic new arrival in New York. All the hopes that Varèse harbored for the arts in America and for his music are audible in this first work that he wrote in his new home. William Grant Still's *Lenox Avenue* and Duke Ellington's *Harlem* both capture sights and sounds of the part of Manhattan north of Central Park that was so central to the emerging "New Negro." Ellington's *Harlem Air Shaft* focuses on a feature of many houses in the city and paints a picture of the experience of living in that vital place.

At the same time as an urban America was replacing the complex nine- teenth-century Eden-wilderness image of the country, composers searched for ways to update and resuscitate the idea of the centrality of the natural place to the nation. As the myth of the American West grew, Roy Harris saddled up and consciously cast himself as a man of the western soil. His overt efforts to emphasize his Oklahoma roots speak to the power of the West in the American psyche. Reluctant to let go of the idea of the United States as nature's nation, Harris, Still, and Grofé all wrote works that celebrated impor- tant natural sites. From Harris's *Cimarron* to Still's *Kaintuck'* and *The Ameri- can Scene* to Grofé's *Mississippi, Grand Canyon,* and *Hudson River* suites, these mid-century Americanist works sustained the notion of a natural America amid the clangorous noises of a city-centered culture.

Because he is the first widely recognized black composer of high-art music in the United States, discussions of William Grant Still's place pieces would benefit from some consideration of the influence of race on his perception of American culture, musical and otherwise. That Still was aware of possessing an experience different from others in high-art music circles is evident in numerous works whose titles don't make overt references to American places, such as the *Afro-American Symphony* or the suite *Africa,* but whose inspiration includes images of places. To understand Still fully, one must consider his place within African American culture; the ways in which race informs one's perception of place is an issue deserving a study of its own. But as Still himself wanted to be judged not as a black composer but as an American composer, the ramifications of his race will not be discussed in this study, except as he brings them up.

In the final decades of the twentieth century, as the environmental movement gained strength in the United States, and the stewardship efforts of its fringe groups were adopted by middle America and even became national policy, composers in large numbers responded by once again looking to natural places as sources of inspiration. No longer the exclusive realm of a few nostalgic nationalists, nature returned to the spotlight and was embraced by a broad spectrum of citizens. But a century of urbanization had left its mark; America's relation to its natural places had changed. While fewer artists, writers, and composers insisted upon waterfalls and mountains as emblems of the nation's unique destiny or as visible signs of God's Edenic polity, citizens returned to the idea of the primary importance of the nation-place and sought its new lessons.

This return to place can be heard in the music of at least three American composers of the last twenty years. They wrote works whose titles point directly to their sources of inspiration, and in more than a few cases those sources were natural ones. Robert Starer's *Hudson Valley Suite* returns to the locus of the first distinctive American school of visual artists and offers a 1983 view of the terrain. Dana Paul Perna turns again and again to America's places, and in doing so pays homage not only to the individual sites, but also to other artists and musicians who earlier captured those places. *Prout's Neck* and *Three Places on Long Island* are just two of many works that isolate places resonant with meaning for the composer from New York. Although Ellen Taaffe Zwilich is best known for her loyalty to traditional abstract forms, her Symphony No. 4, *The Gardens,* is a unique and powerful statement of a current American attitude toward its natural places. Her four-movement work ends with a chorus of children and adults who pledge to "protect our heritage, to nourish our plants and trees, to leave a verdant earth." Just as Still's race could have provided a unique perspective from which to view America's places, so might Zwilich's gender, although she rejects being cast exclusively as a "woman composer."[25] I will leave it to another study to wrestle with the significance of Zwilich's commemoration of a garden, a place regularly associated with flowers, objects historically associated with women.

Works by Steve Reich provide a final exploration of the changing attitudes of contemporary Americans toward their places as revealed in music of the high-art tradition. But in addition to responding to specific physical surroundings, Reich hears the speech melody of Americans who inhabit those places and draws his inspiration. It is the pitch, rhythm, timbre, and cadences of American speech patterns, as well as the sounds of the places themselves, that are the engine behind *The Desert Music, New York Counterpoint,* and *City Life.* The places speak through the people.

At the beginning of the twenty-first century, America's identity no longer depends upon its pristine wildernesses, deafening waterfalls, or iconic canyons. Much as they are places of pride and accompany any visual display of "America the Beautiful," the country has become equally identified with its people and their achievements.[26] At the turn of the millennium, Zwilich's and Reich's unself-conscious depictions of gardens, deserts, and city scenes speak of an evolving and ever more complex relationship between Americans and their places. And as they hear America, we learn something of our own place.

chapter one

America as Niagara: Nature as Icon

ANTHONY PHILIP HEINRICH

The War of the Elements and the Thundering of Niagara

I N 1697 the first known image of Niagara Falls appeared. The engraving was the work of an unidentified Dutch printmaker and was part of a book written by Father Louis Hennepin entitled *Nouvelle découverte d'un très grand pays situé dans l'Amérique*. Hennepin observed the Falls as a member of the expedition of the French explorer Robert LaSalle to America in 1678–82. The missionary priest later devoted two chapters of his travelogue to Niagara. Within two years the book was published in Dutch, English, German, and Spanish, and by the early 1700s several editions circulated.[1]

The art historian Jeremy Elwell Adamson assessed Hennepin's observations: "The geologically ignorant author had described the 'wonderful Downfall' as composed of 'two great Cross-streams of Water, and two Falls, with an Isle sloping along the middle of it.' The 'Gulph' into which the river dropped, he declared, was 600 feet deep. There were no mountains in the vicinity, he noted, and from its commencement at the eastern end of Lake Erie, the broad stream flowed gently over a flat plateau. Unexpectedly and 'all of a sudden,' the river plunged over the 'horrible Precipice,' terrifying the priest with the ferocity of its fall."

Adamson then considered the implications for a visual artist: "Although it is an imaginary view, this initial image nonetheless presents a surprisingly successful solution to the basic question confronting all artists who visited the site itself: how to suggest the vast dimensions of the cataracts and extensiveness of their setting, yet, at the same time, express the psychological impact of the scene. . . . The immensity of the scene is conveyed by juxtaposing small figures against the waterfalls. The 'surprising and astonishing' effect Niagara had upon the mind is suggested by the gesticulating European in the left foreground."[2]

The anonymous Niagara engraving was one of just three illustrations in

17

the book, but it provided the first glimpse of the continent for thousands who had never set foot in the New World.[3] The Falls quickly became the most recognized natural phenomenon identified with North America; they marked the place as unique.

Numerous images followed, portraying the Falls as vast, limitless, powerful, and wild. The wildness of the place was conveyed by variously clad Indians, animals native to the continent including beavers and eagles, and, later on, rattlesnakes—figures that would be adopted as Revolutionary War symbols. Eighty years before the nation existed as a polity, the Falls came to represent America as a vast, verdant, untamed place fraught with danger and full of untapped power.

Over the next two hundred years, Niagara's iconographic power persisted even as its meaning morphed. By the 1820s hundreds of guests were accommodated at Niagara's local hotels. In the same decade that Emerson's essay "Nature" (1836) cast America as the unique site of communion with the universal Being, the Oversoul, Indians disappeared from Niagara images. The wild and exotic Niagara was replaced by the sublime Niagara.[4] Images of Niagara reflected the changing perception of the nation (both its own and others') as it evolved from wilderness outpost to promised land to industrial giant.[5] Thomas Davies, Thomas Cole, John Vanderlyn, John Trumbull, George Willis, Henry Davis, Thomas Chambers, John F. Kensett, Jasper Cropsey, Herman Herzog, Albert Bierstadt, Thomas Moran, John Twachtman, and, most famously, Frederic Edwin Church all painted the Falls, as did a host of lesser names. Their renderings are as different as the moods of the waters.

The flood of visual imagery was echoed in equally ardent efforts to capture the cataract in poetry and prose. Oliver Goldsmith, James Fenimore Cooper, Henry Wadsworth Longfellow, Charles Dickens, Matthew Arnold, and Richard Watson Gilder responded to the Falls and variously interpreted its restless power as the force behind the nation's "uniqueness and promise."[6] Dickens's rhapsody on the Falls that appeared in *American Notes* in 1842 was easily the most oft-quoted description of the cataract. A brief excerpt gives a sense of the tone: "Then, when I felt how near to my Creator I was standing, the first effect, and the enduring one—instant and lasting—of the tremendous spectacle, was Peace. Peace of Mind . . . What voices spoke from out the thundering water; what faces, faded from the earth, looked out upon me from its gleaming depths; what Heavenly promise glistened in those angels' tears, the drops of many hues, that showered around, and twined themselves about the gorgeous arches which the changing rainbows made! . . . I think in every quiet season now, still do those waters roll and leap, and roar and tumble, all day long; still are the rainbows spanning them, a hundred feet below."[7]

This was matched in ardor if not in length by John Quincy Adams's "Speech on Niagara Falls," delivered just days after his visit in 1843. The former president informed the Buffalo audience, "You have what no other nation on earth has. At your very door there is a mighty cataract—one of the most wonderful works of God." He concluded that the waterfall, with its omnipresent rainbow, was "a pledge from God to mankind."[8]

In 1860 the Reverend Edward T. Taylor addressed a gathering of religious leaders in Buffalo, New York, who had taken an excursion to the Falls. His remarks attest to the nationalistic pride still stirred by the natural wonder: "What does it represent? What does it resemble? Does it not resemble our country,—our vast, immeasurable, unconquerable, inexplicable country?" Imbuing the cataract with religious significance, Taylor observed: "After you have said Niagara, all that you may say is but the echo. It remains Niagara, and will roll and tumble and foam and play and sport till the last trumpet shall sound. It will remain Niagara whether you are friends or foes. So with this country. It is the greatest God ever gave to man. . . . Niagara is like our gospel. It never freezes in winter nor dries up in dog-days. You never need to come and go away with a dry bucket. . . . Our gospel is adequate to all the wants of the world. . . . It is as powerful as Niagara!"

With undisguised Manifest Destiny thinking informing his speech, he went on: "It is our own. God reserved it for us, and there is not the shadow of it in all the world besides. I have travelled far, and have seen the best of all the countries of all this world, and there is but one United States of America in the world."[9]

The Civil War would alter the unchallenged national significance of the Falls, but in the late 1870s Longfellow's collection *Poems of Places,* which included at least ten poems by as many writers, testified to the continuing broad appeal of the Falls as an artistic subject. Amateurs joined the Niagara chorus as hundreds of travelers wrote their own original accounts, which were published in local newspapers. Scholars too were "Niagaraized," explaining the changing significance of the natural and cultural phenomenon in articles, dissertations, and books.[10]

A sense of the inspirational power of Niagara can be gleaned from the *Anthology and Bibliography of Niagara Falls* published in 1921 by Charles Mason Dow, an indefatigable guardian of the Falls and a former commissioner of the State Reservation at Niagara. Dow's *Anthology* became its own tribute to the natural phenomenon. In it he reproduced numerous engravings, including the one of the Falls that appeared in Hennepin's volume. He included copies of paintings, maps, excerpts from accounts, and scientific writings, and he listed hundreds of sources containing information on the Falls.

After Louis Hennepin, *Cataracte de Niagara,* Paris, 1757. Courtesy of the Charles Rand Penney Collection.

He hoped his efforts conveyed "some slight idea of the great extent of Niagara literature."[11] The two volumes totaled 1,423 pages.

Dow's second volume opened with a chapter devoted to music, poetry, and fiction. In addition to enumerating the more widely known literary works that focused on Niagara, the former commissioner listed music-related literature inspired by the Falls. While many of the poems are identified as "hymns," they are clearly not intended to be sung. The single musical composition that he cites is one written by the touring Norwegian violin virtuoso and composer Ole Bull, entitled *Niagara.* This unpublished piece for violin and orchestra was composed in New York in October 1844 after a visit to the Falls, and Bull premiered it in public on 18 December of the same year. Bull considered it "the best composition [he had] written," although critics did not agree.[12] In a particularly stinging review of *Niagara,* George Templeton Strong opined: "In the opening of 'Niagara' one might discover (if he knew the subject) the image of a flowing river gradually quickening its current and becoming broken with rapids. Then came a grand explosion from the orchestra, intended to express a cataract, and after that I could recognize no meaning in the piece unless the *artiste* meant to express that he'd gone over the falls with the crash that described them and was drifting about in the fragmentary water below."[13]

A review of Bull's first American concert a year earlier that had appeared in the *Herald* had actually evoked the imagery of Niagara to describe audience reaction: "It was a tempest—a torrent—a very Niagara of applause, tumult, and approbation throughout the whole performance."[14] It would seem that when it came to Bull, Niagaras flowed in all directions.

Dow lists only one other distinctly music-related item, an article by Eugene Thayer (1838–89), the German-trained American organ virtuoso who often accompanied Bull when he toured America.[15] Thayer's four-page study entitled "Music of Niagara" appeared in *Scribner's* magazine in February 1881. It began: "It had ever been my belief that Niagara had not been *heard* as it should be, and in this belief I eagerly turned my steps hitherward the first time a busy life would permit. What did I hear? The roar of Niagara? No. Having been everywhere about Niagara, above and below, far and near, over and under, and heard her voice in all its wondrous modulations, I must say that I have never, for a single instant, heard any *roar* of Niagara."[16]

It gradually becomes clear that Thayer's goal is not merely to argue whether Niagara "roars," a term the author never defines but that a reader infers to mean a loud, uncontrolled noise antithetical to music. Rather, he uses quasi-scientific explanations based upon the vibrations of the overtone series to explain the Falls' sound as the "great diapason—the noblest and completest one on earth . . . the same tone which for ages has ascended in praise of Him who first gave it voice."[17] Thayer therefore not only explains the sound he hears, he identifies it as the voice of God. Using rudimentary charts showing a harmonic series built upon G, comparisons between the height of the Falls and the length of comparatively proportioned organ pipes, and repeated assertions regarding the dependability of his hearing, Thayer explains Niagara's music: "From the first moment to the last, I heard nothing but a perfectly constructed musical tone—clear, definite and unapproachable in its majestic perfection; a complete series of tones, all uniting in one grand and noble unison, as in the organ, and all as easily recognizable as the notes of any great chord in music. And I believe it was my life-long familiarity with the king of instruments which enabled me to detect so readily the tone-construction of this mighty voice of the 'thunder of waters.'"[18]

Not content to address pitch alone, Thayer also clarifies the rhythm of the Falls. "What is its rhythm? . . . Its chief accent or beat is just once per second! Here is our unit of time—here has the Creator given us a chronometer which shall last as long as man shall walk on earth. It is the clock of God!"[19] Thayer provides an example of the rhythm showing a half note at 60, and beats divided into increasingly small groups of threes, perhaps a subtle reference to the presence of the trinity. The author concludes: "What is the *quality* of its tone? Divine! There is no other word for a tone made and fashioned by the Infinite God. I repeat, there is no *roar* at all—it is the sublimest music on earth."[20]

Thayer's remarks are noteworthy for a number of reasons. First is his insistence upon the religious meaning of the Falls: Thayer's pairing of Niagara with a sacred, sublime Deity and his insistence that it was the natural incarnation of God reflected an attitude current in the 1830s and 1840s, and resuscitated in the 1850s by the Hudson River School painters most especially. Yet however passionate this interpretation, it was largely outdated by the last quarter of the century. Realities of the Civil War, dissemination of Darwin's evolutionary theories, and the growing realization of Niagara's potential as a source for industrial power challenged the credibility of a purely sanctified nature. Thayer does update his inspired reading with an evocation of acoustical "facts," a nod to earlier efforts made by others across disciplinary boundaries to reconcile religious interpretation with scientific discovery.[21] But his facts are loosely applied and merely means to an end.

Second, Thayer apparently disregarded what had transpired during the course of the century at the Falls. Henry James, fresh from a September 1871 tour that took him from Toronto across Lake Ontario and to the Falls, chided: "The spectacle you have come so far to see is to be choked in the horribly vulgar shops and booths and catchpenny artifices which have pushed and elbowed to within the very spray of the Falls, and ply their importunities in shrill competition with its thunder." Not content that he had made his point, James continued, "You see a multitude of hotels and taverns and stores, glaring white with paint, bedizened with placards and advertisements. . . . I must say . . . that the importunities one suffers here . . . from hackmen, and photographers, and vendors of gimcracks, are simply hideous and infamous." Acknowledging the artistic significance of the phenomenon, he bemoaned "the abuse of the scene."[22] As John F. Sears summarized, "By the 1860s and 1870s the commercial version of Niagara as a spectacle had threatened to swallow up every other experience of the falls."[23] Niagara had been commodified.

But third, and more specific to a study of music and place, Thayer focused upon the aural component of the Falls, even if he took issue with the word commonly used to describe that sound.[24] Arguing against a roar, Thayer rejected not only the idea that Niagara could make a disturbing noise, but also the very earliest interpretations of the Falls (pre-1820) as a place of frightening wilderness and terrible power.[25] By 1881, however, Thayer's reading had already been thoroughly replaced by Niagara the resplendent, Niagara the transcendent, Niagara the commercial, and Niagara the industrial. "Roar" and "thundering" had assumed positions in a verbal repertoire regularly used to describe the Falls. Thayer's literal interpretation of the term would seem to run counter to those of numerous writers who continued to use the word, but now in a most positive way. The thundering roar became a manifestation of the grandeur and majesty of the Falls, a sound that was beyond containment or analysis. It was no longer a distressful cry but a potent symbol of the power present in the Falls, however that power was conceived.

Unknown to Dow, and apparently also to Thayer, who cited no specific musical works in his essay, three nineteenth-century composers did write pieces inspired by Niagara: Anthony Philip Heinrich, *The War of the Elements and the Thundering of Niagara*, c. 1831–45; William Henry Fry, *Niagara Symphony*, 1854; and George Frederick Bristow, *Niagara: Symphony for Grand Orchestra, Solos, and Chorus*, 1893. They attempted to capture what no visual artist could; their works celebrated the powerful *sound* heard at the Falls.[26] While none of Niagara's musical manifestations ever achieved the kind of renown heaped upon the efforts of Dickens or Longfellow, or most especially upon Frederic Edwin Church's 1857 painting *Niagara*, which cast a spell over much of the United States and Europe and was called "the great painting of the grandest subject of Nature,"[27] musical works inspired by Niagara were yet another barometer of attitudes toward the Falls; they too reflected a changing nation.[28]

They composed large works befitting the colossal spectacle. All of these works required augmented forces and were multisectional, indications of the power and multiformity that composers associated with the Falls.[29] By identifying their works as symphonies, Fry and Bristow conferred prestige upon America's most famous natural phenomenon, as well as on their own compositions.[30] Together these pieces form a distinctive artistic commentary on Niagara and, like their visual and literary counterparts, also speak to the nation's evolving image of itself.

Of art, literature, and music, music was the last to establish a strong national identity. In the earliest years of the colonies, it both flourished and labored under Puritan attitudes, which insisted upon music's moralistic purposes. In the nineteenth century it struggled against the often oppressive influence of European (mostly German) musicians, many of whom first visited the New Found Land as touring artists but increasingly immigrated as professionals who settled in. While their expertise was needed and appreciated at some level, their attitudes toward a nascent American music were not. America might have been the western-most terminus of European exploration, but it did not have to be just one more venue for European musical culture.

Worse still was the case of America's own cultural leaders who, for a variety of reasons, championed European musical values and works over native efforts. In a lengthy review of a concert that took place in Boston in 1846, J. S. Dwight instructed his readers on the many shortcomings of one of the pieces on the program, *Tecumseh, or the Battle of the Thames—a Martial Ouverture—for Full Orchestra,* by Anthony Philip Heinrich.[31] Dwight insisted upon the primacy of organic unity above everything else and held up Beethoven as the model to which all should aspire:

> Beautiful details, sudden fancies, shifting without end, would continually fix attention; but it was not so obvious whither they were leading; no unitary design appeared to cover them. . . . And yet in one sense there was too much design. Too much anxiety to make his compositions clear to every one, has doubtless helped to make them only more eccentric, difficult and unintelligible. In efforts to describe things, to paint pictures to the hearer's imagination, music leaves its natural channels, and forfeits that true unity which would come from the simple development of itself from within as music. Beethoven has no *programme* to his symphonies, intended no description, with the single exception of the *Pastorale:* yet how full of meaning are they![32]

Having dismissed stylistic details as distracting, Dwight next attacked programmatic associations:

> Mr. Heinrich belongs to the romantic class, who wish to attach a story to every thing they do. Mere outward scenes and histories seem to have occupied the mind of the composer too much, and to have disturbed the pure spontaneous inspiration of his melodies. We are sorry to see such circumstances dragged into music as the "Indian War Council," the "Advance of the Americans," the "Skirmish" and "Fall of Tecumseh." Music aiming at no subject,—music composed with no consciousness of anything in the world *but* music, is sure to tell of greater things than these. . . . A series of historical events may have unity enough in themselves to make a very good story; but it does not follow that just that series of subjects, translated into so many musical themes or passages, will still have unity in music.[33]

And yet, in the nineteenth century it was just such subjects and sources that identified American art and literature as distinct. Dwight's insistence upon a purely abstract, organically unified instrumental music composed according to European models assured American composers no original voice. And if there was one thing Heinrich was, it was original.

A wealthy and extremely successful Bohemian merchant, Anthony Philip Heinrich (1781–1861) was also an enthusiastic traveler. In Europe he had visited France, England, Italy, Portugal, Spain, and Austria. He first came to the United States in 1805 "to take a peep at the new world."[34] No record exists of his exact itinerary, but it is quite possible that Heinrich, a lover of nature, would have done as many others were doing at the time and visited Niagara Falls.[35] Such a trek demanded a hearty and adventurous spirit, one that Heinrich would call upon on numerous occasions over the course of the next fifty-plus years. He returned to Europe, but not for long. Through a series of personal miscalculations and a larger financial crisis affecting Europe, precipitated in part by the Napoleonic Wars, Heinrich's business interests suffered. He determined to try his luck in America, selling Bohemian glassware. Savings and sales must have been adequate, at least initially, because by 1810 Heinrich was in Philadelphia directing music at the Southwark Theatre, as an amateur, gratis. By 1811, however, Austria's government went bankrupt and Heinrich was left with no resources. At this point he turned to music as a profession.

Heinrich was back in Europe from 1826 to 1831, and again in 1833, when he spent two years in London before spending another two on the Continent. In 1837 he returned to New York. By 1826 Heinrich was traveling as "the Beethoven of America," a moniker that John Rowe Parker first applied in an article in *The Euterpeiad or Musical Intelligencer,* 13 April 1822.[36] Heinrich genuinely derived much satisfaction from this identification with his adopted land; he was enamored of America—its exotic beauty, its vastness, its power, its opportunities. But he also understood the potential cachet to be derived from an association with the young nation. Various references to "the humble Minstrel of the Western Wilds,"[37] "The Western Minstrel—from the Wilds of Kentucky,"[38] and "The Log House Composer of Kentucky"[39] speak of a conscientious effort on the part of the composer, as well as eager American critics, to market the Bohemian-born merchant/musician as a native spokesman.[40] Heinrich's reference to the famous waterfall in his piece *The War of the Elements and the Thundering of Niagara* would seem to be not only a tribute to the "'sublimest of sublimities,' the terrestrial world's grandest symbol of divine omnipotence,"[41] but also an intelligent marketing strategy for the ambitious composer.

Details surrounding the genesis of Heinrich's *Capriccio Grande for a Full Orchestra,* the subtitle he gave to *The War of the Elements and the Thundering of Niagara,* are sketchy at best. As Andrew Stiller explains in the preface to his 1994 edition of the work, it "was composed sometime between 1831 (known to be the date of Heinrich's first orchestral composition) and 1845, when it appears on a list of works (the "Presentazioni musicali") that Heinrich made at the time. There is no evidence that this work was ever played during the composer's lifetime.[42] There is also no specific program to the music, beyond the phrase "The Thunders of Niagara" at the point in the score marked "Coda."

But there may be some clues to the effect he was after in a description by the American composer and music teacher John Hill Hewitt, who accompanied Heinrich on a visit to President James Tyler at the White House. Heinrich hoped to enlist the support of the president for a large musical piece he was planning.[43] While the work described may be *Jubilee,* "a grand national song of triumph, composed and arranged for a full orchestra and a vocal chorus,"[44] references to "the mighty falls" offer some insight into Heinrich's perception of Niagara.[45]

Hewitt reviewed the afternoon he spent with the enthusiastic composer prior to meeting the president. "Two or three hours of patient hearing did I give to the most complicated harmony I ever heard, even in my musical dreams. Wild and unearthly passages, the pianoforte absolutely groaning under them." And then he described the scene that followed: "At a proper hour we visited the President's mansion. . . . We were shown into the parlor. . . . The composer labored hard to give full effect to his weird production. . . . at times his shoulders would be raised to the line of his ears, and his knees went up to the key-board. . . . occasionally explaining some incomprehensible passage, representing, as he said, the breaking up of the frozen river Niagara, the thaw of the ice, and the dash of the mass over the mighty falls." According to Hewitt, the president, obviously believing he'd given as much time to Heinrich's production as he could afford, "arose from his chair, and placing his hand gently on Heinrich's shoulder, said: 'That may all be very fine, sir, but can't you play us a good old Virginia reel?' "[46] As might be expected, Heinrich was devastated. Therein lies the whole of what might be references to a program for *The Thundering of Niagara.*

No matter which piece Heinrich hammered out for the president, neither work could have received a fair hearing under such conditions. Each required a full orchestra, *Jubilee* also included a chorus, and *The War of the Elements and the Thundering of Niagara* called for a largely augmented percussion section. Beyond the usual timpani, Heinrich had written parts for a bass drum, snare drum, triangle, cymbals, and tambourine; on numerous occasions all six instruments were to play simultaneously. Heinrich's generous brass section— four horns, four trumpets, and alto, tenor, and bass trombones—would also have provided a distinctive timbre to his work, one that no musician, no matter how gifted, would have been able to duplicate on a single instrument.[47]

Starting in the 1820s, visual artists recognized the difficulty of capturing

Niagara's multiple manifestations in a single image or from a single point of view.[48] Putting the Falls into their physical context required acknowledging the larger environment, which, as many painters commented, was noteworthy for its endless flatness; there was little against which to rest the eye. The problem was real: The relatively uninteresting backdrop was an essential ingredient in any painted image if the size, power, and arresting star-like quality of the Falls were to be fully appreciated. Yet incorporating the whole scene required a too-distant vantage point that ultimately lessened the impact of the Falls. A way out of the dilemma was found in multiple images. Beginning in the 1820s, pairs, sets, and series of scenes culminating in Robert Burford's circular panorama of 1833 provided partial solutions to the dilemma of the one-perspective painting.

Music, however, enforced no such restrictions. It was direct in its appeal, immediate in its effects, and dependent for its meaning upon constant motion and change. Multisectional musical works provided ideal forums for contrasting moods. And music could supply the one ingredient missing even from visual images. As a reviewer had observed upon seeing Frederic Church's work for the first time, "this *is* Niagara, with the roar left out."[49] Music could provide the roar. While Heinrich's *Capriccio* is a single, uninterrupted movement, save for two two-measure silences, the numerous tempo and mood changes that characterize the larger piece provide an aural equivalent of multiple perspectives, perhaps the multiple vistas that surrounded the cataract.

"The Thunders of Niagara," Heinrich's semi-autonomous coda to *The War of the Elements,* makes up 174 measures of the 507-measure piece, or just over one-third of the work. It is an unequivocal close to the episodic *Capriccio.* Dwight's observation of "sudden fancies, shifting without end" in *Tecumseh* might also apply to this piece, although *The War of the Elements* has an internal logic that challenges criticisms of formlessness.[50] In 1939 William Treat Upton provided a basic analysis of the piece and divided the larger work into three sections—an introduction, a main section, and a coda.[51] It was clear from his opening remarks that Upton thought highly of the work: "In graceful lyricism contrasting with dramatic fervor, [Heinrich] did nothing better, perhaps, than *The War of the Elements and the Thundering of Niagara.*"[52]

From the opening adagio largo (quarter note at 50), Heinrich's predilection for embellishment and the grand gesture is evident, even if much toned down from the excessive style that characterized his first collections of works from 1820: *The Dawning of Music in Kentucky; or The Pleasures of Harmony in the Solitudes of Nature* and *The Western Minstrel.* Here Heinrich still enjoys a florid melody and colorful harmonic palette (key changes are often unexpected), however, both appear more restrained and his textures are cleaner.

The War of the Elements ends with the roaring power of Niagara's waters; it begins, however, with a more soloistic soundscape, one that seems to be inhabited by twittering birds. Trills, turns, and grace notes in piccolos, flutes and oboes, as well as swooping melodic gestures, call back and forth to one another. Heinrich's experience as a theater orchestra musician informs his highly descriptive musical thinking (see Ex. 1.1).

Unexpected harmonic shifts and numerous fermatas lend spontaneity and drama to the piece; one can almost hear the curtain go up in the early measures of the introduction. Though a strong tonal center is missing, the work is, as Upton observes, "nominally in the key of C."[53] C becomes increasingly important over the course of the work. When a trilled F#7 chord introduces the allegro moderato (quarter note at 120) beginning at measure 17 (the first measure of the second half of the introduction), the listener is jettisoned into B major although the key is not notated by a signature. The initial 4/4 meter changes to 3/4, and a more regular pulse establishes itself. Heinrich interjects twittering, trilling groups of notes that are sustained by fermatas, thereby destabilizing a strong sense of meter but uniting this section with that which had come earlier. The main body of the work commences at measure 33, poco più mosso (quarter note at 144). True to form, rather than unequivocally establishing a home key, Heinrich opens with a diminished seventh chord, this one built on G#, from which emerge solo melodic fragments in oboe, clarinet, and flute (see Ex. 1.2).

In spite of Heinrich's reputation for excessive harmonic activity, cluttered scoring, and too-ornate lyrical lines, "The Thunders of Niagara" includes extended sections of clean textures and simple melodies. Among the most noteworthy moments in the main body of the *Capriccio* is a sixteen-measure andantino beginning at measure 235 (quarter note at 69). The expressive flute solo recalls measures 81–96, when flute, bassoon, and clarinet shared fragments of a similar melody; the larger work is unified by such gestures. Heinrich's lyrical solo halfway through the piece is contained and restrained. The soft espressivo solo follows a lengthy fast section and is immediately preceded by two grand pauses conspicuously marked "silent." (Each is two measures in duration, measures 227–28 and 233–34.) Heinrich's flair for the dramatic is everywhere in evidence. A pizzicato accompaniment in the strings sets off the flute aria; comparison to bel canto opera textures cannot be avoided (see Ex. 1.3).[54]

The rhythmic makeup of the tune recalls similar patterns found throughout the piece, helping to link the otherwise unexpected lyrical interruption with the larger work. Like the first important structural downbeat that connected the opening of the introduction to the allegro moderato, the one lead-

Ex. 1.1: Anthony Philip Heinrich, *The War of the Elements and the Thundering of Niagara*, mm 1–4. Kallisti Music Press edition, © 1994 Andrew Stiller. Used by permission.

Ex. 1.2: Anthony Philip Heinrich, *The War of the Elements and the Thundering of Niagara,*
mm 33–41. Kallisti Music Press edition, © 1994 Andrew Stiller. Used by permission.

ing up to the andantino is also a motion from an F♯7 to a section in B, again
not noted by the key signature. Although local harmonic motion is often
unpredictable and unorthodox in this piece, Heinrich's recollection of an earlier key relationship demonstrates an awareness of large-scale structure and
unity.

An A-flat major seventh chord introduces the final allegro of the main
section at measure 251 (quarter note at 144). If such a chord defies Beethovenian expectations for structural downbeats, it does follow the logic that Heinrich has established for his work. Harmonic, textural, and rhythmic behaviors
recall what has come before and provide the internal consistency for the
music.

At measure 333 Heinrich begins his coda: "The Thunders of Niagara,"
allegro assai, quasi presto (quarter note at 144). Its insistence on C major
provides a unique example of sustained harmonic stability in the larger work.
Softly articulated ascending and descending C-major arpeggios and an unambiguous duple rhythm immediately situate Niagara (see Ex. 1.4).

Trilling flutes and piccolos, and rolling timpani, bass, and snare drums
prepare listeners for a heraldic tutti at measure 344. Fast-moving contrary
motion scalar passages in the strings energize fanfare rhythms in the woodwinds and brass. Drums snap staccato quarter-note beats. Fermatas, so much
a part of the introductory section of the piece, don't appear for more than a

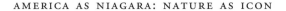

Ex. 1.3: Anthony Philip Heinrich, *The War of the Elements and the Thundering of Niagara,* mm 235–50. Kallisti Music Press edition, © 1994 Andrew Stiller. Used by permission.

hundred measures, and then there is a single one at measure 445.[55] Although the coda begins *piano,* the section is characterized by *forte, fortissimo,* and triple *forte* dynamics.

Heinrich's ever-changing musical soundscape anticipates the subsequent achievement of Frederic Church, who ultimately solved earlier artists' problems of proportion, perspective, and focus by placing his viewer *on* the water, with turbulent currents swirling in all directions.[56] The overwhelming dominance of the water in the seven-by-three-foot canvas allowed for no ambiguity regarding the subject of the painting. The flat landscape became a middleground horizon, with clouds and the essential rainbow suggesting an even larger landscape.

Heinrich provided a composer's solution to the problem of background and foreground, proportion, perspective and focus, although music required that the place be experienced successively, not simultaneously. The introduction and main section of the piece, with their unstable harmonies and thin

Coda: *The Thunders of Niagara*

Ex. 1.4: Anthony Philip Heinrich, *The War of the Elements and the Thundering of Niagara*, mm 333–36. Kallisti Music Press edition, © 1994 Andrew Stiller. Used by permission.

Ex. 1.5: Anthony Philip Heinrich, *The War of the Elements and the Thundering of Niagara,* mm 344–48. Kallisti Music Press edition, © 1994 Andrew Stiller. Used by permission.

textures, provided a musical equivalent to the surrounding terrain: it contained isolated points of interest, but nothing especially dramatic. Heinrich's "warring elements" may well have been the contrast between the relatively benign surroundings and the uncontrollably volatile waters. With the coda Heinrich focused on the superstar of the landscape, the Falls themselves. The solid C-major harmony allows a listener to anchor his aural gaze.

Heinrich reserves his creative energies for timbral effects and sheer quantity of sound. Like Church, Heinrich surrounds his audience with the waters. The open, airy, soloistic texture that dominated the earlier measures is replaced by a thicker, heavier mass in the coda; most of the instruments play most of the time. The effect is a block of sound, like the wall of water itself, solid and strong. One can appreciate the particular appropriateness of percussion to this soundscape. *Fortissimo* timpani, bass, and snare drums provide a firm foundation for cymbal rolls that alternate with tambourine and triangle shakes (measures 385–95) and combine to create a glistening aural spray.[57] A droning brass choir swells to triple *forte* at measure 404. The deep, rich fundamental C-major chord rumbles underneath swirling woodwind and string scales. The power of the Falls becomes music.

Soft, brief, circling figures capture the numerous small whirlpools endlessly rotating in the waters (measures 464–67). Ripples sound in sequences of rinforzando thirty-seconds (measures 480–82). Heinrich's music shimmers; it is in constant motion, and yet rhythmic complexities of the type that characterized his early keyboard and vocal works are absent in *The War of the Elements and the Thundering of Niagara*. Instead Heinrich uses a fast tempo, which is made even faster with a stringendo at measure 490 and the vibratory motions of rolled and trilled sounds to excite his music. He is content with simple dotted figures, a single occurrence of the Scottish snap rhythm (measures 150–51), numerous series of four thirty-second notes, the very occasional syncopation, and a few instances of triplets against eighths and sixteenths. Rhythmically, the piece is restrained; it is neither difficult nor unintelligible, and yet this is among Heinrich's most effective works. Those familiar with his very earliest efforts at composition, *The Dawning of Music in Kentucky, The Western Minstrel,* and *The Sylviad,* might expect an overly embellished work, one weighted down by its own inexplicable flights of fancy, but this is not the case in *The War of the Elements and the Thundering of Niagara.* There is a simple consistency to the elements of the piece, so that in spite of the many mood, key, meter, and tempo changes, it doesn't forfeit overall unity.

If Heinrich's piece reveals his perception of the place, the composer understood Niagara to be a source of thunderous (roaring?) power and strength. For all of its motion and activity, however, he also saw it as a symbol of incontestable stability; the ideal icon for the flag-waving newcomer to the nation. As the Bohemian immigrant composed his own version of America's most famous natural phenomenon, we can hear his energy, his imagination, his passion, and perhaps his heartfelt desire to be identified with the same. It may well be that for Heinrich, Niagara represented not only the physical place, but also his sense of the nation.

34

Ex. 1.6: Anthony Philip Heinrich, *The War of the Elements and the Thundering of Niagara,* mm 402–6. Kallisti Music Press edition, © 1994 Andrew Stiller. Used by permission.

WILLIAM HENRY FRY
Niagara Symphony

Establishing an American high-art music tradition was a protracted process that required the energies of many tenacious participants. Although Heinrich had helped found the New York Philharmonic Society in 1842, his efforts to create an indigenous musical culture were largely focused upon his own compositional activity.[58] Organizing and implementing a more systematic approach fell upon the shoulders of a man thirty-two years his junior who also wrote a paean to Niagara. In 1853 William Henry Fry (1813–64) closed a series of music lectures with what Richard Storrs Willis reported was a "Declaration of Independence in Art": "Until this Declaration of Independence in Art shall be made—until American composers shall discard their foreign liveries and found an American School—and until the American public shall learn to support American artists, Art will not become indigenous to this country, but will only exist as a feeble exotic, and we shall continue to be provincial in Art."[59] Sixteen years earlier, Emerson had delivered an oration before the Phi Beta Kappa Society entitled "The American Scholar," which Oliver Wendell Holmes would label "our intellectual Declaration of Independence." Emerson proclaimed: "Our day of dependence, our long apprenticeship to the learning of other lands, draws to a close."[60] In spite of what they said, folk artists had already broken away from slavish dependence upon European models, with linen weavings, oil and watercolor paintings, and pictorial quilts that captured everyday life in the new nation. William Pierson has argued that a distinctly American architecture developed as early as 1800.[61] The United States was rife with national awareness.

Fry was in the ideal position to advocate for the young nation. The second of five sons of the esteemed Philadelphia printer and publisher William Fry (1777–1855), William Henry possessed an unassailable American pedigree. He could point to an ancestor who spent the winter of 1777–78 with George Washington at Valley Forge, and another who participated in the Constitutional Convention in 1787.[62] His family also enjoyed complete financial security and was highly regarded for its intellectual prowess and support of all things cultural. Though others might have had no forum in which to circulate their ideas, the senior Fry's Philadelphia newspaper, the *National Gazette,* provided an outlet at once personally reflective and publicly acclaimed. The respect that Anthony Philip Heinrich sought throughout a lifetime was the birthright of William Henry Fry, a genuine native son.

But the younger Fry did not rest on inherited laurels. Throughout his fifty-one years, he energetically dedicated himself to the nation's developing culture. As a writer, editor, critic, lecturer, conversationalist, and composer, Fry worked for the cause of American music, insisting that the nation support its own musical creators and creations.[63] Although his musical compositions betray his absorption in bel canto and French opera traditions and have been criticized as too derivative and sounding more European than American, his "eloquence in behalf of American music" remains among his most significant contributions, his "lasting monument."[64]

As a youth in Philadelphia, Fry enjoyed the regular visits of touring opera companies. His devotion to this repertoire eventually resulted in his own composition of five operas and a number of choral and vocal works. In a lecture delivered during the winter of 1852–53, Fry explained: "Vocal music is superior to all others not merely because it is the music of the human voice, but because it carries or should carry clear and precise sentiments expressed in proper and poetical phrases."[65] Fry was himself a gifted vocalist as well as a writer, and these twin interests were well served by early-nineteenth-century opera.[66] But he did more than simply attend performances of visiting companies. In 1841 he and his brothers mounted the first American production of Bellini's *Norma,* in English, thanks in large measure to the work of one brother, Joseph, who had painstakingly translated the libretto years earlier. During those same years William worked on his own first opera, *Aurelia, the Vestal;* it was never performed.

In 1845 he completed his second and most famous opera, *Leonora,* which was produced in Philadelphia at the Chestnut Street Theatre on 4 June and given at least a dozen performances there. Audiences enthusiastically received this first opera in English composed by an American. A heavily revised *Leonora* was revived in 1858 in New York, this time sung in Italian. It was the unsuccessful result of Fry's efforts to interest European companies in his work.[67] Years later Fry admitted his regret that the subject of his best-known work had not been an American one. Such a miscalculation allowed George Frederick Bristow's *Rip Van Winkle* (1855), with its Washington Irving subject, to garner the accolade of being the first American opera.

In 1846 Fry left for Europe, where he would act as correspondent for the *New York Tribune.* While there he traveled to Italy, Switzerland, Germany, the Netherlands, and Belgium, and spent most of a year in London before settling in Paris. Over the course of six years, Fry sent back commentaries on prostitution in England; the restless political situation in France; various popular movements of the time, including socialism and communism; and, of course, the musical scene in Europe. An education at Mount St. Mary's in Maryland, famed for its classical training, and his musical studies with Leopold Meignen, a former student at the Paris Conservatoire who had settled in

Philadelphia, had prepared the young composer-critic to speak with knowledge and authority on a number of subjects. His missives to the New York paper were popular.

It was immediately upon his return to the States in November 1852 that Fry undertook a most ambitious, if not wholly unique, project: a series of lectures.[68] Renting Metropolitan Hall in New York City for ten Tuesday evenings, and soliciting subscriptions to cover the significant costs (estimated at about ten thousand dollars), William Henry Fry launched his music lecture series, one that would include vocalists and instrumentalists of only the highest caliber. He summed up his purposes and goals: "The aim of these lectures will be to present, in a condensed but clear form, an illustrated history of the rise, progress and present state of all departments of instrumental and vocal music—whether sacred, dramatic, symphonic, classic, romantic or national; or of those various kinds which it would be difficult to classify specifically."[69]

In the end the series was so popular that an eleventh lecture was added to the initial offering. They were attended by thousands over a three-month period, and discussed by numerous reviewers who saw the colossal event as a worthy enterprise, if not wholly successful in its execution.[70]

The lecture series catapulted Fry back into the center of the American musical scene, where he quickly became the most public spokesperson for a native musical culture. Over the course of the next few years, Fry engaged in lengthy polemics about musical meaning and value, inspired, in part, by the reception that well-placed critics accorded his music. A spirited public exchange between Fry and Richard Storrs Willis, carried in the *Musical World* and *Dwight's Journal of Music,* followed the Christmas Eve 1853 premiere of his *Santa Claus: Christmas Symphony.* The dispute resonated throughout the nineteenth century as it touched upon nationalism, the nature of art, and the comparative values of abstract and programmatic music. As we shall see, *Niagara Symphony,* while never discussed in the press, raises similar issues.

Fry's controversy with Willis consumed columns of *Dwight's Journal* throughout the early months of 1854. R. S. Willis, much like John Sullivan Dwight, insisted upon the supremacy of abstract instrumental music and faulted the over-long *Santa Claus Symphony* for its failure to follow the four-movement abstract European model. In a letter dated 10 January 1854, Fry replied: "I intend this communication to combat the position which you have taken as to my non-observance of the unities, and to demonstrate that there is no more unity in the four distinct movements of the classical symphony, than in four different novels or different plays by the same author,—that their so-called unity is an illogical absurdity of the founder of the school, and only accepted and admired by those who have not the radical originality to expose the error and who take on trust in music, as in religion, in government and in political economy, all things which bear the sanction of ages."[71]

Sharpening his point, Fry added, "I am an American and was not born in Germany during the last century." But Willis's criticism had not confined itself to an argument for abstract unity; he also chided the composer for the over-programmatic nature of the work and its numerous special effects—including sleigh bells and a cracking whip—descriptive gestures, and familiar melodies, including "Rock-a-by Baby on the Tree Top" and "Adeste Fideles." The work made no pretense to abstraction. At the request of the conductor Louis Antoine Jullien, Fry had written a multipage synopsis of the music for distribution to audience members.[72] This very specific narrative provided Willis with additional ammunition to deride the work. Again Fry responded, this time suggesting that the musical values *he* embraced were reflective of "this country." Like Heinrich, Fry paired his music with America: "In regard to painting eternal nature, I would remark, as applicable to the subject in hand, that the plastic arts, as evolved during our century, have given us new revelations, and so may *descriptive music in this country,* as soon as the mental mumps and measles of national childhood—or the eruptions and fevers of juvenile and provincial-like classicism, are passed away, and we shall believe in nature and not in names."[73]

Fry's caustic remarks tested the bounds of civility in the press and did not advance his cause, but his exasperation was not unwarranted. The title itself, *Santa Claus: Christmas Symphony,* announced that Fry had not intended the piece to be a chastely abstract work, one that would transport its listeners to higher realms of consciousness. Rather, mindful of the season for which it was composed, and of the virtuosic abilities of Jullien's first-chair players, Fry had written a work that celebrated the holiday and the musicians; a jovial Santa was portrayed by a bassoon. In his synopsis, Fry went so far as to name particular orchestral musicians as a way of explaining the roles they played in the program: "It is the Festivities of a Christmas Eve party, children participating: the clarionet of M. Wuille leading to the Dance, which is intended to be one of rollicking gaiety. This movement suddenly changes to another in which the hautboy of M. Lavigne and the flute of M. Reichert take the leading parts."[74] If the work featured flights of fancy, that was all part of his intent. In no uncertain terms, Fry rejected the aesthetic straitjacket forced upon him by Willis and Dwight. As with most artistic debates, this one did not deter audiences from embracing the music they enjoyed. The *Santa Claus: Christmas Symphony* was heard more than any other Fry work in the early 1850s, played more than forty times during Jullien's tour.[75]

If the season justified the theme of his *Santa Claus Symphony,* Fry offered no explanation for choosing Niagara Falls as his next subject, and he provided no program at all to the work beyond the name. This is most unfortunate, as the piece is unique among his orchestral works for its celebration of an American place.[76] Composed just five months after *Santa Claus* and intended for a premiere at a P. T. Barnum Monster Concert in May 1854, the work appears never to have been performed.[77] It is possible that a combination of inadequate rehearsal time, unusual forces, and the after-effects of the very public Christmas symphony controversy caused Fry to think twice about presenting the hastily composed, programmatically titled work.[78] That the piece was never mentioned in the press suggests that it did not get performed. We are deprived of both the composer's and critics' thoughts on what is certainly an effective and provocative work.[79]

It is not even known whether Fry ever visited the Falls; his biographer offers little more than a basic description of the work in a brief synopsis, although he does refer to *Niagara* as "something of a tour de force."[80] But Fry would not have had to see the cataract himself to be sensitive to its national significance: as has been demonstrated, its imagery was inescapable. Years earlier, in 1840, prior to the Fry brothers' production of *Norma* and before William Henry's work in Europe, an impressively large and mobile depiction of Niagara Falls, 200 square feet in all, had been displayed in Philadelphia. A "Moving Diorama of Niagara Falls" was shown at the American Museum in Philadelphia. According to an announcement that appeared in the *Philadelphia Public Ledger* on 24 February 1840, "No painting of the Falls, holds any comparison with this diorama."[81] No record exists to indicate whether Fry took in the show, although his residence in the city, and his work as a journalist for the *National Gazette* at this time, would have made it likely.

While Niagara's role in the national consciousness changed, it remained in the forefront of American iconography throughout Fry's lifetime. By 1850 Niagara had become a tourist mecca attracting about sixty thousand visitors that year alone.[82] However, as Jeremy Adamson explained: "the portrayal of the Falls had lapsed into standardization. With few exceptions, views became predictable and repetitive, lacking expressive power and relying upon established responses."[83] But a group of artists refused to surrender such a powerful subject to hackneyed interpretations and swarming tourists. The 1850s became an especially important decade for reimagining the Falls, as a second generation of Hudson River School painters saw behind the factories, hotels, and souvenir stands that crowded the Falls. It is likely that two artworks in particular caught the attention of the composer-critic William Fry. Together they helped revitalize America's most powerful national symbol.

Among the most effective efforts at mid-century revitalization were two moving panoramas that toured the nation in 1853–54, one created by the Washington, D.C.–born Canadian painter Washington Friend (c. 1820–86), the other by an immigrant landscape artist from Cincinnati, Godfrey N. Frankenstein (1820–73).[84] Moving panoramas were a wildly popular form of nineteenth-century entertainment, seen by hundreds of thousands of people who would spend up to two hours watching a show. They were the direct precursors of twentieth-century movies. Remunerative as well as popular, one such panorama earned more than $100,000 in its first six months on the road.[85] Panoramas consisted of a series of individual paintings that were joined together to form a single very long canvas—some more than 1,000 feet long and 12 feet high—mounted on two large wooden rollers. Scene by scene the canvas was unfurled from one roller to the other, while special lighting, music, and commentary provided a multisensory experience. Because moving panoramas were intended to be viewed from a distance, they were painted with broad brush strokes and in overly bright colors, a contrast to the extremely detailed and subtle work and color of paintings by the Hudson River School landscapists. Conceived more as entertainment than as fine art and often painted by theater (scenery) artists, panoramas were executed with impermanent paints, a situation that has resulted in the near disappearance of examples of this art form.[86]

In 1849 Washington Friend undertook a three-year, 5,000-mile tour of Canada and the United States, sketching natural wonders he viewed along the way. Among a host of depictions of places in North America, his panorama contained a number of Niagara scenes. Once completed, it showed in Canada, the United States, and Britain, providing all who saw it with a sense of the variety and grandeur of the continent. By contrast to Friend's wide-ranging grand tour, all 1,000 feet by 9 feet of the Godfrey Frankenstein panorama were devoted to a single natural phenomenon: Niagara Falls. It took ninety minutes to unwind completely and was accompanied by music and commentary.[87] The result of more than nine years of work and two hundred different sketches, as well as the help of two assistants, it toured extensively in the United States and Britain and eventually wore out; today we are left with only reports of its existence and various scenes published in books and magazines of the time.[88] In the words of a writer for the *National Democrat,* "no locality [had] ever been treated in such a numerous series of views."[89] But as important as the variety of views was their novelty. According to Jeremy Adamson, "The climax of Frankenstein's so-called Metropolitan Niagara was the final sequence of winter views that were 'altogether new and startling,'" essential features if Niagara was to keep the interest of viewers in an image-flooded market.[90]

As Frankenstein's panorama toured the South, it was a source of national pride just as it had been when touring the north. In Savannah, Georgia, the city's *News* dubbed it "the pride of America."[91] In antebellum America, Niagara belonged to the whole nation regardless of region or politics; the power and majesty of the Falls symbolized America's promise. All of this would change with the Civil War. But if Fry had been seeking a subject for musical nationalism at mid-century, there would have been none better than Niagara.

Given Fry's presence in New York when these works toured there, it is inconceivable that he did not know of them or attend a showing of one or both; they were nineteenth-century blockbusters, an essential experience for Americans of his class, culture, and consciousness. They bolstered national pride, a fact that would not have been overlooked. Their contemporaneity with his *Niagara* symphony of 1854 offers one possible explanation for the composition of this solitary American place piece by Fry.

A Musical Panorama

Fry's single-movement symphony showcases his genuine talent for orchestral effects, skills recognized, if somewhat grudgingly, by reviewers of the *Santa Claus Symphony*. His instrumental forces are large and, like Heinrich's, reveal a particular fondness for brass and percussion. A traditional string ensemble is joined by woodwinds, including a single flute, which doubles on piccolo, pairs of oboe, clarinets in B-flat, bassoons, and a single contrabassoon. Of the woodwind instruments only the bassoon is used soloistically, and then only when doubling the second violin line within a full string ensemble (see measures 37–39). The brass family is more generously represented: two trumpets in C, cornets in B-flat, pairs of horns in E-flat and C; alto, tenor, and bass trombones; a tuba; and unspecified numbers of ophicleidi and bombardoni.[92] Fry uses only two types of percussion instruments, but, taken together, their numbers and effects are significant. The score does not specify exactly how many tambori (field drums) Fry requires, but he does write parts for five timpanists playing eleven (!) timpani pitched to G, A-flat, A-natural, B-flat, B-natural, C, D-flat, D-natural, E-flat, E-natural, and F♯.[93] Fry used his large brass and percussion sections to produce an always full, round, and resonant sound, even when the dynamic level hovered at *pianissimo*.

The piece, approximately thirteen and a half minutes, is continuous and divides into three large sections: (1) an opening: Largo assai, grave measures 1–35, followed by più mosso con impeto measures 36–64; (2) a middle section that combines elements of both an Italian brindisi and a more sober choral aria, which extends from measures 65 to 79, is repeated, and followed by a four-measure transition.[94] This leads back to (3) a *da capo* with *fine* at measure 64. Over the last eight measures of the *da capo* (measures 57–64), the composer indicates "Rit. molto (second time only)."[95] Fry's choice of an A B A form supplied formal unity, at least at the structural level. As will be shown, it also served programmatic purposes.

Given the size of the brass and percussion forces and the subject being described, one might expect the piece to begin loudly and forcefully. But the exact opposite is the case. Four of the eleven timpani, those pitched A, C, E-flat and F♯ rumble an indistinguishable opening chord *pianissimo*. For four measures, the audible but nearly unidentifiable sound surrounds a listener with its soft, gradually increasing swell. Bassoons, bass trombone, oficleidi, bombardoni, celli, and contrabass enter with *piano* tremolos at measure 5. Divisi viola join at measure 6, with everyone reinforcing the diminished harmony of the timpani.

Fry is careful in his instructions to the timpanists: At measure 11, he reminds player number four to mute the E-flat timpani in preparation for a *fortissimo* E natural six measures later; and then again at measure 19 he reminds the player to mute the E-natural in anticipation of an upcoming E-flat.

At measure 13, the entire brass ensemble, and oboes, clarinet, and bassoons, emerge on a C-major chord; here the piece reaches a *forte* dynamic. But this is only a foretaste of the larger, more dramatically triumphant C-major chord and theme that explode triple *forte* at measure 23.[96] It is hard not to think of Haydn's *Creation,* a work that was extremely popular in America throughout the first half of the nineteenth century, with its similarly glorious arrival at C major coinciding with the line "'Es werde Licht!' und es ward Licht." Haydn approaches the tonal denouement via a chromatic ascent in the soprano, while Fry works through an extended series of diminished chords. Whether intended or not, the musical association of Fry's symphony with Haydn's famous oratorio paired Niagara Falls with divine creation, an idea that was still popular among many quarters at mid-century and, thanks to the revitalizing efforts of a second generation of Hudson River School painters, would become even more so.[97]

But while this harmonic event might recall Haydn's 1798 work, Fry's timbral choices anticipated the brass-heavy exultant sounds of much later pieces: Wagner's *Die Walküre* of 1870 and Verdi's *Requiem* of 1874 among them. And beyond timbral similarities, the theme that emerges at measure 23 of *Niagara* also shares a descending, arpeggiated shape with the bass line of the "tuba mirum" of that Mass. Though Fry descends through a C-major arpeggio and Verdi traverses an A-flat minor one, dynamic levels, timbral choices, and the overall powerful mood of both pieces makes for similarly effective moments within larger pieces. Regardless of Verdi's religious title, his work, like Fry's, was theatrical (see Ex. 1.7).

On numerous occasions in the course of the *Niagara* symphony, a listener is struck by Fry's instrumental combinations: this is a music of color and effect. While in Europe, Fry had attended concerts conducted by the celebrated French composer-critic Hector Berlioz, a master of the newly named discipline orchestration.[98] Although there is little hard evidence of a friendship between the two men during these years, Fry's appreciation for Berlioz's gifts as an orchestrator was clear in remarks made years later. In a *New York Tribune* review of an 1863 concert in which Berlioz's *Harold in Italie* was performed (conducted by Theodore Thomas), he noted, "Hector Berlioz is a Frenchman—a composer of distinction in the instrumental walk . . . of course there is evidenced all the orchestration of a superlative master in the use of musical instruments." Later in the review the critic enthused, "the ecstatic finale of Harold gave a fine chance for the multiform simultaneous traits of musical coloring or instrumentation, the whirl of violins, the strident wrath of the brass, the clash of cymbals, the shrieks of the little flutes and all the agonies and ecstasies of the soul in communion with physical nature aroused."[99]

In much of *Niagara* the entire ensemble "whirls" and "shrieks." If Church's 1857 painting became famous for its masterful depiction of multiple swirling waters, Fry made a noble attempt to capture the same in sound. This is music of motion. Strings are well suited to the long, fast, scalar passages that Fry wrote for them. But some might question the practicality of measures-long, whirling thirty-second-note runs demanded of trumpets, oficleidi, and bombardoni (see Ex. 1.8). Such writing challenges even the technically brilliant instrumentalists of today; one can only imagine the obstacle these passages would have presented to the lesser-trained musicians of Fry's time. Perhaps this was another reason the piece was not performed.

But if Fry was not particularly sensitive to practical considerations regarding brass instruments, he did succeed at creating incessant momentum and a thoroughly saturated sound mass. He covered the pitch range from string basses to piccolos. When the brass start up their running figurations, Fry adds the entire woodwind ensemble to the mix. As the scales rise into the realm of multi-leger lines above the treble clef, piccolos, flutes, and oboes shriek in the vortex of a musical Niagara. Fry also uses the continuous roll of field drums to create an effect akin to splashing water, a relatively high-pitched, white noise–like sound familiar to anyone who has spent much time around the surf. While Fry might not have shown all the signs of a polished orchestrator, his ambitious and creative handling of orchestral instruments surely earns him the sobriquet of America's first native-born symphonic composer.

Fry's musical whirlpool climaxes at measure 45 before dissipating nearly completely at measure 54. It is followed by a ten-measure iteration of a single A-diminished chord that starts out triple *forte* at measure 55 and decrescendos to a triple *piano* at measure 64. This signals the end of the first section, which will also form the close of the piece the second time through.

Measures 65 to 79 provide a soft, gentle, lyrical interlude; woodwinds and brass are marked espressivo. The passage resembles a slowed-down drinking song, or a bel canto choral aria, complete with pizzicato string accompaniment. Both of these genres would have been familiar to the opera-loving Fry. But reminiscent as it is of such models, Fry's orchestral aria is not built upon simple four-square phrases answered by four-measure phrases. A fifth measure, which repeats a fragment of the previous measure, is added to each of the phrases, and then both are followed by a third group of five measures that draw from the third and fourth measures of the initial phrase (see Ex. 1.9).[100]

Though Fry provides a key signature of three flats, the interlude is solidly in A-flat, as is indicated by the numerous D-flat accidentals added to the score. The aria cadences with an arpeggio in A-flat and then repeats. Like the reiterated diminished chord built on A that closes out the first section, Fry follows this second section orchestral aria with four measures of an arpeggiated A-diminished chord that lead directly back to the da capo. Each measure of this transition starts softly and crescendos to a *fortissimo,* heightening the tension and suggesting a continuation of the drama, although what occurs can't be anticipated.

A return to the beginning means a return to the nearly inaudible rumblings of the timpani. The juxtaposition of the *fortissimo* ending of the transition and the *pianissimo* beginning of the *da capo* makes for a startling and extremely theatrical, if not wholly satisfying, effect. There is little to connect the serene song of the second section with the bombastic arpeggiated theme that dominates the surrounding sections. One seeking organic, teleological music will surely be disappointed. But harmonically the piece is unified; beginning, middle, and end share the same diminished chord.[101] By grounding his piece in a single harmony, even one as unstable and ambiguous as a diminished chord, Fry holds his disparate musical ideas together. The distinct sections of music, it could be argued, aptly represent the multiple aspects of Niagara that painters found so hard to capture in a single image.

Once again, whether intended or not, Fry's use of the same repeated chord to begin and end his piece suggests the constancy of the natural phenomenon. Listeners come upon the Falls as they come upon his piece, with sounds that are soft and mysterious, and they leave the Falls and the piece the same way. Fifty years later, Charles Ives would depict eternity using a similar approach

Ex. 1.7: William Henry Fry, *Niagara Symphony,* mm 13–26. Fleisher Collection of Orchestral Music, Free Library of Philadelphia.

B * Original has Alto Trb. and Tuba I as 8ve higher in bracketed section.

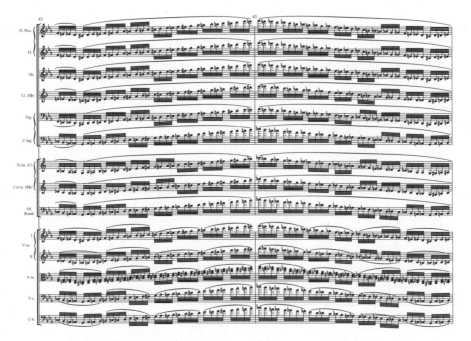

Ex. 1.8: William Henry Fry, *Niagara Symphony,* mm 42–43. Fleisher Collection of Orchestral Music, Free Library of Philadelphia.

in his piece *The Unanswered Question.* In both works auditors enter into an extremely quiet musical environment, experience the musical scene, and exit without having altered the original environment, although they might themselves be changed. Perhaps Fry was suggesting the same about Niagara: Regardless of decades of commercializing and commodifying, the essence of the Falls was beyond human alteration. The efforts of the 1850s painters, from Friend to Frankenstein to Church, to revitalize this reading of the Falls found a sympathetic spirit in William Henry Fry.

Fry's music is filled with sounds similar to those of contemporary European composers. His choice of diminished harmonies and the arpeggiated announcement of C major recall Heinrich's *War of the Elements and the Thundering of Niagara,* a work unpublished and unperformed at the time.[102] Striving to create an original American music, Fry nonetheless worked with the sounds of the established traditions. The tradition loomed large. As Michael Broyles has observed, Heinrich, while writing music based on a folk-variation technique, desired it to be measured against the high-art tradition, and "therein lay his aesthetic undoing. In attempting to do so he created a

Ex. 1.9: William Henry Fry, *Niagara Symphony*, mm 65–69. Fleisher Collection of Orchestral Music, Free Library of Philadelphia.

dichotomy of his own making."[103] While championing as vehemently as anyone in his time the urgent need of an original American music, Fry could do little better than write within the European tradition in his own compositions and encourage others to seek a truly national voice. At the very least with the *Niagara Symphony,* he turned toward the celebration of an American subject and attempted to contribute to a larger national artistic effort to preserve that icon. It is one of the ironies of America's music history that Fry's patriotic prose was read by large audiences on both sides of the Atlantic, but his single attempt at musical nationalism was most likely never heard.

GEORGE FREDERICK BRISTOW
Niagara: Symphony for Grand Orchestra and Chorus

Still another nineteenth-century American took on Niagara as the subject of a large musical work. A contemporary of Fry's and the director of instrumental and vocal music at Fry's lecture series, George Frederick Bristow (1825–98), the third of America's first symphonists, wrote a hybrid instrumental-choral work titled *Niagara: Symphony for Grand Orchestra and Chorus.*[104] Like Fry, Bristow was an outspoken advocate for American composers and American music. At the same time as Fry was conducting his public battle in the press over the goals of his music, Bristow took on the Philharmonic Society for its anti-American practices, which, he claimed, excluded American composers from having their works performed on Philharmonic concerts. Targeting the German musicians who made up a large number of professional musicians in the country, Bristow accused them of "little short of a conspiracy against the Art of a country to which they have come for a living."[105] It is not surprising that years later, Bristow too should turn to the earliest national icon as inspiration for a piece.

Though he composed it in 1893, Bristow had to wait until 1898 for its first scheduled performance. Then a premier worthy of the grand subject was planned. *Niagara* would be the last large work that Bristow completed. With this piece the composer, conductor, teacher, author, and advocate for American music and musicians offered a final nineteenth-century word on the Falls, one that reflected his deeply religious, patriotic, and conservative values. In 1961 an even later American composer, Ferde Grofé, created what is to date the last purely orchestral tribute to Niagara Falls. This work will be taken up in a subsequent chapter.

Of Heinrich, Fry, and Bristow, Bristow was the most thoroughly trained musician; the product of a musical household, he devoted his life to the art.

Frederic Edwin Church, *Niagara*, 1857. In the collection of the Corcoran Gallery of Art, Washington, D.C.

Winslow Homer, *The Artist's Studio in an Afternoon Fog*, 1894. Reproduced courtesy of the Memorial Art Gallery of the University of Rochester, R. T. Miller Fund.

George Frederick was born to Anna and William Bristow, who had come to the United States from England early in the 1820s. William quickly became a leader in the musical life of Brooklyn, New York, assuming the roles of conductor, church organist, theater musician, and teacher of various instruments, including the piano. It was with his father that George Frederick began lessons on piano and organ. Later he studied harmony with Henry Christian Timm, a German immigrant keyboardist who served as the president of the Philharmonic Society from 1848 through 1863, and when the violin virtuoso Ole Bull was on tour in America, Bristow studied violin with him.[106] At twelve years of age, he joined the Olympic Theatre Orchestra as a violinist (this was the same ensemble in which his father played clarinet), and in 1842, when just seventeen, Bristow became a member of the first violin section of the New York Philharmonic Society, a group he stayed with until 1879.[107] His skill and versatility as a performer are apparent from his appearances on numerous occasions as both a violin and a piano soloist with the Philharmonic.[108] In addition to his duties with that organization, Bristow was one of the native musicians chosen by Antoine Jullien to augment his orchestral forces when the French conductor came to America, and he accompanied Jenny Lind when she was on tour. His warm feelings toward Jullien would result in his second symphony being dedicated and named for the conductor: the *Jullien Sinfonia.* The native New Yorker was literally and figuratively in the center of what was quickly becoming America's cultural capital.

Busy as he was with orchestral obligations, Bristow's interests went beyond purely instrumental music. In 1851 he became the conductor of the New York Harmonic Society, a large amateur choral group in the city. For his inaugural concert with the society on 11 December 1851, he directed Haydn's *Creation.* The chorus from the ubiquitous oratorio would be performed again by the Harmonic Society under Bristow's direction at the inauguration of the Crystal Palace on 14 July 1853.[109] Along with Handel's *Messiah,* the *Creation* became a staple of the society's repertoire. In keeping with his dedication to the promotion of native works, during the course of his twelve-year tenure at the Harmonic Society Bristow programmed pieces by a number of Americans, William Henry Fry and himself among them.[110] Linked forever by music historians as America's first symphonists, Fry and Bristow crossed paths regularly in mid-century New York as they energetically strove to create an American musical culture.

Before his career as a choral conductor came to an end, Bristow conducted two additional groups, the Mendelssohn Union (from approximately 1867 to 1871) and the Harlem Mendelssohn Union (1871–73). His involvement with these groups had a direct impact on his compositions; two-thirds of the works he composed between 1852 and 1879 were for voice, a clear change from his earlier preference for instrumental composition.[111] Bristow's move toward vocal music reflected the popularity of these societies and their repertoire, his active involvement with them, and his own best chance of having some of his pieces performed. The *Niagara Symphony* reflects all his associations, orchestral and vocal.[112]

Blessed with seemingly endless energy, in 1854 Bristow added to his already full schedule the duties of music teacher for the New York Public Schools. It was his teaching, no doubt, that inspired him to write a number of instruction books: *The Cantilena* (1861) and *The Cantara* (1866), and a translation of *Ferdinand Beyer's School for the Piano-Forte* (1866). He also contributed to two collections of pieces, *Melodia Sacra* (1852) and *The Centennial School Singer* (1876), and he published an organ method book entitled *George F. Bristow's New and Improved Method for the Reed or Cabinet Organ* (1887). After 1879 and his retirement from the New York Philharmonic Society, teaching, both privately and in the public schools, consumed the majority of Bristow's time and energy. Dedicated until the end to educating his nation to the cause of music in America, George Frederick Bristow passed away in a classroom.

While William Henry Fry used the bully pulpit of the press to rail at a nation unresponsive to its native musicians, Bristow acted on the charge and assumed the mantle of American composer. Understanding what seemed to come only late to Fry, Bristow turned to a variety of American subjects for his pieces. Perhaps his most successful work was one based upon a popular Washington Irving tale, his opera *Rip Van Winkle,* composed between 1852 and 1855. Bristow and his librettist added a love story to the plot, thereby assuring the requisite tenor-soprano duet; according to the program, the change was "approved" by the author.[113] But having satisfied convention, the opera still didn't hold together. Musical action was interrupted numerous times with spoken dialogue; the opera resembled a pastiche of sentimental songs. According to Delmer Rogers's dissertation, the work was much too long (four hours) and suffered from the absence of any unifying musical ideas "that would help organize the opera as a whole."[114] Bristow and a new librettist would revisit this opera years later, but it never achieved an enduring place in the repertoire.

Other works that celebrated American subjects included two overtures: the *Columbus Overture* of 1861 and the *Jibbenainosay Overture,* written in 1889. The title of the latter comes from an 1837 novel by William Richard Bird entitled *Nick of the Woods, or, The Jibbenainosay.* In the story, a Quaker frontiersmen whose family is massacred becomes the devil or Jibbenainosay of the woods. It is a story that lends itself to all sorts of melodramatic musical effects.

Rogers observes the similarity of this character to those found in James Feni-more Cooper's *Leatherstocking Tales,* another source of nationalistic litera-ture.[115] Still other of Bristow's pieces refer to the nation and its people quite conspicuously in their titles: *Souvenir de Mount Vernon: Grand Valse Brilliante,* of 1861; *The Pioneer: A Grand Cantata,* written in 1872; *The Great Republic* of 1880, a work scored for soloists, chorus, and orchestra; and a series of piano pieces entitled *Plantation Pleasures* and *Plantation Memories,* written in 1894–95. But it is the *Niagara Symphony,* opus 62, with its soloists, chorus, and orchestra, its enormous proportions, and its sacralization of a specific icono-graphic American place, that goes beyond mere flag-waving nationalism and comes closest to being a bona-fide place piece. With this work Bristow joined a centuries-old tradition of artistic tributes to the Falls, even as that tradition was nearing its end.

After the Civil War, belief in Manifest Destiny waned. It was hard to sell America's nature as pure and sublime when picturesque rolling pastures had become carnage-strewn battlefields, when the steel beams of railroads laced miles of virgin plains. Niagara suffered too in the postwar years, both in its physical environment and as a symbol of a unified America. The Falls, like the Hudson River School painters who had immortalized it, was closely iden-tified with the North, an association that did not endear it to the peoples of the defeated Confederacy. In addition, exploitation by commercial venturers in the area directly surrounding the falls made a mockery of the idea of a nation sacralized through its natural beauty. In response to America's more sober, perhaps more honest, awareness of itself, painters turned away from grand, universally resonant depictions of natural sites to more intimate and personal ones. Niagara Falls, which had been "the pride of America," was now stripped of a single national meaning; it no longer symbolized a unified vision.

An engraving that appeared in *Harper's Weekly* in 1873 captured the multi-farious perceptions of the Falls; it is titled "Niagara Seen with Different Eyes."[116] The artist Arthur Lumley surrounds the Falls with discrete groups of people, each situated on a different ledge or in a different crevasse close by the waters. In the center is an American Indian family. Written in the foam of the waters just above them is "The Indian appeals to the Great Spirit." They are seemingly the only people present, among more than twenty who populate the scene, who view the Falls with any kind of awe or reverence, and perhaps a touch of sadness. Everyone else—a geologist, a painter, soldiers, sailors, patriots, a poet, lovers, a "practical business man," a blushing bride, a sentimentalist, and a group of tourists—looks out over the Falls devoid of wonder, with no recognition of the others. Each is content with his own

Arthur Lumley, *Niagara Seen with Different Eyes,* from *Harper's Weekly,* 9 August 1873. Courtesy of HarpWeek, LLC.

vision. Lumley makes the point clear with numerous captions superimposed upon the work: "with the eye of the geologist," "with the eye of patriotism," "with the eye of love," "with the eye of the tourist." While the Falls are valued by everyone present, they have no inherent significance, they carry no national message. As Elizabeth McKinsey concludes: "The meaning one might read is a function of one's own attitude and condition. Any single meaning would seem to be merely arbitrary."[117]

But even amid countless vendors, enterprises, and tourist haunts, the earlier meaning of the Falls would not completely evaporate like so much sea spray. Most immediately the Falls provided an object lesson for settlers heading west who took with them vivid memories of the commercial callousness that had all but destroyed Niagara.[118] They could save the West from a similar fate, intercede to preserve what remained of America's nature before it had all been compromised. Their efforts became a matter of national pride, national prestige. Eventually they would help to energize Niagara's reclamation. As the preservation historian Alfred Runte observes, "A country that sought its antiquity in natural landmarks could not, at the same time, allow those landmarks to be despoiled."[119] The national shame of Niagara was the beginning of its redemption. It would take two full decades after Appomattox to reclaim the cataract for the nation, and even then it would be a different Niagara, one fashioned by a landscape architect. But the Falls would rise again, and this was the context in which George Frederick Bristow wrote his final symphony.

First discussions regarding the "restoration" of Niagara took place as early as 1869, when Frederick Law Olmsted visted the Falls with his partner Calvert Vaux; Henry Hobson Richardson, an architect; and William Dorscheimer, a New York State district attorney. Olmsted, who had gained worldwide fame and respect for his design of New York's Central Park in 1858 and his efforts to preserve the Yosemite Valley and Mariposa Grove in California in 1862, led the charge. He was joined by an equally famous figure, Frederic Edwin Church. The group attempted to focus attention on the plight of Niagara and the need for intervention. By comparison, Yosemite and, later, Yellowstone National Park were relatively easy projects, as their natural beauty was intact. Niagara, however, presented multiple problems: it was administered by two different countries and their local governments, the province of Ontario in Canada and New York State in the United States, and it was already developed by various individuals and businesses. This would require confiscating much of the land through the exertion of eminent domain over vast areas of the site in question.

Olmsted's and Church's initial efforts failed to excite support; a war-weary nation had bigger projects to consider. It would take another ten years and the 1878 initiative of the governor general of Canada, Lord Dufferin, to get the project moving. Dufferin formally proposed to New York's governor, Lucius Robinson, that the two sovereignties create an international park.[120] That it took Canada to motivate the United States to save its most celebrated national icon must have been a source of embarrassment and frustration to those who had been working for years to stimulate interest in the project. One can't help wondering to what degree pride motivated the U.S. response.[121]

The outgoing New York governor set the wheels in motion, and in the early months of 1879 the state legislature authorized a survey of the Falls. Once again Olmsted was a key player. In a report issued to the state, the influential architect envisioned an environment that increased "the influence of the scenery" and encouraged a visitor to follow "his natural and healthy individual intuitions."[122] He emphasized the need to plant rows of trees so that all man-made structures would be hidden; as much as possible visitors should feel that they were in a park. As John F. Sears observed, "Olmsted's plan for the reservation made room for the genteel tourist again, but defined the proper experience of the Falls as picturesque contemplation rather than sublime excitement."[123] The Falls would be denatured.

It would take another six years and a lengthy media campaign to win legislative approval (in 1883) before the Niagara Falls State Reservation opened in 1885. Three years later Ontario opened its own park. As Frederic Church's *Niagara* had forced mid-century viewers to look again at the cataract and see it as if with new eyes, Frederick Olmsted's parklike vision of the grounds reshaped the very setting of the Falls and rescued Niagara as a national symbol, albeit a significantly revised one. Olmsted succeeded in civilizing nature, and in doing so created a national icon that has endured.

The resuscitation of Niagara Falls at the end of the century was not exclusively a rear-guard action, nor was it the sentimental clinging to outdated national images that it might initially appear to be. At the same time that the newly dedicated park was becoming established, as its newly planted trees were taking root and providing the canopied paths envisioned by Olmsted, the United States was casting aside its provincial image and emerging as a world player. Accompanying this rise in stature was a newly invigorated sense of nationalism. Numerous end-of-the-century celebrations and exhibitions showcased the burgeoning power. In an age of European expositions, the nation's own World Columbian Exposition of 1893 in Chicago, complete with its classical-Greek-inspired White City, brought the United States to center stage.[124] Here was a showcase for America as an industrial leader and a unique cultural entity. It was in 1893, as the nation mounted its first international retrospective and while pride in America's accomplishments and promise was at a peak, that Bristow wrote his symphony.

This was also the year that Mark Twain wrote an essay lampooning Niagara, not as the natural phenomenon that he clearly valued, but as an overused cultural object susceptible to the nation's changing needs. He titled his sketch "The First Authentic Mention of Niagara Falls: Extracts from Adam's Diary."[125] Twain set the Garden of Eden at Niagara with Adam and Eve as bickering honeymooners, thus making the Falls a symbol of the fall of man.[126]

Casting his tale as a marital tiff, Twain unloads his verbal shot and in the process attacks the very notion of Niagara as the symbol of a divinely destined nation. In Twain's story, Adam is distressed that Eve ceaselessly moves about the "estate" naming things and thus commodifying them. He had had his own ideas about where he was before she came on the scene, but Eve constantly corrects him. "The new creature," he says, "calls it Niagara Falls—why, I am sure I do not know. Says it *looks* like Niagara Falls." He wishes she'd stop following him around and "stay with the other animals." Exasperated by his helplessness, Adam complains: "The naming goes recklessly on, in spite of anything I can do. I had a very good name for the estate, and it was musical and pretty—GARDEN-OF-EDEN. Privately, I continue to call it that, but not any longer publicly. The new creature says it is all woods and rocks and scenery, and therefor has no resemblance to a garden. Says it looks like a park, and does not look like anything but a park. Consequently, without consulting me it has been new named—NIAGARA FALLS PARK. This is sufficiently high-handed, it seems to me. And already there is a sign up: KEEP OFF THE GRASS. My life is not as happy as it was."[127]

Twain challenges Olmsted's transformation of Niagara from what was once a rugged, proud, natural site into a rule-bound, domesticated, parklike scene. Using Adam and Eve's problematic relationship, he pokes fun at the idea of Niagara as a romantic honeymoon destination, a role it played since the third decade of the century. It is no accident that in Twain's tale the Falls have been domesticated by the "first wife." The author simultaneously undermines and reinforces all sorts of assumptions.

It was in this highly charged atmosphere of reinvigorated nationalism, growing interest in preservation, and turn-of-the-century cynicism that Bristow wrote his work. There is no mention of the *Niagara Symphony* having been composed for the Chicago Exposition, and the 1 September 1893 completion date that appears in the manuscript may have precluded it from being presented there. The event was well under way by that time.[128] The composition of such a large work requiring festival-size performances this late in Bristow's career does, however, raise the question of inspiration and motivations. His *Niagara: Symphony for Grand Orchestra, Soloists, and Chorus* was anomalous among the smaller religious works he was writing on a regular basis in the final years of his life.

Niagara was scheduled for performance 11 April 1898, under the auspices of the Manuscript Society of New York, an organization conceived in August 1889 by a small group of composers and musicians that eventually included George Chadwick, Arthur Foote, Edgar Stillman Kelley, Edward MacDowell, and Horatio Parker, among others. This group joined together "for the purpose of promoting the composition of good music in America" and "the frank and free criticism of one another's compositions."[129] In its earliest years the society sponsored public and private concerts showcasing members' works. It grew steadily to include music supporters as well as composers, changed the structure of its governing body to accommodate its growing membership and vision, instituted a requirement that all applicants for "active membership . . . should submit a manuscript in polyphony writing," and required the contribution of "a manuscript composition to the library of the society."[130] This creation of a library indicates an organization with a sense of its historical role.[131]

Society-sponsored concerts were the most visible and public sign of the young organization's support of American music. The impact of Antonín Dvořák's three years in America (1892–95) as director of the National Conservatory in New York, and his challenge to the nation's composers to look to indigenous sources, reinforced earlier admonitions by Fry and Bristow to write American music, although they had offered no such specific suggestions for native materials. The visitor's urgings became apparent in the music programmed on Manuscript Society concerts. One given on 3 December 1896 included *Indian Rhapsody* by Paul Miersch, an overture entitled *In the Sunny South* by Henry Schoenefeld, and a pair of *Negro Idyls* by Henry F. Gilbert. A review that appeared in *The Pianist* singled out the *Indian Rhapsody,* a work "written on motifs derived from the songs and dances of the Ute Indians," as "the hit of the evening."[132]

But by January 1897, the society's *Bulletin* revealed a problem that was to grow only more difficult to solve. Even though the society was financially healthy, and the treasurer boasted that the organization had never closed a year with a single member behind in dues, the board expressed great concern "in obtaining a sufficient choice of suitable manuscripts for performance." Officers announced an addition to the by-laws that opened the doors to "members of other societies of American composers [whose works] may at the discretion of the music committee be placed on the programs of the public concerts and private meetings of this Society."[133] By the early years of the twentieth century the society listed more than nine hundred members, but it also began to suffer the pangs of dissension among its ranks. It limped along sponsoring fewer and fewer concerts and eventually disbanded in 1918, but not before it had demonstrated the "necessity of cooperation in promoting American music."[134]

Bristow was a board member of the Manuscript Society between 1894 and 1896, and he had a hand in arranging public programs sponsored by the society.[135] It was while he was a member of the public programs committee that Bristow had his Mass in C performed at a Manuscript Society–sponsored concert on 8 January 1895. His *Niagara: Symphony for Grand Orchestra and Chorus* was scheduled for performance on 11 April 1898. Stories in the Manuscript Society's *Bulletin* from January and March 1898 reveal plans for a grand event: "a chorus of 200 voices, several eminent soloists and the Seidl Grand Orchestra, all under the auspices of the Manuscript Society of New York," and conducted by Bristow himself. Two months of rehearsals readied the various performers.[136] Neither of the stories could have anticipated Anton Seidl's unexpected death from food poisoning on 28 March 1898, just two weeks before *Niagara*'s scheduled performance. All of New York mourned the passing of its celebrated conductor.[137] One would assume that the *Niagara* extravaganza would have drawn the attention of even the most distracted critics and observers had it taken place. The absence of any reviews in the

New York Times or *New York Herald Tribune* almost certainly means that plans were changed.

The Music of Niagara

If there were no title to guide a listener's thinking, it is doubtful that the subject of Bristow's programmatic symphony would be immediately obvious, at least up to the final choral movement, where the text leaves little question. Unlike the Fry symphony, whose augmented percussion arsenal immediately signaled something magnificent and grand, Bristow's instrumentation is not especially unusual: a pair of flutes, the first of which is called upon to play piccolo; oboes; clarinets in B-flat; two bassoons of which one is a contrabassoon; four natural horns, crooked variously in C, G, E-flat;[138] a pair of trumpets in C; three trombones, the third of which is doubled by a tuba; timpani initially tuned to D and A (later tuned to E-flat and B-flat, and C and G); and a complement of strings, including first and second violins, viola, cello, and string bass.[139]

The symphony opens with a solo trumpet call that starts off loudly and gradually diminishes over eight measures to a *pianissimo;* it could easily herald any highly dramatic work. The trumpet's alternating Cs and Gs delineate a general tonal area, but not the precise mode. Modal space will be traversed in Bristow's grand symphony much as it was in Beethoven's Fifth Symphony, which begins in C minor and ends in C major. Given the length cast by Beethoven's shadow over all composers writing symphonic works in the nineteenth century, similarities would not have been lost on Bristow. The use of C major among the three Niagara symphonists may speak as much for the preferences and capabilities of instruments and instrumentalists as it does for any specific association with the Falls. Unlike Eugene Thayer, none of the composers made a case for the Falls sounding in a particular key.

The fanfare dies away, and the first movement allegro gets under way *pianissimo* at measure 9 with horns, violins, and violas reiterating C. The music surges with chromatic runs that cascade over bar lines; dotted hieratic rhythms are replaced by measures of triplets that propel the music forward. Similar motions characterize the entire movement. While Bristow's timbral palette is relatively muted and conservative, he shows many late-nineteenth-century musical preferences, including a refusal to remain within purely diatonic orbits. Within moments of beginning, chromatic runs cascade over bar lines, and consecutive measures of triplets propel the music forward. The entire movement is characterized by similar gestures. If Bristow sought to create a musical equivalent to the incessant heaving motions of the Falls, he succeeded; the music surges. But there is little else to suggest that this piece is about the Falls.

Clarinets introduce a second movement, adagio, in A-flat major. The slower tempo and 12/8 meter suggest a more lilting quality than was found in the opening allegro. Bassoons, horns, and then the rest of the woodwinds create a soundscape traditionally associated with natural scenes. At measure 8, strings join in con espressione. Without comments from Bristow we are left to speculate upon the programmatic focus of this movement, if any was intended. Bristow obviously sticks with conventional symphonic tempo expectations by writing a fast first movement and a slower more lyrical second one.

But whether he sought to depict the more parklike setting that now framed the Falls or something even more specific, suggesting the romantic honeymoon destination Niagara had become over the century, is unknown. There are no metronome markings or internal tempo or mood indications within the movement to suggest any programmatic associations, or that Bristow wanted to move beyond the slow tempo he had established at the outset. On the other hand, ten key changes, six of which are accompanied by meter changes, and one instance of an additional meter change without any change of key, provide harmonic and rhythmic flexibility and interest to what might otherwise be a too restful moment of repose. By the end of the second movement, the piece has moved to C major.

A maestoso third movement in C major recalls the dotted rhythms of the first movement and introduces voices for the first time. Bristow's years as an organist, choir director, and church musician become evident as he interpolates the tune of "Old Hundredth," crosses out the familiar words to the doxology that he had originally written underneath, and substitutes new words: "Let every power of heart and tongue/Unite to swell the fateful song/While age and youth in chorus join/And praise the majesty divine." In an allegro section that follows, Bristow quotes from Handel's "Hallelujah Chorus," complete with the repetitions of the text "King of Kings," which are then followed by the word "Niagara." This is the first clear indication that the piece is about the Falls. While both Heinrich and Fry captured the sounds of the Falls with greatly expanded percussion sections and dynamic compass, Bristow confined Niagara to his text; it bears his message.

Bristow's clearest references to conflation of religion and Niagara are most obvious in the final allegro movement. In the following text excerpt, he compares the commingling waters of the Great Lakes with the supernatural form of a peri, thus immediately elevating the subject from the mundane to the otherworldly.

Superior, Huron, Michigan, and Erie with little Clair commingling,
    commingling like a Peri.
Superior, Huron, Michigan, and Erie with little Clair commingling,
    commingling like a Peri.
Superior, Huron, Michigan, and Erie, Superior, Huron, Michigan and
    Erie,
With little Clair commingling like a Peri,
With little Clair, little Clair commingling like a Peri, a Peri.

[*Musical Interlude*]

Speak! Waters deep and blue,
Speak! Waters deep and blue,
Why do ye gather, why do ye gather, why do ye gather why do ye,
To take this fearful leap?
To take this fearful leap?
Seek ye a mother?
Seek ye a mother, seek ye a mother?

[*Musical Interlude*]

Is this your roaring? Never, never ceasing,
Is this your roaring? Never, never ceasing,
And ever to the listening ear increasing?
And ever to the listening ear increasing?
For treacherous, Atlantic's bosom crying.
For treacherous, for treacherous Atlantic's bosom crying, crying.
Seek ye her briny breast with tears and sighing?
Seek ye her briny breast, seek ye her briny breast, with tears and sighing?
Tears and sighing, tears and sighing? And sighing? And sighing?
Sighing? Sighing? Sighing?

[*Musical Interlude*]

At this point the tempo changes to allegro furioso, and a bass chorus joins in, followed by sopranos and a solo quartet.

Thou cataract, thou King thou impetuous leaping, impetuous,
Combine ye all, combine ye all, your diapasons blending.
Combine ye all, your diapasons blending, Your diapasons, diapasons,
    blending,
Combine ye all your diapasons, Combine ye all your diapasons,
Combine ye all your diapasons blending.

[*Brief musical interlude*]

For the final stanza the tempo changes back to maestoso, the tempo that signaled the initial vocal part. As the grand symphony moves toward its end, voices reiterate a series of unison Cs.[140]

> To praise your God, to praise your God, to praise your God in anthems
>   thus ascending.
> To praise your God, to praise your God,
> To praise your God in anthems thus, thus ascending, thus ascending.

The penultimate stanza's references to "diapasons" recalls Eugene Thayer's 1881 article "Music of Niagara," where he explained the sound of Niagara as the "great diapason—the noblest and completest [*sic*] one on earth."[141] The analogy, however, would have been a natural one for Bristow, who, like Thayer, was an established church musician and organist. Consistent with his conservative compositional style, Bristow exhibits a nostalgic desire for a Niagara that is more in keeping with its earlier symbolism than with its current reality. Just as the World Columbian Exposition showcased America as the incarnation of progress and change, so it also strove mightily to reassure a wary nation of its stability and valuation of tradition. The complete coalescence of nature and religion, and the elevation of the Falls to the position of a holy symbol in *Niagara: A Grand Symphony,* recalls attitudes of an earlier time, although in Bristow's rendering blatant patriotic references are not apparent. This is a work of reassurance.

Aspiring to join ranks with nineteenth-century symphonists whose works strove for transcendence, Bristow instead weighed down his Niagara with sentimental, religious prosy. Rather than elevate the Falls, the backward-glancing, end-of-the-century American composer only called attention to the dissonance between the romance and the reality. Ironically, his sincere but stale phrases represented only too well what had become of the Falls. As Niagara was itself engineered, tributes to the Falls became hackneyed. For Bristow, clinging to a belief that Niagara was beyond manipulation or commodification, the Falls could be God's own chorus. But in reality God would have to compete with the power plants to be heard and seen. Niagara required the intervention of Olmsted and Church and a group of politically savvy idealists to refashion and recreate what had once been natural wildness and beauty. Tourists had to be coaxed along carefully created scenic paths in the park that was now Niagara.

When the establishment of the New York State Reservation in 1885 protected the Falls proper, developers sought to circumvent restrictions on uses of the waters and divert sources above the cataract to supply increasing demands for power. If these demands were unchecked, the Falls faced the very real possibility of being waterless. It would eventually take a series of treaties negotiated over a forty-four-year period between the United States and Canada to guarantee the equitable harnessing of Niagara's power supply and the preservation of "this great work of God."[142]

Although Bristow's grand symphony ostensibly celebrated the divine magnificence that was Niagara, the work ultimately succumbed to its own mawkish expression, just as the Falls had succumbed to greedy developers and souvenir stands. Both the music and the natural wonder were packaged. Clinging to such a romantic view of the Falls amid the nation's first decade as an international power broker, and at the same time as the Falls were in danger of quite literally being drained dry, speaks not only of Bristow's personal attachment to a bygone vision of America, but also of a similar view held by large numbers of Americans who were fearful of change and reluctant to let go of an earlier, more comfortable reading of their nation.

Separated by fewer than sixty years, the Niagaras of Heinrich, Fry, and Bristow represent the tumultuous changes experienced by the United States during the nineteenth century as it grew from a newly organized polity to a recognized world power. The various and bountiful physical endowments that had distinguished the New Found Land and been credited with defining a uniquely forthright and resourceful American character grew less and less essential to the nation's self-image as it proved its mettle as an innovative industrial leader. At the beginning of the century, Heinrich identified himself with a nation whose pride was tightly bound to its places. His "Thundering of Niagara" was the composer's own membership badge. Fry emerged on the scene as the country strove to create a culturally distinct consciousness and voice. The *Niagara* symphony was Fry's contribution to the broader artistic effort to reimagine the most famous natural icon as the symbol of national identity. Bristow spoke of an age only too aware of change. Ignoring the depth and breadth of America's transformation and the concomitant effects on the waterway, he took refuge in a religious-romantic vision of the Falls. His nostalgic paean speaks of an age in which large numbers of citizens desperately struggled to hold their footing.

Together, Heinrich, Fry, and Bristow contributed rare musical offerings to the larger Niagara chorus. In so doing they proffered three personal readings of the Falls that gave voice not only to their own values and ambitions, but also to national values and ambitions. When Niagara next inspired a full-length instrumental work, its composer would not be able to ignore the changes that had occurred.

chapter two

From Country to City in the Music of Charles Ives

THE HOUSATONIC AT STOCKBRIDGE

As Frederic Edwin Church and Frederick Law Olmsted quietly struggled to restore Niagara's iconographic status, as the Colonial Revival movement in architecture popularized building styles of the late eighteenth century, and as groups such as the Society for the Preservation of New England Antiquities (SPNEA) organized across the nation to protect a vanishing cultural heritage, Charles Ives (1874–1954) grew up in an established, old-Connecticut family, one dedicated to preserving Puritan values and pursuing liberal causes.[1] Graduating from Yale in 1898, the same year that Bristow died, Ives too was uncomfortable with social, political, and technological changes that threatened all aspects of life as he knew it. Yet, unlike Bristow, who remained tied to nineteenth-century compositional values, within a few decades Ives wrote music that would be considered among the most radical of any composed by an American. His century-straddling life embodied the tensions felt at the time throughout Western culture between Victorian right-wrong moralizing and modern inclinations to question all tradition: he manifested them both.[2] A strong sense of family, civic duty, service, and responsibility made him a leader in the insurance industry in the years immediately following the Armstrong investigations of 1905.[3] His writings on the philosophical underpinnings of life insurance and his instructional methods for new agents were essential to the success of Ives and Myrick, the agency that he founded in 1908 with his partner, Julian Myrick. They are still cited in business courses today. At the same time as he was regarded as a respected founder of modern insurance practices, Ives was characterized as a noisemaker, a musical iconoclast, a composer-dilettante and dabbler—and only years later as America's greatest composer.

His father, George Ives, was an accomplished instrumentalist, bandmaster, teacher, and musical experimenter. Both he and Horatio Parker, a European-trained composer and organist and the first music professor at Yale University, provided Charles with thorough training in composition. They refined and polished Charles's innate musical mind. Having secured his financial independence in business, Ives was free to write music that cottoned to no one's tastes or standards but his own. And he did. He composed while commuting on the train, in the evenings, and on weekends, but he was no weekend composer. Nor was he a dabbler or dilettante. Even in his most raucous and ostensibly chaotic works, Charles Ives was an inspired craftsman completely in charge of his materials and loyal to his ideas. He saw no conflict in his multifaceted life; on the contrary, Ives believed his life was full and whole.[4] That he chose to chart his own compositional course and to write the music he heard rather than the music that others wanted to hear was not a cranky choice, but a personal necessity. Ives personified Thoreau's drummer—instinctively, resolutely marching to his own beat. Familiar with the works of the Concord woodsman, Ives had a bit of Thoreau in him.

Although most of Ives's works were unknown—either ignored or rejected—while he was alive, beginning twenty years after his death his music gradually took its place at the center of American musical scholarship and the larger musical culture. Today Ives is an essential figure in a growing pantheon of great American artistic minds; he is a national figure who wears his Made in the U.S.A. label proudly.[5] Unlike many artists and musicians at the turn of the century who traveled to Europe for training and an environment they felt was conducive to creativity, Ives looked to his own culture for inspiration and guidance.[6] He missed no opportunity to champion his nation and its culture in his prose, poetry, and music. In the tradition of Heinrich, Fry, and Bristow, he also found an unmistakable way to identify a piece of music as being about America. Beyond using familiar tunes, Ives found an enduring reference to cherished ideas and values in American places. Memorializing places subdued the passage of time and enabled Ives to traverse the distance from powerful events of the past to potent experiences in the present, both for himself and for the nation. Musical evocation of places could amplify and suspend single moments in time and compel listeners to reconsider their awareness of experiences associated with places, both personal and national experiences. Ives's references to places as both geographical and temporal markers locate his connection with America.

In dozens of pieces Ives referred to places that were meaningful to him, to his country, and, by extension, to the larger world. Among the composers treated in this book, not since Anthony Philip Heinrich had an American artist used America's places as points of reference as often as did Ives. If the

Bohemian-born Heinrich used such references to legitimize himself as an American composer, Ives often used American place references to legitimize America. The sheer number of Ives's place pieces requires a word of explanation.

A Taxonomy of Place

A most basic taxonomy of works shows Ives's place pieces to be of two types: those that refer to places in their titles (*Ann Street, Central Park in the Dark, From Hanover Square North,* to name only three), and those in which place is clearly involved but not identified in the title (*Calcium Light Night, The Circus Band, The Indians,* among others). Within each of these groupings are a number of subcategories: titles naming *specific* places; those that name more general regions or places (*At the River, Down East,* and *From the Steeples and the Mountains*); those that distinguish places that are American from those that are European; and works that focus on more "extraterrestrial" sites (*The Unanswered Question: A Cosmic Landscape* and the *Universe Symphony* are examples).

In the case of songs, texts clarify the connection between place and piece either by the setting of the narrative or by the suggestion of a dialect that is regionally specific. Both are at work in Ives's song *Charlie Rutlage.*[7] For instrumental works devoid of specific place references in their titles, Ives's commentary often clarifies relationships between sites and sounds. He situates the third and fourth movements of the *Concord Sonata, The Alcotts* and *Thoreau,* very specifically in *Essays before a Sonata.*

Inherent within the two basic classifications are more subjective groupings that attempt to get at Ives's relationship to the places memorialized. Was the site the locus of a deeply personal experience that Ives sought to capture, or did he aspire to the role of the detached observer or recorder of events? There is a conceptual difference between an artwork that aspires to documentary and one that makes no effort to suppress subjectivity, even though intentions might not be obvious or audible in the finished work. Distinctions become fuzzy as all creators to some extent modify, filter, and reshape the subjects they handle.[8] In a few instances Ives's remarks in his autobiographical work, *Memos,* illuminate his relationship to and position within a place, but at other times this remains more ambiguous; always an observer and eyewitness, sometimes he is a more active participant. Still other pieces show the composer blending elements of recollection, dream, and reality. His songs *Tom Sails Away* and *The Things Our Fathers Loved* acknowledge the obscurity of boundaries between that which is real and that which is imagined, and question the essential nature of any experience.[9] In an age of William James and Sigmund Freud, such questions were not unusual.

In a limited number of pieces, Ives focuses upon particular sounds heard at particular places: in each of these works, the sounds associated with the place are the primary motivation for the work. The aural environment provided the raw materials for his experimental piece *Over the Pavements*. In cases such as this, Ives's emotional response to the place seems not to be the main focus, even though the automaton-like effects he creates may, in effect, criticize city life. In a few other works, natural aural phenomena are the most significant aspect of a place; in *From the Steeples and the Mountains*, Ives celebrates place as pure sound.

A last subcategory includes those works that use places to frame compositions. These are Ives's journey pieces.[10] While the journeys may not involve identifiable locations, these works focus on physical or mental movement from one place or condition to another. Changing places, or leaving and returning to a place, becomes a metaphor for growth, motion, and development, most often of an emotional or spiritual nature. *The 'St. Gaudens' in Boston Common (Colonel Robert Gould Shaw and His Colored Regiment),* and "Putnam's Camp, Redding, Connecticut" manifest such place-as-journey thinking.[11]

Although places are not always associated with specific sounds in Ives's work, the places that he commemorates are invariably sensorially rich. In a number of pieces place is intimately bound up with sights, as well as with sounds. As becomes evident, just as Ives himself resists easy categorization, these classifications or subgroupings are not mutually exclusive.

Pride of Place

Ives was drawn to places that had elicited literary and artistic responses from others, just as Heinrich, Fry, and Bristow had been drawn to the oft-cited Falls at Niagara. Secluded river banks, pulsating urban parks, the abandoned encampments of Revolutionary War soldiers, crowded train stations, and historic city commons became musical stages for the many and varied dramas that were America. Contrary to the once-popular perception that Ives identified exclusively with his nineteenth-century New England roots, his works show him to be responsive as well to the city he made his home for his last fifty years. In many ways, Ives's life and music reflect America as the nation moved from identifying itself as the mythical sylvan Eden to the modern, urban Mecca.

As discussed earlier in this book, through the mid-nineteenth century,

America's bounteous natural gifts provided a focal point for native writers, artists, philosophers, politicians, and business entrepreneurs intent on distinguishing their young nation from Europe. They championed the country's size and variety, its pristine wildernesses and limitless possibilities: its certain divinity. Works of the Hudson River School painters provided, perhaps, some of the most obvious evidence of these values. Ives also idealized the American landscape, deftly conflating America, nature, and religion with his music. *The Housatonic at Stockbridge,* the third movement of Charles Ives's orchestral set *Three Places in New England,* celebrates an idyllic Massachusetts river. Here is an equivalent of the glowing oils of Frederic Edwin Church and Asher B. Durand. Its brevity—barely four minutes and just forty-four measures of music—makes it apprehensible and memorable. Yet the limited absolute dimensions belie the work's enormous impact. The compressed temporal scope, in part, actually *intensifies* Ives's expression; so much happens in so short a time that listeners reel in a sonic wake.

The power of *The Housatonic* grows out of a palpable tension between dynamic and static musical elements: between a penetrating melodic trajectory that insists upon forward motion (the drama) and an imperturbably grounded rhythmic and harmonic anchor (the place). Stasis, as an elemental and structural component of many twentieth-century compositions, works against the powerful harmonically driven organicism that characterized almost all nineteenth-century Western art music. In this regard a river, with its constant and often turbulent motion, confined within the limited space of its banks is the perfect embodiment of such conflicting elements.

Of the three places that Ives commemorated in his *First Orchestral Set, The Housatonic at Stockbridge* is unique in two important ways: first, for its eventual arrangement as a song, and second, for its focus on a natural site.[12] Though Ives is a participant in the idyll, and sounds from a church are man-made, as will be shown, in *The Housatonic* people are understood in relation to nature; it dominates the landscape.[13] In both earlier movements, significant historical events that occurred at each of the sites inspired and shaped the compositions from the finest details to the grossest motions. No such historically resonant events happened in the Housatonic River Valley, although the river was a valuable natural resource and one that had been important to the early development of the Northeast. Although all three movements are unequivocally programmatic pieces, the program that Ives created for *The Housatonic* is about the natural scene. The place becomes significant in its own right; it is its own story. Ives concentrates his energies on sonifying the rich environment that he had experienced on a summer's day in 1908.

In *Memos,* Ives explains the impetus for *The Housatonic.* He emphasizes the sensory feast that he and his bride, Harmony, enjoyed as they walked through the Elysian hillside of Berkshire County: "The last movement, *The Housatonic at Stockbridge,* . . . was suggested by a Sunday morning walk that Mrs. Ives and I took near Stockbridge, the summer after we were married. We walked in the meadows along the river, and heard the distant singing from the church across the river. The mist had not entirely left the river bed, and the colors, the running water, the banks and elm trees were something that one would always remember."[14]

The Housatonic valley clearly impressed the susceptible groom, for, according to the composer, within days of returning from the trip, he "sketched the first part of this movement for strings, flute, and organ."[15] The immediacy of Ives's action is but one indication of the strength of his response; the music is another. Here are sounds so moving that at times they seem to defy containment within the score. But personal and private as the experience was for Ives, the river valley had evoked similarly impassioned responses in others, and Ives was aware of some of these. As it turns out, the impetus behind his musical memorial was perhaps not as purely spontaneous as his reporting of it might suggest. He did, after all, compose a piece whose melodic scansion fit neatly with the verses of a poem entitled "To the Housatonic at Stockbridge," written by Robert Underwood Johnson, a poet with whose works Ives was familiar. But beyond Johnson's paean to this particular waterway, rivers were a regular subject of artistic rhapsodizing.

Water

Water has played a principal role in discussions of place and in explanations of creation since the earliest recorded histories. It has been construed as the very source of life and as a symbol of the constant and changing forces that power life. Western readers are perhaps most familiar with Biblical stories and their references to waters that flooded and ravaged, as well as to waters that protected, nourished, and sanctified. A brief survey of a Bible concordance reveals dozens of references to the word. Protestant hymnody overflows with texts that make overt references to water. "Shall We Gather at the River," "Throw Out the Life-Line across the Dark Wave," "In the Sweet Bye and Bye, We Shall Meet on the Beautiful Shore" are all hymns with water references that Ives borrowed and used in other pieces. And, of course, water is *the* symbol of purity and new life in the Christian sacrament of baptism.

As a member of a religious family, and as a professional church musician, Ives was well acquainted with the Christian significance of water. Additionally, spiritual associations with water would have been reinforced by nineteenth-century writers and Transcendentalist philosophers with whose work Ives was also familiar. The Ives family interest in Transcendentalism could be traced back to Charles's grandmother.[16] One family story has Ralph Waldo Emerson staying with the Iveses when he lectured as part of the Danbury Lyceum series. Charles was most interested in the writings of Emerson and Thoreau, of all the Transcendentalists, and he attributed particular personal significance to the latter.[17] In *Walden* (1854), Thoreau's pond is the central image within the woods, one that mediates between the sky and the earth, one that signifies purity and perfection, one that mirrors heaven. References to Biblical times and religious themes fill descriptions of the pond. Thoreau hypothesizes the pond's existence "when Adam and Eve were driven out of Eden," and assumes that it "obtained a patent of heaven to be the only Walden Pond in the world."[18] The pond as mirror is an essential image for Thoreau:

> In such a day, in September or October, Walden is a perfect forest mirror, set round with stones as precious to my eye as if fewer or rarer. Nothing so fair, so pure, and at the same time so large, as a lake, perchance, lies on the surface of the earth. Sky water. It needs no fence. Nations come and go without defiling it. It is a mirror which no stone can crack, whose quicksilver will never wear off, whose gilding Nature continually repairs; no storms, no dust, can dim its surface ever fresh;—a mirror in which all impurity presented to it sinks, swept and dusted by the sun's hazy brush,—this the light dust-cloth,—which retains no breath that is breathed on it, but sends its own to float as clouds high above its surface, and be reflected in its bosom still.[19]

That it captures heaven is made clear in Thoreau's depiction of the iced-over pond of winter. Having cut through the snow and ice to reveal the "quiet parlor of the fishes, pervaded by a softened light as through a window of ground glass," Thoreau concludes: "heaven is under our feet as well as over our heads."[20] Thus the waters of Walden Pond sanctified the woods and put God in place close by Thoreau's cabin. Ives's portrayal of the Housatonic River, with its mists and elms (and, not incidentally, sounds wafting from a distance, an issue treated in great detail by Thoreau), is not unlike the one painted by Thoreau at Walden Pond. It is easy to imagine Ives bringing his recollections of *Walden* to bear on his musical rendering of the Housatonic. The Sunday morning walk in the meadows provided the young New York businessman with a Thoreauvian experience.[21] Thoreau's symbolic uses of nature and water, however, were not unique in nineteenth-century American literature.

God and Nature

God in nature and nature as the sign and symbol of God were essential tenets of Transcendentalism as articulated by Emerson. His seminal essay "Nature" (1836) was nothing short of a hymn to the sanctity of nature. To experience nature was to experience God. In this famous passage, Emerson locates God in the woods: "In the woods, we return to reason and faith. There I feel that nothing can befall me in life,—no disgrace, no calamity (leaving me my eyes), which nature cannot repair. Standing on the bare ground,—my head bathed by the blithe air and uplifted into infinite space,—all mean egotism vanishes. I become a transparent eyeball; I am nothing; I see all; the currents of the Universal Being circulate through me; I am part or parcel of God."[22]

The moral seems clear: we lose and find ourselves in nature, in God. But the new-world philosopher had no monopoly on such thinking. Belief in the union of God and nature inspired Hudson River School painters as well. Their canvases glowed as if backlit, and still waters provided moments of serene repose; nature offered a contemplative refuge. In the second of a series of letters on landscape painting published in *Crayon* in 1855, Asher B. Durand commended the study of nature to all who would paint: "I refer you to Nature early, that you may receive your first impressions of beauty and sublimity, unmingled with the superstitions of Art. . . . There is yet another motive for referring you to the study of Nature early—its influence on the mind and heart. The external appearance of this our dwelling place, apart from its wondrous structure and functions that minister to our well-being, is fraught with lessons of high and holy meaning, only surpassed by the light of Revelation."[23]

Beyond the abstract spiritual qualities attributed to nature, nature was also often likened to a church. In 1858 the draughtsman and naturalist Heinrich Möllhausen referred to the forest, with its water and rocks, as a holy place. He observed: "Here, as amidst the wilderness of waters, in the dark primeval forest, among the giant mountains, Nature builds a temple that awakens feelings not easily to be expressed; but the pure joy we feel in the works of the Almighty Master may well be called worship. . . . The fact that clear springs so often gush out amongst the rocks amidst these grand scenes, inviting the wanderer to rest near them, may even suggest the idea that hard rock has been thus smote and the water made to gush forth, to detain man the longer before these natural altars."[24]

American writers and artists consciously and conscientiously emphasized the connections between nature and God, and in so doing encouraged generations of citizens eager to see their nation as a place uniquely consecrated by the Almighty. If God and nature formed an indivisible unity, God, nature, and art formed an aesthetic trinity that influenced American thinking for the first half of the nineteenth century; it was a particularly useful construct for a culturally fledgling nation. With a God-permeated nature, America's plenitude of place was a sure sign of the Creator's generous beneficence toward the new land. Manifest Destiny was apparent to all who had eyes to see.

Such thinking had multiple uses. Beyond inspiring national confidence, and art and literature in the nineteenth century, it justified the formation of government-sponsored exploratory parties that charted the edges of the territory. It enticed settlers. It encouraged the laying of railroad track across the continent. It helped the federal government rationalize its policies toward Native peoples, including the removal of tens of thousands of American Indians from their lands to send them westward, thereby making room for eager pioneers and entrepreneurs. By the end of the century, however, new concerns regarding what many perceived to be unchecked American imperialism (especially as regards the United States' involvement in the Spanish-American War) called into question the earlier religiously rooted and mandated nationalism. That the more romantic notion of America was losing credibility and usefulness by the last quarter of the century did not diminish its presence or power in Ives's own life and thought. Ives clung to his beliefs.

Nature in the Housatonic Valley: "The Palestine of New England"

Though various rivers inspired literary and artistic meditations, the Housatonic River and the valley surrounding it were singled out on numerous occasions by writers and painters who lived in the area. The reverent poem by Robert Underwood Johnson was well known to Ives.[25] A study of this source suggests that the composer was most likely aware of the works of others as well. In the earliest published edition of the *First Orchestral Set* (Mercury, 1935), Ives selected twenty-two lines from Johnson's sixty-six-line poem and presented them facing the first page of the third movement.

Johnson's poem had originally been published in 1897, as part of a collection of patriotic works entitled *Songs of Liberty, and Other Poems*. It had appeared numerous times in later compilations of his works.[26] Johnson used his rhymed couplets to stress America's uniqueness (as it was manifest in nature), and to caution those who insisted that the Housatonic was merely equivalent to pastoral waterways in England. He denied that any comparison was possible: "Beware their praise who rashly would deny to our New World its true tranquility. . . . Surely, serener river never ran." For Johnson the Housatonic was incomparable; it outshone its European counterparts and epitomized America's strength and promise. America's nature was qualitatively superior.

Here was a theme shared by Emerson, Thoreau, and Hudson River School painters; it was one cornerstone of the nineteenth-century American myth. Ives believed it too, although he did not set these particular lines in his song.

While the influence of Johnson's poem on Ives's music will be discussed more fully, it is important to note at this point that in his text Johnson made a subtle reference to another poem and another poet. The third stanza devotes ten of its fourteen lines to singing the praises of "thy Homeric bard," Bryant, who years earlier had written his own tribute to the Housatonic waterway. Johnson pays tribute to Bryant as he interrogates the river:

> Art thou disquieted—still uncontent
> With praise from thy Homeric bard, who lent
> The world the placidness thou gavest him?
> Thee Bryant loved when life was at its brim;
> And when the wine was falling, in thy wood
> Of sturdy willows like a Druid stood.
> Oh, for his touch on this o'er-throbbing time,
> His hand upon the hectic brow of Rhyme,
> Cooling its fevered passion to a pace
> To lead, to stir, to reinspire the race!

In the second decade of the nineteenth century, William Cullen Bryant (1794–1878) wrote a poem entitled "Green River"; it celebrated a small stream that fed the larger Housatonic. Johnson made a passing reference to the subject of Bryant's poem in his own second stanza, in the line "Convoyed by two attendant streams of green . . ." A comparison of Johnson's poem "To the Housatonic River" and Bryant's work "Green River" leaves little doubt that the earlier sixty-four-line poem of rhymed couplets provided a model for Johnson's later sixty-six-line work. For Johnson, the shared pastoral surroundings and the ultimate union of these two bodies of water meant that they were one and the same. Although the poems differ in many ways, they also share a range of references and express their sentiments similarly.[27]

Ives's inclusion of Johnson's tribute to Bryant in his own careful reduction of the poem, and his later setting of the poem as a song, are endorsements of Johnson's sentiments and perhaps an indication that Ives knew the Bryant poem as well. Though Ives included the Bryant lines in his reduction of the poem, they are not part of the text that he set years later in song, nor is there any melodic correlation for these poetic lines in the instrumental or vocal versions of *The Housatonic at Stockbridge*.

One wonders if Ives was familiar with other Bryant works associated with the Housatonic. In addition to writing "Green River" and other poems, Bry-

Engraving from a painting by A. F. Bellows, *The Housatonic,* 1873.

ant also edited a large two-volume work entitled *Picturesque America.*[28] Among numerous chapters exploring "the mountains, rivers, lakes, forests, water-falls, shores, canyons, valleys, cities, and other picturesque features of our country," there is a twenty-nine-page section devoted to the "Valley of the Housatonic." It includes twenty-three drawings by J. D. Woodward and an engraving from a painting done by A. F. Bellows.

Especially interesting to Ives's 1908 reminiscence of the scene, which included the sounds of a hymn tune wafting through the air from "the church across the river,"[29] is the Bellows painting: a bucolic setting of the Housatonic, complete with a church steeple across the river in the background. There is no ambiguity in this work regarding the peaceful coexistence of religion and nature.

A few excerpts from the text convey the tone of the prose that accompanied the artwork: "The gray, misty gleams of the young morning harmonized well with the broad, pale shimmering of the river that was merging—consciously, it may be—its individuality into the wide waste of waters beyond it. . . . The change from quietness to romance in the aspects of the Housatonic Valley, from its broad mouth upward toward the hills, if less rapid than that of the cool, gray dawn into the warm and shadowless beauty of the day, was still not less real."[30]

It seems that the writer of the text, W. C. Richards, like Ives, was taken by the morning mist. He clarifies later that this scene described the Housatonic wending its way through Stockbridge specifically. "On leaving Stockbridge, the tourist can scarcely venture to promise himself a beauty beyond that he has already enjoyed; and this may be suggested without disparagement to the varied scenery of Northern Berkshire."

The author also makes clear his sense of the region's spiritual significance and ultimate perfection: "It may hardly be doubted that the rare and numerous attractions of this whole region—so aptly called 'the Palestine of New England'—are crystallized, in excess of loveliness, around Stockbridge as a nucleus. If this verdict had gathered something of weight to the judgment from the acknowledged union in Stockbridge of all the forces—natural, historical, social, intellectual, and religious, alike—which have given to Berkshire its enviable renown, the influence would be, nevertheless, legitimate and just."[31]

Ives's supremely personal encounter with the Housatonic Valley in summer 1908 may indeed have provided the necessary impetus to compose his piece, but paintings, poems, and prose had earlier captured the scene. By memorializing the river at Stockbridge in his music, Ives joined forces with other writers and artists who had already identified and hallowed the spot. Ives joined in a tradition that celebrated nature and the American place as something uniquely sacred.

Poetry and Music

Though Ives waited until 1921 to arrange the song version of "The Housatonic at Stockbridge," it is clear from the close fit of the melody with selected lines from the text that his first conception of this work in 1908 was animated not only by a personal experience with the place, or even by picturesque sketches and romantic prose, but specifically by Johnson's poem. Ives ultimately set fourteen of the twenty-two excerpted lines that he reproduced in the 1935 edition.[32] The brackets in the excerpt below surround those lines that do not appear in the song.[33]

"The Housatonic at Stockbridge"

Contented river! In thy dreamy realm—
The cloudy willow and the plumy elm . . .

[Thou hast grown human laboring with men
At wheel and spindle; sorrow thou dost ken; . . .]

Thou beautiful! From every dreamy hill
What eye but wanders with thee at thy will,

[Imagining thy silver course unseen
Convoyed by two attendant streams of green. . . .]

Contented river! And yet over-shy
To mask thy beauty from the eager eye;

Hast thou a thought to hide from field and town?
In some deep current of the sunlit brown
[Art thou disquieted—still uncontent
With praise from thy Homeric bard, who lent
The world the placidness thou gavest him?
Thee Bryant loved when life was at its brim; . . .]

Ah! there's a restive ripple, and the swift
Red leaves—September's firstlings—faster drift;
Wouldst thou away, dear stream? Come, whisper near!
I also of much resting have a fear;
Let me tomorrow thy companion be,
By fall and shallow to the adventurous sea!

In Ives's composition, excerpts of poetry are set to gradually enlarging musical phrases. By selecting so few lines from the first and longest stanza, he eliminated Johnson's verses that were devoted primarily to historical comparisons and patriotic boasting. The composer would have wholeheartedly endorsed the poet's sentiments in this regard—especially as they provided a comment on one of Ives's favorite topics, the limits of the old world and the limitlessness of "Our 'New World'"—but the lines clearly lay outside what Ives wished to focus upon in this work. His subject here was the reconciliation of forces and the achievement of unity that is possible in the natural place—mankind with nature, power with peacefulness, the local with the universal, God with man. The Housatonic River Valley embodied this ideal for the composer, and his piece captured it in a unique artistic utterance.

The Musical Place

But how does a composer convey the primacy of place or the sanctity of nature in a textless music? What substitutes for inspired visual images of mountains, or heavenly light bathing a sylvan setting, or crystalline pools of cleansing water such as filled the canvases of Albert Bierstadt, Frederic Edwin Church, Thomas Cole, and Asher B. Durand? What offers the specificity of detail that glistens on the pages of the best descriptive writers? The first question might be: How does music capture place at all?

As a temporal art—an art form that unfolds in time—much Western music is ideally suited to narrative; it tells stories well. The musical tradition that Ives inherited was premised upon predictable harmonic motions, trackable temporal sequences, and a dominant, single trajectory that determined the hierarchy of all elemental relationships and behaviors. It was goal-oriented music: the goal was announced at the beginning and achieved near the end. Here is music that conveys action. But depicting a place, a stationary location, works against this most basic musical impulse to move on. To fully appreciate a place, to capture it in the mind's eye, the observer must resist the urge to move on, must temporarily forget a goal; the observer must stand still. This requires a different approach to composition, one that emphasizes being somewhere rather than getting somewhere, one that insists that a composer reconsider the relationships between harmony, rhythm, and melody. Using techniques that Robert Morgan has termed "spatial," Charles Ives created room for a musical place.[34]

Musical Techniques

Ives's spatially conceived place pieces employ harmonic stasis, circular melodic and rhythmic structures, a weakened sense of lapsed time, and large-scale musical structures that seem to defy or temporarily negate conventional objectives. At times *The Housatonic at Stockbridge* uses all of these techniques. Here Ives creates an intimate marriage of poetic image and sound, with basic ideas for the music coming from Johnson's unsung text.[35]

The calm of the "contented river" is epitomized in the barely audible opening with its few recurring pitches, gentle lilting tempo, and conjunct, circling melodic line. The flowing waters are present in triplet subdivisions (difficult to discern at first) and a half-cadence that together push the music through and over bar lines, moving directly from one strong beat to the next.[36] Forward motion is discernible even though it appears reluctant; tensions between spatial and lineal techniques invigorate the music. But it is essential that Ives's peaceful soundscape not be just any bucolic scene: a degree of specificity, while difficult to achieve, is desirable. In order to capture his recollection of church music wafting through the air (and to get God into nature), Ives needs an obvious reference. He finds this religious touchstone in a hymn tune, which plays an increasingly important role in the resolution of the work.

Although the text of Johnson's poem does not scan perfectly with the hymn tune that Ives borrows, "Dorrnance" is noteworthy for its compatibility with Johnson's poem in the ways in which it conveys both individual words and larger issues.[37] Listeners unfamiliar with Protestant hymns will nonetheless recognize the tune as being hymnlike in style; it most certainly invites reflection.

Ives's first melodic reference is to the *end* of the hymn. When the tune enters, Ives quotes the final phrase of "Dorrnance." True to his years of experience as a church organist, he introduces the tune by lining out its last phrase

DORRNANCE, 8.7.8.7.

Stanzas 1–3, WALTER SHIRLEY, 1725–1786
based on JAMES ALLEN, 1734–1804
Stanza 4 from COOKE and DENTON'S CHURCH HYMNAL, 1853   ISAAC B. WOODBURY, 1819–1858

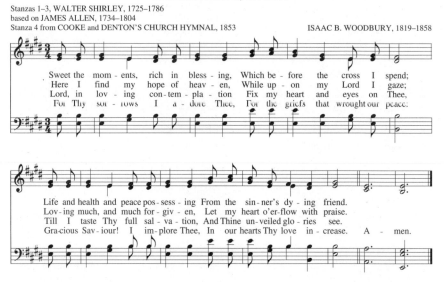

Ex. 2.1: "Dorrnance."

before starting at the beginning of the melody. When one considers that the essential rise of the melodic line in the final phrase of the hymn is echoed and magnified in the dramatic closing of the piece, it appears that Ives is providing both a logical beginning to his work and a preview of the piece's (and the river's) ultimate course. The hymn tune is a microcosm of the movement.[38]

Ives sought to capture the lushness and depth of the environment, and so instructed instrumentalists, on no fewer than six occasions, to throw sounds "into the background" or make them appear as "a distant sound."[39] The effect of distance on sound was a long-standing concern for Ives, and for his father before him, and for Thoreau before them both. Convinced that a sound heard from a distance was not the equivalent of a soft sound, Ives used specific instrumental timbres, positioning, and combinations to create the effect of layers of sounds. In the course of the work, a particular instrument may be of primary importance and command attention or hover in the background shrouded by other sounds. Ives's subtle mastery of orchestral timbre is everywhere apparent in *The Housatonic at Stockbridge*. Listeners are intended to linger a while where they are and absorb as much of the multilayered environment as they can. Ives uses spatial techniques to focus attention on what is occurring all around.

The Musical Background: Rhythm

In order to convey the "dreamy realm" of Johnson's opening line, the complex environment of the Housatonic Valley had to emerge sounding rich but not excessively crowded. Any suggestion of sonic cramming would undermine the blissful calm that Johnson and Ives strove to depict. But serene stillness was only one manifestation of the Housatonic. To achieve the initial desired effect and leave room for a metamorphosing river, Ives crafted a piece in which he methodically introduced new elements to the sonic canvas. His gentle approach invited listeners to slowly observe the landscape and join in his remembered walk. He worked as a watercolorist might, first applying a wash to the paper, filling in the background, and only gradually moving out to the foreground of the work. Painting with sounds, Ives established the place by working from background to foreground. Given the ubiquity of the river in Ives's conception of the place, he painted it first.

But the river was no simple object; its static and dynamic aspects were not always apparent or discrete, and then sometimes they emerged simultaneously. What appeared to be a calm and contented stream at one vantage point became a powerful, churning waterway a few miles off. The river demanded a flexible voice that could embody and project its multiple personae. Ives unified the waterway by confining it to a single instrument family, the strings, but he created room for its multifaceted personality by writing rhythmically variegated music for separate instruments. Here is one musical manifestation of the river's coexisting static and dynamic features.

The power of the river resides in the lowest string parts, which move most slowly. An open fifth in the string basses and cellos creates an echoing resonance that persists for nine measures before it is momentarily interrupted. An organ pedal doubles the string bass line, providing an unwavering hold on a C♯. (The organ was present in Ives's earliest conception of the piece, and it seems an especially appropriate instrument for a memory that includes sounds from a church.) This is Ives's sonic anchor on which outside forces will tug. The more spontaneous motions of the river gurgle on the surface of the water in the highest strings, which move most quickly. Between these two extremes of activity, upper celli and violas move at gradually increasing rates of speed in relation to the basses. This rhythmic stratification is visible in the opening measures of the score. A similar layering is present in Ives's dynamics. The higher the string part and the smaller the note value, the softer the dynamic level.[40]

In spite of the relentless activity of the higher strings, their muted, legato undulations impress an auditor not with their exertion, but with their calm:

here is the river at Stockbridge—drifting, hushed, untroubled. Any sense of agitation or disquiet is absent. Musical "progress" concedes to the fluid web of circular gestures; for the moment at least, forward motion appears to be captured. Pitch patterns adjust to rhythmic changes and quietly whirl. By combining slowly revolving motions with deep drone-like sounds, Ives focuses our attentions on this moment, this place.

Multiple circular patterns are an important component of Ives's spatial techniques because they inhibit the sense of linear movement. A reader does not have to be fluent with music notation to appreciate such patterns in the viola line pictured in Ex. 2.2.

Viola music slowly, softly spins in small sonic whirlpools, the result of carefully organized rhythm and pitch patterns whose repetitions are perceived almost subconsciously by the listener. The slow tempo (adagio molto), soft dynamic level (*mp-pppp*), and density of the string texture make identifying any discrete pattern difficult. But repeating sequences, such as those found in the viola music, unify the individual lines and provide the musical logic of the piece. Measures 1 to 7 of the viola line form a large cycle of pitch and rhythm patterns that begin again at measure 8.

One of the shortest patterns comprises a series of six pitches that occurs thirteen times before being interrupted.[41] The pitch pattern of the viola line, E-D-D#-E-D-C#, which begins on beat one of measure 1, rotates within the triplets and enters one-third or two-thirds beats earlier each time it reappears.[42] The pattern is interrupted only to resume at measure 15, beat three, where it continues as before to beat one of measure 21. When the viola pitch pattern finally quits at measure 21, it is replaced with an oscillating figure in the oboe, and a tenacious six-note pitch pattern in the flute that takes its cue from the opening music of the second and third violins.[43] Over the course of the work it becomes apparent that the early river music provides a source for later musical developments, and that all aspects of the environment are filtered through and understood in relation to the sound of the omnipresent river.

Simultaneous with the viola's recurring six-note pitch series is a repeating note-value pattern that is also easily visualized.

Musical fig. 2.1: Note-value pattern of the opening of the viola line.

Ex. 2.2: *The Housatonic at Stockbridge*, mm 1–8.

In each pair of patterns, quarter and eighth notes combine to form alternating rhythm patterns. In the first occurrence of the pitch pattern, the note-value pattern begins with a quarter note that is followed by two tied eighths, a single eighth, two tied eighths, and two quarter notes. In the second occurrence, the note-value pattern begins with an eighth note that is followed by a quarter, two tied eighths, a quarter, an eighth, and a quarter. By modifying the notation of the tied notes in the two patterns, we can create an arrangement that reflects the actual aural experience of the rhythms.

Musical fig. 2.2: Aural experience of the pattern of the opening of the viola line.

A new grouping also emerges. This new pattern occurs three times within each pair of pitch patterns. The shorter patterns evenly divide the twenty-one pulses of eighth notes into three groups of seven pulses each.

Musical fig. 2.3: Three seven-beat patterns of the opening of the viola line.

This inner rhythmic pattern is reinforced by a pattern of accents that stress the first note in the pattern. Recurring accents also create their own smaller, more circumscribed pitch patterns that rotate among three accented notes: E-D-D♯, E-D-D♯, E-D-D♯. (E-D-D♯ is the beginning of the six-note pitch pattern referred to earlier.)

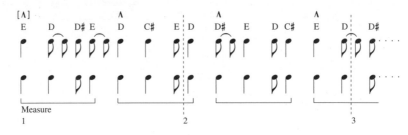

Musical fig. 2.4: Recurring accented pitch patterns of the opening of the viola line.

Though the muted viola part is lodged in the center of the string ensemble, its accented notes do penetrate the surface of sound. The audible recurrence of the pitch E in the opening measures of the music, and its strategic accenting on beat one—implied in measure 1, but actually notated at measure 8, where the largest pitch and rhythm cycle begins a second time—foreshadows the importance of this pitch in the second half of the work, and illuminates the final descending third, G♯ to E, that ends the entire piece.[44] Though the piece does not confine itself to a key (such a practice would require too much harmonic determinism and demand a dominantly linear approach), certain pitches play important roles in guaranteeing the harmonic logic of the work; E is an important melodic pitch.

The viola line and the oscillating figures of the surrounding string instruments embody the simultaneous and synchronous, "spatial" qualities of the place that Ives sought to capture in his music. While important characteristics of these patterns will inform later musical behavior, the early string activity doesn't demand specific immediate responses; there is no sense of inevitability associated with these cyclic patterns. This is the nature of cyclic patterns. For all the attention paid to a few select pitches, there is no urgent pull toward a key, and their ultimate function is unclear. Even though the music unfolds *through time,* the implied and diachronic qualities of the music that are essential to a perception of a strong linear motion have been neutralized for an extended moment *in time.*

From Background to Middleground

Even in the first two lines of the cello music, where Ives indicated that the instruments were to be "strong enough to throw [the] upper strings into the background," the rocking half notes of the upper divisi part move so slowly that it is difficult to interpret their motion as anything more than a minimal musical respiration. Ives secures the stillness of the valley in these first two measures. It is only when bassoons enter to double the cello line at measure 3 that listeners turn their heads. Although the bassoon music flows naturally and effortlessly from the string music that precedes it, its distinctive timbre and promise of a genuine melodic idea sound significantly different from other musics that are occurring simultaneously. By identifying the river with the string family, and by having the hymn tune emerge from both the low strings and the low woodwinds, Ives creates a logical transition for listeners; he creates an aural path that draws listeners into the work. With the introduction of Ives's paraphrased hymn tune, the calm river music wends its way into the background of the landscape and the auditor considers other aspects of the Housatonic Valley.

To treat issues of conciliation in this brief piece, it was imperative that Ives create audibly autonomous musical components early on in the work. Multiple, discrete spheres of polyphonic activity were an important characteristic of Ives's spatially conceived works, and an essential aspect of the richness and depth of experience that he depicted in this particular place piece. The variety of sounds and sights that Ives heard and saw while on his morning walk comes to life in music that grows gradually larger and more complex. He applied a complementary but distinctive middleground to the sonic canvas by introducing new timbres; the move was diverting and deft.

Creating the Middleground: Timbre

An exploration of timbre illuminates one way in which Ives balanced the static and dynamic elements of this piece and this place. The opulent atmosphere of Ives's idyll comes to life in instrumental colors that distinguish aspects of the place. But discrete areas of activity must also sound as if they are parts of a whole and flow effortlessly from one to another. The integrated sound mass has to contain the potential for separation.

An example of how Ives accomplished this occurs early in the piece in the dexterous transfer of musical materials from one instrument family to another. At measure 3, when bassoons gently join with cellos to introduce "Dorrnance," they intensify the melodic material of the strings without dramatically altering the color of the sound. They subtly emphasize an aspect of the music that auditors might otherwise overlook. The chameleon-like quality of the bassoon timbre makes it the perfect instrumental intermediary between the low string sound at measure 3 and the impending French horn entrance at measure 6. While the bassoon provides a palpable connection between the river music and the rest of the aural environment, it also makes possible the eventual separation of sounds that is essential to an accurate portrayal of the multidimensional river valley. As the bassoon prepares listeners for a change in focus, the entrance of the French horn appears as both a natural outgrowth of the aural environment and a distinctive aspect of that world.

The French horn was an instrument long associated with musical depictions of outdoor scenes. In choosing this instrument for his pastoral soundscape, Ives stayed within canonic norms. But he was not swayed by historical precedent alone. His chief interest lay in the color of the horn sound, which was capable of flowing effortlessly from the bassoon timbre that preceded it. Having created a smooth connection from string to woodwind to brass, Ives was now able to separate background, middleground, and foreground strata from each other.[45]

Using French and English horns, Ives fashioned a pastoral duet whose gentle tone and expansive temporal quality are reminiscent of Berlioz's English horn and oboe dialogue in the "Scène aux champs" of *Symphonie fantastique*. While Ives's duetlike format and his choice of timbre are in keeping with established European models, his choice of the hymn tune "Dorrnance," by the nineteenth-century New England composer Issac Baker Woodbury (1819–58), was not; it made his pastoral scene distinctly American. Ives chose an American tune to pay tribute to an American river.

In measures 6 through 20, Ives focuses attention on a brass-woodwind "call and response." He guarantees a degree of autonomy for this stratum by instructing the English horn at measure 8 to play sufficiently loudly to keep the strings in the background.[46] The penetrating double-reed timbre accompanied by the increased volume of the French horn assure that the hymn tune will be heard within the more static sonic mass. The English horn part is also reinforced by rhythmically and harmonically supportive *pianissimo* trombones; their synchronized efforts assure the overall consistency and uniformity of this brass-woodwind sphere of activity.[47] The breadth of the physical environment is audible and visible in the wide-open spacing that lies between string music and hymn tune music.

Although the melodic line is clearly related to the harmonic foundation of the lowest strings—the C♯ drone creates a triadic root for the melody pitches—the significant distance between the strings and the woodwinds suggests that the melody is truly floating freely through the air as Ives recalled, "from the church across the river." In addition to hearing the actual sounds of this environment, listeners can hear the space between the sounds. Readers familiar with a children's toy called the Viewmaster have experienced seeing the space between the various scrims used to create its three-dimensional images. Ives achieves a similar effect with ambits of sound.

Like the multifaceted river, the surrounding environment contained an assortment of subtle colors and shades. Ives symbolizes its variety in pairs of instruments that are gradually introduced and spotlighted. The first of these pairs, French and English horns, illuminates the sensitivity to timbre and range that Ives demonstrates throughout this piece. Although listeners do not often mistake the two for each other, in certain tessituras the horns produce remarkably similar sounds. A good example is the transition from French to English horn that occurs midway through the musical phrase at measures 7 and 8. Since one of the most characteristic qualities of the French horn is the unmistakably brassy sound of its attack, Ives wisely allows the French horn sound to decay before having the English horn enter. The lower range of the English horn, while sounding distinctly like a double reed instrument, also sounds very much like the middle range of the French horn. With the overlap in timbres occurring when it does, the transition from French horn to English horn is easy and inconspicuous. The difference in their sounds is enough to provide variety to the tonal palette, while their similarity assures that both instruments will be perceived as belonging to the same stratum of activity, an important consideration if Ives is to avoid confusing listeners.

A similar case can be made for Ives's handling of the timbres of flutes, and oboes and clarinets when they enter at measure 21, and for trumpets and trombones when they join the ensemble with melodic material at measure 34. By separating instruments into groups with complementary timbres, Ives clarifies spheres of activity in his place pieces. The practice becomes an essential aspect of the composer's spatial techniques as they are applied in the work. But because this piece demands a conciliatory denouement, the separate strata that have been so carefully created will eventually need to move toward interaction and integration.

Creating the Foreground: Melody

Ives's environment by accretion allows auditors to experience the valley as he and his wife did on their walk—slowly—gradually taking in more and more of the surroundings. The deliberate pace gives Ives the opportunity to firmly establish different realms of activity for consideration before moving on. In fact, pacing is so important to the correct manifestation of this pastoral scene that Ives waits until the midpoint of the movement to unveil the foreground—when he does, the sounds come from an unexpected source. As flutes, oboe, and clarinets appear in measure 21, the foreground appears to have emerged; it has not. The new timbre and higher register combined are not powerful enough to offset the nature of their musical material, which rotates in patterns reminiscent of the opening viola music. Since Ives has relegated circular music to the background once before in this piece, these similar patterns become part of that background as well, and emerge as secondary in focus to the linear hymn tune. By recasting instrumental roles, Ives thwarts any expectations that the foreground will emerge from the new ensemble.

Starting on the fourth beat of measure 22, first and second violins, which had been part of the background through measure 21, now become the foreground with a new rendering of "Dorrnance." Ives informs us that the river is capable of more than dreamy meandering: it can also harness its energies and chart an unequivocal course. The instruments that interpreted the river now interpret the hymn on their own terms. While such a timbral role change might threaten the notion of carefully constructed discrete spheres of sound, that does not happen. Listeners depend upon Ives's painstakingly deliberate portrayal of multiple, simultaneous areas of activity to sustain them through the shift. Rather than signal an end to timbral sovereignty, the introduction of high woodwinds heralds a new focus in the work.

With the upbeat to measure 23, the piece enters its second half. New sounds invite a fresh look at the valley. For the first time, the descending major third incipit of the hymn is heard at a different pitch level from the previous three appearances—G♯ descending to E over a C♯ pedal, instead of F descending to D-flat. The palpable rise from F to G♯ not only introduces a new intensity to the piece, it moves the melody to the pitch level found in numerous sources of the hymn. The minor-key harmonization of the tune (the E is heard as a minor third over the C♯ pedal) also reflects a restlessness in the river that Johnson refers to in line forty-five of his poem and that Ives sets: "Contented river! And yet over-shy to mask thy beauty from the eager eye; Hast thou a thought to hide from field and town? In some deep current of the sunlit brown." This is Johnson's first hint that the river is more than a placid stream; it is Ives's first suggestion as well.

At measure 23 there is a noticeable increase in sound. For the first time, upper-string instruments remove their mutes and increase their dynamic level; though they begin at *mezzo forte,* they quickly increase to *forte.* The greater volume is matched with more assertive articulation. Replacing the long, beat-obscuring legato phrases are three consecutive accents on the opening notes of the tune; there is conviction behind this utterance. Directions for playing the line non tremolo guarantee a strong, unwavering voice for the violin's melody. The tune, which had been submerged in the cello line, now makes its second appearance, riding confidently on the surface of the music. As the melody has moved to "the front" of the string ensemble, the river moves from the background into the foreground of the sonic canvas.

Reconciliation in the Valley

With the once-static violins energetically embracing the dynamic hymn, Ives begins the process of musical reconciliation that is the essence of the piece. If in the first half of the movement the hymn represents a discrete force, separate from nature, starting at measure 23 that force is transformed and absorbed by nature. In fact, by measure 23 the violins' hymn is thoroughly surrounded by and connected to the constant hum of nature: violas and harps swirl rotating patterns underneath the melody, while flutes, oboes, clarinets, and celesta circle above. As if to drive home the commanding hold that the violins have on the linear material, they alone sing the hymn tune for over eight measures.

When violins finish their tune, Ives recalls the river's other temperament by reintroducing the earlier spatial music to the four-part string group. The violin's flexible motions, from spatial to linear back to spatial music, free French horns to play a part other than the hymn incipit (with which they have been closely identified) and permit flutes to venture, momentarily, into the realm of lineal music. Horns and flutes combine to announce the climactic closing of the piece.

At measure 33, the music alters its course and enters into an increasingly turbulent passage. Ives's piece transports listeners from Johnson's once "dreamy realm, . . . by fall and shallow to the adventurous sea." Like the poet who confidentially admits to the river a fear of "much resting," Ives's music also seems to fear too much complacency. Distancing itself from its placid beginnings, the last quarter of the piece is as agitated as the first was tranquil.

Starting at measure 34, new timbres, increased tempos, augmented dynamics, and denser textures set out on an unstoppable course. As the music surges to the foreground of the sonic canvas, all of nature seems to shudder with its newly discovered power. Trumpets and trombones take over for the violins and negotiate the wave of sound, using "Dorrnance" to chart the course. The brass are among the few instruments whose sound can penetrate the thunderous cascade. River water shivers and spills in the sounds of tremolos and glissandi. Powerful, synchronized pulses pump through the orchestra and push the music forward at regular intervals; boundaries between discrete spheres of activity are washed away as the once separate musics mingle and move toward a common goal—"the adventurous sea." As the physical environment is overwhelmed by the river, the aural environment is saturated with sound. Music fills every opening in chromatic, registral, and temporal space.

Were the piece to stop at measure 42, a listener could surmise that the river's thunderous surge to the sea had washed away all memories of the more pastoral aspects of the Housatonic Valley. Indeed, the final lines of Robert Underwood Johnson's inspiring poem leave readers with just that impression. But Ives's piece is not about restless, eclipsing power, nor is it concerned exclusively with adventure to the great unknown. (It is not about the victory of linear compositional techniques over spatial techniques either.) What drives this place piece are the conciliatory possibilities in the Housatonic Valley that reveal themselves to the composer and to willing auditors of that environment. The final two measures of the piece clarify Ives's idea.

At measure 43, as the chromatic crash of music suddenly dissipates, sounds of the contented river softly reemerge from the violins. Their entry on G♯ provides an important reference point for listeners who, consciously or not, recall this pitch as signifying a return. The first significant use of G♯ as melodic material occurred at measure 3, where cellos and then bassoons entered with the final phrase of "Dorrnance." Prior to this, G♯ acted as an essential harmonic component in the upper voice of the two-part pedal point that grounded the piece. The violins' hymn tune solo at measure 23 entered on the second significant melodic use of G♯. Now, in addition to the return of G♯, the reappearance of C♯ in the basses at measure 43, though soft and muted, offers a harmonic recollection and hint of stability. The return of C♯ reminds listeners of the lower voice of the pedal point that prevailed through significant portions of this piece. The reemergence of these two pitches at this final moment in the piece is structurally significant and musically symbolic.[48]

Such constancy is an important anchor in a piece that on first glance seems to change so much from its quiet opening to its bombastic closing. At the climax, in the midst of its most wrenching musical expression, the river recalls its gentler nature; the hymn tune incipit emerges apparition-like in a sonic sea spray, sung at the familiar pitch level, supported by the expected harmonic foundation. This New England waterway is capable of both power and peacefulness, change and constancy. Contradictory as these qualities may appear, they are harmonized by their presence in one entity, the Housatonic River. The appropriateness of the water image becomes clear.

Issues of rapprochement stimulate other aspects of Ives's piece. For a majority of the work the transient hymn tune appears to have wrested the spiritual spotlight away from the river, but the final two measures confirm the source of spirituality for Ives. Persuasive as the sounds from the church are, they are merely a point of reference; the real source of spirituality can be traced to nature. If no fully fleshed-out expression of Ives's Transcendental beliefs exists in his prose at this time, perhaps *The Housatonic* can be considered a musical statement of his understanding of that movement. God, as represented by Woodbury's hymn tune, is immanent in nature, in American nature, in the American place. Nature and man relate and respond to each other with their music; they are engaged in an ongoing dialogue. To know God, one must know nature. Though tensions exist between them, man remains inextricably bound to nature, just as the hymn tune remains bound to the river music.

And finally, the Housatonic Valley symbolized another quality, one that was of utmost importance to this American composer. The river embodied a personal and local connection to the universal. Fed by streams in the quiet hillsides of the Berkshires, wending its way through small hamlets and towns, the New England river nonetheless flowed inexorably to the anonymous sea. What originated as a personally significant, local place joined energies in time with a universally shared property. The liquid medium allowed no boundary lines, no separations between what was local and what was universal; the river contained both qualities simultaneously. The universal being was immanent in the local, in the individual. In *The Housatonic at Stockbridge,* Ives asserted the importance of America's natural place as a locus of spiritual revelation. Like the Hudson River painters who saw temples amid trees, baptismal fonts in serene pools, and natural altars etched within rock formations, Ives heard the distant echoes of a hymn in the intervening atmosphere. The nineteenth-century aesthetic trinity of God-nature-art had a voice.

FROM HANOVER SQUARE NORTH, AT THE END OF A TRAGIC DAY, THE VOICE OF THE PEOPLE AGAIN AROSE

Charles Ives has been so closely identified as a nineteenth-century New Englander and a Yankee tinkerer that a systematic consideration of his ties to other types of places has not occurred.[49] We have neglected to consider the influence of a second, equally powerful environment that Ives voluntarily embraced. From the summer of 1898 until the day he died, 19 May 1954, Charles Ives was as much a denizen of contemporary urban America as he was of the romantic rural countryside.

Though Ives often disparaged New York City,[50] his practice of maintaining a residence in the city throughout his adult life, and his decision to spend major portions of each year at that residence after he retired from business in January 1930, attests to his involvement with the nation's foremost cultural scene.[51] Although Ives regularly sought the quiet refuge of his country home and acreage, his return to Babylon at predictable intervals every year suggests, at the very least, an attachment to city life that he was unwilling to break.[52] For had Ives wanted to sever his relationship with that place, he most certainly would have. His fluid movement between urban and rural places became an essential feature of his adult life; the composer-businessman was bicultural.[53] Ives's life boasted a wealth of influences; because he composed from his experience, his music did too. In addition to celebrating historic New England sites and bucolic New England scenes, the music also commemorated crowds of busy New Yorkers and the clangorous noises of city life. For the successful businessman-composer, rural and urban places were equally vital and legitimate sources of inspiration.

Two pieces in particular illustrate Ives's involvement in the urban place: *Central Park in the Dark,* composed in 1906 and later grouped with *The Unanswered Question* as one of *Two Contemplations,*[54] and a piece that Ives went on record as naming "one of the best that I've done": *From Hanover Square North, at the End of a Tragic Day, the Voice of the People Again Arose*. It was "assembled [and] reworked c1919 from material composed c1909–1919."[55] Ives's generously detailed commentary provides essential information regarding his motivations and goals for this second work.

By the time Ives wrote *From Hanover Square North,* he was a successful middle-age businessman and a seasoned New Yorker. The years since his 1898 graduation from Yale had seen his marriage to Harmony Twichell and the formal establishment of the Ives and Myrick insurance agency. Ives's decade of bachelorhood, 1898–1908, and early years of marriage were a period of personal mobility, artistic productivity, emotional satisfaction, and professional achievement. A half-dozen changes in residence, the continuous composition of music, and the steadily increasing prosperity of his business attest to a man thoroughly engaged in a busy and rewarding life. Though Ives would probably have resisted identification as a New Yorker, *From Hanover Square North* reveals an appreciation that particular types of meaningful human interactions existed, perhaps exclusively, in the city. *From Hanover Square North* captures an actual moment that Ives shared with his fellow New Yorkers.

His portrayal of Hanover Square in the third movement of the *Second Orchestral Set* reflects the crowded, mobile, protean urban landscape in individual moments and in the overall form of the piece.[56] Ives captures the activity and the complex, fomenting energy that has defined the modern city since the early 1900s. The location is the essential backdrop to the story that he wants to tell, for it could take place nowhere else. But perhaps even more important than picturing the urban environment is sonifying the drama of the people who undergo a powerful collective experience there. Whereas *The Housatonic* is a piece that celebrates a natural place and in that way is very much in keeping with traditional nineteenth-century portrayals of America, *From Hanover Square North* is a place piece that concentrates more on a human drama within the newly important urban landscape.

Unlike other places that Ives commemorated whose *natural setting* often supplied some specific aspect of the program, Hanover Square was *only* important because of the human drama that occurred there. Nothing of local, regional, or national historical import took place at the "El" station. Nature as it appeared in Ives's three New England pieces, or as it was portrayed in *Central Park in the Dark,* is missing in this piece. From the opening measures, Ives tells us the city was man-made and that people defined this place. Absent the bucolic setting, and the promise of nature, people turned to one another for spiritual sustenance. In both *The Housatonic* and *Hanover Square,* a human receptor provides the orientation point for our understanding. This receptor is similar to the human figure in a landscape painting who provides scale and perspective to the towering mountains and endless vistas. By calling upon his memories of the day in May 1915 when the passenger liner *Lusitania* was sunk, Ives focuses upon a moment of profound human cohesion that was possible only in the "unnatural" urban setting, and he finds God in man.[57]

The Program

Ives's commentary in *Memos* on the genesis of *From Hanover Square North* is perhaps the most generous of any he provides for his pieces. It offers an assessment of the relative worth of the piece, a detailed explanation of the events, times, and places involved in its creation, a description of the scene that Ives wanted to capture, and a judgment of the lasting value of different types of music. For all these reasons it bears reprinting:

> The last movement, in my opinion, is one of the best—that's not the same as saying that it's any too good—it's simply saying that, as far as I'm concerned, I think it's one of the best that I've done. There's a personal experience behind it, the story of which I will now try to tell. We were living in an apartment at 27 West 11th Street. The morning paper on the breakfast table gave the news of the sinking of the Lusitania. I remember, going downtown to business, the people on the streets and on the elevated train had something in their faces that was not the usual something. Everybody who came into the office, whether they spoke about the disaster or not, showed a realization of seriously experiencing something. (That it meant war is what the faces said, if the tongues didn't.) Leaving the office and going uptown about six o'clock, I took the Third Avenue "L" at Hanover Square Station. As I came on the platform, there was quite a crowd waiting for the trains, which had been blocked lower down, and while waiting there, a hand-organ or hurdy-gurdy was playing in the street below. Some workmen sitting on the side of the tracks began to whistle the tune, and others began to sing or hum the refrain. A workman with a shovel over his shoulder came on the platform and joined in the chorus, and the next man, a Wall Street banker with white spats and a cane, joined in it, and finally it seemed to me that everybody was singing this tune, and they didn't seem to be singing in fun, but as a natural outlet for what their feelings had been going through all day long. There was a feeling of dignity all through this. The hand-organ man seemed to sense this and wheeled the organ nearer the platform and kept it up fortissimo (and the chorus sounded out as though every man in New York must be joining in it). Then the first train came in and everybody crowded in, and the song gradually died out, but

the effect on the crowd still showed. Almost nobody talked—the people acted as though they might be coming out of a church service. In going uptown, occasionally little groups would start singing or humming the tune.

Now what was the tune? It wasn't a Broadway hit, it wasn't a musical comedy air, it wasn't a waltz tune or a dance tune or an opera tune or a classical tune, or a tune that all of them probably knew. It was (only) the refrain of an old Gospel Hymn that had stirred many people of past generations. It was nothing but—*In the Sweet Bye and Bye*. It wasn't a tune written to be sold, or written by a professor of music—but by a man who was but giving out an experience.

This third movement is based on this, fundamentally, and comes from that "L" station. It has its secondary theme [and] rhythms, but widely related, and its general make-up would reflect the sense of many people living, working, and occasionally going through the same deep experience, together. It would give the ever changing multitudinous feeling of life that one senses in the city. This was completed and all scored (as it stands now) in the fall of that year, 1915.[58]

In a way not unlike what he'd done in *The Housatonic,* Ives used a hymn to reconcile human beings and place, and he introduced religion as the mediator of people and their environment. Thus he charged a song about a different place, an allegorical place, "a [more] beautiful shore," with the power to unite the divergent city people and his piece.

A brief look at the hymn "In the Sweet Bye and Bye" reveals important basic musical elements of *From Hanover Square North.*

The sixteen-measure hymn contains a verse and refrain of equal length. The verse has four distinct phrases, each of which begins with an identical rising major third upbeat pattern of dotted-eighth and sixteenth to the downbeat quarter. The refrain has a similar pattern of rising thirds in dotted rhythms, but three of its four musical phrases begin with minor thirds. The fourth phrase of the refrain ignores the prevailing rhythmic and directional patterns completely and returns to the major third of the chorus. In addition, it reverses the ascending third to a descending one and flattens out the dotted rhythm into a pattern of two equal eighth notes. Notable as these last phrase changes are, they are not significant enough to challenge the defining features of the tune: rising, step-wise major and minor thirds, and the dotted rhythms.

The internal consistency of the musical material and the limited number of distinctive gestures make this hymn an ideal vehicle for Ives's dramatic purposes. We can believe a random assortment of people effortlessly joining voices in this simple tune. Significantly, the text of the hymn is especially

IN THE SWEET BYE AND BYE

("There's a land that is fairer than day")
SOURCE: *Gospel Hymn and Tune Book*, no. 437.

Ex. 2.3: "In the Sweet Bye and Bye"

befitting the particular events that Ives attempted to capture. References to a better life awaiting believers on another shore are eerily appropriate for victims of this nautical disaster.[59] As the text of the hymn unites seekers of a paradisiacal dwelling place, the characteristics of the tune unify Ives's musical tribute. The organizational role of the hymn is disclosed as the piece evolves.

Setting the Scene

Ives establishes the multiple, competing aspects of the city place by initially separating the instrumental forces into a "distant choir" and a "main orchestra": he creates the equivalent of visual perspective. He allows us to hear behind the foreground sounds by keeping each of the ensembles relatively autonomous. As he did in *The Housatonic at Stockbridge,* he lays in the background sounds first; in *Hanover Square* this means securing the music of the distant choir. This is a uniquely colored ensemble: the offstage orchestra of the distant choir consists of a single horn in C, chimes, a harp, piano, two violins, one viola, and four or more basses in addition to the vocal ensemble. Immediately we perceive a difference between the natural Housatonic River Valley environment and that of the urban El station: It is essential to Ives's conception of the man-made city that even the background sounds include a human presence.[60] As in *The Housatonic,* the very slow tempo and extremely soft dynamics the opening measures elude traditional rhythmic and har-

Hanover Square Station, 1878, from a sketch by Theo R. Davis. Collection of the New-York Historical Society, negative no. 64942.

monic categorization; it is hard to distinguish exactly what is being heard or how to measure it. As is the case with many of Ives's place pieces, listeners enter upon music that is already under way.[61] But the texted intonation that begins *Hanover Square*—"We praise Thee O God, we acknowledge Thee to be the Lord, all the earth doth worship Thee"—where individual words penetrate our consciousness as discrete elements and so call attention to the vocal line and the omnipresence of people, distinguishes this place. It is unlike other place pieces in this regard, but for the most part the opaque opening music manifests itself more as a composite effect than as a collection of individual, identifiable components. The distant choir acts as part of a unit.[62] For Ives, cities and people are inseparable; people define cities.

Of the seven instruments in the distant choir, only the horn calls attention to itself in any way resembling the voices. But even it acts more as a shadow to the voice line than as an independent agent. The relationship between voices and horn is itself blurred and ambiguous. The background distant choir becomes the constant elements of the city, including humming traffic noises and the "many people living, [and] working . . . together."[63]

As with musical backgrounds in other pieces, the persistence of this one throughout the course of the work does not always guarantee its audibility. Though place must be established at the outset of the work, once defined it can withdraw into the sonic scenery and become part of the larger canvas; it becomes the stage for the program. Unlike Ives's other places, however, where people interact to some degree or other with the natural world, Hanover Square Station is uniquely and exclusively a place for people. As such, voices are basic elements in this place.

For all its uniqueness, the piece shows compositional techniques similar to those observed in *The Housatonic at Stockbridge.* The density and unity of the opening of *Hanover Square* result from the vertical alignment of numerous static features—pedal points, ostinati, narrowly circumscribed pitch pools—and important similarities among the eight contributing lines. Like the city itself, the music is crowded, both harmonically and rhythmically; it is a struggle to separate individual instrumental gestures by timbre or register, since so many of their motives are similar. Horns, chimes, harp, piano, voices, violins, viola and basses of the distant choir create a "widely related" but unquestionably unified whole.[64] This unity, which is not immediately apparent, derives from the hymn tune "In the Sweet Bye and Bye." Unknown to listeners when they first come upon the piece, the chanted vocal line subtly prepares them for the approaching human drama and the emerging hymn that will share with the chant the characteristic rising third.

The dizzyingly kaleidoscopic activity of the city, however, does not have to negate the impact of individual moments upon a keen observer. And so it is with the music. From deep within the muffled chromatic mass of the opening of the piece, a few distinct pitches and intervals come forth. The pitch F that conveys the majority of Ives's intoned text is an important touchstone early in the piece.[65] The uniqueness of the texted vocal line within the larger sonic canvas assures its audibility; from the beginning the human presence at Hanover Square is spotlighted (see Ex. 2.4).

The intoned F combines with other pitches to create additional musical markers. At the end of the phrase "We praise Thee O God, we acknowledge Thee to be the Lord," and on the final word of the second phrase, "All the Earth doth worship Thee," the F cadences downward to D, calling attention to a second clearly audible pitch but, more important, to the minor-third interval separating the two. This is one of two intervals that characterized the initial upward sweep of the intonation "We praise Thee." The pitches D and F, and the minor third interval that separates them, are significant in other instrumental parts as well, as in the chimes' and basses' music, where F and D circle repeatedly as part of an ostinato. Although the very low register of these instruments makes precise pitches nearly inaudible, they reinforce others that we can hear. Not coincidentally, this is the same pattern of pitches found in the lowest notes of the circling piano music. Ives's belief in Emerson's underlying metaphysical unity may be manifested in these small details of musical construction.[66]

The horn eventually echoes the cadential minor third gesture in its enharmonic equivalent E♯ to D, but not before it presents a significant challenge to the dominance of F (E♯) and the minor-third interval. The horn makes its debut with three unequivocal F♯s at measures 4 to 6 and insists upon descending major third cadences at measures 7–8 and 11–12. It only gradually works its way toward E♯ (F) and a final minor-third cadence at measures 13–14 and 19–20. The rising third gesture that characterizes important phrases of the hymn appears for the first time in the horn line at measures 12–13 and 17–18 as F♯, G, A, but having not yet heard a hymn fragment, its association with the hymn is unclear at this point. Ives foreshadows what is to come.

Circling music of the piano line reinforces the horn by sounding F and F♯, sometimes playing one, sometimes the other, sometimes both simultaneously. The combination of the piano F/F♯ pitches and the harp's open fifth on D and A ensures that important major- and minor-third tensions remain present even if they are not always consciously perceived.[67] The piano is charged with the simultaneous duties of clarifying and obscuring pitches and intervals.

Violins and viola are part of the obfuscating forces; their pitch series are characterized by semitones, major and minor thirds, and prominently placed Fs and F♯s.[68] Though the characteristic intervals of the hymn appear abundantly (if hidden) in the early measures of *Hanover Square*, the dotted rhythm identified with the upbeat to seven of eight phrases of the hymn tune is absent completely. In place of the distinctive and compelling long-short-long gesture, Ives begins his piece with a maze of motions. Ambiguity of pitches and intervals is reinforced by rhythmic ambiguity.

Ives creates the rhythmic equivalent of a photographic double exposure by avoiding precise synchrony between rhythmic articulations.[69] Various metrical patterns penetrate one another but are prevented from aligning because of asymmetrical groupings, ties over bar lines, and unexpected stresses. (See opening measures of the distant choir.) A mélange of accents, echoes, and pre-echoes results. In the same way that multiple neighboring pitches weaken a

Main Orchestra tacet until [B]

Ex. 2.4: *From Hanover Square North* (3d mut. of *Orchestral Set No. 2*), by Charles Ives, mm 1–19. © 1971, 1978, 2001 by Peer International Corp. International rights secured. Used by permission. All rights reserved.

accelerando
12
Horn
[mp]
Chimes
Harp
Piano
Intoned
Vns.
Va.
(all)
Db.
pp

16
Horn
Chimes
Harp
Piano
Intoned
Vns.
Va.
Db.

solid pitch center, shifting patterns within a fluid rhythmic scheme obscure precise beats. Traditional downbeats disappear in this metrical mixture, where Ives sought to picture "the ever changing multitudinous feeling of life that one senses in the city."[70] Like the scene it portrays, the music of the distant choir is characterized by fluidity and fluctuation. Though there is constant harmonic and rhythmic motion, there is no sense of ultimate direction or inevitable progress.

The inability to distinguish individual components may appear to challenge their significance, but distinctiveness is not necessarily the primary value. Ives is after the larger texture of the city. In *From Hanover Square North*, he first establishes the existence of numerous different elements; details of their relationships will develop in time. Just as the kinship between individual New Yorkers is not immediately evident even to themselves, initially common qualities in the music are hidden from auditors.[71] The music, like the place, vibrates with an oscillating collective energy that only gradually reveals its nature and power.

Revealing the Drama

In order to capture the communal experience that he recollects, Ives has to leave the spinning, spatial music that defined the place and turn to more traditional, linear techniques of musical composition. The body of the work becomes the drama that Ives witnessed. While the opening intonation provides a vague and temporary linear focus, it disappears with the chorus by measure 11. Its distant sound also works against its being heard as the dominant feature of the soundscape. The voices serve their purpose by focusing attention on the human aspects of the place and the drama, which are the real subjects of this piece. Although no other single linear trajectory materializes to guide listeners through the work in quite the way the intonation did, Ives creates a compellingly logical piece by following a different compositional course.

By combining and overlapping fragments of the generative hymn, Ives etches a fractured, multifaceted linear channel through the piece. Although we hear more and longer identifiable fragments of the generative hymn, it is not until the end of the work that the entire hymn refrain is evident. The piece moves from complexity to clarification, albeit a richly complex clarity. The musical consensus that emerges is an analogue of the newly discovered human consensus that has existed all along in the city, unbeknown to its inhabitants. Ives's music is a symbol of the experience presented in its own terms. J. Peter Burkholder refers to the resulting musical structure as cumulative form: "a thematic, non-repetitive form in which the principal theme is presented, not at the beginning as in traditional forms, but near the end."[72] Musical fig. 2.5 lays out Ives's multilinear scheme.

After nineteen measures of place-defining distant-choir music, the main orchestra enters for the first time at measure 20. As in many other Ives place pieces, important dramatic action occurs only after a setting is in place. Cellos begin on B-flat, with a rhythmically neutralized version of the hymn tune's rising third in whole and half notes. The clarinets follow at measure 23, with a speeded-up echo of the cello entrance. Their faster tempo actually encourages listeners to think of the rising pitches as melodic, perhaps even as the incipit to a song, whereas the larger note values of the cello line did not lend themselves to such speculation. But listeners must wait until measure 24, when the solo piano and cello provide the characteristic dotted rhythm of the hymn, to associate the rising third gesture with the tune "In the Sweet Bye and Bye." It would appear that Ives has missed no opportunity to make his point that his piece is about elements coming together. The important melodic thirds and the identifying rhythmic components of the hymn are separated in their initial appearances, much as the peoples of New York are emotionally separated from each other without the nudge of a communal crisis. Even something as unified as this hymn is made up of a number of separate elements that must be brought together by circumstance.[73]

As the solo piano beats the dotted rhythm on a series of Fs, the first identifiable pitch of location now becomes the first identifiable pitch of action. The important minor third emerges between that F and the D pedal point sustained by the basses, which are both interpreted within the context of the B-flat first introduced by the celli. Meanwhile, from the muffled distant choir, the piano's repeated and accented F♯s are audible, simultaneously providing the major third with the pedal D. As important pitches and intervals are reinforced, Ives begins the slow process of piecing together the hymn.

As in *The Housatonic at Stockbridge,* once the scene is set, instrumental timbres are carefully and gradually introduced and layered upon one another. In *Hanover Square,* Ives establishes each instrument and its hymn fragment: cello, clarinet, piano, violins, brass, flutes. He captures the multitonal singing of the impromptu train-station chorus in a series of hymn tune fragments, each of which has its own idea about key.[74] Though ultimately auditors may not be able to separate individual lines within the resulting composite sound, listeners will know that they exist and as a result will be better able to understand the complexity of the situation—musical, social, and historical.

Soon after the main orchestra enters, the distant choir retreats to the recesses of our consciousness; it truly becomes the background, the place for the

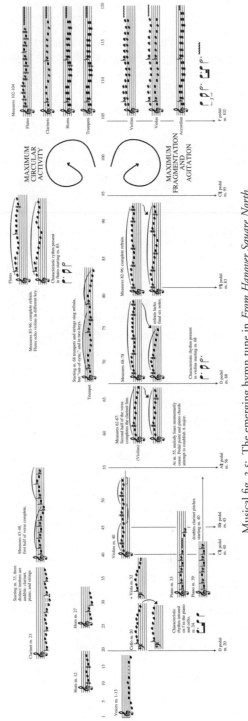

Musical fig. 2.5: The emerging hymn tune in *From Hanover Square North*.

drama. Attentions are refocused on the new foreground music, which, like the material of the earlier distant choir, initially resists traditional rhythmic coordination. As he did in *The Housatonic,* Ives moves to consider the foreground of his soundscape only after establishing its relationship to the larger sonic canvas. But as instruments explore fragments of the hymn tune, sometimes individually and sometimes joining forces for a moment, it becomes clear that over time they are capable of a more sustained, rhythmically synchronized effort.

By measure 33, clarinet, solo piano, viola, and cello are all involved with fragments of the hymn. As parts of the melody overlap and echo, listeners hear the tune from different vantage points, much as people at the train station must have heard it. Once again, a sense of musical progress results from the accretion of musical activity. But in *Hanover Square,* progress also results from the growing realization that a familiar hymn tune is evolving simultaneously in numerous locations. The cumulative effect will far exceed individual expectations. The unilinear trajectory that sufficed for centuries as the principal path of large-scale musical logic is inadequate to this task.

Simultaneous linear progressions overlap and create a moving line as variegated in its tone color as are the city sights and sounds that inspire it. Ives connects the distinctive timbres of the orchestral palette in a multilinear trajectory and projects this against the constant hum of the distant choir. He pieces together the hymn using gradually lengthening fragments of chorus and refrain material. (The emerging hymn tune appears in Musical fig. 2.5.)

What starts out as a three-note incipit in the French horn grows to the entire opening phrase of the verse at measure 20 in the cello, and at measure 23 in the clarinet. At measure 43 the main orchestra piano offers its own reading of the phrase, but on a new pitch level that is then picked up and doubled by the clarinet. Ives expands the fragment to include the second phrase of the verse. Underneath this layer of activity, violins enter with a short fragment of the verse in D. Their oscillating recitation, D-E-F♯-E-D-E, prepares the way for the piano and lower strings to establish A as a new harmonic area at measure 55. Seven measures later, violins complete the work begun by the clarinets and present the second half of the verse; they remain in D. Halfway through the piece, Ives is halfway through the hymn.

Having completed the verse, Ives presents the refrain. At measure 68, violins and trumpets launch into a polytonal out-of-phase refrain fragment (trumpets in F, violins in D). Important pitches and intervals introduced at the beginning of the piece still function as unifying devices at the halfway mark. Violins begin with a complete rendition of the refrain in D major at measure 82. One measure later, the pedal changes to F and flutes enter with their own version of the refrain in F major. The F/F♯ tension originally presented in the distant choir has now moved into the main orchestra. By measure 97, *Hanover Square* is a whirl of rotating hymn tune fragments, none of which prevails. But unlike similar soundscapes that Ives created in *Central Park in the Dark* or its companion piece, *The Unanswered Question,* both of which appeared to exhaust themselves in musical chaos and frustration late in the works, the moment of maximum agitation in *Hanover Square,* measures 97–102, actually congeals individual efforts and produces a quasi-unified rendition of the seminal hymn. The generative idea behind *Hanover Square* demands a different outcome from that of *Two Contemplations.* From the densely packed sound mass that fills the place emerges the multi-voiced refrain to "In the Sweet Bye and Bye": the voice of the people arises. Major and minor thirds and dotted rhythms—the important characteristics of the hymn—sing out in a perfectly out-of-tune and out-of-step chorus.

Ives mediates a traditional unilineal approach to composition with a later more spatial mode and thus captures the human drama that took place at Hanover Square. Though each mode is eclipsed by the other at some point in the work, there is no question but that ultimately the two are coexisting and dependent upon one another for meaning and substance. Without the constant hum of the city as background, the full impact of the people's achievement could not be realized. As Ives's singing commuters board trains for their trips home, the hymn tune fades, but the sounds of the place remain. An F pedal in basses and cellos supports reiterated F major triads in the piano and recalls the opening intoned pitch. Lingering C♯s keep tensions—human and musical—alive.

As the piece seems to move away from us, morendo, *pppp,* uncertainties linger in the music, much as uncertainties persisted after the Treaty of Versailles. While the opening vocal line of *Hanover Square* chanted F, competing pitches and intervals weakened its power to assert inevitable harmonic motions or goals. Ultimately, listeners appreciate that the tensions present at the beginning of the piece portend musical behavior that persists through all 119 measures of the work. The ambiguity in harmonic and rhythmic domains that greeted listeners at measure 1 also wafts in the air as the final sounds dissipate.[75] Using purely musical means, Ives instructs us that there are no easy solutions to the historical situation or its artistic manifestation. But thanks to his reconstruction of the hymn and the gentle layering of its component parts, the persistent dissonances and blurred metrical schemes that needed arbitration at the outset of the piece achieve a degree of resolution and equilibrium at the end.

Though "In the Sweet Bye and Bye" ultimately emerges in full glory, it never appears in a neatly harmonized, well-tailored rendition. At climactic measure 102, where instruments finally join together in the refrain of the hymn, they insist upon singing the song in their own key(s), no doubt creating a sonic equivalent that is closer to what Ives heard on that memorable day than any well-rehearsed, uniformly rendered, proper performance could be. What started out as confusing ambiguity ends up as profound richness. Although it is hard to conceive of any musical consensus emerging from the sonic amalgam of the opening measures, Ives manages to create a persuasive closing that is all the more powerful because of its honesty, its fidelity to the historical drama. Loyalty to the generative idea was paramount to Ives.

The unique multilinearity of *From Hanover Square North,* the piece, emerges directly from the particular spatial qualities of Hanover Square, the place. Auditors witness a reconciliation of musical spheres that is as moving and internally consistent as any traditionally closed musical ending. Ives's piece succeeds because his musical and dramatic ideas are fully reflexive. It is no wonder that he was especially pleased with this work. Ives's tension-filled conclusion is an accurate representation of how he and his fellow commuters must have felt as they collectively contemplated the possible resonance of this single momentous human and political catastrophe. The composer-business-man wrote his work as one who shared in a soul-stirring national experience. Reflecting upon the eventual costs of World War I, with its annihilation of a generation of young men among the 10 million who died, listeners cannot help wondering at Ives's prescient statement and stand in awe of his musical achievement.

On the Significance of Trains

Ives was a frequent and vocal critic of technology. Those who are attached to the myth of him as the crusty curmudgeon like to tell the story of an elderly Charles Ives shambling among the fields surrounding his West Redding home, angrily poking his cane skyward as an airplane buzzed overhead. An award-winning film chronicling the life of the composer makes much of this incident, at the same time suggesting he is quite dotty.[76] Testimonials by Ives's friends and acquaintances that recall his disparaging of radios and other modern-day contrivances also feed the characterization of a technophobic codger. And there is truth in all these portrayals. Ives resented the intrusion of modern technology. He feared surrendering control to unknown forces. He questioned unchecked "progress," as his proposed chamber set entitled *The Other Side of Pioneering: Side Lights on American Enterprise* made clear.[77] There was much happening in the first decades of the twentieth century to legitimize and feed such skepticism. If nothing else, World War I proved that technological advances could turn on themselves in the most brutal of ways. What was to say that radio, the telephone, or an automobile might not do the same?

And so it is noteworthy that Ives chose to capture this historical moment at Hanover Square with its essential setting at an elevated train station, and with the train itself such an important agent of the drama and inspiration for the sounds. Els were symbols of urban modernity. But trains were also among the most important symbols of *nineteenth-century* America, and one with which Ives was comfortable. This particular modern symbol, a source of inspiration for numerous twentieth-century artists and composers, held warm memories for the composer and for the nation, even if the focus of its setting had changed.[78]

The railroad was introduced to America with horse-drawn cars of the Baltimore and Ohio Railroad in 1828. Two years later, steam-powered trains transported goods and people. Within forty years the first transcontinental railroad was complete, and by the early 1880s more than 128,000 miles of tracks connected the nation. The iron horse was ubiquitous. The railroad was an essential player in the Civil War and was responsible for opening up markets throughout the continent. It generated millions of dollars in revenues. But not all citizens immediately perceived the railroad as a step forward. Along with enlarging the nation's marketplaces, it became the locus of numerous public battles among its financial backers: corruption was rampant. Others feared the intrusion of the noisy, smoke-belching machine into their otherwise unsoiled land.[79] With so much riding on the rails in the nineteenth century, it is no surprise that trains found their way into the nation's art, literature, and music.

Henry David Thoreau heard the trains from his cabin at Walden Pond and wrote about them in *Walden* (1854). He mused on the commerce being conducted on the rails and the connective power of the train: "I am refreshed and expanded when the freight train rattles past me, and I smell the stores which go dispensing their odors all the way from Long Wharf to Lake Champlain, reminding me of foreign parts, of coral reefs, and Indian oceans, and tropical climes, and the extent of the globe. I feel more like a citizen of the world."[80] The railroad was not without its intrusive qualities for Thoreau, yet it was also a humbling reminder of his place within a larger sphere and a symbol of the degree to which the entire country had come under the spell of the anthropomorphized "race now worthy to inhabit it." "They go and come with such regularity and precision, and their whistle can be heard so far, that the farmers set their clocks by them, and thus one well conducted institution regulates a whole country. . . . To do things 'railroad fashion' is now the by-word."[81] Ives would have been familiar with the scenes Thoreau painted and the sentiments he expressed.[82]

Among the most persuasive nineteenth-century proponents of the "fierce-throated beauty,"[83] however, was the country's first great urban poet, Walt Whitman. According to David S. Reynolds, a Whitman biographer, "he enthused over the swift, powerful train, which he called America's furthest 'advance beyond primitive barbarism.'"[84] In the poem "Passage to India" (1870), Whitman offered a paean to technology in his very first stanza: "Singing my days,/Singing the great achievements of the present,/Singing the strong light works of engineers,/Our modern wonders, . . . The New by its mighty railroad spann'd,/The seas inlaid with eloquent gentle wires."[85] According to Reynolds, "Whitman was coming to believe that the cultural unification he had been seeking might be achieved through the technological-industrial feats Americans were celebrating."[86] "Passage to India," however, was not a unique celebration of railroads among Whitman's oeuvre. Reynolds cites "The Return of the Heroes" and "Song of the Exposition" as two other poems that "gave technology an almost transcendental significance."[87] He goes on to observe, "More than two decades before the 1893 World's Columbian Exposition in Chicago, in which religion and technology were memorably joined, Whitman sang hymns to the modern age."[88] It is perhaps noteworthy that in September 1893 Ives traveled by train to that exposition with his uncle Lyman Brewster and would have seen for himself the massive effort to meld technology with a new national identity.

Whitman was perhaps the most famous spokesperson musing on the railroad's place in American culture, but he was certainly not alone. A cursory search of railroad-related materials generates thousands of citations in documents ranging from historical timetables and railway maps to stories covering train wrecks, collections of songs, catalogues of exhibitions of railroad art, records of societies for the preservation of historical stations and memorabilia, and bibliographies of the railroad in literature. One such reference book by Frank P. Donovan is *A Brief Survey of Railroad Fiction, Poetry, Songs, Biography, Essays, Travel and Drama in the English Language, Particularly Emphasizing Its Place in American Literature.*[89] This testament to "railroadana" divides the literature into four major periods in American history: 1830–90, inception and growth; 1890–1910, the Golden Age; 1910–30, period of decline; 1930–40, renaissance. Donovan observes that railroad literature often celebrates the especially courageous trainmen and is closely tied to the idea of settling the West, with all of the attendant danger, romance, and glamour: "Other than soldiering there were few occupations more hazardous than railroading, especially in the old link-and-pin days." Railroad songs, like railroad literature, were "concerned with feats of strength, endurance, and courage that like as not end in tragedy."[90] Because the West was so important in shaping America's identity in the nineteenth century, the railroad became especially associated with the emerging nation. If Niagara Falls had been the most important natural phenomenon to achieve iconographic status in the first half of the early nineteenth century, then the train was the most important man-made symbol of the developing nation as the century unfolded.[91]

This is borne out in the visual arts, where lithographers and numerous photographers such as Carleton E. Watkins and A. J. Russell made the railroad an essential ingredient in their new-world landscapes. Frances (Fanny) Palmer's color lithograph *Across the Continent: "Westward the Course of Empire Takes Its Way"* (1868), made famous by Currier and Ives, shows a train heading westward and leaving Indians on horseback waiting to be engulfed by the smoke. This is among the most famous of their prints. Photographers, often hired by railroad companies or already employees or speculators themselves, documented "man's progress into the wilderness . . . [and] the powers of civilization" with their works.[92] The Hudson River School painters Asher B. Durand, George Inness, and Jasper F. Cropsey, among others, included the new Pegasus in their paintings. Cropsey's *Starucca Viaduct, Pennsylvania* (1865) depicts a wholly integrated landscape *cum* railroad in the most romantic of ways. A train gracefully curves through the mountains that overlook the Susquehanna River, echoing the shoreline below. Its steamy plume merges with a soft blue sky that casts gentle light across the middleground waters. In the foreground and wrapping the edges of the painting are trees and greenery. Two observers, one standing, one reclining, accompanied by a dog, look out from a promontory at the entryway of our visual path and contemplate what many of the nineteenth century dubbed the "Eighth Wonder of the World." Was Cropsey pressured by artistic conventions to reconcile the seemingly dissonant spheres of technology and nature, or did he believe that the two could peacefully coexist in America's landscape? Does this work "signify the symbolic fusion of man and nature through Mind—secular invention subsumed into the larger creation," as the Hudson River School scholar Barbara Novak suggests?[93] Are we to believe that technology is a natural aspect of America?[94] Regardless of their motivations, artists and photographers quickly accommodated the machine in their garden. As to Cropsey's painting, Susan Danly concludes, "The railroad thus appears in an idealized setting, suggesting the easy assimilation of new technological forms into the aesthetic mode of the picturesque."[95]

Charles Ives, born just five years after the golden spike joined the Union

Pacific and Central Pacific railroads at Promontory, Utah, had fond memories of trains from his childhood, as John Kirkpatrick recorded in *Memos:*

> As Charlie and Mossie grew up, one of their greatest delights was finding that their father had never outgrown the capacity to enjoy things the way they did. As Ives wrote years later, they used to play train, about 1884—"the Ives Bros. R.R. under the clothes line . . . two barrels on the wash bench, an old stove pipe and the dinner bell . . . the cab was part of a chicken coop. . . . Father always entered into it seriously . . . and would just wave and never stop to talk while the train was going full blast. At that time I remember he was practising the violin. . . . father discovered that staccato passages and arpeggios could be made to sound like the clicking of the car wheels. . . . So he . . . rode in the rear passenger car for the whole trips . . . the noise of the wheels always stopped at the stations.[96]

Memories of trains conjured up memories of his beloved father.

As an adult, Ives used the technology he played at as a child. Like many wealthy businessmen, Ives commuted on the New Haven line from New York to his Connecticut home. He kept an intermittent diary of his travels to work and back. He also memorialized trains in two compositions that make references to railroads of one type or another: *The Celestial Railroad,* and *From Hanover Square North, at the End of a Tragic Day, the Voice of the People Again Arose.* The first is a fantasy for solo piano based on the Hawthorne story of the same name, in which a railroad ride is offered to passengers as an easy way to heaven. In the dreamlike story, passengers ultimately find themselves close enough to heaven to see the Celestial City across a river, but they end up exiting the train and being ferried to hell instead.[97] The allegorical tale would seem to condemn technology and the easy ride that it promises. (Those pilgrims who seek heaven by foot actually arrive at their destination.)

From Hanover Square North, however, provides a different set of passengers with a different kind of ride. In this work Ives realizes the possibilities of blending art, technology, and religion in a most positive way. He sets his drama at an El station and incorporates the motions and sounds of a train to depict a transcendent moment. There is no hint in Ives's commentary that this is a condemnation of technology; rather it appears to be a tacit recognition of the integral role that technology plays in modern life. In the city, technology, as manifest at the El station, has brought together people who would otherwise be disconnected. The locus of technology becomes their meeting ground. As passengers board the train singing the hymn tune, the rails take them beyond their individual worries and present place.[98] The train brings them together, where they find their common hope in religion, and then transports them with visions of a journey to "a beautiful shore." Technology has enabled transcendence.[99]

chapter three

Urban Places: Iconic New York

AARON COPLAND
Quiet City and *Music for a Great City*

A ARON Copland was born in 1900 just sixty-five miles away from Charles Ives's hometown, but the Brooklyn neighborhood where he was reared represented a different world. Although the two musicians were unalike in backgrounds and temperament, Copland was among the very first champions of Ives's music. In 1932 he programmed a set of seven Ives songs to be sung by Hubert Linscott at the Yaddo Festival, and in 1934 he wrote an article about Ives's music that appeared in *Modern Music*.[1] A grateful Ives wrote to Copland after the festival and mentioned looking forward to meeting him. The meeting never occurred, but Copland's respect continued for the man who had, in his own words, "the courage of a lion." Among Copland's last works is a piano piece entitled *Night Thoughts (Homage to Ives)* written in 1972.[2]

As much as Copland the composer was identified with the West, thanks to his widely popular ballets *Billy the Kid* and *Rodeo,* he remained a creature of the city. And he captured two sides of that environment in two very different pieces: *Quiet City* and *Music for a Great City.* Aaron Copland's relation to the urban place evoked in *Quiet City* is complex, in part because the city suggested in the title is not purely of his own design. Rather, it is an environment fundamentally shaped by the author Irwin Shaw for his 1939 play *Quiet City.* Copland's chamber suite *Quiet City* had three sources: his association with the experimental ensemble Group Theatre for which Shaw created the work; his deep and abiding friendship with its founder and director, Harold Clurman; and his sympathy with social and political issues of the 1930s, which were at the heart of all Group Theatre productions.

Quiet City was a timely piece, written for a play that was particularly reflective of the larger social and cultural climate of the late 1930s.[3] Here was a play wrestling with issues of class and the disparity of wealth in the decade of the Depression, immigrant assimilation and anti-Semitism, and worker struggles in an era when many felt, in the words of the brother of the protagonist, like "by-products of the machine of the city."[4] It was also a work of special personal meaning to the composer, marked in unique ways by his close ties with multiple people involved in its conception. Howard Pollack summarizes Copland's connection to Group Theatre personnel as follows: "Copland counseled the Group on musical matters, located benefactors, composed incidental music, and, within his very limited means, offered donations. Like only a few other artists outside of theater, he became a Group associate. He regularly attended rehearsals and performances—he spent much of the summer of 1933 with the company—and became pals with Kazan, Lewis, Meisner, and especially Odets."[5]

Aesthetically, *Quiet City* was a challenging project, one that invited Copland to revisit a place he'd already memorialized in an earlier work and one that forced him to consider in a single piece issues of fantasy and reality and past and present action.[6] The play called for flashbacklike scenes, quick changes of venue, and numerous instances of voices and sounds being heard from afar. Additionally, *Quiet City* provided a forum for the musical expression of America as reflected in an *urban* place, an environment Copland knew well but which, until the beginning of the twentieth century, was not frequently summoned to symbolize the nation.

The 1930s proved to be a decade of reconsideration for the United States. The near-manic, self-indulgent individualism that followed the end of World War I—the Jazz Age—and that characterized much of the 1920s came to a screeching halt with the economic crisis that began in 1929. Such a life appeared hollow—a dead end for meaningful growth and progress in the nation. In the arts it was hard to justify the luxury of abstract thought when those around you were reduced to selling apples and chestnuts on street corners to live. The essential loneliness of American life had to be counteracted.[7] Composers of the 1920s (the ultra-moderns), many of whom had been committed to seeking the new, often simply for its newness, now consciously looked beyond the extremes of modernism for modes of expression that spoke to larger numbers of people about real issues.[8] Writers and musicians turned their attentions to the cause of creating works with broader social relevance and appeal. The arts, they insisted, could no longer stand outside life; they had to participate in and reflect it. Artists had to become responsible to more than just themselves or an elite coterie of supporters. The arts, if used properly, could become "an integral part of American cultural and intellectual life."[9] The arts could change life. It was within this more sober, serious, and socially responsible idealistic environment that Group Theatre came to life.

The seeds for its conception had been planted not in the 1930s but years earlier, and Aaron Copland had been there. He and a relative by marriage, Harold Clurman, roomed together and became inseparable friends during a three-year European sojourn, 1921–24.[10] Initially based in Paris, the two young men absorbed all they could of modern European culture. Clurman, having interrupted his course work at Columbia for the jaunt, attended the Sorbonne, where he focused upon French civilization studies. Copland studied composition—first, during the summer of 1921, with Paul Vidal, and then for the next three years with Nadia Boulanger in the newly formed American Conservatory at Fontainebleau.[11] Clurman and Copland frequented cafés and attended concerts and receptions together; they shared their enthusiasms for all that was French—literature, art, and music—although Clurman, in particular, found French theater disappointing in comparison with strides being made in the other arts.[12] In his 1945 monograph on the Group Theatre entitled *The Fervent Years,* Clurman recalled that theater seemed less connected to daily life: "The composers and the painters are searching for new words, so to speak, new forms, shapes, meanings. Aaron Copland tells me he wants to express the present day, he wants to find the musical equivalent for our contemporary tempo and activity. Where is the parallel to all this in the theatre?"[13]

Clurman and Copland coveted the reflexive relationship they believed existed between French culture and French arts, and they determined that they would take it upon themselves to create an equally vital and integrated artistic culture for their own country. According to Clurman, "we both knew when we returned from Europe in 1924 that we wanted to be spokesmen of our generation in American arts."[14] Copland set to work, realizing his goal with the composition of *Music for the Theatre* in 1925 and the Copland-Sessions concerts starting in 1928; Clurman founded the Group Theatre in 1931.[15]

Because of Copland's warm affection for Clurman, his heartfelt belief in their shared hopes for America's cultural life, and his involvement in various aspects of the theater ensemble from its earliest days, composing incidental music for *Quiet City* became a project with special meaning. Here was an opportunity to make a highly personal, politically charged, socially relevant comment about the difficulties of contemporary urban life. Here was an opportunity to integrate American life and American art. Clurman approached the formation of his collaborative company with a near-fanatical zeal, and Copland supported him by acting as a human sounding board, attending organizational meetings, and arranging contacts with potential donors.[16]

But Clurman had grander ideas for his troupe. Rather than see the ensemble as merely a training ground for actors, he sought to use it to explore a larger question: "the theatre's reasons for being." The Group's purpose, he "reiterated time and again, would be to combine a study of theatre craft with a creative content which that craft was to express. To put it another way, our *interest in the life of our times* must lead us to the discovery of those methods that would most truly convey this life through the theatre."[17] He also emphasized the need for philosophical unanimity: "Here the individual actor would be strengthened so that he might better serve the uses of the play in which *our common belief* was to be expressed. There were to be no stars in our theatre, not for the negative purpose of avoiding distinction, but because all distinction—and we would strive to attain the highest—was to be embodied in the production as a whole."[18]

The more-or-less permanent company of just under thirty actors, directors, writers, and other theater types coalesced during a ten-week summer residency at Brookfield Center, Connecticut, beginning on 8 June 1931.[19] They immediately began work on Paul Green's drama *The House of Connelly,* which would become their first production when they returned to New York.[20] Two weeks into the residency, Clurman launched a series of lectures that developed his philosophy as he had outlined it in earlier organizational meetings. The Group became a near-complete world for its members. As an intense collaborative venture, however, one dependent upon sustained intimate interactions among highly charged, socially committed artist-activists who often lived as well as worked together, the ensemble was a volatile organism.[21] From its inception and throughout the 1930s, the Group weathered a number of near-fatal crises—personal, professional, financial, and philosophical.

By 1938, however, Group Theatre was back on track and had amassed a sizable following of subscribers. The revenue base they provided, though tenuous, allowed Clurman and his two codirectors, Cheryl Crawford and Lee Strasberg, to devote the Group's own funds to mounting works of a more experimental nature, which were scheduled for Sunday run-throughs. It was in this capacity that Irwin Shaw's *Quiet City* was given its few performances.[22] The Group's collective social conscience embraced Shaw's tale, whose theme, in Clurman's words, was "the recurrent one of the troubled conscience of the middle class that cannot quite reconcile itself to its life in a distraught world."[23] In his biography of Aaron Copland, Howard Pollack offers a fuller gloss of the work, one that provides details of the play that Copland might have found personally resonant. "Quiet City is about a half-Jewish, middle-aged businessman, Gabriel Mellon, who has rejected his liberal Jewish background and his youthful dream of becoming a poet, Anglicized his name, married a wealthy socialite, and assumed the presidency of a large department store. His beloved brother and alter ego, the nervous, frustrated, and unconventional David Mellinkoff, awakens his social conscience and artistic aspirations with his trumpet playing. . . . Gabe . . . imagines 'the night thoughts of many different people in a great city,' along with, at key moments, his brother's trumpet playing."[24]

One wonders why Copland wrote music for this particular Group Theatre play. In 1936 Kurt Weill wrote the music for their production of Paul Green's play *Johnny Johnson,* and at the same time as Group Theatre was mounting *Quiet City* (April 1939), Paul Bowles wrote the score to a second play, *My Heart's in the Highlands,* by William Saroyan. Thanks in part to Copland's involvement with the Group, it had access to multiple, talented composers within his circle. That Copland may have agreed to write incidental music "to help out his cash-strapped friends,"[25] as Pollack suggests, is certainly possible and in keeping with Copland's altruistic inclinations, but he might also have been motivated by other impulses: his desire to try to capture a place, a time, and a situation with which he had some personal acquaintance.[26] Although there are distinct differences between Gabe Mellon's situation and Copland's, in 1939 the composer was thirty-nine years old (the character Gabe was thirty-five), and both were middle-aged and Jewish. As a liberal homosexual male, Copland stood outside mainstream America much as Gabe Mellon did.[27] Copland's family (originally Kaplan) owned and managed a successful department store in Brooklyn, where he had worked as a youth. Correspondences between events in the play and his own life would have been impossible to overlook. Although angst weighs on Gabe and David, angst was not Copland's style; reflection was. *Quiet City* might have provided an opportunity to revisit a place he knew well, the place he had first considered in *Music for the Theatre* almost fifteen years earlier. [28]

As a native of Brooklyn, Copland was familiar with urban sounds. He knew the exhausted nocturnal silences and the hollow, contained echoes so different from those that bounce between mountains in a range or traverse wide-open spaces. He experienced the ragged, jazzy rhythms pulsating from the streets. He breathed the upbeat tempo. These were the sounds of modern life that he was committed to capturing. In addition, Copland lived with the collective memory of sounds from past lives—musics brought from homelands left behind. The intimate knowledge of ancient and modern repertoires stood him in good stead when he tackled Shaw's play, with its theme of reconciliation of one's past and present. But beyond an awareness of the sounds of a city, Copland must also have understood the isolation that one feels when surrounded by hundreds of thousands of people—an isolation that is both profoundly alienating and wholly necessary if one is to maintain, in Thoreau's words, any margin to one's life. It could be argued that Copland's impenetrably sunny disposition was in part a manifestation of his mastery of city survival skills; few people, if any, got beyond the public persona. If accounts by his intimate friends are accurate, even in that realm he maintained his margin.[29]

Given his upbringing and training in New York and then Paris, Copland wrote *Quiet City* as an informed insider, as someone well acquainted with urban angst even if he did not yield to it himself.[30] That the piece suggests introspection and encourages the same in its listeners is undeniable. Time and time again, David's trumpet playing is used to make Gabe (and all listeners) think. Shaw intended the trumpet to "arouse the conscience of his fellow players and of the audience."[31] How much Copland's lonely, mournful instrumentalist's sound is a representation of his own personal relationship to city life and American culture, and how much the composer simply created a convincing sonic persona for Shaw's character and message, is impossible to determine without Copland's corroboration, and he offered none. We can assume, however, that there is a sympathetic composer behind the sounds.

When Shaw's play was withdrawn because of insoluble production problems, Copland salvaged his music and created the chamber work for strings, trumpet, and English horn or oboe, which he completed it in fall 1940 in Lenox, Massachusetts. In its original conception as incidental music to a play, Copland had expressed a desire to write music that "would evoke the inner distress of the central character."[32] Numerous cues to the text of the play written within the rough sketch of the incidental music reveal Copland's efforts to wed music and drama.[33] By any measure, the music is an empathetic response to Shaw's storyline. But the "inner distress" of Gabe Mellon may well have also projected the social concerns of the Group and reflected the larger mood of the 1939–40 world scene, poised as it was on the brink of the second global confrontation in twenty years. Regardless of the degree to which *Quiet City* illuminates Copland, it does illuminate America and American life around 1940. As such, the place-evoking title of the piece becomes important. In unexpected ways, details of the music argue a conflation of the larger American place and city culture. It may be that by the mid-twentieth century, cities provided the most concentrated expression of American culture: the temper of the city *was* the temper of America and, perhaps by extension, an expression of the temper of the economically distressed, midwar world. Copland may indeed be America's musical spokesperson of that age.

Within the first four measures of *Quiet City*, Copland offers up one of his signature sounds: widely spaced fourths and fifths moving wedgelike—softly, slowly, and unequivocally. Mode-defining thirds fill out the sonic palette. The music is vintage introspective Copland, that side of him revealed perhaps for the first time in his 1920 piano pieces *Three Moods*, in particular the one entitled "Wistful."[34] From the vantage point of the twenty-first century, a listener can't help being struck by the similarity to another famous Copland incipit, that of *Appalachian Spring* (1944), which also opens meditatively, first with an ascending major triad and then with the introduction of fourths. Both works begin by quietly delineating harmonic space. Both also establish peaceful, slow-moving environments for their dramas, and both break that initial mood with interjections of highly charged, rhythmic solo lines. In *Quiet City*, string and woodwind music makes way for a nervous trumpet intonation; in *Appalachian Spring*, the bucolic soundscape is interrupted by unison strings singing a spirited tune that is quickly taken up by other instruments. Over the course of a half-century we have grown comfortable connecting Copland's wide spacings and transparent textures with the idea of the expansive American continent.[35] But in *Quiet City*, the familiar, open harmonies and textures do not depict the generous spaces of the nation's natural landscapes. Here the sounds so often associated with America's physical abundance suggest the opening up of a more confined space, a more interior place, a man-made place, circa 1940.[36]

The overwhelming interiority of *Quiet City* marks the suite as among Copland's most personal expressions; listeners sense that they are getting close to the private man, whether or not this is true.[37] But the mood is achieved using techniques similar to those employed by Charles Ives in his numerous contemplations of places: extremely soft dynamics (*pp*), slow tempi (slow, half note = 60), and long note values (whole and half notes, and strategically placed fermatas) minimize auditors' concern with the passage of time and maximize their sense of being somewhere.[38] The opening of *Quiet City* sets the stage for the drama that unfolds; these peaceful surroundings, however, are not wholly benign. As in the opening to Ives's homage to the sacrificed soldiers of the Massachusetts 54th Regiment of the Civil War in *The "St. Gaudens" in Boston Common (Colonel Robert Gould Shaw and His Colored Regiment)*, Copland uses a hesitant on-off rhythmic figure in the lower strings to unsettle the soundscape of *Quiet City*. There is something ominous in the hushed pizzicato, poco marcato articulations ticking below. A stuttering trumpet intonation beginning at measure 14 (Copland indicates "nervous, mysterious") grows out of this rhythmic motion. The trumpet tentatively announces the drama.[39]

Though it is not the purpose of this study to hypothesize regarding the myriad meanings of Copland's use of specific instruments, it is instructive to consider the significance of the trumpet and its evocations in *Quiet City*. They are many and potentially important. In the original context of the piece, the trumpet was the instrument of Irwin Shaw's thoroughly unhappy character

David Mellinkoff, and so an essential component of the play.[40] But it is also the instrument that Copland used for a "nervous" solo in his 1925 work *Music for the Theatre*.[41] His Prologue to *Music for the Theatre* indicates four times in the first fourteen measures that the first trumpet is to play "*forte,* sharp, fast, clear, nervous." The source of nervousness in *Music for the Theatre* is not clear, although Copland uses the term to describe the mood of the entire second movement as well: "This is a short, nervous dance." An obvious difference between the instructions to the trumpeters in the two pieces involves dynamic levels: *Music for the Theatre* operates at a self-confident, sometimes cocky *forte* level much of the time. In addition, within the fourth movement, "Burlesque," Copland indicates that the solo trumpet is to be played "grotesco," a far cry from the almost self-effacing tone assumed at the outset in his incidental music to the 1939 play.[42] In the earlier piece, the trumpet's presence can be attributed to its prominent role in pit orchestras and Copland's desire to capture an authentic sound for his theater suite. The composer, however, also understood its connections to jazz, as his explanatory note makes plain: "In this work the two Trumpets each use two different kinds of Sourdine: the ordinary orchestral Sourdine and the harsh Sourdine used in Jazzbands."[43] Within a year of his return from Paris, Copland paired the trumpet with theater in general and with jazz more specifically—two phenomena closely associated with urban settings, and, in the case of the latter, especially exemplary of the new world.[44]

Although it is not obvious why the trumpet solo ought to sound nervous in *Music for the Theatre* (except perhaps that Copland seemed to prefer an edgy effect in many pieces), the instrument's association with jazz might help to explain his instruction to play nervously in *Quiet City*.[45] In addition, in numerous remarks Copland acknowledged the presence of Jewish chant influences in *Quiet City,* and they are audible.[46] But quite aside from the widely spaced intervals characteristic of Jewish chant, the opening fanfare sounds shofarlike in its distant call to auditors, Gabe Mellon among them. The music is soft and then dissipates, as if coming from afar. Indeed, if one considers Shaw's story, the distance suggested is both spatial and temporal. We hear the echo of David and Gabe's spiritual homeland and its traditions; we hear their memories. As the trumpet vacillates between repeated Cs and B-flats, auditors experience varying degrees of repose and tension against the strings' pedal-tone C, a musical analogue to the ambivalent peace that Gabe Mellon has achieved in his new world environment. David's trumpet call reminds and challenges Gabe in the most basic ways.

While the trumpet fanfare repeats in closer and closer succession, background strings increase the rate of their stinging unison Cs, surface rhythm

117

builds, and each stuttering statement seems emboldened. At measure 21 the trumpet breaks from its narrow pitch, rhythm, and dynamic confines— moving from a major second to a major eleventh and from *mezzo piano* through a crescendo, and slides into a rifflike figure. In a matter of moments, the trumpeter leaves behind the old world and embraces a bluesy jazz sound.[47]

Ex. 3.1: *Quiet City,* mm 14–21. © 1941 by the Aaron Copland Fund for Music, Inc. Copyright renewed. Reprinted by permission of Boosey and Hawkes, Inc., sole licensee.

Copland's evolving trumpet call becomes the musical encapsulation of Gabe Mellon's story—sacrifice of tradition and assimilation into a foreign culture—a story reflecting those of many immigrants who come to American cities. We hear the trumpeter testing out a new personal voice. It is no wonder that the music initially sounds tentative, nervous. Copland's hybridized Jewish-Jazz fanfare articulated early-twentieth-century culture for large numbers of city dwellers in America who had not been included within the founding fathers' predominantly Protestant and rural vision of the nation.

Copland's original incidental music was scored for very few instrumentalists, which kept costs minimal for his Group Theatre colleagues. Four musicians—a pianist, a trumpeter, and two clarinetists, who also doubled on bass clarinet and saxophone—provided all the music. When the composer reworked his score, he kept only the essential trumpet, but he substituted a string orchestra for the piano parts, removed the two clarinets and the bass clarinet and saxophone, and added an English horn or oboe (if no English horn was available).[48] Eliminating the saxophone, an instrument closely associated with modern American cities through its presence in jazz ensembles, appears to be consistent with the composition of Copland's other urban soundscapes. Neither *Music for the Theatre,* written for a small orchestra in 1925, nor *Music for a Great City,* commissioned by the London Symphony Orchestra and scored with a greatly enhanced percussion section in 1964, uses the saxophone. Substituting the more traditional English horn brings the piece within the fold of standard orchestral instrumentation, where we would expect to find the double-reed woodwind instrument. There are, however, additional advantages to this change. Although Copland insisted that the English horn was added as a practical consideration—to provide the trumpeter with necessary breathing space—its particular selection from among all possible instruments carries additional evocations as well.[49]

Copland's use of a woodwind instrument, a brass instrument, and a string ensemble resulted in a clean, audible stratification of timbres. An argument could be made that the saxophone, a hybridized wind-brass instrument, is not as unambiguous in tone color as the other instruments Copland employed and so might compromise the timbrally distinct spheres that seemed to be his goal.[50] In addition, by 1939 the saxophone was closely associated with jazz bands. While *Quiet City is* a piece about urban America, it is not meant to be a study or critique of jazz per se. As incidental music to a play this would be clear: the story would make it so. When, however, the piece became a freestanding concert work, the role of the saxophone would not necessarily be obvious. By eliminating this instrument, Copland eliminated the potential confusion. He could refer to jazz to the limited extent that he required with the trumpet but avoid any suggestion that this was a jazz-inspired or focused work.

Strings provided a neutral backdrop for the sometimes tender, sometimes spirited dialogue between the English horn and the trumpet, much the way Ives's strings offered a background for the questioning trumpet and answering woodwinds in *The Unanswered Question.*[51] The distinct tone qualities of the trumpet and English horn, including their different abilities to attack, color, and penetrate a soundscape, make them ideal participants in the musical and dramatic exchange that ensues. Both instruments, however, also have long-established programmatic associations within Western art music. In addition to their modern connection to theater and jazz, trumpets were traditionally used to evoke military and religious situations.[52] Woodwinds, especially double-reed instruments, are showcased in numerous compositions depicting more bucolic scenes.[53] Although Copland might deny any considerations for his instrument choices beyond the most practical timbral ones and the inherited story line, their historic associations go beyond his acknowledged intentions and are part of the Western high-art music tradition.

How do these diverse sounds resonate within Copland's urban landscape? What is the role of the historically rustic English horn in an evocation of the city? *Quiet City* opens with four measures of strings followed by English horn, which echoes the viola's melodic gesture: an ascending perfect fourth answered by a descending minor third. Though timbrally distinct from the strings and so clearly audible in spite of its pianissimo entrance, the English horn reveals its relation to the background music by appropriating this important melodic motive. At the same time, the second violin plays a broadly spaced two-note figure, which anticipates the trumpet's twitchy two-pitch motion that will emerge at measure 14.

While Copland develops essential motivic relationships, he also marks out the piece's harmony, which emerges as more complex than the key signature suggests. The one-flat signature indicates F major, although the piece finishes by reiterating a series of Cs—the dominant of F, the pitch of the pedal tone, and the note that received the most "air time" during the opening and closing fanfare sections. The pitch C and the C-minor mode dominate measures 73–87, whereas A pedals anchor measures 94–113, before the music lifts upward from a brief D pedal to an ostinato pattern: E-flat, A-flat, B-flat in the string basses. The pitch F is showcased only briefly, if very dramatically, at measures 146–49. Here the trumpet exaggeratedly crescendos ascending octave Fs, which the English horn echoes. Both crescendos are followed by sudden *pianos,* a gesture that calls attention to itself. But rather than a belated acknowledgment of F as the key of the piece or as resolution into that key, the motion is followed immediately by a return to an abbreviated version of the opening measures of the piece with their emphasis on the pitch C. The same C pedal grounds the close of the piece, as the English horn descends a fifth from G to C and all instruments converge on the note, with the lowest strings plucking pizzicato Cs. In traditional theoretical terms, it is difficult to determine which pitch represents the tonic and which the dominant: it is hard to know which is home. In the broadest sense, the open ending speaks to all unresolved dilemmas, Gabe's and others'.

While delineating the harmonic parameters of the piece, Copland's first thirteen measures also serve programmatic ends by suggesting the complex relationship of protagonists (instrumental and human) with each other and their environment. When the trumpet enters with its "nervous, mysterious" Cs, the music sounds distinctly different from that which came before, and yet it also sounds inevitable; it is separate while connected. The opening C echoes the first note of the viola and English horn entrances. Its stuttering utterance challenges the serene mood that had prevailed. As Group Theatre tackled the real-life drama of the times in its productions, Copland's carefully integrated music addressed the internal conflicts of the play's principal characters.

Within the confines of the harmonically unresolved piece, Copland introduces two modal melodies. Pollack describes the first as "suggestive of Gabe's nostalgia for his youthful aspiration," and the second as "the music associated in the play with Gabe's painful relationship with his father, Israel."[54] Both tunes share a fondness for sevenths and thirds and so sound related, and both tunes involve the English horn and trumpet in a dialogue, with one and then the other taking the lead.

In Gabe's "nostalgia" music (beginning at measure 33), the English horn introduces a tune that the trumpet echoes at measure 40, and then expands upon at measure 46.

Ex. 3.2: *Quiet City*, mm 33–39, Gabe's nostalgia music. © 1941 by the Aaron Copland Fund for Music, Inc. Copyright renewed. Reprinted by permission of Boosey and Hawkes, Inc., sole licensee.

The English horn reenters at measure 55, with the theme in diminution. It quickly introduces rhythmically intensifying triplets, which the trumpet commandeers and makes its own. The trumpet indulges in an eight-measure *forte* solo starting at measure 64, before segueing into the more agitated second melody at measure 73. Here the strings assume a greater role, as their double-dotted rhythm intensifies the momentum and they join with the trumpet and then the English horn to create the fullest and most integrated texture of the piece. At measure 85 the trumpet reintroduces the fanfare figure, and then at measure 88 it recalls its bold solo from measure 64 (see Ex. 3.3).

Auditors witness the growing importance of the trumpet's role within the larger soundscape. Without access to the story line, one can imagine Gabe Mellon becoming more accustomed to his new-world environment as the trumpet grows more comfortable interacting with horn and strings. The text,

Ex. 3.3: *Quiet City*, mm 73–93, second melody. © 1941 by the Aaron Copland Fund for Music, Inc. Copyright renewed. Reprinted by permission of Boosey and Hawkes, Inc., sole licensee.

however, tells a different story. Gabe ultimately denies his poetic soul, turns his back on his family, and goes along with the advice of his calculating vice president. But as the curtain falls the trumpet dominates the theater, "wonderfully clear, wonderfully promising, wonderfully triumphant."[55] While the text tells of a human tragedy, the music promises a victory still to come. The masses will have to be their own heroes.

The final iteration of the nostalgia theme is prepared for by a duet, first among the strings (measure 95), and then between strings and English horn (measure 105). At measure 124 the trumpet articulates an ever-louder fanfare figure, which reintroduces a diminuted *fortissimo* version of the melody first heard at measure 33. This time stately strings (marcato, *ff*) lead the way, trumpet and English horn obligatos comment, and all three come together at measure 133 on a *sff.*

Copland works back to a reiteration of the opening of the piece via a modified fragment of the nostalgia theme. When the trumpet reenters with its fanfare figure, "as at first," Copland mutes the instrument as if to place it even further in the distance, perhaps in Gabe's memory. The strings' C pedal diminishes from *piano* to *pianissimo* to triple *piano* to quadruple *piano* before Copland indicates morendo. A foreshortened return of the on-off rhythmic pattern pulses, and all instruments come together to fade from our hearing.

Knowing the story line of Shaw's play, and with the help of Copland's sketches for the incidental music, we can understand dramatic action as it is revealed in musical behavior. Copland tells us that David's trumpet is the embodiment of Gabe's "inner distress," the psychological conflict caused by the successful new-world entrepreneur turning his back on his heritage and dreams. But the trumpet becomes more than that, as the instrument also conveys associations with the modern world exemplified by American cities, much as it did in *Music for the Theatre* and as it would in *Music for a Great City*. Pitting it against the bucolic-sounding English horn creates a contrast between country and city, and between past and present. The synchronic and diachronic qualities of music allow it to do both simultaneously.

By contrast, these same cinematic qualities of Shaw's story, with its juxtapositions of different places and times, reality and fantasy, numerous scene changes, and unwieldy number of characters, presented insurmountable problems for Group Theatre in 1939; eventually the ensemble abandoned the work. But Copland was able to reconcile multiple times and places in his chamber suite by selecting instruments and music rife with associations. In *Quiet City* he integrated then and now, the real and the imagined, and rural and urban in a seamless utterance. He argued the centrality of the city to modern America.

Aaron Copland returned to evocations of the city in 1962, when the London Symphony Orchestra commissioned him to create a work celebrating their sixtieth anniversary. He turned to music written a year earlier, for a Hollywood film whose action was set in New York. According to the composer, "the nature of the music in the film seemed . . . to justify extended concert treatment . . . [although] no attempt [was] made . . . to follow the cinematic action of 'Something Wild.'"[56] As Howard Pollack notes, Copland "originally intended to title his suite from the film *Music for New York* but changed it to *Music for a Great City* in deference to the London Symphony Orchestra."[57] In his biography with Vivian Perlis, Copland explained that "the 'great' in the title meant large and noisy."[58] Whether it was in response to

Copland's remarks regarding his original title for the work or because British reviewers were making a subtle criticism of the cacophonous nature of parts of the piece, "every critic mentioned that the precise locale of the 'great city' in the title was Manhattan, not London"; Copland was pleased with their observation.[59]

In notes accompanying a recording of *Music for a Great City,* Copland explained the large-scale structure: "The four movements of the work alternate between evocations of big city life, with its external stimuli, and the more personal reactions of any sensitive nature in the varied experiences associated with urban living. 'Music for a Great City' reflects both of these aspects of the contemporary scene."[60] Although the composer asserted a balanced treatment of both the external and more internal aspects of city living in this work, *Music for a Great City* seems decidedly weighted toward the former. Not even in the second movement, entitled "Night Thoughts," or in the quieter moments of the fourth movement, "Toward the Bridge," does a listener experience the sense of contemplation, introspection, isolation, or personal longing that characterizes the very private *Quiet City. Music for a Great City* is Copland's public comment on urban life; in size, in performing forces, in dynamic compass, it is a large gesture.

In contrast to *Quiet City,* with its intimate dimensions and chamber instrumentation, *Music for a Great City* boasts a large orchestra with a percussion section whose size and variety is worthy of Edgard Varèse. Five musicians manage an arsenal of nineteen different instruments, including: a snare drum, tenor drum, conga drum, a pair of timbales, a bass drum, wood block, temple bells (both high and low), sandpaper, maracas, ratchet, cymbals (both suspended and crash), a gong, glockenspiel, xylophone, and vibraphone.[61] Timpani, harp, piano, and celesta provide additional tone color and support. Both woodwind and brass families are augmented as well. Copland uses his generous resources to create an opening movement that is powerful, dissonant, angular, diverse, pulsating, complex, and loud: the music begins *fortissimo.* He captures the New York a visitor might encounter when emerging for the very first time from the subway to the light of day at Forty-second Street. With the initial chord of "Skyline," the city energetically and confidently asserts itself. Although there are quieter and more lyrical interludes, the same opening mood concludes the movement, and twenty-four minutes later closes the entire piece.

When asked about those qualities of music (his own and others') that made for an "American" sound, Copland cited what he thought was a general fondness for percussion among the most obvious features. He also talked of a "zippy rhythm that nobody but an American would dream up."[62] By these standards, his instrumentation for this piece provided him with all that he might need to create an American work. It is no wonder that British critics heard Manhattan and not London.

The first movement is kaleidoscopic in its motion from one musical event to the next. Although it may not follow the original action of the film, the music recalls the cinematic technique of splicing. Declamatory fanfare figures preceding rehearsal 4 butt up against syncopated dance rhythms that give way to Stravinskian ostinati at rehearsal 6.[63] Jazzy percussion appears at rehearsal 16. The entire movement relaxes at rehearsal 26 with a lyrical woodwind and string interlude, but this is soon interrupted by the fantastical sounds of the celesta and flute at one measure after rehearsal 29; glockenspiel and vibraphone join the ensemble and reinvigorate the rhythm. From that point until the measure-long pause that precedes rehearsal 37, eighth notes pulsate continually. The music embodies and radiates energy. At rehearsal 37, Copland indicates "As at first," and motives heard earlier in the movement return. The same ragged rhythm introduced at rehearsal 4 and four measures before rehearsal 20 reappears at rehearsal 38. Stravinskian ostinati pound starting one measure before rehearsal 40. The movement comes to a screaming, triple *forte* dissonant end, with near-complete saturation of chromatic space. One can feel the steel construction that shapes so much of the city and undergirds Copland's musical "Skyline."

Expressive melodic fragments and a very slow tempo characterize the second movement, "Night Thoughts." When dynamics reach beyond the *piano* to *mezzo forte* range that dominates the movement, they do so only briefly, and then the music sounds more tragic than bold. (See especially two and four measures after rehearsal 53.) Here is contemplative music from the film score functioning as the lyrical second movement of a traditional symphonic structure. In all of *Music for a Great City*, "Night Thoughts" comes closest to *Quiet City* in acknowledging a human presence within the urban landscape, although this might be an Everyman rather than a particular individual such as Gabe Mellon. A preference for woodwinds and muted strings, open textures, and a simple scalar melody makes the music sound vulnerable, a condition not explored at all in the inflated, thudding first movement. But whereas in the 1939–40 *Quiet City* long melodies were assigned to soloists, here families of instruments explore and exchange ideas. There is a near-constant dialogue. At rehearsal 48, soft and tender counterpoint contrasts woodwinds and strings simultaneously, and thereafter instruments take turns. It is the communal nature of "Night Thoughts" that makes it less an individual story and more a general statement made by "any sensitive nature." The piece is remarkable for successfully sustaining a quiet mood for a period of more than six minutes without significantly developing or contrasting musical materials. The same idea circulates, dreamlike. We are reminded of Copland's comment that the music is not intended "to follow cinematic action," and, indeed, narrative is all but absent in "Night Thoughts." In its place, however, is an extended meditative moment.

The complete absence of percussion in "Night Thoughts" is more than balanced by its dominance of the third movement, "Subway Jam." Bass, conga, tenor, and snare drums; suspended cymbals played with a variety of techniques and brushes and sticks; and timbale and woodblock energize the fast-moving and at times frantic piece. Here is Copland's answer to traditional expectations for a third-movement dancelike piece. A cowbell, sounding much like the clanking bell of a train, is the only programmatic element that locates the jam session in the subway. While percussion drives the music, trombones and then trumpets, horns, and bassoons get off pointed, terse, syncopated asides. *Forte, fortissimo,* and then triple *forte* dissonant glissandos from horns, trombones, and trumpets swipe at the driving rhythm.[64] The piece seems something of a contest between brass and percussion. Nothing approaching a melody develops within the pounding three-minute movement, although a brief interlude beginning at rehearsal 70 that includes pairs of oboes, clarinets, and bassoons keeps the accumulating momentum from careening out of control. As in the first movement, there is little ambiguity about the location of Copland's underground jam. Instrument choice, syncopated rhythms, growling brass, near-manic energy, and an in-your-face delivery capture the aggressive pace of New York. One can't imagine such behavior in London's "tube."

"Toward the Bridge" is Copland's alternately tragic and wild conclusion to his cityscape. If the fourth movement is intended to suggest "more personal reactions," it does so boldly. The large, agitated *forte* opening creates a tense background for the woodwind and string dialogue that ensues at rehearsal 78. This expressive conversation evokes moments of the second movement, in which the same instrument families were featured. However, the intense trumpet solo that enters at rehearsal 81, as well as the marcato fanfare figure at five after 84, also conjures up memories of *Quiet City,* where the trumpet was the signifier of the distressed protagonist (and ultimately the triumphant masses) of Irwin Shaw's drama. As in "Skyline," the final movement is a cinematically constructed series of musical images that quickly displace one another. After a rhythmically fluid opening, at rehearsal 85 a faster, more decisive pace establishes itself. At rehearsal 88 the tempo is quickened yet again. Nineteen measures of sixteenths create a motoric rhythm that erupts into a full-blown dance at rehearsal 92. Snare and conga drum, high and low timbale, and high and low cowbells enter *forte* and lend their collective voice to articulating the dotted, syncopated rhythm that takes over. It would seem that the subway jam session is not quite over. Ultimately cymbals, xylophone, wood block, claves, temple bells, slap stick, triangle, gong, vibraphone, and glockenspiel join in the clangorous fray.

Without the aid of the film to provide coherence to the score, Copland employs music alone to integrate and synthesize materials and gestures from earlier movements into a final, culminating statement. References to the second and third movements have already been suggested. Using large forces, ostinato passages, dance-inspired rhythms, and a dynamic compass similar to that of the first movement, Copland also ties together "Skyline" and "Toward the Bridge." He employs a measure-long rest (one before rehearsal 100) that acts as an analogue to that of the first movement (one before rehearsal 37). In both cases, the silences act to interrupt accumulating momentum and prepare listeners for a closing statement. More subtly, the ascending arpeggio that follows rehearsal 100 recalls that which appeared at measure 5 of "Skyline," and the collective descending passage at one after rehearsal 102 echoes similar motions at measure 3 of the first movement. Like the quivering mass of sound that closes "Skyline," the climax of "Toward the Bridge" is a dissonant *sff* chord filling the airways; tenor and conga drum offer their final shots. Copland's great city is a place of dynamism and variety. Aggressive, energetic music collides with meditative, expressive interludes. Throbbing rhythms that characterize urban life are never far from the surface of this piece. In its bombast and tenderness, the work captures the extremes of the city experience.

Pollack has suggested that *Music for a Great City* is "arguably Copland's culminating cityscape."[65] And if sheer size is the standard by which his urban place pieces are judged, such is the case. *Quiet City,* however, may be the more convincing of the two works. There is a sincerity of expression that fills every moment of the smaller piece that is lost in the bombast and braggadocio of the bigger work. To what degree this is true, or is attributable to the empathy that Copland might have felt for Shaw's story or to the closeness he felt to the struggles of the times, can only be surmised. But if programming and scholarly attention are any indications, Copland's quieter, if more distressing, urban world is the more convincing place.[66]

EDGARD VARÈSE

Amériques

In 1915, five and a half years before Aaron Copland set sail for Paris, a young French musician joined a group of his artistic countrymen and escaped to the place they saw as the new center of modernist thinking, New York. While American composers still sought the imprimatur of European training, first in Germany and then later in France, Edgard Varèse and a number of French artists understood the value of America as a source of new materials and new possibilities. Taking advantage of all that the international political scene afforded him, Varèse quickly established his credentials as a musical force in the New World. As Heinrich had done decades earlier, he celebrated his new home with a piece named for the place. Edgard Varèse's orchestral work *Amériques* (1918–21), like Aaron Copland's *Quiet City,* involves a complex relationship between composer and musical subject. But the sources of the complexity are quite different. Whereas Copland connected with the city place and the generating narrative in numerous personal ways as an insider, Varèse approached his subject first from a distance. The French title announces his outsider's perspective; its plural form hints at possibilities yet unknown to the émigré.

As was the case with many Europeans born in the last decades of the nineteenth century, Varèse's image of America had been formed by reading Washington Irving, James Fenimore Cooper, and Walt Whitman, and by envisioning the vastness of the territories described in their works. According to Paul Rosenfeld, Varèse even imagined sounds to accompany Cooper's tales: "the feeling of the prairies became associated in his mind with the sound of a piercing, bitter-high whistle."[67] Louise Varèse cited "that legendary America" that her husband and others brought with them, replete with "Indians, high skies, endless horizons and space!" But Varèse's vision of the New World was not mired in purely romantic images. During the early years of World War I, he was influenced by American films that were shown throughout Paris.[68] Olivia Mattis refers in her dissertation, "Edgard Varèse and the Visual Arts," to "documents [that] reveal that in late 1915 Varèse formed a triumvirate of New York dreamers with Valentine Gross and Jean Cocteau, and that together they went to see Pearl White on the big screen." They saw *Les Mystères de New York,* the French title given *The Exploits of Elaine.* Mattis goes on to explain: "Varèse shared his friends' excitement at the possibilities offered by America's fresh terrain, and was even called 'the angel of New York,' by his artist friends."[69] His arrival in December 1915 put him into direct contact with the dreamed-of place. A warm reception and immediate integration into circles of artist-immigrants, as well as the enthusiastic support of New York's wealthiest patrons, meant that Varèse quickly found a home amid the skyscrapers, even if a language barrier initially prevented him from participating in all aspects of American life.[70] According to Paul Rosenfeld, it was Varèse the European immigrant who became the "poet of the tall New Yorks," who best captured the energy of modern culture as it was manifest in that most modern of cities.[71]

Noteworthy in these remarks, and in numerous others that Mattis provides, is the assumption that for Varèse, and indeed for his entire circle of modernist friends, "America" was synonymous with urban, industrialized, iron-girded New York, and vice versa. This represents a change in perspective of enormous significance. As noted previously, through much of the nineteenth century, America had been identified almost exclusively with its spacious open lands, its magnificent canyons, mountains, and rivers, its not-to-be-equaled waterfalls: its Edenesque nature. Concomitant with that view was one that characterized cities—closely associated with Europe—as enervated, corrupted, and contaminated. America could turn with pride to its pristine wildernesses and unspoiled nature and claim moral superiority, which it did.

Now, in the opening decades of the twentieth century, there was a new "modern" vision of America, a new nature that was being extolled, a man-made nature, the nature of the city.[72] Starting as early as the 1890s, this new nature had been celebrated in a series of photographs by Alfred Stieglitz. *"Spring Showers, New York"* captures rain beating on a glistening sidewalk and street. A single young tree tethered within its wrought-iron cage stands gracefully in the foreground, while a lone street-sweeper, just behind it and to the left, combats the elements. Carriages splash through the middle ground, and tall buildings shrouded in mist and fog offer a mountain-evoking backdrop. As in so many Hudson River School paintings in which an individual is strategically placed within the work to provide a sense of scale and comment upon the man-nature duality, one gets the sense that Stieglitz's brave sapling and lone street-sweeper do the same. The relationship between man and nature, however, has been complicated. Man is still small, but so too is nature, at least our old idea of nature, at least in comparison with the *new* nature.[73]

At the same time as early-twentieth-century American artists and photographers turned to their urban environment, with its pulsing vitality and steely, sharp-edged profile, European immigrants brought their own city-centered culture with them to the United States. Once associated with tired European traditions, the city, especially New York, now exemplified modernism in the New World.[74] Although America's expansive land and seemingly endless nature were still valued and became important subjects for many progressive photographers (Ansel Adams perhaps being the most famous), the city became the symbol for the newly mature nation.

In 1931, the historian Frederick Lewis Allen emphasized the gradual urbanization of America. He observed that with the end of World War I, "urban tastes and urban dress and the urban way of thinking . . . [conquered] the

Alfred Stieglitz, *Spring Showers,
New York,* 1900. The Minneapolis
Institute of Arts, Gift of Julia
Marshall.

whole country."[75] The United States no longer had to emphasize its distinctiveness by hawking its natural endowments; starting at the turn of the century, the nation could participate as an equal in the larger, increasingly industrialized world culture. In a climate that valued internationalism over provincialism, Varèse's French-inflected cosmopolitanism made him the American musical modernist's modernist. Starting in the earliest years of the twentieth century, America would promote itself and be promoted as the center of international culture, and New York City was the epicenter.

Given Varèse's enthusiasm for his adopted land (he became a United States citizen in 1927), that he should title his first work begun in the United States *Amériques* seems natural. Here is a personal paean and, as it turns out, a not unwise political move.[76] Varèse saw himself as bringing contemporary music to America, which he believed suffered under the weight of its dependence upon German musical culture.[77] The version of contemporary music that he brought would, of course, include a healthy dose of his own, a situation that would eventually prove problematic for some of his American peers.

The Armory Show in 1913 had determined that America was receptive to contemporary art and, given the emphasis on French works, particularly receptive to French culture. Frederick Allen observed, "art collectors went in so wholeheartedly for the work of the French moderns and their imitators that the United States became almost—from the artistic point of view—a French colony."[78] In a 1977 article that Elliott Carter wrote for an exhibition entitled "Paris–New York," commemorating the opening of the Pompidou Center in Paris, the American composer considered Franco-American musical relations in the early decades of the century and concluded that "the efforts of French musicians who had become established [in America]" had been responsible for "a great deal of contemporary music being played."[79] When Varèse arrived in the United States late in 1915, there was great enthusiasm for anything French, and he capitalized on this in numerous ways. His timing was fortuitous. As Carol Oja put it, "he exploited his nationality mightily."[80] But by 1918, the year in which Varèse began sketching *Amériques,* the war was over and much of the nation was weary of Europe; they were "tired of applauding the French."[81] Allen noted "the growing apathy of millions of Americans toward anything which reminded them of the war." He explained: "They were fast becoming sick and tired of the whole European mess. They wanted to be done with it."[82] *Amériques* seems to have been a wise and sensitive title, given Varèse's enormous personal ambitions and the political realities of the time.

For all the place-specificity suggested in the title, however, *Amériques* referred to more than a topographical entity or a national demarcation. In the composer's words, "I did not think of the title *Amériques* as purely geographic but as symbolic of discoveries—new worlds on earth, in the sky, or in the minds of men."[83] For Varèse, these discoveries were very specifically related to music. Here in the New World, he could create his new world of sounds. But if in his mind *Amériques* was larger than simple geography, Varèse did think of *Amériques* through the specific prism of New York City, the place he would come to refer to as "ma ville."[84] In 1929 Alejo Carpentier wrote on the significance of the piece to the composer:

> North America impresses him with a sensation of vastness and extent, he says. In passing, one can cast an absent-minded glance from the window of a railroad train at the largest waterfalls on earth. In the depths of canyons, there are cities creating their own storm. . . . For him, New York is neither jazz nor "musical comedy," nor even Harlem dives. He stands apart from those ephemeral characteristics of this new world, but feels himself profoundly moved by the tragic meaning which he perceives in the implacable rhythm of its labor, in the teeming activity of the docks, in the crowds at noon, in the bustle of Wall Street. . . . *Amériques* begins to ripen. Encouraged by the possibilities for its realization, Varese conceives the work on a vast scale. He will not attempt to create a score that will convey the external or picturesque side of American life, but rather throw himself courageously into the discovery of new horizons.[85]

Four years earlier, after hearing *Intégrales* in 1925, Rosenfeld had made a similar point: "Varèse never has imitated the sounds of the city. . . . He has come into relationship with the elements of American life, and found corresponding rhythms within himself set free. Because of this spark of creativeness, it has been given him to hear the symphony of New York."[86] And hear it he did. In his mind, Varèse distinguished himself from other composers by refusing to depict scenes or copy sounds.[87] Varèse's relationship with New York, according to the composer and the press, went deeper than aspiring to mimicry: he breathed its spirit; his exhalations were his music.

Such complete identification of music and subject became an issue for Varèse as he fought to separate himself from other modernist artistic efforts. The composer was particularly sensitive to the issue of imitation and art, and he stressed repeatedly that the two were antithetical. He dismissed programmatic music outright: "Don't connect my music with anything external or objective. Don't try to discover a descriptive program for it. Regard it, please, in the abstract. Think of it as existing independently of literary or pictorial associations."[88] And when his music was compared with that of the Italian Futurists, Varèse was vehement in distinguishing between the creations of

"Marinetti and his noise-artists"[89] and his own: "Italian Futurists, why do you merely reproduce the vibrations of our daily life only in their superficial and distressing aspects? My dream is of instruments that will obey my thought—and which, by bringing about a flowering of hitherto unsuspected timbres, will lend themselves to the combinations it will please me to impose on them and bow themselves to the demands of my inner rhythm."[90]

His close personal association with Dadaist artists and his frequent mention in *391,* Francis Picabia's Dadaist journal, called into question his freedom from such influences and seemed to suggest a degree of sympathy with that movement's ideals. However, a letter that Varèse wrote in 1965 to an inquiring Ph.D. candidate downplayed the connection: "I have been called a Futurist, a Dadaist, a Cubist composer—erroneously I believe. I have always avoided groups and isms. . . . As for the Dada movement, I had several Dadaist friends, Tzara and Marcel Duchamp among them. However, in music I was not interested in tearing down but in finding for myself new means by which I could compose with sounds outside the tempered system that existing instruments could not play. Unlike the Dadaists, I was not an iconoclast."[91]

Mattis's painstaking research, which included uncovering numerous letters from Varèse to Picabia, questions the credibility of such denials. That Varèse rejected "isms" seems clear. Like a majority of twentieth-century artists and composers, he wanted to be considered original, without peer, without ancestor. As Mark Rothko later insisted, "Real identity is incompatible with schools and categories, except by mutilation."[92] Yet the similarities between Varèse's musical goals and the artistic goals of the Cubists, Futurists, and Dadaists are not easily dismissed and, given his close ties with numerous artists espousing such views, seem almost futile to deny.[93] The difference between their views and his own might be one of tone and motivation rather than of basic tenets. Clearly, at no time did Varèse intend his works to be "celebrat[ions] of nonsense and frivolity," as did his Dadaist peers;[94] he was not "anti art," although he believed old conceptions of art were inappropriate for the twentieth century. And his factory noises were not mere interpolations of existing industrial sounds, as they were in others' works, although audiences were not always able to make such distinctions without being told.[95] In spite of catcalls and jeers that greeted his music, Varèse took himself and his work seriously.[96] His unrelenting seriousness may have been a reaction to the carnival atmosphere that surrounded many modern music events including numerous piano recitals being given in New York at the time by the Futurist pianist and composer Leo Ornstein, who drew large, often extremely animated crowds. As Varèse's fellow Frenchman Erik Satie baited audiences with his audacious aesthetic philosophies and music, Varèse took another tack, a scientific, highly intellectualized one. By 1955 the visual artists had made peace with the lasting values of such movements, yet as late as 1965 Varèse was unable to reconcile himself to the ways in which his music had embodied many of the forms and techniques of Dadaism (and Futurism) without necessarily championing the original negative or humorous motivations of those groups.[97] Varèse also took seriously his role as a prophet of contemporary music in the New World.

Varèse, however, was interested in more than simply bringing musical modernism to America; his motives were not all altruistic or idealistic. America was a symbol of beginning, and of release from the poverty and malaise that afflicted Europe. America meant freedom and possibilities. Varèse was not only running *to,* he was escaping *from.* America represented quite literally new opportunities, new possibilities, new worlds. That being the case, Varèse imbued America and *Amériques* with perhaps greater than usual hopes for the realization of his ambitions—artistic, political, and otherwise.

Besides Varèse's sweeping dismissal of programmatic music and traditional narrative forms in general, and specifically of the idea that *Amériques* actually described something in particular, the composer avoided discussing the existence of any extramusical *motivations* for writing the piece. For Varèse, music was its own subject, its own reason for being: it represented only itself. And yet, at least on some emotional level, the piece was made possible by his immigrant's experience, whether it became a specific program or not.[98] What were the artistic possibilities that the New World unleashed for the "New York dreamer"? It is useful to briefly consider five basic categories: space, power, perspective, movement, and control.

1. Space Building upon nineteenth-century romantic visions of America as a land that was infinitely capacious, *Amériques* is the musical incarnation of Varèse's twentieth-century concept of "bodies of intelligent sounds moving freely in space."[99] *Amériques* is conceived on an enormous scale. It revels in untethered movement through a seemingly limitless expanse. If the work were a canvas, it would be of the 12-by-25-foot variety. If it were a piece of sculpture, it would tower beyond human scale. In this sense, *Amériques* shares much with the romantic symphonic tradition; it is Varèse's most romantic surviving piece. It is long in duration—twenty-plus minutes of uninterrupted sound—and it exploits pitch range from piccolo to string bass. It is extreme in its dynamic compass as well, with alternately crashing quadruple *fortes* and whispering, muted quadruple *pianos,* and is abundantly large in its performing forces: it requires forty-five woodwind and brass instruments, including heckelphone, contrabassoon, contrabass trombone, and contrabass tuba, as well as two harps, a full complement of strings, two sets of timpani, and sixteen different nonpitched percussion instruments played by nine percussionists.

While neoclassicists extolled the virtues of transparency, simplicity, and clarity, Varèse clung to a symphonic orchestra that was Mahlerian in its size and sound. Both the place and the *idea* of America provided Varèse with the space he needed to explore his massive conception.

2. *Power Amériques* is painted with big brushes and bold strokes; it is virile and muscular. Even in those moments when single instruments or small ensembles surface or linger exposed, they speak directly and clearly. Instances of this instrumental "frankness" abound in the piece, but a few examples will suffice: the opening alto flute solo and its numerous iterations refuse to speak softer than a *mezzo forte* and, on one occasion, at measure 43, enters poco *sf;* soloistic entries by piccolo, clarinet, and trumpet at measure 41, a horn choir at measure 85, and a trio of oboes at measure 153 all enter *fortissimo* and get louder. There are few instances of instruments assuming subservient roles. There is nothing timid about the work. At times one feels as if the composer has an aerial view of his soundscape and sees 360 degrees in a single glance; he is in complete control of all he surveys. We hear that confidence. If the opening flute solo provides a relatively human and personal orientation point, it is not a stationary one. The fragmentary solo, even while staying with the same timbre, morphs via an extremely subtle diminution of durations. Power, confidence, and forthrightness describe the music that reflects Varèse's America.

Jonathan Bernard observes that "an accelerando takes place" not through the imposition of any tempo change, but as the result of an overall shortening of the melodic figure.[100] As the piece comes more fully into focus, the melodic fragment emerges in different colors. At measure 60 the trumpet commandeers the melodic idea, recasting it with its brass timbre and augmenting its rhythm to form a broader statement.

At the moment in the piece when auditors might be inclined to consider the melody motivic and the source of formal unity, Varèse drops it altogether. The idea, like its creator, resists confinement by materials or traditional expectations. Having freed itself from having to develop motivic materials, the piece explores other musical ideas.

3. *Perspective* One senses that Varèse, like his painter-contemporaries Wassily Kandinsky, Joan Miró, and Paul Klee, was naturally disinclined to see a single horizon point. He created the musical equivalent of multiple focal points and embraced discontinuity even as his unique sound unified all his works.[101] In contrast to the Copland and Ives pieces considered earlier, *Amériques* has no discrete background, middleground, or foreground layers; there is no single aural path. After the introductory flute passage, Varèse forgoes extended periods of conventional melody and accompaniment texture, al-

though on numerous occasions different instruments are showcased. With one exception, all sounds are brought to the surface and cut through and around each other on the same plane. The exceptional instrument is the siren, which by its nature emerges as if coming from a distance. Kandinsky's 1923 painting *Accented Corners No. 247*, with its blocks of light and dark flashing colors and numerous penetrating planes, provides a possible visual analogue to *Amériques*. In 1913 the visual artist explained: "Painting is like a thundering collision of different worlds that are destined in and through conflict to create that new world called the work."[102] At many points during Varèse's piece, one hears *Amériques* as a "thundering collision . . . destined . . . to create that new world."

4. *Movement*   Even during moments of relative calm, *Amériques* throbs, and we are inside the sound being pushed along. Neither the music nor its auditors are allowed to rest. Starting at measure 2 and continuing intermittently throughout the 535-measure piece, subtle pulses emanating from a variety of instruments act as heartbeats for the musical organism. Even when the music turns relatively lyrical rhythm is quietly conspicuous.

Absent, however, are long stretches of audible, predictable (confining) meter. In their place are juxtaposed measures of six and five and four and three and seven beats, within which intricate rhythmic patterns jostle with each other for duple and triple organizations of time. A reliable pulse frees Varèse to move in and out of groupings. The constant, complex rhythmic soundscape of *Amériques* creates a believable analogue to New York City's own jostling rhythms. Whether this was Varèse's intention is not necessary to determine.

Even when a time signature lingers over a number of measures, asymmetric groupings and unpredictable entrances obscure the meter.[103] On only two occasions does Varèse indicate more than one time signature simultaneously: at measures 484–85, where 5/4 occurs with 15/8 and 4/4 occurs with 12/8, all resolving to 4/4 at measure 486; and at measures 500–501, where the same combinations of meters appear, but this time the 12/8 meter persists until all instruments take up 3/4 at measure 510. In both these cases the eighth-note meters are simply subdivisions of 4/4, so there is no real juxtaposition of different meters. At all other times, various instrumental parts are written in the same meter. Combined with rapidly shifting meters, tempos morph no fewer than fifty-three times, with presto characterizing the longest sections of unchanging tempo.[104] For Varèse, "Rhythm is the element in music that gives life to the work and holds it together. It is the element of stability, the generator of form."[105] Rhythm enlivens and energizes *Amériques;* it is pervasive and palpable.[106]

5. *Control* Without sounding wholly calculated, *Amériques* sounds most carefully constructed. We are listening to a sonic environment deliberately shaped by an individual answering only to himself; we are listening to Varèse as much as to America(s). His hand is everywhere in the score. In addition to precise dynamic markings for every entrance of every part, and constant metronome markings and tempo guidelines to aid in the exact transition from one section to another, Varèse instructs his players *how* to play their parts: *incisif, très en dehors, dolce poco esitante, très serré, agité, clair, sec et mordant, sans nuances, très intense, très rude, sauvagement.* While *Amériques* explores a wide range of expression, the precise articulation of any expressive state is dictated by the composer. Even in moments of frenzied activity, Varèse's controlling hand is audible. (Perhaps a "clenched fist" would be a more apt image.) At measure 503, as the piece nears its cacophonous end and all instruments are at triple *forte,* Varèse explains to his trumpet players the exact notes of the trill he wants and adds *stentati e pesantissimi.* Throughout the piece and especially during the final outcry, one senses Varèse's determination to overcome boundaries—of pitch, of harmony, of form, of expectation. He thrives upon the adversarial relationship. Not content to merely fill our soundscape, Varèse overwhelms us with its presence.[107] We sense a battle between man and environment. If the piece suffers from anything, it might be a surfeit of will. It is decidedly the work of the man who once declared: "I dream of instruments obedient to *my* thought . . . [that] will lend themselves to the exigencies of *my* inner rhythm."[108] Varèse's dauntless style is as much the subject of his music as are the sounds themselves.[109] This is America through the eyes and ears of Edgard Varèse.

On almost every level, *Amériques* challenges traditional musical expectation, description, or analysis.[110] If Varèse sought to make an unambiguous statement about the newness of the New World, he did it by the very uniqueness of his piece. Certainly at the time of its composition, there was nothing like it. Here is a work that behaves according to its own rules, much as the fledgling nationals did when they unloaded British tea into Boston harbor or refused to comply with the Stamp Act.[111] Perhaps more amazing than the singularity of Varèse's vision, however, was that he accomplished his feat using largely traditional instruments. That said, it is essential to point out that the percussion section was unusual in its size and variety, and instruments were played in novel ways. *Amériques* requires no fewer than two timpanists and nine other percussionists. The instrumentation to the 1973 Colfranc edition (actually a reduced and substantially altered version of the original score) devotes half a page to percussion alone. It is worth listing to appreciate the size and timbral variety of the arsenal: two sets of timpani, xylophone, chimes, three triangles, three sets of sleigh bells, low rattles, a glockenspiel, a lion's roar, multiple whips, a tambourine, three gongs, a celesta, three bass drums including one played with a wirebrush, crash and suspended cymbals, castanets, and a snare drum. And then there is a siren. The siren is described as being "deep and very powerful, with a brake for instant stopping affixed to a solid base."[112]

Linton Martin's review of the 1926 premiere conducted by Stokowski devoted almost as much space to audience reaction as to musical description. Martin's opening line sets the tone of his remarks: "Ultra-modern music was provided in sensational style by both orchestra and audience at the Philadelphia Orchestra concert in the Academy yesterday afternoon." He mentions "jeers and cheers, hisses and hurrahs . . . sedate-looking ladies resort[ing] to catcalls, discordant whistles mingled with prolonged hisses." The article recalls descriptions of the *Sacre* premiere in Paris thirteen years earlier, or the riot that accompanied Satie's *Parade* in 1917, although by 1926 carnival-like concerts were regular occurrences on both sides of the Atlantic. Only in the third paragraph does Martin attempt a description of the cause of the commotion: " a piece . . . that manages to make more variegated noises than might be believable." The reviewer admits that "it is easy and the obvious observation to say that it suggests the assorted sounds of New Year's Eve and Fourth of July, of New York's Times Square and a barnyard simultaneously, or march and murders." Yet Martin allows that there is something beyond just noise: "Its spiritual significance is cryptic: but the fact remains there is more to the 'music' than a mere jumble of sound produced by sirens, slapsticks, all sorts of percussions and the regular orchestral instruments, although the composer has apparently overlooked including dishpans, steam riveters, and blasting machines." Clearly the sheer noise of the piece was impressive. But Martin also perceived a "distinct mood" and "original rhythms," and harmonic schemes that had "shape and progression." After noting two march sections and a melancholy episode, he admitted that he was troubled by the monotonous length of the piece.[113]

If Varèse's audience didn't fully understand or appreciate his piece, he had at least succeeded in getting their attention. And he had caused his reviewer to think of New Year's Eve and Fourth of July and Times Square, all New World associations: the "noise" sounded American. Satie had used instruments called *sirène grave* and *aigüe* in *Parade* in 1917, but Varèse used sirens for the first time in his own work in *Amériques*.[114] Their characteristic unbroken series of pitches was of great interest to the composer. Here was a sound source free of the baggage of tradition, which would attach itself to woodwinds, brass, or strings in trying to create the same glissando effect.[115] Though many pointed to New York City as the inspiration for the sirens in *Amériques,* Varèse denied such limited readings. In a response published two days after Martin's review, he explained:

> This composition is the interpretation of a mood, a piece of pure music absolutely unrelated to the noises of modern life, which some critics have read into the composition. If anything, the theme is a meditative one, the impression of a foreigner as he interrogates the tremendous possibilities of this new civilization of yours. The use of strong musical effects is simply my rather vivid reaction to life as I see it, but it is the portrayal of a mood in music and not a sound picture. . . . Now, as to the use of unusual sounds throughout the piece. I do that to avoid monotony. I employ these instruments with a definite fixed pitch to serve as a contrast in pure sound. It is surprising how pure sound, without over-tones, re-interprets the quality of the musical notes with which it is surrounded. Actually, the use of pure sound in music does to harmonies what a crystal prism does to pure light. It scatters it into a thousand varied and unexpected vibrations. It is often said that I am bringing geometric elements into the field of music. Sudden stops, sharply broken intensities, exceedingly rapid *crescendi* and *diminuendi* give an effect of pulsation from a thousand sources of vitality.
>
> To be modern is to be natural, an interpreter of the spirit of your own time. I can assure you that I am not straining after the unusual.[116]

Varèse had been fascinated by the possibilities of an unlimited pitch spectrum long before his arrival in New York. Childhood memories of train whistles heard from a distance, early studies of Hermann Helmholtz's *On the Sensations of Tone,* and his stimulating friendship with Ferruccio Busoni during his last years in Berlin were perhaps greater influences upon Varèse than was the immediate physical environment that appeared to give birth to *Amériques.*[117] In a lecture entitled "Spatial Music" delivered at Sarah Lawrence College in 1959, Varèse recalled his first experiments with sirens and whistles when he was about twenty years old. With Helmholtz's ideas as inspiration, he used unorthodox instruments to create what he later called "spatial music."[118] In the same lecture Varèse explained, "My first physical attempt to give music greater freedom was by the use of sirens."[119]

In light of these early experiments, it would be shortsighted to limit the meaning of sirens in *Amériques* to evocations of emergency vehicles racing through Manhattan. According to Claire R. Reis, however, it was just such an event that may have played a large role in the creation of *Hyperprism* and possibly became the impetus behind the sirens in *Amériques.* Reis recalled a rehearsal that took place soon after Varèse had completed *Hyperprism:*

As he was conducting a rehearsal in his studio a sound that was new to his ears came from the street, the siren of a fire engine dashing past his house. Rushing to the window, he leaned out and listened intently. Then, turning back to the musicians, he announced, "The rehearsal is over; I'll call you soon." Without waiting for them to pack up their instruments and leave, he clapped on his hat and coat, and dashed out the door and off through the streets to the nearest fire station. There he announced flatly to an astonished fireman, "You must lend me one of your sirens for a concert!" He was advised to wait until the district chief returned.

The chief was intrigued by the request, but sirens had only lately been replacing bells on fire engines, and it seemed unlikely that any would be let out.[120]

Reis goes on to explain Varèse's initial failure to procure the siren from the fire station and his subsequent success with the Department of Acoustics at Columbia University: "To his delight . . . they had such a siren. Sympathetic to his desire to experiment musically with it, they lent it to him. He then called the men back into rehearsal on *Hyperprism*."[121] Given Varèse's claim to an early interest in sirens, the recollection calls into question whether the sound was truly "new to his ears" in 1922.[122]

The excitement that Reis observed could well have been Varèse's realization that he finally had access to a mechanism capable of producing the sound he wanted.[123] That this incident took place in 1922 means that it might have resulted in a change to the original *Amériques* score. According to the Varèse scholar Professor Chow Wen-chung, "*Amériques* was composed mostly from 1918 through 1921 with the score copied in 1922, in the midst of some challenging years, with the launching of the New Symphony Orchestra and the International Composers' Guild."[124] It is possible that the siren was actually added to the score of *Amériques* after its initial conception but prior to its 1922 "original" scoring. In this scenario, sirens would appear in both the original version of the score and the revised version of 1927.[125] Such a reading does not contradict Varèse's claim that sirens were more than programmatic representations. It seems clear that sirens liberated sound for Varèse: that here was a new "instrument" for a New World.[126]

The siren's infinite pitch spectrum freed musical thought. The power of a tonal center reliant upon relationships between twelve arbitrary semitones was undermined. Traditionally articulated forms, which had depended upon a harmonic hierarchy anchored in a single home key, lost their appeal. As assumptions regarding the behavior of pitch, harmony, and form were challenged at every turn, the ready-made structures for understanding any composition became ineffectual, useless. Varèse might argue that his motivations were not iconoclastic, much as Schoenberg rejected the term "atonality" because of its negative connotations, but in both cases the sounds, their relationships and implications, and a listener's understanding of the music could only be judged against the background of what was known, and this was like nothing anyone knew. If, however, Varèse's music is not *about* throwing off old ideas but rather *is* its own subject, then *Amériques is* newness. The title becomes not merely a cosmic reference, but a symbol of something concrete and real. *Amériques is* Varèse's New World.

And how does Varèse construe his "new worlds on earth, in the sky, or in the minds of men"? It would seem with a heavy dose of French culture. From timbral preferences evident from the opening flute solo of the piece to numerous Stravinskian melodic and rhythmic fragments scattered throughout the score to his all-consuming concern with tone color effects, Varèse's debt to French musical culture is in the forefront of our listening experience. His emphasis on newness as a value in its own right, on rejecting old notions of art, and his eschewing codification and analysis while insisting that the artwork is its own subject are rallying cries of the Cubists and Dadaists. On the other hand, his focus upon rhythm, according to Copland the most identifiably American of musical elements, suggests a composer listening carefully to his immediate environment. Varèse's title might indicate an outsider's French perspective on America, but it also reveals a French presence *in* America. As such, *Amériques* becomes a remarkably timely place piece. It celebrates the newly sanctified urban landscape of early-twentieth-century America while simultaneously documenting the reality of a larger American culture fixated on anything French.

Over the next thirty-five years Varèse wrote pieces that took advantage of developing technologies. He not only expanded upon traditional acoustical sounds but also explored sounds made possible by electromagnetic tape. He explored ways of combining audio, visual, and architectural elements. In retrospect, *Amériques* becomes merely the starting point of Varèse's exploration of "new worlds on earth, in the sky, or in the minds of men." Which raises the question: Are all of Varèse's pieces about the new horizons and the new possibilities afforded him in the New World? Are they all about America? Are they all place pieces?

DUKE ELLINGTON
Harlem Air Shaft and Harlem

New York is a dream of a song, a feeling of aliveness, a rush and flow of vitality that pulses like the giant heartbeat of all humanity. The whole world

revolves around New York, especially my world. Very little happens anywhere unless someone in New York presses a button!

New York is its people, and its people are the city. Among its crowds,
along its streets, and in its high-piled buildings can be found every mood,
sight and sound, every custom, thought, and tradition, every color, flavor,
religion, and culture of the entire earth.

And if I am asked to describe New York, I must think in musical terms,
because New York is people, and that is what music is all about. This in-
credible city embraces all humanity within its structure, whether resident
or visitor, and joins each new heartbeat with her own throbbing pulse.[127]

The city that inspired Ives, Copland, and Varèse became an endless source
of inspiration for another American composer, Duke Ellington. His musical
tributes to the place would provide a wholly new perspective. By the early
decades of the twentieth century, New York had achieved iconographic status
within the Western arts world. In poetry, in paintings, in photographs, it
became the new symbol of America's promise: it signified the future. Unlike
many rural towns, the city was not home to an ethnically homogeneous population or dominated by a unifying set of traditions or type of architecture,
even though omnipresent images of skyscrapers suggested that tall angular
buildings were the only profile to be found in the place. Within the twenty-
two square miles of Manhattan island, a variety of neighborhoods coexisted.
Edward Kennedy "Duke" Ellington (1899–1974) trained his eye and ear on a
distinct neighborhood within New York City, one not known for its iron-
girded towers but rather for its clubs, dance halls, and churches. In the process, he revealed unique aspects of the American urban landscape.[128] Ellington
introduced the people and culture of Harlem to the world.[129] In spite of tours
that took him around the country and the world, he claimed the adopted city
as his home until he died in 1974.[130]

It was into the complex environment of old and new values, the National
Association for the Advancement of Colored People (NAACP), the Universal
Negro Improvement Association (UNIA), and the broader cultural movement
that came to be known as the Harlem Renaissance that Duke Ellington arrived in 1923. Harlem became the young band director's first home base in
New York, and it turned out to be a wise choice. All the best jazz musicians
and clubs were there. As had his hometown of Washington, D.C., at the turn
of the century, New York now boasted the largest black population in the
nation, and Harlem was the center of that population. The young musician
struggled and even returned to Washington briefly, but he came back to Harlem. For all the career opportunities that the city promised, it also afforded a

good time for a young man on the move, "a playground in which he and his Washington friends romped each night."[131] Inspired by this northern enclave of Manhattan Island and the experiences of those who peopled it, Ellington enlarged immeasurably the notion of what constituted the American place. A brief comparison with Charles Ives, Aaron Copland, and Edgard Varèse clarifies Ellington's unique perspective on urban America, and begins to explain the power of a piece he titled *Harlem*.[132]

Charles Ives, clinging to nineteenth-century notions of what was *real* America and wearing his old-family pedigree proudly, had come to see the urban place as the embodiment of that which was corrupt and unwholesome. Although he resided in the city for fifty-six years, and lived at various addresses from Greenwich Village to the Upper East Side, he resisted embracing the city wholeheartedly. So closely had he identified himself with his New England roots that he regularly retreated there.[133] On a few occasions, however, Ives acknowledged that all was not lost in the city. As has been shown in *From Hanover Square North,* he redeemed and memorialized urban culture by depicting a diverse group of people who came together in a time of crisis at an elevated train station. Both the El and the cross-section of society could have been found only in cities. The people transcended their environment and their differences by joining together in song. Ives allowed his personal feelings, as reported in his commentary, to be transferred to the larger crowd.[134] He objectified his urban experience.

Aaron Copland was a true product of the city. Although he traveled extensively in Europe throughout his life, took trips to the Southwest, and visited Mexico and Cuba, Copland was forever a New Yorker.[135] His youth was shaped by the sounds and experiences of an ethnically mixed Brooklyn neighborhood. *Quiet City,* written for Irwin Shaw's play, spoke for and about all those who came to the urban Mecca at the turn of the century and attempted to reconcile their old-world ways with the New World. This work reveals a personal connection and understanding of the place that is palpable. Brooklyn, one of New York City's five boroughs, lies to the southeast of Manhattan island at the southern end of western Long Island. The Brooklyn and Manhattan bridges connect it to Manhattan. Although Brooklyn is part of the city, it stands outside it as well; it offers a perspective on the more active and infamous borough to the west. Copland's *Quiet City,* while not a tribute to a specific Brooklyn neighborhood or ethnic group, is a meditation on the cultural, social, and economic dissonances so apparent in cities, a theme understood by hundreds of thousands of immigrants, and the overriding message of Shaw's play.

Edgard Varèse was born in Paris and came to New York in 1915, having experienced both rural and urban environments earlier in his life. His biographer Fernand Ouellette has detailed the impact that Varèse's childhood stays with his aunt and uncle in Villars had upon the receptive young boy. Ouellette observed that although the small village had none of the standard musical organizations, "there was a train whistle to be heard in the distance, the splashing of the Saône, the wind blowing over roofs and through the grass and trees." He tells of a childhood experience that found its way into Varèse's music: "One night, the young Varèse was awakened by a long C sharp rending the silence. It was the whistle of a train as it passed close by the village. It was not until much later, after his arrival in New York, during the period when he was living on West 14th Street, near the docks, that he was to rediscover that high, whistling C sharp of his childhood."[136] Such memories provided Varèse with an appreciation for the country and its open, sound-transforming distances. He would cite the memory of train whistles across the countryside as a source of his interests in pitch continuums.

Later, studies in Paris and Berlin brought him directly in touch with Europe's urban arts scenes and a type of intellectual stimulation that existed only in metropolitan areas. To visit New York City was his goal. Once he arrived, he declared he had found his home. Varèse saw New York as the only possibility for a real modernist art culture. Here was a place free of the shackles of Europe's malaise and traditions. The New World needed only to be awakened to its potential. For Varèse, New York represented intellectual and artistic possibilities. While he attempted to promote himself, and succeeded at least initially in securing patron support and a conductor's platform, his dictatorial manner was not well received by native musicians and the coworkers upon whom he depended. As much as he adopted the city as his own, Varèse remained a Frenchman on American soil, and so spoke of America as an outsider.

Duke Ellington was American by birth, and exclusively urban by experience and inclination. Of the four composers discussed in this chapter, Ellington and Copland are most alike in this regard.[137] He was born one year before Copland, in 1899, in Washington, D.C., a city described at the time as "the undisputed center of Negro civilization" in America.[138] Raised in the black upper-middle-class northwest section of the city and staying there throughout his youth and early twenties, Ellington drank deeply of a refined and aspiring family culture and a cultivated black community. He was doted upon by an adoring mother who encouraged her son to believe he was special and could become anything he wanted. Although he didn't complete high school, Ellington did learn important lessons about taking pride in his black heritage and finding his way in a white world.[139] Washington, D.C., provided numerous models of black men who succeeded as professionals. His aspirations were in keeping with his upbringing and his environment.

Edward Kennedy Ellington was an urban American with no connection to the northeastern pastoral tradition that was so valued by Ives and was so much a part of the early nation's identity. Nor did Ellington have much in common with any southern rural tradition, except perhaps that which was commuted through black religious traditions. Even in this domain, however, Ellington's beliefs were mediated by his urban environment and his attendance as a youngster at both his mother's Baptist church and his father's more formal John Wesley African Methodist Episcopal Zion church.[140] Although the composer-bandleader remained religious throughout his life, his views toward spiritual matters incorporated his larger world experience and went well beyond southern black religious practices.[141] Ellington brought a decidedly different perspective to the American musical landscape.

Though modernists around the world saw New York City as home to a newly freed international artistic aesthetic, Ellington understood both Washington and New York as enclaves of empowered black Americans. Aside from the artistic and intellectual opportunities that lay within city boundaries, Ellington saw possibilities for himself and the people he represented, for he always saw himself as a spokesperson of his people. In Stuart Nicholson's words, Ellington could use his music to comment upon "the plight of the Negro in an America divided by racial inequality."[142] Harlem was a chance for "the new Negro" who was just coming into his own, and Ellington made the most of his propitious timing.[143]

Later in his life, Ellington would write a number of extended symphonic works that detailed the history of blacks in America and celebrated his own heritage.[144] But an early piece that he wrote in 1926 with Bubber Miley bore a title that recalled where black Americans had been most recently: "East St. Louis Toodle-O." The title was a potent reminder. On 2 July 1917 East St. Louis, Illinois, was the site of a massacre of black Americans unequaled in its violence. According to a report issued at the time, "four hundred thousand dollars' worth of property was destroyed, nearly six thousand Negroes driven from their homes, and hundreds murdered, a number of them burned alive in houses set fire over their heads." A few weeks after the massacre, thousands of Harlemites staged a silent protest march down Fifth Avenue in New York.[145] In using this piece as his theme song for a number of years, Ellington subtly kept racial consciousness in the forefront of his work.[146]

Between 1914 and 1918, thousands of black workers and dozens of black writers, poets, artists, and musicians fled hostile northern cities and the South, with its repressive Jim Crow laws; many migrated to the Harlem district of

New York. The Harlem Renaissance was a flowering of black culture unlike anything that had occurred in the United States to that date. One need list only some of the participants in the movement to appreciate the convergence of talent: Langston Hughes, Zora Neal Hurston, James Baldwin, Claude McKay, Countee Cullen, Arna Bontemps, and Aaron Douglas. Jazz, however, like other progressive black-focused activities, was not fully embraced by all blacks. There was a rift between older, middle-class, and socially elite blacks on one side and a younger, less established group who frequented the club and café scene on the other. Animosity also existed between many black Americans and American West Indians who did not share the same history. Some saw ragtime and the blues, with their early associations with brothels, and jazz, with its humor-laden grunts, growls, slides, and moans, as steps backward, a not-so-faint echo of the minstrel shows. Such musical activities mocked the strides that had been made to lift up a struggling race.

Blacks throughout the nation became divided between those who advocated a black separatist or nationalist movement—led most conspicuously by Marcus Garvey in the late Teens and early Twenties—and those who supported a strategy of integration and equality, whose position was articulated by W. E. B. Du Bois.[147] In a fifty-year career, Duke Ellington would help develop, define and dignify jazz as an art form and then eventually decide to drop the word from descriptions of his music, finding it too restrictive for his increasingly lengthy and ambitious creations.[148]

Ellington never wavered in his dedication to the cause of black people in America, but a public disagreement in January 1951 with local strategies of the Richmond, Virginia, branch of the NAACP caused him great distress. It all turned on concert seating. Dr. J. M. Tinsley, president of the Richmond chapter, called attention to seating policies that favored blacks to stir up anti-segregation sentiments.[149] Dr. Tinsley noted that the city-owned Mosque Theater allotted the "'best seats in the house' to colored people" at certain concerts, which he interpreted as "discrimination against whites." He encouraged association members to boycott. According to an article in the *Afro-American*, "Observers [saw] this as a master stroke. . . . Dr. Tinsley . . . succeeded in convincing a large segment of the white population that race segregation penalize[d] not only colored citizens, but that . . . whites [were] victimized by the same Un-American practice."[150]

Local concert promoters were opposed to such tactics and urged the Richmond NAACP to "take its fight for civil rights to the courts, not resort to boycotts."[151] They also encouraged Ellington to appear as scheduled, thereby taking a stance against the NAACP; instead, he canceled the concert altogether, claiming his feelings were hurt. While Ellington was sympathetic to

many of the association's goals, he was incensed that their action had inter-
fered with his band members' earning their livings. This too, he argued, was
a form of discrimination. Although he had been made a life member of the
NAACP in 1939 and had appeared in honorary capacities as a representative
of that organization, he was publicly chastised in the *Afro-American* for his
willingness to play for segregated audiences. In the heated exchanges that
occurred, many also took issue with a comment Ellington made that seemed
to suggest blacks were not entitled to equal treatment in America: "We ain't
ready yet." Though he later explained his remark as meaning that black
Americans did not yet have the economic clout to insist upon their rights, the
damage had already been done. Ellington was accused of forgetting his own
people, of seeing himself as above them. It was only years later, throughout
which time Ellington continued to contribute to the association, that the rift
was mended. In 1957 the NAACP again awarded Ellington its Scroll of Honor
(an award he had received in January 1951, just prior to the canceled Virginia
concert), and in 1959 they presented Ellington with the Spingarn Medal for
"the highest or noblest achievement by an American Negro during the preceding year or years."[152] Little could Ellington have known when he arrived in
New York that "Harlem's Aristocrat of Jazz," the insider who perhaps more
than anyone else brought dignity and honor to jazz, would for a time be
perceived as a pariah among his own people. If his son Mercer's observations
are accurate, the entire episode with the NAACP had a lasting impact on his
father's willingness to involve himself in political and racial issues.

But none of this could have been foreseen when Ellington came to New
York. Within six months of his arrival he had played at three important clubs,
the Lafayette Theater, Connie's Inn, and Barron Wilkins' Exclusive Club. He
had taken part in a recording session for Victor and had performed at least
once over the radio. Ellington also had met numerous important musicians,
among them Willie "the Lion" Smith, James P. Johnson, and Fats Waller,
masters of stride piano, all of whom would have a direct impact on his developing keyboard style. Although this period was not an uninterrupted string
of successes, it did position Ellington to take advantage of opportunities that
were to come his way.[153]

Harlem became a symbol to the world of black artistic and intellectual life
at the same time that New York City rose to prominence as the undisputed
center of modernism: the convergence was auspicious. As Carol Oja notes:
"American modernism and the Harlem Renaissance were closely intertwined,
perhaps most fundamentally in a shared sense of historic opportunity."[154]
Each was self-consciously aware of the moment. In addition, jazz had much
to offer musical modernists who were outspoken in their disdain for tradition

147

and etiquette. Here was a music that defied proper behavior. It held special promise for those modernists interested in primitivism, a strong current in the movement. The modernists' enthusiasm for jazz was evident in Florenz Ziegfeld's response to a critical review of *Show Girl*. An excerpt from the lengthy rebuttal talks about the appeal of "syncopated music" in general and the prestige of Ellington in particular as early as 1929: "It was probably foolish of me, after spending so much money on a large orchestra, to include a complete band in addition, but the Cotton Club Orchestra, under the direction of Duke Ellington, that plays in the cabaret scene is the finest exponent of syncopated music in existence. Irving Berlin went mad about them, and some of the best exponents of modern music who have heard them during rehearsal almost jumped out of their seats with excitement over their extraordinary harmonies and exciting rhythms."[155]

At the same time as cutting-edge, high-art composers such as Varèse were reconsidering the very structure of music, the rhythms of jazz bands presented a new focus for those who were trying to escape the yoke of a tonally dominated, harmonically driven European musical aesthetic.[156] With traditional artistic values seemingly exhausted and the notion of progress challenged at every turn, it didn't matter the source of the primitivism; this was a powerful new value for composers. Supercharged rhythms and ear-stretching harmonies became the sounds of urban, industrial society. Primitive sounds became modern ones. "Jungle music," with its muted and growling brass, spoke of a culture far removed from the well-behaved world of symphony halls.[157] Here was a legitimate source for an American art and music; here was a source for a modern aesthetic. Rhythm, the musical element singled out by Copland as distinguishing American music, was at the heart of jazz. While closely associated with primitivism, jazz would also eventually be perceived as the product of a more mature culture, a more complex culture, a faster-paced, high-energy, urban culture: a culture that didn't rely upon romanticized interpretations of pristine wildernesses to convince the world of its seriousness and worth.[158] Here was a music that spoke of America's coming of age. European composers arriving in the States for their first visits in the 1920s singled it out as representing "the core of American music."[159] Although jazz had its roots in the South and would later develop numerous regional styles, for years the physical core of jazz was anchored in Harlem.

Over a period of five decades, Ellington captured Harlem in pieces whose titles proudly sported its name: *Harlem Flat Blues* (1929), *Blue Harlem* (1932), *Drop Me Off in Harlem* (1933), *Jungle Nights in Harlem* (1934), *Harlem Speaks* (1935), *Echoes of Harlem* (1936), *Harmony in Harlem* (1938), *The Boys from Harlem* and the *Blue Belles of Harlem* (1939), *Harlem Air Shaft* (1940), *Heart of Harlem* (1945), *Shades of Harlem* (1957), and *A Night in Harlem* (1962), among others.[160] His most fully developed musical commemoration of the place was his piece *Harlem,* alternately titled *Harlem Suite, Harlem Symphony,* and *A Tone Parallel to Harlem,* written between 1949 and 1950. Altogether, Ellington's Harlem pieces described the people, places, and moods that he associated with this city within *the* city, a place he knew from the inside.[161] With his music he spoke of and for an urban culture not specifically addressed by Ives, Copland, or Varèse.

If titles are clues, one indication of Ellington's intimate knowledge of the place is his 1940 piece *Harlem Air Shaft.*[162] As anyone who lived in a city building prior to central cooling or heating knows, the air shaft was an essential internal source of fresh air and ventilation, often located just off the kitchen or the bathroom or both. A sash window with some kind of obscuring opaque glass provided privacy when closed and allowed for air circulation when opened. In summer months, the predominantly brick homes became unbearably warm; privacy was then often sacrificed for the small bit of moving air that an open air shaft window provided. But fresh air was not the only thing to circulate in the shaft. Sounds and smells from neighboring houses and apartments also mingled and wafted about. It was easy to know what someone else was eating for dinner, and neighbors could easily overhear altercations from adjacent residences. Occasionally, animated conversations were carried on among neighbors via the acoustically live air shaft. The brick and glass chute became one large mixing board with no one at the controls.[163] The air shaft provided a distinctly urban experience. Duke Ellington supplied a lengthy program for his piece:

> So much goes on in a Harlem air shaft. You get the full essence of Harlem in an air shaft. You hear fights, you smell dinner, you hear people making love, you hear intimate gossip floating down. You hear the radio. An air shaft is one great big loudspeaker. You see your neighbors' laundry. You hear the Janitor's dogs. The man upstairs' aerial falls down and breaks your window. You smell coffee. A wonderful thing, that smell. An air shaft has got every contrast. One guy is cooking dried fish and rice and another guy's got a great big turkey. Guy-with-fish's wife is a terrific cooker but the guy's wife with the turkey is doing a sad job. You hear people praying, fighting, smoking. Jitterbugs are jumping up and down, always all over you, never below you. That's a funny thing about jitterbugs. They're always above you. I tried to put all that into Harlem Air Shaft.[164]

James Lincoln Collier speaks for many when he finds *Harlem Air Shaft* to be among Ellington's most successful musical pictures. In describing the piece, he relies on Ellington's program to help explain musical behavior: "The intro-duction signals what is to come. It is made of three quite disparate musical fragments, which, as they succeed each other abruptly, shift the mood exactly as in an airshaft when at one moment we smell the fish and at the next the roast turkey. The main body of the piece continues to mix and match con-trasting, frequently jarring elements."

Collier then tracks the various players and their contributions to the musi-cal mix:

> Muted brass playing a bugle figure against creamy unison saxophones; Nan-ton growling over the saxophones; trombones with Barney Bigard's clarinet flying over them. Particularly felicitous are episodes in the second chorus. In the previous chorus the bridge was played by Nanton growling over long chords by the saxophones. The second chorus opens with similar long chords, while the rhythm drops out to give the effect of the "break" so common in early jazz. We expect something similar to what went before, but this time, after four bars, Cootie, open horn, dives in as the rhythm section takes up. Then, as he begins to get up momentum, the saxophones suddenly take another break; and so it alternates through the bulk of the thirty-two bars.

In a closing paragraph, Collier distinguishes the descriptive scenario for *Harlem Air Shaft* from those of other programmatic Ellington works: "The piece ends with a rousing chorus in which the airshaft is filled with flying objects: saxophone and brass all go hell-for-leather as Bigard screams over-head, as he had done so often for Duke in the 1930s. 'Harlem Airshaft' works as program music in a way that others of Duke's pieces do not. In fact, the abrupt shifts in it would seem merely disruptive without an understanding of Duke's intention."[165]

The last observation is questionable, since the piece holds together even if analysis yields what seems to be a series of initially unrelated parts. This is music that does not depend upon the development of related themes to make sense; it is born of contrast and juxtaposition. Prior to the "three . . . disparate musical fragments," Ellington sets the mood with a cool piano and string bass introduction that begins with a four-note motive that is taken up and modi-fied by the brass. Ellington's connections are subtle. The full orchestra enters, only to be quickly disassembled into its constituent parts—first saxes speak and then the brass—as if Ellington wanted to separate the characters in his musical tableau.[166] A solo trumpet emerges as the narrator of the scene.[167] His opening four-note motive recalls that which Ellington used to introduce the piece. This gesture will function in both solo and accompanimental roles, not developed in the traditional sense, but simply recalled. Ellington's smooth alternation and blending of solo trumpet, brass choir, and saxophone and clarinet show him to be a master of his orchestral palette. His gifts as a painter reemerge as he manipulates tone colors. A consistent upbeat tempo prevails, although percussion refrains from asserting itself at any time in the three-and-a-half-minute piece.

Harlem Air Shaft becomes a three-way conversation among the solo trumpet, the brass, and the winds. And a polite conversation at that. On multiple occasions the solo trumpet softly laughs: these reappearances help unify the work and keep the mood cordial and relaxed. Not until the end do voices rise above a well-modulated dynamic level. Then brasses scream, a suspended cymbal reverberates, and all forces become more assertive and defined. But even at the climax Ellington avoids suggesting hostile conflict; instead we hear boisterous, active, lively, multifarious Harlem. Precisely because of the "unconnected connectedness" of Ellington's opening sax and brass materials, *Harlem Air Shaft* convincingly captures the heterogeneity of sounds and styles that is New York.[168] While not integrated and unified in a traditional sense, the music, like the best heterogeneous cities, works; it sounds good.[169]

By the time Duke Ellington wrote *Harlem* in 1949, he had seen his name in lights on Milwaukee's city hall, won numerous awards both individually and with his band, received the first of his fifteen honorary doctorates, and was on his way to becoming a cultural ambassador to the world.[170] Although Harlem tenements and their air shafts would remain one part of his experience, he had moved beyond that vital, if circumscribed, world. Changing with him, Harlem too had moved beyond its glory days of the Twenties and Thirties, even if not in the same positive direction.[171] In many ways Ellington's *Harlem* would be a tribute to a bygone place and era.

But Duke Ellington's piece was not the first extended artistic tribute to Harlem. A 1929 all-black Broadway play entitled *Harlem,* by William Jourdan Rapp and Wallace Thurman, was widely reviewed in the New York press. Nor was Ellington's musical memorial the first of its kind. Although no evidence exists to suggest that he had William Grant Still's *Lenox Avenue* in mind when he wrote *Harlem* or was even familiar with the piece, the two works share similar programmatic frameworks and moods. Although Still will be discussed more thoroughly in the following chapter, possible relationships between these two pieces warrant a brief exploration of *Lenox Avenue* here.[172]

In 1937 CBS commissioned Still, the nation's most respected black composer, to write a piece for its radio orchestra. He responded the next year with *Lenox Avenue,* a suitelike orchestral work that included a chorus and narrator, with a text written by Verna Arvey.[173] Later that same year, the suite was

Sargent Johnson, *Lenox Avenue,* 1938. Drawing, 10½ x 14½ inches. William Grant Still and Verna Arvey Papers (MC 1125), Group 4, series 7, Special Collections, University of Arkansas, Fayetteville.

adapted as a ballet and premiered by the Dance Theatre of Los Angeles. The piece depicted the varied sights and activities one might encounter in the 1930s along the famous Harlem byway. An introductory narrative sets the tone for the piece: "Lenox Avenue, at first it looks like Beale Street, or Decatur Street, State Street, or Central Avenue, or any of the main Negro thoroughfares in the United States. But then you see a different world, a different atmosphere, because this avenue cuts through famed Harlem. Let's take an evening stroll down Lenox Avenue and see it through the eyes of a musician."[174]

Still describes the passing crowd, some of whom are in "flashy suits" while others show the signs of poverty. He sees those who are "living fast," others who are "neat and wholesome," "tired people, rushing people." He hears "sirens screech and subways rumble . . . a Harvard accent, then a southern dialect, and yet again the screech of a West Indian." The narrator characterizes them as a "motley crowd." The introduction closes with an ingenuous assessment of the place: "But here in Harlem, folk laugh in the face of tragedy, and aching hearts respond to joyous music. A blend of fun and anger, love and laughter and religion all on Lenox Avenue." Though it is not the purpose of this study to scrutinize such a simple summation of 1930s Harlem culture, the introduction is noteworthy for its avoidance of any potentially contentious issues related to the place, including issues of race and discrimination, which were a constant theme from the mid-teens onward in the daily life of the dominantly black population. Such issues remained concerns for Still throughout his adult years. Text interpolated within the body of the music does little more than touch upon such problems.[175] Given Still's unique position in the New York high-art music scene, perhaps he decided that a nationally broadcast radio piece was not the forum for didacticism or campaigning.

Still's *Lenox Avenue* is divided into eleven sections: "The Crap Game," "The Flirtation," "The Fight," "The Law," "Dance of the Boys," "Dance of the Man from Down South," the extremely popular "The Old Man (The Philosopher)," "The Mission," "The House Rent Party," "The Orator," and a finale that recalls the music of the mission section one last time. Ellington's *Harlem* has a series of descriptive sections as well. Like Still's introduction, Verna Arvey's good-natured, optimistic narrative spends little time on highly charged political issues. No doubt Still understood that he was writing for a mostly white national audience and appreciated that if he used the radio as a soapbox for racial arguments, his opportunities for similar commissions might be curtailed.[176] According to Arvey, letters received by the station commenting specifically upon the *Lenox Avenue* broadcast of 23 May 1937 indicate that Still knew how to reach his audience; only 6 of 117 letters offered any criticism.[177] Still's depiction of *Lenox Avenue* notwithstanding, the importance of this street to Harlem culture, especially as a locus of black *political* activity, cannot be overstated. One would have to believe that Still chose this street not simply because it "cut through famed Harlem" (so does St. Nicholas Avenue), but because it was of great symbolic importance to black Americans, even if that fact is simply assumed.[178]

Lenox Avenue runs north from Central Park up to the Harlem River. According to Jervis Anderson, Lenox at 135th Street was a regular gathering place of "political and race radicals" who made their speeches using "Harlem soap boxes and stepladders." "It was one of the major radical forums of black America."[179] In addition, Harlem's famed dance halls and nightclubs—the Savoy, the Cotton Club, the Radium Club, to name only three—were clustered around Lenox Avenue. Equally important to the culture of Harlem as politics was religion. The Abyssinian Baptist Church, home to the largest and wealthiest black Baptist congregation in the world, was on 138th Street between Seventh Avenue and Lenox.[180] Then as now, religion and politics were never far apart; in Harlem they would be accompanied by a distinctive musical soundtrack.

On two occasions, Still includes church bells and congregational singing in his sonic travelogue; the second time the chorus sings to a jazzy beat, a nod to Harlem's musical culture. Prior to this religious reprise, however, is the section entitled "The Orator," Still's one acknowledgment of political activity in Harlem. The narrator explains: "That sidewalk orator doesn't seem exactly to belong on Lenox Avenue, but he has an audience. He's crying out against evils and raising his voice in an impassioned plea for universal brotherhood. Some listen because it's cheap entertainment, but others are absorbed in every word he says." Still treads most carefully around the subject, recognizing the presence of the orator-agitator but not quite reconciling his appearance on Lenox Avenue ("doesn't seem exactly to belong on Lenox Avenue"), even though historically this would be exactly where such activity would take place. Still's reluctance to treat this aspect of Harlem culture is made clear when he closes the twenty-plus-minute piece with a return to the placating introductory remarks: "Dusky faces, dusky smiles, where folks laugh in the face of tragedy and aching hearts respond to joyous music." Thus he acknowledges tragedy and heartache but soft-peddles their effects on the "dusky" Harlemites.[181]

In 1938 William Grant Still was a successful black composer operating within an almost purely white world. In addition to composing his own works, he had arranged for Paul Whiteman and conducted the Los Angeles Philharmonic at the Hollywood Bowl. Studies with George Whitefield Chadwick in Boston and then with Edgard Varèse in New York made him uniquely qualified to participate in high-art circles—a situation that was both a blessing and a curse. As Oja summarized it: "Still was the only African American composer among the modernists. . . . often fully on the inside, . . . but always aware of his race. Still constantly faced expectations to produce work that in some way reflected his racial difference. And even though the modernists on the whole embraced him enthusiastically, he still had to function in a world where racism could be loudly articulated."[182] Things were only slightly different in Ellington's world of jazz.

In the ten years between *Lenox Avenue* and *Harlem,* the famed uptown center of America's black culture saw a decided downturn. If Still's piece idealized the place, it did so just after the neighborhood's reputation crested. By the time Ellington composed his tribute, Harlem was a mere memory of its halcyon days. There had been a number of reasons for the change.

According to Anderson, "by 1950 many of those who helped to make Harlem the most brilliant black city in the world had died—depleting the reservoir of idealism and exemplary achievement that had nourished the community's positive sense of itself." Many others simply relocated. The arrest in 1931 of nine black youths in Scottsboro, Alabama, on bogus charges of raping two white women radicalized both blacks and whites in Harlem. Racial tensions increased. Riots in 1935 and 1943 diminished Harlem's appeal as a social destination, especially for whites. When the Cotton Club moved down-town in 1936 and other clubs closed, there was little incentive to visit Harlem. Anderson quotes a Harlem newspaper columnist of 1949: "Nobody comes to Harlem anymore. Nobody seems to care. . . . Only a few places offer anything approaching a show, and even so it's nothing like the days when 'Harlem jumped.'"[183] But Harlem would never completely fade, not as long as its churches remained, and they did. Ellington pointed to their presence in his program, which, like Still's earlier work, referred to the place in its heyday.

Ellington's *Harlem* was commissioned by the NBC Symphony Orchestra and premiered on 21 January 1951 at the Metropolitan Opera House as part of a benefit concert for the NAACP. That same year Langston Hughes wrote his poem "Harlem" and acknowledged the more volatile aspect of the city; the one that Still and Ellington so carefully avoided.[184] Ellington's fifteen-minute, one-movement work was the focal point of the benefit concert.

In keeping with his predilection for descriptive music, Ellington offered a commentary to help listeners through the work. This was the narrative version of a more schematic list of twenty section titles that he had devised to identify various aspects of the work.[185]

Harlem is a place, you know, in New York City, on Manhattan Island, between 110th Street and 145th Street. It's bordered on the west by the Hudson River, on the east, by the East and Harlem Rivers, and it's a rather nice community. It was originally settled by the Dutch, but right now, of course, they have some exceptionally handsome people who live there. But in spite of our beauty, we are really so good in Harlem that we are even represented in Congress by a Minister.

And so we sort of take you on a tour, on Sunday morning starting down at Central Park and going up Seventh Avenue through the Spanish neighborhood up through the business district to a West Indian [district], and it's Sunday morning, and you know. And there are more churches in Harlem than there are cabarets. And everyone is on their way to church, dressed nicely and very polite and everybody's in a good friendly sort of mood, and they're greeting each other.

We can see in the distance across the street a very chic chick who's standing on the corner under a lamp post . . . and she too is in a friendly mood. You may see us as we are in an Elks parade, or a Masonic parade, you may see a funeral go by, or you may even recognize the sound of our making our social significance demands. And this is Harlem.[186]

One can imagine the bandleader's rich, smooth baritone as he introduces the piece to an audience. Without addressing racial issues head-on or suggesting serious social unrest, he makes a case for the beautiful black people found in present-day Harlem. Tongue-in-cheek, he speaks of the "goodness" of the population and for proof refers to the prominence of churches and Harlem's representation in Congress by a minister (Adam Clayton Powell Jr.).[187] He acknowledges different neighborhoods—Spanish and West Indian—and the "friendly" women standing on corners, and the possibility that we will see (and hear) a parade or some political speech. As in *Harlem Air Shaft*, Ellington was interested in demonstrating the variety of people and activities that defined the place. This was no monochromatic people, this was no monochromatic place. The tone poem provided generous space to expand upon the initial concept.[188]

In *Harlem* Ellington participated in a tradition of crossover works that emerged in the 1920s and that he helped expand in the 1940s.[189] But unlike others who contributed to the hybridized genre—George Gershwin, George Antheil, Aaron Copland, Paul Whiteman, William Grant Still, Ferde Grofé, to name just a few—Ellington came at symphonic jazz not from a background in classical training or performance but from the jazz side of the equation. One of the most important creators and definers of jazz in the 1920s and 1930s, Duke Ellington became one of the refiners of the style in the 1940s and 1950s.[190] As Ellington had observed early in his career when talking about various musicians, there were the "readers" and "ear cats." Though he eventually honed his own music reading skills, Ellington had started out using his discriminating ear and going with the sound. That he was aware of these different approaches and traditions when writing *Harlem* is obvious in Maurice Peress's notes to the piece:

> Duke, a master title-giver, described the work as a concerto grosso for Jazz band and symphony orchestra. He similarly described his *Queenie Pie*—already a wondrously ear-catching name—as an *opera comique*. While neither of these works exactly fits the classical description, their subtitles nevertheless help raise one's expectation for more than just another Broadway musical or jazz-inspired orchestra piece.
>
> *Concerto grosso* was more likely Ellington's way to get his orchestra into the center of Toscanini's celebrated NBC Symphony. This would assure that the music would be interpreted in a true jazz style, but it does not fulfill the traditional idea of a concerto grosso wherein the group—the Duke Ellington Orchestra—is pitted against the symphony.[191]

For all this self-consciousness, *Harlem* comes across as a spontaneous musical utterance; there is nothing contrived or strained in the work. This in spite of the fact that Henderson and Peress's scoring required an oversized (and potentially unwieldy) ensemble incorporating both jazz band and orchestra: three flutes, with the third doubling on piccolo; two oboes; English horn; two clarinets; bass clarinet; two bassoons; four horns; five saxes, including two altos, two tenors, and a baritone; four trumpets and two trombones, to be played with a variety of mutes; a tuba; traps to be played with numerous brushes and sticks, timpani, and assorted percussion; a harp, and a full complement of strings including a solo string bass, for which Ellington stipulated, "no amp."[192] Unlike Still's earlier work, in which text connected the programmatic sections of the piece, Ellington's musical ideas flowed unencumbered.

The work is unified melodically through the interplay of a pair of musical ideas, which are separated by a plaintive clarinet solo. The first is a two-note, descending minor third interval, which Ellington insisted actually articulated the word "Harlem." The muted solo trumpet speaks "Harlem" three times, slowly. One senses that Ellington wanted the trumpeter (and perhaps the audience) to roll the word around in his mouth, to play with it, to taste it (see Ex. 3.4).

The motif is taken up by saxes, horns, and strings, and then treated seductively by a solo clarinet at rehearsal letter A. Trumpets and saxes answer the motif with a relaxed (Ellington indicates that they are to play "warmly") response heralding the appearance of the entire ensemble, save the uppermost woodwinds. Harlem (and *Harlem*) is introduced slowly and deliberately. The music of this section never exceeds a moderate swing tempo (quarter note = 120).

One measure after rehearsal letter O, a solo clarinet starts up a mournful tune; the rest of the ensemble drops out. It is joined at rehearsal letter P by horns and saxes and a thudding, pulsing cadence that beats in the timpani and low strings. Ellington creates timbral, textural, dynamic, and structural contrast equivalent to the relief offered by the slower, more lyrical internal movement of a concerto (see Ex. 3.5).

The second idea is a more fully developed blues melody evocative of the slow, strutting march tunes that one might hear at a New Orleans funeral parade. (Ellington refers to this section of the piece as an Elks parade.) A trombone introduces the "felt hat solo" (Ellington's phrase) about two-thirds of the way through the piece at rehearsal letter Q. The instrumentalist is instructed to play "freely," "not sentimentally" (see Ex. 3.6).

The syncopated melody is characterized by rising and falling major and minor thirds, which provide a clear and audible link to the opening two-note "Harlem" motif. During the course of the fifteen-minute work, Ellington spotlights each of the ideas separately. Then at rehearsal letter R, winds and brass join in a moment of counterpoint as the piece works toward a climax.

157

Ex. 3.4: Duke Ellington, *Harlem,* mm 1–5, "Harlem" motif in trumpets, © 1952 (Renewed) by G. Schirmer, Inc. (ASCAP). International copyright secured. All rights reserved. Printed by permission.

Ex. 3.5: Duke Ellington, *Harlem,* clarinet idea at letter O, © 1952 (Renewed) by G. Schirmer, Inc. (ASCAP). International copyright secured. All rights reserved. Printed by permission.

Ex. 3.6: Duke Ellington, *Harlem,* blues march tune, © 1952 (Renewed) by G. Schirmer, Inc. (ASCAP). International copyright secured. All rights reserved. Reprinted by permission.

Close intervalic relationships between the two-note motif and the more fully developed theme, along with Ellington's instincts for timbral blends and contrasts, create a closely integrated and compelling work.

Important as melodic, intervalic, and timbral relationships are, however, it is Ellington's treatment of rhythm that propels *Harlem* through its paces. Tempo is in a constant state of flux, unwilling to be confined. In most cases transitions are smooth and seamless, prepared for by poco ritards or indications to "broaden." At other times Ellington writes in more abrupt switches, often following a fermata, or he simply instructs the musicians to "Swing it!" Like altering kaleidoscope images, sometimes rhythm changes are subtle, and at other times they completely transform the landscape. Always *Harlem* is informed by dance—an appropriate quality, given the place being memorialized. While Harlem had its famous dance clubs, its churches too were venues for the swaying and hand-clapping that accompanied singing. On two occasions Ellington indicates the names of particular dances: bolero (at rehearsal letter B1) and rhumba (at rehearsal letter E), perhaps a nod to the Spanish and Cuban citizens of Harlem. But even when no precise dance is identified the music pulses, it moves, it swings. Ellington gets his rhythmic ideas across to the orchestral musicians with parenthetical reminders, "hard accents" or "big back beat." Like Varèse's *Amériques,* the score is laden with instructions how to play. As he approaches the percussion cadenza (one measure before rehearsal letter Y), Ellington coaches his musicians to play "grandly" (rehearsal letter W), and then maestoso (one measure before rehearsal letter X).

Maurice Peress recalled a rehearsal of *Harlem* with the Symphony of the New World, where upon reaching the cadenza Ellington commanded the percussionist "take us all the way back to Senegal."[193] If there was ever any question regarding Ellington's ideas concerning the roots of jazz, this moment in the piece provides the answer. The ten-measure "Summary" that follows is a fully involved, bold, and blaring assertion of self.

Although Ellington wrote no piano part for this work, his distinctive sound is everywhere in the piece—from the plunger-muted trumpet opening to the sweetly dissonant sax ensemble at rehearsal letter T. This is a tribute not only to the place, but also to one man's experience of that place. We hear Harlem through Ellington and appreciate that it is difficult to separate the two. Sensitive soloistic writing butts up against big band effects; growling and whinnying trumpets, tom-tom drums that let loose, and sparring winds and brass screaming in the final moments brand this work vintage Ellington.

In treating a program about Harlem symphonically, Ellington validated the place in much the same way Charles Ives had validated the vernacular tunes and topics that he chose to set in numerous orchestral sets, sonatas, songs, string quartets, and symphonies. Like Fry and Bristow years earlier, these composers honored and legitimized American culture by insisting that its symbols and sounds were worthy of serious treatment within the most highly regarded musical genres. Ellington expanded this idea even further. In bringing jazz to Carnegie Hall and the Metropolitan Opera House, Ellington validated America, jazz, and himself. And in so doing, he elevated them all.

chapter four

Beyond the City:
Rivers, Canyons, and Plains

WILLIAM GRANT STILL
Kaintuck' and *American Scenes*

> The United States themselves are essentially the greatest poem. . . . Here is
> not merely a nation but a teeming nation of nations. . . . The largeness of
> nature or the nation were monstrous without a corresponding largeness and
> generosity of the spirit of the citizen. . . . His spirit responds to his country's
> spirit . . . he incarnates its geography and natural life and rivers and lakes.
> —WALT WHITMAN, *Leaves of Grass*

While large numbers of photographers, artists, writers, and composers embraced urban sites, stories, and places as the new archetypes of America, others
clung to more rural symbols. As the nation developed a more modern sense
of itself and its place within the world and located the center of that emerging
urban consciousness in New York City, many composers continued to promote a national identity anchored in the land and its promise of America's
uniqueness and potential. Among the most active in this pursuit were three
men born in the last decade of the nineteenth century: Ferde Grofé (1892–
1972), William Grant Still (1895–1978), and Roy Harris (1898–1979).[1] For
composers just making their marks between the wars, a time when nations
actively jockeyed for power, social and political exigencies played powerful
roles. It is perhaps not surprising, then, that for Still and Harris in particular,
ideas about place got tangled with more general questions of patriotism and
nationalism.[2] Regardless of how modern the nation had become, it was hard
to argue with the enduring power of America's physical endowments, and
calling attention to the land tied one to it. When Still commemorated five

regions of the country in the series *The American Scene,* and when Harris celebrated "the West" in a piece named *Cimarron,* there was more at stake than simple pride of place. Such works symbolized and solidified one's loyalty, one's Americanism. The notion was not all that different from that which had guided Heinrich nearly a century earlier, although now there were additional political ramifications.[3]

It is difficult to tease out and separate motivations for individual musical works beyond the incentive of a commission, although composers often provided voluminous commentary, both written and oral, explaining themselves.[4] The temper of the times worked on composers as it had throughout history on all creative artists, often in ways unknown to the individual. For different reasons, all three composers turned away from the international overtones of the experimental modernist movement and aligned themselves with music that was much more accessible and comfortable. All three composers were awarded numerous commissions, and at different times the music of each of them enjoyed great popularity. At mid-century, these more traditional composers kept American places in the forefront of the nation's listening public. Although they were close contemporaries of Copland and Ellington, they carved out very different paths. Harris, Still, and Grofé all spent long periods of time in the West, and this may be part of it; for them, America was more than the modern urban scene.[5] Inspiration varied: it could have been pure love of the land, personal attachments to particular places, a sense of patriotism that gained strength through close associations with national landmarks, or little more than calculated self-promotion. Yet as individuals and as a group, these composers demonstrated the enduring power of America's geography to shape and define a national identity.

William Grant Still, whose *Lenox Avenue* has already been discussed, wrote close to twenty place pieces in a variety of genres. Throughout his composing career, he was inspired by places, from an early orchestral piece entitled *American Suite* (pre-1916) to radio and stage works such as *Lenox Avenue* (1937–38) and *Highway 1, USA* (1962). He composed an orchestral tone poem, *Dismal Swamp* (1936), celebrating that feature of Virginia and North Carolina, and another for the 160th birthday of Los Angeles in *Old California* (1941). He celebrated the broader nation in the fifty-minute, multisectional *American Scene* (1957), wrote the impressionistic piano and orchestra work *Kaintuck'* (1935), and created works for voice and piano such as *Bayou Home* (1944), *Mississippi* (1948), and *Arkansas* (1940s–50s). Among these works some were commissioned by institutions—as was *Lenox Avenue* by CBS radio; others were in response to individuals. *Old California* was composed at the request of Werner Janssen; another, *Kaintuck',* was one of two pieces that Still offered to the League of Composers for a commission.[6] Others evolved on their own. Together they capture the country, from marshes to mountains, cities to swamps, east to west.

Still was born in Woodville, Mississippi. His mother moved with him to Little Rock, Arkansas, after his father died; William was just a toddler. He spent his entire youth in Little Rock benefiting from the more cosmopolitan, enlightened, and racially progressive environment that characterized that city, even though it too would succumb to worsening conditions for black citizens during his family's time there. Yet the move was an auspicious one. Woodville, Mississippi, just north and east of the Louisiana border, would forever be synonymous with a series of racial confrontations that had taken place in the 1870s. Situated in an overwhelmingly black county in southwestern Mississippi, Woodville had been the scene of a controversial and violent election in 1875. An 1876 Senate inquiry into the allegations reported numerous instances of fraud and even murder perpetrated against the city's black citizens. Testimony revealed that as many as fifty blacks had been killed, some by hanging. The attitudes that had encouraged those incidents died hard. Carrie Fambro Still, born in 1872, had come to Woodville upon marrying Still's father. She sought a different environment in which to raise her young son, and she found it in Arkansas.[7] William Grant Still would remain there until 1911, when he left to attend Wilberforce University, in Ohio.

According to Willard B. Gatewood, although Little Rock was racially segregated, it boasted "a cosmopolitan character unusual in Arkansas, and much of the South." At the time that Carrie and her son arrived, "the lines had not yet been rigidly drawn. Interracial association still existed to an extent that had virtually disappeared in the rural districts of the state."[8] There were "mixed neighborhoods," and it was in one of these that the Stills settled. In 1904 Carrie Still, having become a highly respected teacher and activist, married Charles B. Shepperson, himself a well-regarded member of the black community. Their home became a meeting place for the multiple cultural and literary societies that thrived in the city. In addition to this enriched environment, Still recalled his stepfather's large collection of opera recordings as his introduction to that genre. He was also given violin lessons and taken to numerous theatrical and musical performances. In his reminiscence entitled "My Arkansas Boyhood" Still spoke warmly of his stepfather's role in his artistic education: "He initiated and fostered in me a love for the stage which has never died."[9] But his musical education, though grounded in the high-art tradition, was not confined by it. As Gatewood points out, Still's maternal grandmother, Anne Fambro, a former slave, exposed him to "black folk music with her regular singing of spirituals, hymns, and other songs."[10] His education in black music traditions intensified in 1916, when he spent the summer in Memphis, Tennessee, with W. C. Handy playing and arranging band music. Handy's firm, Pace and Handy, would publish "at least ten early Still songs and arrangements."[11] From W. C. Handy, William Grant Still learned the basics of what would become classic blues tradition. It was one of many musical discourses upon which he drew in creating his own compositional voice.[12] Although Still insisted throughout his life upon his identity as a composer of serious music (in the high-art tradition), from a young age he was also conscious of other repertoires and traditions. This awareness only grew over time.[13]

Still went to New York in 1919, four years after Edgard Varèse and four years before Duke Ellington. Throughout the 1920s he amassed a range of musical experiences that represented a wide spectrum of traditions. He arranged for some of the most popular orchestras and musicians of the time, among them Eubie Blake, Sophie Tucker, and, later, Donald Voorhees and Paul Whiteman. He played in numerous bands, and in the pit orchestra for Sissle and Blake's African American theater piece *Shuffle Along* (1921–22). It was in 1922, while this show was on tour in Boston, that Still studied privately with the German-trained American composer George Whitefield Chadwick, who was then director of the New England Conservatory.[14] After returning to New York, Still went to work for the Black Swan Phonograph Company in 1923. Quite serendipitously, he ended up studying composition with the most famous ultramodernist of the time, Edgard Varèse. Varèse had sent a letter to Black Swan soliciting names of young black composers who might be interested in studying composition with him as part of a personal scholarship program he was initiating. Still came upon the letter and put himself forward as a candidate. He deeply appreciated the guidance of this modernist champion, who encouraged him to seek musical forms different from those commonly used in the white concert tradition and made possible multiple performances of his works through Varèse's own organization, the International Composers' Guild.[15]

Still's modernist efforts were generally well received, even while reviews of his music seemed always to include a racial reference or component. Paul Rosenfeld's 1925 review of *From the Land of Dreams* is representative of the kind of "double-consciousness" or expectation that characterized Still's audience:[16]

> *From the Land of Dreams,* the work for small harmonic orchestra and voices instrumentally treated by William Grant Still, well known for his excellent orchestration of many negro [*sic*] revues, adds another member to the grow-

ing company of American musical embryonics. Still has learned much from Edgar Varèse, his instructor, although he has not yet quite learned to speak out freely: a certain absence of freedom in the use of his ideas limits one's enjoyment, and the material of the first two sections of his composition is insufficiently contrasted. But Mr. Still has a very sensuous approach to music. His employment of his instruments is at once rich and nude and decided. The upper ranges of his high soprano have an original penetrating colour. And the use of jazz motives in the last section of his work is more genuinely musical than any to which they have been put, by Milhaud, Gershwin, or any one else.[17]

The following year, a review of the chamber orchestra tone poem *Darker America* appeared in *Musical Courier*.[18] Its writer couldn't help pointing out the novelty of Still's race within the milieu: "The actual high spot was a new work by that greatly gifted Negro composer, William Grant Still. . . . He already has a splendid technic and is obviously full of ideas. Just at present his ideas are clouded by modernistic harmonies (i.e., dissonances) which spoil them. However, there is no doubting the man's power, and his music on this particular occasion was like a bright spot amid a lot of muddy grime."[19]

When Still discovered that the more dissonant idiom of the ultra-modernists was not fully sympathetic to the musical message that he sought to communicate, the racial themes he hoped to address, and could not be reconciled with his desire for a more accessible music, he found another forum and champion in Howard Hanson and his newly created American Composers' Concert series at the Eastman School in Rochester, New York.[20] Over the years Hanson premiered numerous works by Still, many revealing the composer's movement away from a self-consciously modernist approach and toward his more "racial music." Hanson premiered Still's most famous work in this idiom, the *Afro-American Symphony*, in 1931.[21] As Gayle Murchison has noted, the success of this symphony gave Still the authority to speak for African American music.[22] In essays and lectures appearing in a variety of journals, including *The Baton, Revue internationale de musique, Musica, Opportunity,* and *Etude,* Still used his position to educate the public, whites and blacks alike, to the aesthetic values of jazz and the blues as well as spirituals.

He spoke as a composer who appreciated the emotional depth and unique harmonic form in the blues: a twelve-bar structure that bore little resemblance to the more common four- and eight-bar phrase lengths that characterized many western tonal music forms. By using this distinctive harmonic and temporal framework, along with the call-and-response gestures that typified many black musical genres, Still left a black imprint on his music. But he did not claim these musical resources for himself alone, nor did he want to be confined to their use because he was a black composer. In the spirit of ecumenism that characterized so much of Still's thinking and music, he saw these resources as among many available to all American composers. Here were additional tools for creating American music. During this period and throughout Still's next self-described "universal idiom," Howard Hanson was an ardent supporter and friend. He remained so until Still's death in 1978.

Although Still had moved far away from his Mississippi birthplace and its deep South culture, if titles of pieces are any indication, he maintained a warm spot for the state. An opera entitled *A Bayou Legend* (1941) is based on a tale from Biloxi, Mississippi; regarding a band piece *From the Delta* (1945), Still was quoted as saying, "This is the first time that I have tried to express in music the romance of the Delta country in my native state of Mississippi."[23] A variety of songs celebrating the "bayou state" attest to a continuing affection for the landscapes and legends of his birth. While Still might have had to grow into an appreciation of his black musical heritage, once that had occurred, he needed little encouragement to memorialize it. But as the earlier list suggests, Mississippi was not the only place that Still turned into sound.

A lifetime of place-inspired music reflects Still's susceptibility to his surroundings and a deep love of his country, both as an idea and as a physical entity. Of the composers covered in this study, it is likely that William Grant Still spent more time living in and visiting more places in the United States than did any other. He was insatiably curious about the nation, an appetite that was encouraged and satisfied, at least to some extent, by his fascination with the road. According to Still's daughter, Judith Anne Still, her father simply "loved to drive."[24] He drove from New York to California in the mid-Thirties, and once established there, he took trips up and down Route 1, reveling in the beauty of the West Coast.[25] Judith Still recalls car trips as regular family activities when she was growing up.[26] She says that a later trip involved Still and his wife Verna Arvey driving from Los Angeles to Taos, New Mexico, where they spent time among the Navahos absorbing the scenery and culture. This excursion eventually bore musical fruit in *The American Scene*, fourth suite, "The Far West," third movement, entitled "Navaho Country."[27]

Another example of Still's love of the road and the places it took him manifested itself in his response to a request in 1962 by Fabien Sevitzky, a Russian-born conductor and longtime friend. Sevitzky asked Still to write a short opera to be produced at the University of Miami. The composer chose an unusual backdrop for a high-art genre when he set his opera *Highway 1, USA* at a gas station along the famous East Coast road that stretches from the Florida Keys to Presque Isle, Maine. (Highway 1 goes right through Miami.)

It premiered the following year.[28] The title alone conjures images of the great distances (in miles and cultures) that one can traverse by car, a familiar theme in the era that gave birth to Jack Kerouac's 1957 novel, *On the Road,* and to the television show *Route 66*. Arvey's brief description of the opera suggests additional meanings inherent within *Highway 1, U.S.A.:* "The music was Billy's, the text mine, and the plot our own. We wrote about ordinary people with a reasonable problem [two brothers and their conflict], people who live in the America of today, who love each other, and who share the aspirations of most American families. It was a simple plot, but a dramatic one."[29]

The highway became the set for the drama of "ordinary" Americans, a nation of people always on the move. The highway is both a democratizing agent and an extremely resonant national symbol. Travel is no longer the exclusive province of the wealthy; anyone can go anywhere in America, both literally and metaphorically. As the idyllic landscapes of the Hudson River School painters had marketed a vision of America as limitless, natural, and available in the mid-nineteenth century, manufacturers of automobiles used the familiar trope of the vast expanse of the nation, now combined with the open road, to sell their products in the mid-twentieth century. One can appreciate the degree to which cars, travel, and America were conflated in 1950s and 1960s thinking in a jingle sung by Dinah Shore, as she signed off her weekly television program. Smiling broadly, the pert, blond entertainer faced the camera and energetically pointed a finger toward her television audience, singing: "See the U.S.A., in your Chevrolet, America is asking you to call; drive the U.S.A. in your Chevrolet, America's the greatest land of all." The rationing of gasoline that had accompanied World War II was a thing of the past. Driving and seeing the United States became signs of victory, prosperity, and patriotism. William Grant Still's and Verna Arvey's intense patriotism was reinforced by their country's romance with the open road.

Years before *Highway 1, U.S.A.,* a train trip through Kentucky had provided the inspiration for a different place piece, the tone poem *Kaintuck'*. Judith Still explains that her father probably collected and noted ideas for the piece while riding a train to visit family in the Southeast.[30] Around the same time, the League of Composers commissioned a work from Still.[31] According to Catherine Parsons Smith, "Still offered *Dismal Swamp*, written in a style that retained traces of his 'modernist' idiom, and the more populist *Kaintuck'*. Claire Reis [the League's administrator] chose *Kaintuck'* as the piece to be dedicated to the league, which in fact did not perform either piece."[32] When Still got back to California, he finished the work and dedicated it to Verna Arvey. It was premiered on 5 May 1935 in Los Angeles, with Arvey as the piano soloist. Written just a few years earlier than *Lenox Avenue, Kaintuck'* shows the versatile composer creating very different kinds of music in response to very different kinds of places. William Grant Still knew both urban and rural America.

Those who have described *Kaintuck'* seem to disagree as to whether the sounds are intended to be evocations of moonlight or of sunlight glinting off Kentucky's famed bluegrass.[33] Indeed, the opening minute of the piece, with its dreamy, impressionistic wash of colors, could evoke either end of the day. In an article by Frederick Yeiser that appeared on 22 March 1936 in the *Cincinnati Enquirer,* Still was quoted as saying: "Several years ago, when going from Cincinnati to Lexington on what was then the Queen and Crescent Railroad, I was so greatly impressed by the beauty of the country that I decided to attempt at some future time to describe in musical terms my reaction. And it is my feeling of peacefulness, and the more active emotions inspired by the more rugged sections that I seek to present in the piece."[34] The music is in no hurry to move on; listeners are lulled by the slow tempo, repetitive rhythms, seemingly directionless harmonies, and soft dynamics. One is reminded of many of Charles Ives's place pieces, in which the composer weakens a listener's concern for an unfolding narrative and etches out a particular locale using just such techniques. Although Still initially appears to be concerned with nothing more than creating beautiful effects and painting a musical landscape, he subtly introduces essential rhythmic motives, interval relationships, and pitch elements that will shape the entire piece.

The solo piano opening of *Kaintuck'* shimmers. Still achieves this effect through very deliberately paced chromatic alterations of chords, juxtaposed major and minor seconds and thirds, and widespread transparent textures. A slow-moving, chromatically descending melodic fragment "singing sweetly" is tucked into the inner voice of the piano part. The music is weightless; it floats.

Ex. 4.1: *Kaintuck',* mm 1–4. Courtesy of William Grant Still Music. Used by permission.

The opening, while notated in G major, sounds harmonically ambiguous, and for good reason. Measure 1 begins with a hybrid ninth chord (E-G#-B-C#-D-F#) spread out over both hands and five octaves. Measure 2 introduces a different extended chord collection. There is no obvious motion to a tonic. An open fifth (C-G) on the downbeat of measure 5, however, signals a change in course. The music traverses a series of fifths, and the twelve-measure introduction closes with another ninth chord, this one built on G.[35] The same pitch G and a pair of ninth chords eventually close the piece.

At measure 6, about thirty seconds into *Kaintuck'*, Still introduces and immediately repeats an important intervallic motive: a rising second, in this case a minor second. It balances the descending chromatic pattern of the melodic fragment. The notation of the piano part in three staves conceals this motive from the eye, but the significance of this gesture is apparent to the ear.[36] The rising second returns at strategic moments throughout the piece;[37] ten measures from the end of the piece its direction is reversed, it is expanded to a major second, and the final G is approached from an upper A. The piece fades away.

At the same time as melodic and harmonic elements are ambiguous in the opening measures, forward momentum is also thwarted by a rhythmic pattern that seems to run out of energy each time it repeats itself. The following figure combines the rhythms of the top two staves of piano music and represents the rhythm as it is heard by a listener, as a series of eighth-note motions:

Musical Fig. 4.1: Rhythmic pattern.

This rocking pattern anchors the first five minutes of the piece; thereafter the pattern subdivides, the tempo increases, and rhythm takes on a whole new role.

The opening of *Kaintuck'* plays with our expectations for works written for orchestra and piano. In earlier models, such as traditional solo concertos, the orchestra introduced materials and then the soloist joined in.[38] Even George Gershwin's *Rhapsody in Blue* (1924), a most celebrated one-movement orchestral and piano work, followed the expected pattern of entrances, although the opening clarinet glissando announced that it *was* a different kind of piece.[39] In Still's tone poem, the soloist leads and the orchestra follows.

When the orchestra enters, it takes up the basic melodic and rhythmic materials, including the melodic fragment now played by the celli deeply embedded in the orchestra, and the piano retreats to a support role. Still forefronts the minor second interval, repeats it several times, and recasts it with jazz-inflected harmonizations. The music gradually gains speed and momentum through a syncopated reinterpretation of the eighth-note pattern that pushes the piece forward.

Musical Fig. 4.2: Rhythmic pattern.

While *Kaintuck'* is uniquely its own and reflective of a completely different spirit from that of the urbane, swaggering, and showy *Rhapsody in Blue,* the presence of piano and orchestra coupled with syncopated rhythms and blues-like harmonies, the similar durations (both pieces are indicated to be about fifteen minutes long), and introductory passages of comparable length make comparisons between the two works natural. This observation is not meant to suggest that Still consciously imitated Gershwin's work; I don't believe he did. Given statements that the former made about the latter, it would seem out of character. But symphonic jazz works shared harmonic, rhythmic, and timbral preferences regardless of individual musical materials, and these basic qualities are audible in *Kaintuck'.* Such jazzy, modern sounds initially appear ill at ease within the dreamy, pictorial opening. And then we recall the genesis of the work: a train trip through Kentucky. Five minutes into *Kaintuck'* brass and percussion emerge, the tempo increases, and the ever-flexible eighth-note pattern changes once again. With little effort, one can hear the rhythm of a train chugging along the railroad tracks. Piano figuration adds a "clicking" effect suggestive of the rotating wheels.[40]

Musical Fig. 4.3: Rhythmic pattern.

Still works his way back to the opening mood of the piece via a subdued piano cadenza. (The score indicates: "This cadenza must not be rushed.") Here again the composer thwarts traditional behavior. Rather than build dramatic intensity through a display of pianistic pyrotechnics, as would be typical, Still uses the cadenza to transition back to the calmer and more contemplative condition of the first minute of the piece. But as trains take us

170

from one place to another, Still's ending is not quite a literal return to the starting point. A repeated interval of a second recalls the important interval that characterized the opening, but it is now the descending one, a closing gesture, the one that characterized the overall motion of the melodic fragment. It is now moving from B-flat to A to arrive at G, the tonal center that appeared to elude our hearing until the end of the first section. The work drifts off with soft, low G octaves and a pair of muted major and minor ninth chords suspended above. The train trip through Kentucky provided William Grant Still with both adventure and opportunities for sustained reflection "depicting his emotions as [he] passed through a certain section of Kentucky on a misty summer day,"[41] much as train trips do today. Both are present in *Kaintuck'*.

Still's patriotism is often discussed in conjunction with the strong, public anti-communist stance that he and Verna Arvey articulated beginning in the 1940s; both ideas get conflated with the notion of place. When his patriotism is considered thus, it appears to be a late development, a reaction to political exigencies, and one perhaps exacerbated by the composer's increasing sense of rejection by the most powerful musical circles in the Northeast. But an inclination to celebrate his nation via place seems part of Still's makeup early on, as the existence of *American Suite* attests. Catherine Parsons Smith refers to it as "Still's earliest-known multimovement work for orchestra" and dates its composition as "no later than early 1916."[42] *American Suite* predates the overt nationalistic movements of the 1930s that converted even the most radical of the ultra-modern composers to the cause, as well as the McCarthyism of the late 1940s and early 1950s, which through its intimidation tactics increased patriot rhetoric tenfold. The piece anticipates Still's expanded racial awareness, which emerged when he worked for the first time with W. C. Handy in Memphis during the summer of 1916. *American Suite* and *The American Scene,* composed more than forty years apart are pieces whose titles reveal William Grant Still's long-standing interest in the idea and place called America. Patriotism, anticommunism, and place come together.

Much has been written about Still's anticommunist position because he and his wife spoke and wrote much on the issue themselves. For Still, communism and race were closely connected problems facing America, and he was not alone in this opinion. In May 1949 he addressed the issue of communism at St. Mary's College, in Los Angeles, as part of a talk on problems facing composers of serious music: "I turn now to one tremendous problem that confronts only those composers in our country who are loyal Americans. It is a problem created by the opposition of Communists to all who do not subscribe to their beliefs; a unique problem in that individuals responsible for it cover up so effectively their affiliation with the party.[43]

Still made an even more explicit statement in a talk entitled "Communism in Music," which was presented to the chamber of commerce in San Jose, California, in May 1953; the speech was recorded. He sketched his view of the importance of music to the Soviet agenda in America. He enumerated a "series of coincidences" experienced personally that suggested to him the presence of a "carefully planned campaign on the part of leftists" to make things "uncomfortable for loyal Americans." He talked about "gangsterism in art." And then he named composers who he believed were pawns of the Soviets, knowingly or not. Among them were Roy Harris, Aaron Copland, Leonard Bernstein, Marc Blitzstein, Kurt Weill, Oscar Hammerstein II, Ira Gershwin, and Hans Eisler. He bemoaned that Douglass Moore of Columbia University, in other ways such an admirable gentleman, appeared on "UnAmerican" lists. He recalled that Henry Cowell had been well received in Russia during his tour there, and "regarded as a fellow revolutionary."[44] He stressed his concern for the power these men wielded over America's cultural life as writers, teachers, composers. He cautioned about the ways in which titles and dedications could be used for propaganda purposes. Still closed his speech with a comment on communism and the "racial angle" by observing that for decades, "American Negroes" had been especially targeted by communists as the group that would lead their cause. He concluded that because he had opposed their plans and rejected their overtures to bring him into the fold as a prominent Negro musician, he had been especially targeted. "So both musically and racially I have been opposed."[45] Such a reading, not without some basis in fact, helped Still make sense of his diminishing popularity.

In her essay "'Harlem Renaissance Man' Revisited: The Politics of Race and Class in Still's Late Career," Parsons Smith considers how Still might have arrived at his communist plot theory.[46] She tracks the changing reception that Still's music experienced over the course of the 1940s, noting the patronizing criticisms of Blitzstein and Copland that appeared in prominent music journals, as well as Still's rejection of the Composers' Collective's efforts to incorporate folk idioms without recognizing his own earlier work in that area. Parsons Smith details Still's difficulty with the perception that his music was not "racial" enough, even though the composer had dedicated his life to pursuing integration, assimilation, and universal brotherhood and was vehemently against any kind of black-white opposition or separatist movement. Still did not want to be confined to the role of the spokesman composer, unless it was as a spokesman for all of America.

In addition to the arguments that Smith puts forth, there may have been other, outside influences shaping William Grant Still's thinking. Ultimately, Still's perception of the political situation and his relation to it may have been strengthened by views expressed in *The Crisis,* the journal of the NAACP, with which Still was familiar.[47] His publicly stated opinions were in keeping with that "party" line. When W. E. B. Du Bois founded the journal in 1910, it, like the association, was committed to integrative and assimilative policies. *The Crisis* stressed education as a way to bring black Americans into the dominantly white culture.[48] Fighting Jim Crow laws, whether they were enforced in prisons, the armed services, the Metropolitan Opera, churches, or, more famously, schools, was a major campaign of the association and its journal, from their inception through the Fifties.[49]

But in the April 1948 issue of *The Crisis,* articles and editorials specifically concerned with the communist threat to America's black population began to appear with increasing regularity. An editorial entitled "Keep an Eye on the Communists" compared Czechoslovakia's takeover with the ways in which "for many years American Communists have been trying to 'sweet talk' American Negroes." Two months later, another editorial clarified its position: "NAACP branches should be instruments for carrying out the NAACP program, not that of any political party, and . . . our readers should be alert on this point."[50]

The May 1949 issue carried a scathing criticism of the once-idolized actor and singer Paul Robeson and observed, "The vast majority of [American Negroes] soured on him when he began mixing the Communist Party line with 'Water Boy.'"[51] In October of that year, Robeson was blamed for riots in Peekskill, New York, which critics claimed were provoked by his concert. *The Crisis* found itself in the awkward position of defending the rights of the communists to assemble while faulting New York's governor Dewey for failing to anticipate the inevitable confrontation between incensed veterans and the singer's communist followers. During the following year headlines such as these appeared: "Communist Smear," "The Moscow Ghetto," and "American Negro Problem in the European Press," with explanatory comments such as, "The propaganda war between Russia and the USA gives timely interest to this article." There was a lengthy story by Walter White in the August–September 1950 issue, "The Negro and the Communists."[52] White laid out his understanding of the role that communists had played in the famed Scottsboro case: communists "capitalize on Negro unrest in the United States." "Communist tricks" had tried to undermine the efforts of the NAACP in the case. In a paragraph subtitled "Remedy for Communism," White asserted: "There is but one effective and intelligent way in which to counteract Communist efforts at proselytizing among American Negroes, and that method is drastic revision of the almost chronic American indifference to the Negroes' plight. . . . In brief, the only antidote to the spread among American Negroes of revolutionary doctrine is even-handed justice."[53]

The next year Herbert Hill wrote his own exposé of communist tactics directed at American Negroes, in an article entitled "Communist Party, Enemy of Negro Equality."[54] After detailing the history of communist attempts to weaken America by advocating that Negroes separate from the U.S. government, Hill concluded: "To preach separation . . . is to advocate a more vicious form of segregation."[55] Still had always been disinclined toward any policies or practices that separated the races, that pitted black against white. These and other articles encouraging Americans to "fight against godless Communism" kept the issue hot for years.[56]

It was in this environment that William Grant Still assessed his own situation and interpreted his diminishing status. It was also in this environment that, later in his life, Still composed and arranged a number of pieces celebrating the nation: *To You, America* (1951) was commissioned by the U.S. Military Academy at West Point; he arranged *America: A Vision* (1953), a piece by Mabel Bean; and in *The American Scene* (1957), an extended work, he provided a musical tour of different regions.[57] A series of folk suites composed in the 1950s and 1960s presented songs from various cultures and folk idioms in the Americas. Knowledge of the larger cultural-political climate helps one to understand Still's later place pieces celebrating the United States.

The American Scene, composed in 1957, is an orchestral work comprising five separate suites. Each has a different dedicatee and offers a musical depiction of some aspect of the United States. Although it is not discussed in any of the literature on the piece, a subtitle, "Five Suites for Young Americans," that appears on copies of the score suggests the quasi-political agenda informing the piece. When the work was premiered on 20 January 1959, only one movement, "Tribal Dance," from the suite "The Old West," was performed. In ensuing years other movements from different suites were combined, programmed, and played over radio and in various cities. But Still's music waited until 18 November 1990 to be played in its entirety; this took place in Memphis, Tennessee. The breadth of Still's sense of America as a place (and perhaps his experience of it as well) is suggested in the titles:

Suite 1. The East

    I.   On the Village Green (Graceful Dancers)
    II.   Berkshire Night (Tranquillity)
    III.   Manhattan Skyline (New York, the Gracious City)

Suite 2. The South

I.   Florida Night (Soft Loveliness)
II. Levee Land (Birthplace of Blues and Spirituals)
III. A New Orleans Street (The Festive Spirit of Yesterday)

Suite 3. The Old West

I.   Song of the Plainsmen
II. Sioux Love Song (Based on a Sioux Melody)
III. Tribal Dance

Suite 4. The Far West

I.   The Plaza (Los Angeles) (Latin American Charm and Grace)
II. Sundown Land (A Mysterious Land, Far beyond the Golden West)
III. Navaho Country (Based on a Navaho Melody)

Suite 5. The Southwest: A Mountain, a Memorial, and a Song

I.   Grand Teton (A Symbol of America's Strength)
II. Tomb of the Unknown Soldier (Our Boys Will Never Be Forgotten)
III. Song of the Rivermen (They Sing of the Mississippi)

The suites favor those regions where Still spent significant periods of time: the South, the East, and the West, with the western half of the nation receiving most attention. Perhaps this is an indication of his preference for those climes and the proportion of his years spent there. In two pieces, "Sioux Love Song" and "Navaho Country," Still indicated that his music was based on indigenous melodies. Given his sensitivity to white composers borrowing the music of their black colleagues without attribution, it is good to see him acknowledging his own sources.[58]

Still developed a general curiosity about "expressing American ideas" in music during his studies with Chadwick, but if he was looking for reinforcement of his interest in American Indian music, he had to look no further than his friend the Los Angeles composer Charles Wakefield Cadman (1881–1946).[59] Cadman shared many of Still's opinions regarding communism, as well as his love of opera. Born in Pennsylvania, Cadman moved to Los Angeles in 1917. Prior to his arrival there he had become deeply interested in Native American music, recorded it, and arranged collections of tunes and dances. Still arrived in New York in the same season that Cadman's Indianist opera *Shanewis* was produced at the Metropolitan 1918–19. A decade later it was broadcast over NBC radio; it is possible that Still heard this program. In 1922 Cadman's operatic cantata *The Sunset Trail* premiered in Denver, Colorado. Still would have been encouraged by Cadman's operatic successes and taken them as a sign that his own operas stood a chance of being performed. Both men sought to fuse their nation's European musical inheritance with other indigenous and African traditions to create an American music.

Still was also aware of the efforts of another, older contemporary composer interested in American Indian music, Arthur Farwell (1872–1952). Still's library contained a copy of Farwell's 1901 collection published by G. Schirmer, entitled *American Indian Melodies Harmonized by Arthur Farwell.* While living in California, Farwell became Roy Harris's composition teacher and enthusiastic promoter. But beyond his role as personal booster of Harris, Farwell had secured his place in American music history as the founder of Wa-Wan Press (1901–11), which provided an outlet for American composers, especially those who used indigenous sources. Farwell's press was the principal publisher of many American composers, including Cadman and Farwell himself. Direct and indirect reinforcement from these two, combined with Still's own efforts to educate himself about American Indian music, provided the composer with some background for his *American Scene.*

Suite 4, "The Far West," reveals Still's embrace of America's numerous cultures within a single brief suite: the first movement, "The Plaza (Los Angeles)," is inspired by the echoes of Latin America that one can hear in that city; the last movement depicts the sounds of Navaho country. They are separated by a dreamy meditation on lands that lie beyond the West. The suite's dedication to the Pasadena Inter-racial Woman's Club acknowledges Still's hopes for an integrated America.[60] Still demonstrated his sensitivity to orchestral timbre with instrumental choices and combinations that evoked each of the cultures, while his unencumbered melodies revealed his lyrical gifts so often commented upon by reviewers. As Murchison observes: "Still's musical aesthetic placed an emphasis on melody and music that an audience could find easily accessible"; *The American Scene* is wholly accessible.[61]

Still instructed his instrumentalists to play "The Plaza" "daintily." High woodwinds articulate a soft, gentle, rhythmic figure, which is answered delicately by staccato strings.

Additional instruments join in and the timbral call and response continues its polite exchange, never exceeding a *mezzo piano* dynamic level. Xylophone octaves glisten; one can almost hear the sunshine glinting off the plaza. At the pickup to rehearsal 4, Still introduces a sweeping, slightly syncopated melody in the upper strings that fits neatly with the rhythmic motive heard in the first measure. The Latin presence is everywhere in the rhythm of the tune.

The melody never rises above *mezzo forte* and reaches that level only momentarily before returning to its soft-spoken *mezzo piano.* At the pickup to

Ex. 4.2: *The American Scene, The Far West: The Plaza,* mm 1–4. Courtesy of William Grant Still Music. Used by permission.

rehearsal 5, Still recalls the opening rhythm with a subtle use of maracas and claves. (In case the cultural reference has been missed thus far, these instruments clarify the inspiration of this piece as Latin American.) The broad string melody returns for a second chorus, now sung an octave higher. As the pitch rises, dynamic levels increase as well. This second iteration moves from *mezzo forte* to occasional *fortes,* but always maintaining an easy, graceful sway. The presence of mutes on trumpets (which make a very brief appearance and then are to be played "elegantly"), and lower strings, assures that the increased volume of sound does not precipitate a change of mood. The piece is not looking to make a profound statement, but rather to capture a pleasant scene. At rehearsal 7 the opening alternating patterns of woodwinds and strings reap-

Ex. 4.3: *The American Scene, The Far West: The Plaza,* melody at rehearsal 4. Courtesy of William Grant Still Music. Used by permission.

pear, only this time with augmented woodwinds. As the piece fades away on the pulses of the sixteenth-note rhythm, castanets click a first and final gesture, and a curtain is drawn on the tableau. The piece lasts just over two minutes, and yet in that brief span William Grant Still has evoked aspects of a rich musical culture, one that has benefited from influences beyond the traditional European ones that so dominated America's early musical history.

"Sundown Land" is a melancholic meditation between the two rhythmic framing movements. Soft gong strokes introduce the work, hang in the air, and then dissipate. The flute sings a dissonant, weary melody. Like "The Plaza," this movement confines itself to a quiet dynamic world never venturing beyond *mezzo forte*. But where the first sounded light and easygoing, the softness of "Sundown Land" suggests enervation, uncertainty, and resignation. Again Still is a master melodist, clearing an aural path for even the least musically sophisticated listener to follow. As a final melodic fragment outlines an ambiguous tritone, the music seems to point to an unknown future "far beyond."

Still ends his "Far West" suite with a lively, upbeat evocation of Native American culture complete with tom-toms, rattles, and bells. In "Navaho Country" mutes are eliminated, sharp accents articulate strong rhythms, and for the first time the music soars in the *forte* and *fortissimo* range. If the second movement appeared hesitant and uncertain, this is firmly grounded and self-assured. Series of open fifths in the horns and melodic fifths in the strings, all set off by ascending trombone glissandi and pounding tom-toms, combine to create a spacious musical landscape that, while not necessarily authentic, served at the time to conjure aural images of "Indians" for many composers—Dvořák and Ives included (see Ex. 4.4).[62]

Musical materials are extremely limited but gain their power by repetition and intensification. Throughout the two-minute movement, rhythm is monotonously constant. Every measure of the score, save three measures preceding rehearsal 19, contains an accent on beat 1. With a tempo of a quarter note at 144, this means that accented beats occur with fast-paced regularity.

A fragmentary melody emerges at rehearsal 17 in piccolo, flutes, and clarinets. It rides upon strings thumping out their accented downbeat rhythms. Woodwind and brass answer the melody with a two-measure response that echoes the sixteenth-dotted-eighth rhythm that characterizes the "tune" (see Ex. 4.5).

Pitting instrumental families against each other is a favorite device of Still and one that he uses to great effect. The five-plus-two-measure melody begins again an octave higher and then repeats with a modified ending. Eight measures before rehearsal 19, Still composes a broad hemiola that reinterprets the unceasing pulse as a big two. Without giving up the repetitive rhythm he

Ex. 4.4: *The American Scene, The Far West: Navaho Country*, mm 1–4. Courtesy of William Grant Still Music. Used by permission.

breathes life, and much needed contrast, into the piece. He repeats this gesture before returning to the opening string material, which is now combined with the stuttering sixteenth-dotted-eighth rhythm in the high winds. It is at this point that Still includes three muted trumpets whose repeated *forte* fanfare figurations add both volume and intensity to the piece as it drives to its end. At the last measure cymbals join in for the first time, and the music crescendos to a final *fortissimo*.

Although Still commandeers rhythms, tunes, and instruments often associated with American Indian music, he combines these with other more traditional sounds to create an authentic American hybrid. Orchestral harps and bowed string instruments of the type Still uses in "Navaho Country" have no place in this particular Native American culture. The same can be said of the woodwind and brass instruments that he employs, although wood flutes would have been possible. Still's fast triple meter is also questionable. The overwhelming majority of Navaho music is in duple. Such obvious deviations from the most basic expectations of Native American music call into question the validity of Still's tribute to the Navahos. And yet, Still was not seeking to educate his public or to present an ethnomusicological study of America's

Ex. 4.5: *The American Scene, The Far West: Navaho Country,* rehearsal 17. Courtesy of William Grant Still Music. Used by permission.

native people. His intention was to suggest the breadth of America, its places, and its culture; his hope was that through his music, he might bring its diverse peoples together. Purists might find his use of musical stereotypes damaging, but for the audience Still was hoping to reach, these were sounds they understood; they spoke of a version of America in which they believed.

ROY HARRIS

Cimarron

Tapping into a vision of the nation that Americans were eager to embrace, regardless of its completeness or basis in reality, proved to be the specialty of

Roy Harris (1898–1979), a contemporary of William Grant Still. He capital-ized unabashedly on the still-resonant agrarian myth of national settlement and on Frederick Jackson Turner's related frontier thesis. Among twentieth-century composers, few have exhibited a more self-conscious Americanism than Harris. Not given to subtlety or equivocation, Harris's often proprietary remarks on the topic drew strong responses from the press. He made much of his log cabin roots and sharing a birthday with Abraham Lincoln: "The shadow of Abe Lincoln has hovered over my life from childhood. This was, I suppose, inevitable, for the very simple reason that my birthday fell on the national holiday honoring Lincoln's birth."[63] A 1935 *Time* magazine article seized upon the phrase "Log Cabin Composer" for its title, thereby reinforc-ing Harris's connection to the president and, coincidentally, to Anthony Philip Heinrich, the early nineteenth-century Bohemian immigrant first iden-tified by that expression and another who had been determined to portray himself as thoroughly American.[64] Inevitable or not, Harris parlayed his coin-cidence of birth into a type of divine sanction.

In 1940 the composer and critic Virgil Thomson charged: "No composer in the world, not even in Italy or Germany, makes such shameless use of patriotic feelings to advertise his product. One would think, to read his pref-aces, that he had been awarded by God, or at least by popular vote, a monopo-listic privilege of expressing our nation's deepest ideals and highest aspirations."[65] Given the political climate of the time, with totalitarian re-gimes deciding the appropriateness of various types of music to their individ-ual causes, Thomson's comparison of Harris with composers in Italy and Germany was particularly pointed. Harris's popularity peaked in the 1930s and 1940s, an era when a premium was placed on developing a national musi-cal idiom, a voice that was unmistakably American. He enthusiastically re-sponded to that climate, and the climate responded to him. Thereafter, even after such flag-waving movements had gone out of favor, Roy Harris was still closely identified with musical Americanism.

He consistently evokes the nation in his music. Many of his more than two hundred works refer to the idea and ideals of America in a general way; occasionally, however, Harris binds those ideas to a specific place. In such instances he moves beyond musical nationalism to a celebration of the Ameri-can places with which he was personally familiar.[66] Over a career that spanned five decades, Harris set the poetry of the American writers Walt Whitman, Vachel Lindsay, and Carl Sandburg. In 1929 he wrote *American Portrait;* this was later followed by *When Johnny Comes Marching Home: An American Over-ture* (1935), based upon the Civil War song by Patrick S. Gilmore, and *Ameri-can Creed* (1940), both for orchestra; and *American Ballads* for solo piano

(1942–45), two sets of works inspired by such tunes as "Streets of Laredo," "Wayfaring Stranger," and "Black Is the Color of My True Love's Hair." His Symphony No. 4, "Folksong Symphony" (1940), the only one of his symphonies to include a chorus, was based upon American folk songs culled from John A. Lomax's collection *Cowboy Songs and Other Frontier Ballads* and Carl Sandburg's *An American Songbag.* His sixth symphony (1944) was inspired by Lincoln's Gettysburg Address. Roy Harris's one-movement *Epilogue to Profiles in Courage: JFK* premiered in 1964. In the last decade of his life, Harris was especially concerned with the environment and with race and discrimination in America. *Whether This Nation,* a work for chorus and orchestra written in 1970, and his Bicentennial Symphony of 1976 reflect his sensitivity to these issues.

Harris championed his country in a general way, yet he also helped to perpetuate one of its favorite myths—a myth of the American West. Although as a composer he was best known for symphonic and chamber works, perhaps no piece better reflects Harris's identification with the West than his first symphonic overture for band written in 1941, a work entitled *Cimarron.*

In choosing the name *Cimarron,* Harris associated his piece with a range of references that included, among other things, an infamous western territory, a popular novel by Edna Ferber, and an Academy Award–winning film.[67] According to notes accompanying Harris's score, "*Cimarron* relates one of the most stirring tales of the early American frontier"; it celebrates the last land rush into the Oklahoma territory, a region popularly known as Cimarron Country.[68] Harris dedicated the piece to his native state of Oklahoma.[69] For one born in the town of Chandler, Oklahoma, in 1898, the word "Cimarron" would conjure myriad images. The Lincoln County area had been settled in 1891 during one of six land rushes that took place between 1889 and 1895. Harris drew upon stories told by his parents, the already richly embroidered myths of the American West, and the conscious efforts of critics and friends to shape a composer-persona vested in the frontier.[70]

It seemed to matter little that Harris's mother, Laura Broddle, was English by birth and had met his Iowa-born father, Elmer Ellsworth Harris, in Lake Arrowhead, California, a town less than eighty miles northeast of Los Angeles; in Roy Harris literature, they were Oklahoma pioneers and Harris was a child of that soil.[71] Nor did Harris or the critics bent on packaging him as fresh from the prairies distinguish between the West as a compass direction, or geographical region, and "the West" as a cultural construct.[72] Myths mixed with reality.[73] Although Harris's parents moved *east* from California to Oklahoma sometime between 1891 and 1895, lived there until 1903, and then returned to the Golden State when Harris was just five years old, their journey eastward was in effect a move to "the West." California may have had gold and been the farthest one could venture before encountering the Pacific, but "the West," as any red-blooded American citizen knew, meant cowboys, and the Oklahoma territory was teeming with both cattle and cowboys. In the American imagination, Oklahoma was much farther west than California. (California was also home to cowboys, but they had perhaps been eclipsed by the 1848 gold rush.) In Harris literature, Oklahoma would become the source of his Americanism.

Selling Harris's "westernness" often meant downplaying or recasting other important influences. The most conspicuous of these were his three years of study in Paris (1926–29) with Nadia Boulanger, initially made possible by the financial backing of that most New York of patrons, Alma Wertheim. It is conceivable that Harris could just as easily have marketed himself as a European-trained modernist as a man of the Oklahoma territory, had the social and political climate of Depression-era America been different. Beth E. Levy has systematically traced Roy Harris's westernization and cites numerous examples of the process as they appeared in contemporary books and journals. Among the "first steps on Harris's westward migration" that she notes are remarks made by Paul Rosenfeld in his 1929 book, *An Hour with American Music*. Where "the young Oklahoman" was characterized as rugged and heroic, "one of the chief potentialities of American music." Rosenfeld used that most powerful of western icons, the cowboy, when he noted "a certain irregularity and looseness" in Harris's melodic contours. He likened this musical behavior to "a body reeling from side to side, staggering a little and yet never actually losing its balance." He reasoned, "cowboys walk in that fashion, extremely awkwardly and extremely lithely; and so personal a piece as the scherzo of Harris's sextet brings to mind nothing so much as the image of a little cowboy running and reeling about on the instruments, toppling but never falling." Rosenfeld, a modernist critic, also linked Harris's Scotch-Irish heritage with the American folksong tradition, and particularly with cowboy ballads, and concluded "very few American composers, indeed, very few composers throughout the world, give greater promises of growth than this awkward, serious young plainsman."[74] Fully aware of Harris's European studies and New York connections, still Rosenfeld identified Harris as a "plainsman" and zeroed in on his Oklahoma birth.

Three years later Arthur Farwell wrote the first important scholarly article on Roy Harris, the catchword of which was "vitality." Harris had studied with Farwell in California for about a year in 1924. The two grew to be close friends, and Farwell became Harris's greatest champion. By 1932, with only a single Harris work published, Farwell claimed that "a peculiar feeling of *vital-*

ity attaches to the mention of [Harris's] name"; Farwell detected a "mental *vitality* and breadth" and Harris's "determination to work out a new, *vital* and creative way in every musical sphere."[75] In summing up Harris's rhythmic innovations, Farwell noted that "such effects give much of Harris' music an overflowing restless energy which stirs the blood and lifts the hearer, if indeed he can follow, to new levels of *vitality*." Finally, Farwell made the important connection between Harris's vitality and the West. Explaining the source of the composer's "new vision of music's potentialities," his teacher-champion pointed to "his spiritual standpoint, the free Western soul's sense of what life is today in its most *vital* realizable meaning."[76] The notion of vitality, organicism, growing from the soil, would eventually help explain Harris's theory of musical organicism and "autogenesis," Harris's term for "the principle underlying [his] concept of form."[77]

Farwell's emphasis on the West was not accidental or unprompted. On numerous occasions during the course of his studies in Paris and thereafter, Harris wrote to Farwell. His letters expose alternately a humble idealist and a man in possession of a remarkably inflated ego. The complete correspondence also reveals both composers' concern with the need for America to develop its own musical culture, "a new *Great Culture* of the world," and, not incidentally, Harris's appropriateness for the job.[78]

Preparations for Farwell's *Musical Quarterly* article prompted additional exchanges, letters in which Harris, building upon the image already circulating in the press, encouraged his teacher to focus on his westernness: "I especially hope that you will stress the Western influence as opposed to the Eastern European influence."[79] He reminded his teacher of the earlier Rosenfeld comments and of John Tasker Howard's assessment in his 1931 book, *Our American Music:* "In some respects Roy Harris is the white hope of the nationalists, for this raw-boned Oklahoman has the Southwest in his blood. And he puts it into his music."[80] Farwell followed Harris's lead. His article explained: "Leaving his original West, he went abroad to steep himself in technical resources. Now he feels the urge to go back and identify himself again with the Western earth-rhythm, the Western social consciousness, to refresh and reinforce his original vision and integrate it with his newly gained expressional resource."[81] The West becomes the new mantra. Harris's years "abroad" are reduced to an extended technical exercise; the name of the famous French pedagogue with whom he studied is never mentioned at all. Thereafter, Harris's western pedigree was assumed.

Over the next decade the western theme would echo in comments by Nicolas Slonimsky and Henry Taylor Parker, and in another John Tasker Howard book, *Our Contemporary Composers,* in which the author made plain the hopes riding on the man from Oklahoma: "When he first appeared on the scene, in the late 'twenties, he seemed the answer to all our prayers. Here was a genuine American, born in a log cabin in Oklahoma, like Lincoln, tall, lanky, rawboned, untouched by the artificial refinements of Europe or even the stultifying commercialism of cosmopolitan New York; a prophet from the Southwest who thought in terms of our raciest folk-tunes. Small wonder that we called him the white hope of American music."[82]

Here, Harris's years in France were not simply downplayed or ignored, they were denied. Physical comparisons with Abraham Lincoln, the greatest American hero since George Washington, were offered up; Harris was no longer merely a composer, he was a prophet. While the frontier was but one of the many environments in which Harris lived, it was *the* place with which he identified and was identified. Beginning in the 1930s, as America's musical modernists turned away from their insular, dissonant, international idioms and embraced a more nationalistically informed and accessible musical discourse, Harris understood the valuable cachet of his natal West in defining himself as American. As the eastern vanguard *studied* folk songs, he simply recalled them from his youth. In no uncertain terms, Harris assumed the intellectual equivalent to the *droits de seigneur* when it came to identifying with this region of the country. What better composer to write *Cimarron?* The "city boys" could never be legitimately western.[83]

The Many Manifestations of Cimarron

Among the most "western" of western places in American myth was the region now known as Oklahoma; it was here that the word "cimarron" came to life again and again. The Cimarron is a river running close to seven hundred miles from northeast New Mexico through Colorado and Kansas to the Arkansas River in northeastern Oklahoma. Today tourists can walk along portions of the "Dry Cimarron Scenic Byway" in New Mexico, but in the nineteenth century the trail along the often parched river was one of the major wagon train routes to the West. Violent storms, unreliable water supplies, and the presence of Indians made travel along this route extremely dangerous.[84]

In addition, Cimarron was a city in southwestern Kansas where a bloody confrontation took place on 12 January 1889. Townsfolk fought over which city, Cimarron or Ingalls, would receive the honor of being named the county seat. Backroom deals were cut, records were spirited away, a man was killed, others were wounded. The governor sent in the militia, and eventually Cimarron won. This was only three and a half months before President William Henry Harrison opened two million acres of territory for the first Oklahoma land run, on 22 April 1889. With Dodge City just twenty miles to the east, here were the stomping grounds of Bat Masterson, Wyatt Earp, and Doc Holliday, just a few of the men whose real actions and activities fueled the legends that would grow around them.[85]

In still another incarnation, *cimarron,* a Spanish word meaning "wild" or "untamed," was used to identify the two-hundred-mile-long panhandle region of the Oklahoma Territory once known as No-Man's Land.[86] It was also the name of the westernmost county in the panhandle, home to miles of the Santa Fe trail, and, at nearly five thousand feet, the highest point in the territory, the Black Mesa. The county bordered Texas to the south, New Mexico to the west, and Colorado and Kansas to the north, the only one in the country to border four states. The Cimarron was traditionally Indian territory (as was all of Oklahoma), home to the plains Indians: the Osage, Arapaho, and Comanche, among others.[87] This was a land of fertile prairies and endless plains—and roaming horse thieves and other criminals. White men who ventured into this ungoverned domain in the middle years of the nineteenth century did so at great risk. Conditions were primitive and Indian confrontations commonplace. The Comanche were especially protective of their territories and aggressively fought intruders, killing more whites in proportion to their numbers than any other tribe. Given the treatment that many Indians had received at the hands of white men in the early decades of the nineteenth century, the depth of their hostility toward pioneers was understandable, even if their killing sprees were not. Of all the North American Indian groups, the plains Indians would be the last to capitulate to white encroachment. Their actions would help keep Indian issues in the news well into the early decades of the twentieth century.[88]

Those pioneers who waited until the land rushes of 1889–95 to settle the territory were only slightly less daring than their mid-century predecessors. Though Indian confrontations may not have been as great a threat as thirty-five years earlier—a result of U.S. government policies that systematically "relocated" Indians, thus minimizing the likelihood of encounters—the basic challenges to survival that accompanied forays into this territory provided all the materials needed for adventure tales and legend making. Stories of Roy Harris's parents being among the later groups of pioneers staking their claim in one of the final land rushes, Harris's birth in a log cabin, his being brought up on corn bread and sweet milk—all became part of the composer's myth. Like many novels set in the West, the story of Roy Harris was one that mixed fact and fiction. However, a propensity for hyperbolic prose paired with a peripatetic lifestyle may be authentic manifestations of Harris's real frontier roots.[89]

More often than referring to a specific river or county or confrontation, however, "cimarron" was used to refer to the general region; people talked of "Cimarron Country." The name was synonymous with images of the frontier—open land, rugged men, strong women, brave scouts, resourceful settlers, dangerous natives, lonesome cowboys—America at its earthiest. In turning to the West, Harris drew from his own personal history and capitalized upon the nation's fascination with that image-rich region. He understood the symbolic power of the West as representing the most American of places, and he used his association with it to promote himself as the most American of composers.[90] While Harris did have a legitimate claim to his western persona, he also consciously manipulated it and benefited from the cachet attached to the West, a cachet that developed and coalesced in the final decades of the nineteenth century.

At the beginning of the twentieth century, two myths of the American West prevailed: one closely associated with Buffalo Bill and his Wild West Extravaganza, which portrayed cowboys and scouts violently wresting the region from natural and native foes; and a second summarized by the historian Frederick Jackson Turner, who, in his thesis on the significance of the frontier, pointed to pioneers, farmers, and merchants peacefully settling the wilderness in steady waves expanding across the nation.[91] The land grabs of 1889–95 were among the last waves, although they differed from more gradual settlement patterns in the nature of the territory being claimed, the widespread organization of the efforts, the eclectic mix of participants, and the frenzied speed of their accomplishment. Different as these explanations were, both William Cody and Frederick Jackson Turner focused on the unique role that nature played in helping shape the American character. Europe may have had cities and cultivation, but America had nature—nature in embarrassing abundance. The Cimarron Country land rushes, when the U.S. government gave away millions of acres to those fast and clever enough to claim it, were evidence of that abundance.

Turner's 1893 thesis, conceived and delivered just four years after the initial Oklahoma land grab, provided many Americans with the first systematic explanation of their growing nation and culture. Although Turner's thoroughness was a matter of debate, it was nevertheless an explanation rooted in the soil.[92] The dissemination of his vision was quick and widespread. Nineteenth-century writers, artists, philosophers, politicians, and business entrepreneurs agreed that the western frontier was what made America unique. And if the young University of Wisconsin historian didn't get the word out, a genuine western scout known as Buffalo Bill did.[93] By all accounts, Buffalo Bill's Wild West Extravaganza was the most successful entertainment of its type, a three-hour spectacle of calf roping, bareback riding, sharpshooting, and Indian fighting. It featured a cast of hundreds. Hundreds of thousands of spectators on both sides of the Atlantic saw their mythical cowboy hero.

It was Buffalo Bill's version of the West that dime novelists of the 1880s and 1890s seized upon; their ability to create mythical figures and situations using the scantiest measure of fact was matched only by the public's insatiable appetite for such stories.[94] These works provided a model for Harris's own autobiographical fantasy. But novels set in "the West" began earlier than Buffalo Bill's appearance on the scene. Among the very first dime novels were those published by Erastus Beadle in New York in 1860, with the most famous of the western novels, Edward S. Ellis's "Seth Jones; or, The Captives of the Frontier," appearing that year.[95] Soon, similar tales of adventure and romance set in various locations fed the ready market of soldiers on the fronts. A summary of their success appeared in an announcement 20 December 1864: "Up to April 1st, an aggregate of five millions of Beadle's Dime Books had been put in circulation, of which half at least were novels, nearly a third songs, and the remainder hand-books, biographies, etc. . . . The sales of single novels by popular authors often amounted to nearly forty thousand in two or three months."[96]

By the 1880s Beadle's dime novels had begun to feel the effects of competition, but tales of the West continued to sell. In large measure this was because of William Cody's presence in the cultural consciousness. Beadle's *Half-Dime Library* was still published every Tuesday in the 1880s and sold by local newsdealers and at railroad stations. Its stories typically ranged in length from eight to fifteen pages. Later, in the 1890s, Beadle's *Dime Library* stories increased in length, a few running as long as forty-five pages. A stable of authors churned out dozens of adventure stories, and though the setting for the tales was not restricted to the American West or even the United States, that region of the country inspired the overwhelming majority of titles. The historian John T. McIntyre observes: "Fascinating people came into the old romances of the frontier. The noble savage made his first appearance in these fictions, as did the hunter with his wondrous love of the woods; footprints became important things for, perhaps, the first time in history. This type of story . . . was the first absolutely American thing; it had rooted itself deeply and, as can be seen, persists in various forms today."[97]

John W. Osborn, one of the more productive authors in Beadle's stable, listed "The Brand Burners of Cimarron," "Cactus Burr: The Man from Hard Luck," "Old Buckeye: The Sierra Shadow," and "Gold-Dust Dan, the Trail Patrol" among his many offerings. Buffalo Bill–inspired tales were so plentiful that they warranted their own category within the Beadle *Library:* columns and columns of titles were listed. Colonel P. Ingraham wrote most of these stories, although Buffalo Bill was credited with writing some of them himself. Not only was the western scout-turned-showman on the road with his extravaganza, he was also at his desk writing a version of the West that would live on once the spectacular show had closed.[98] Cody's death at age seventy-two in 1917 resonated across the nation: President Woodrow Wilson wrote a letter of sympathy, Chief Jack Red Cloud of the Oglala Sioux Indians of South Dakota sent condolences, and the State of California sent "an official Resolution in Memoriam" expressing "its appreciation of the courage and fearlessness of this, our last frontiersman."[99] Harris did not need to invent such a persona for himself, he needed only to assume a role ready-made in fact and fiction.

The dime novels contained all the essential ingredients for perpetuating the romantic myths of the West, as Osborn's story "The Brand Burners of Cimarron" demonstrates. It is set in the fictitious locale of Tiptop City, Oklahoma, a town "fairly thronged with people." Readers immediately learn of the exotic mix of folks who inhabit the place: "Ranchmen, farmers, traders, Indians, and Negroes made up the motley crowd."[100] An outlaw band intent on stealing and rebranding a herd of cattle descends upon the frontier town. The intruders kidnap and hold for ransom important citizens of Tiptop, including the requisite young woman. There follows a dizzying series of plot twists and turns, multiple escapes from certain death, battles at corrals, horse chases, heroic rescues, and shoot-outs. It is only through the brave actions of a posse headed by Pawnee Bill, "a quarter-blood who was the deputy marshal," that the outlaws led by Spanish John are ultimately trapped "and thus . . . one of the most dangerous bands that ever infested fair Oklahoma destroyed."[101] In Osborn's tale, a "quarter-blood" is accorded hero status; this was not always the case in a time and place better known for its disparaging attitudes toward Native Americans. Pawnee Bill's mixed heritage did make him a more exotic character, and someone well equipped to negotiate the cultural clashes that were a regular feature of frontier life.

But romantic heroes were not all that distinguished the West. The place itself, boasting a topography unlike anything in the East, took on its own significance. Sometimes the novels contained poetic descriptions of the land, as does the opening paragraph of Frederick Dewey's "Cimarron Jack, the King-Pin of Rifle-Shots; or, The Phantom Tracker, a Tale of the Land of Silence."[102] "It was a sultry, scorching day on the banks of the river Gila—very sultry and silent. The sun in the zenith looked whitely down and the yellow banks reflected its rays fiercely on the sluggishly-creeping warm river. Away over the flat glistening plain reigned the utmost silence. As far as the eye could reach it saw nothing—only dead level, dead heat, and dead silence. Here, mile upon mile from civilization, hundreds of miles away from any habitation, this vast wilderness stretched away—always level, always hazy, always silent—a spectral land."[103]

In almost all cases, authors combined elements of fact and fantasy. In Dewey's tale the Gila River is real, but the land is *ghostly,* a place of immense nothingness. Osborn's town of Tiptop is fictitious, but the Oklahoma Territory is an actual place. Such blended approaches to telling the story of the West remained the norm well into the twentieth century. It might be argued that the West grew even more real as fact and fiction wove themselves together.

To understand the inspiration behind Harris's piece, one needs to appreciate the singular importance of land rushes to Oklahoma's history. His *Cimarron* is as much about that series of events as it is about any other aspect of the West, as his program note attests. Perhaps the most engaging source of this history is a novel by Edna Ferber published in 1929; it too was entitled *Cimarron*. Ferber prepared her readers for the mythlike quality of her story with a matter-of-fact foreword. Readers quickly learned how much the West was dependent upon legend.

> Only the more fantastic and improbable events contained in this book are true. There is no attempt to set down a literal history of Oklahoma. All the characters, the towns, and many of the happenings contained herein are imaginary. But through reading the scant available records, documents, and histories (including the Oklahoma State Historical Library collection) and through many talks with men and women who have lived in Oklahoma since the day of the opening, something of the spirit, the color, the movement, the life of that incredible commonwealth has, I hope, been caught. Certainly the Run, the Sunday service in the gambling tent, the death of Isaiah and of Arita Red Feather, the catching of the can of nitro-glycerin, many of the shooting affrays, most descriptive passages, all of the oil phase, and the Osage Indian material complete—they are based on actual happenings. In many cases material entirely true was discarded as unfit for use because it was so melodramatic, so absurd as to be too strange for the realm of fiction.
>
> Anything can have happened in Oklahoma. Practically everything has.[104]

Edna Ferber (1885–1968), a Michigan-born member of New York's urbane Algonquin Round Table, had no personal connection with "the West," but she understood the powerful stories contained therein.[105] Her knowledge of Oklahoma history was the result of a ten-day trip to the state and meticulous research. But according to a *New York Times* story, beyond her research skills her success as a novelist could be traced to "her love of the United States (which she found 'varied, dazzling and unique') and to a somewhat uncanny ability to project herself into any environment."[106] Ferber's 1924 novel *So Big,* set in turn-of-the-century Chicago, won a Pulitzer Prize. In 1926 the Midwesterner explored Mississippi River life in *Show Boat,* which was adapted as a musical in 1927 by Jerome Kern and Oscar Hammerstein II, and was made into films in 1936 and 1951. In 1929 Ferber trained her eye on another American story as it played itself out in Cimarron Country. She captured the flavor of the people and the place with keenness usually reserved for insiders. She took time to create sympathetic characters and comment upon conditions peculiar to the Oklahoma Territory. Her novel was adapted to film in 1931 and won Academy Awards for best picture and best screenplay. *Cimarron* was also nominated in five other categories, including best actor (Richard Dix) and best actress (Irene Dunn, who also starred in *Show Boat* in 1936). It was the first western genre film to be so honored.[107] A 1960 remake of the film testified to America's long romance with the West.

Ferber's *Cimarron* revolves around the actions of a fictitious pioneer named Yancey Cravat, one of the early boomers of the Indian territory, a composite character who personifies the West. As with John Osborn's Pawnee Bill, no one in the novel is certain of Yancey's history: "They say he has Indian blood in him. . . . He was raised in a tepee; a wickiup had been his bedroom, a blanket his rope. . . . He had dwelt, others whispered, in that sinister strip, thirty-four miles wide and almost two hundred miles long, called No-Man's Land as early as 1854."[108] His sympathy with the plight of the Osage Indians feeds the settlers' curiosity. Yancey is larger than life—the editor of the frontier-town newspaper *The Oklahoma Wigwam,* a preacher, a lawyer, and a one-man moral crusade. He strides around the region dressed in an oversize *white* hat and high boots. Long before Superman was a hero, bullets were bouncing off Yancey Cravat. He often speaks in measured verse. Yancey, however, is also an adventurer, a restless mover, a man who can't be tied down to a single place. In the course of the story he leaves his family on multiple occasions, being gone five years at one time and twenty years at another. His lengthy absences draw out unsuspected strengths from his loved ones, most especially his wife, Sabra. He is a powerful presence throughout the novel, whether on the scene or not.

In both fiction and reality, the West was a land where people could go to make or remake their fortune, where they could make or remake their identity. It was a place to start up or start over, again and again. As such, the specific details of a person's history were of less consequence than in the old-family, *Mayflower*-conscious East. The absence of systematic record keeping in the region may have been as much a cause as an effect of this attitude. The Harris biography, with its numerous uncertainties regarding his early years, benefits from this condition.

When Yancey, just back from "The Run" of 22 April 1889, tells his story, we learn something of Roy Harris's folklore heritage.

> Folks, there's never been anything like it since Creation. Creation! Hell! That took six days. This was done in one. It was History made in an hour—and I helped make it. Thousands and thousands of people from all over this vast commonwealth of ours . . . traveled hundreds of miles to get a bare piece of land for nothing. But what land! Virgin, except when the Indians had roamed it. "Lands of lost gods, and godlike men!" They came like a procession—a crazy procession—all the way to the Border, covering the ground as fast as they could, by any means at hand—scrambling over the ground, pushing and shoving each other into the ditches to get there first. God knows why—for they all knew that once arrived there they'd have to wait like penned cattle for the firing of the signal shot that opened the promised land.

Ferber's pairing of the frontier with the promised land recalls the power of Manifest Destiny thinking during much of the nineteenth century. America was not only a political or geographical entity, it was also a religious promise. And, like religion, America welcomed all true believers. A hint of the democratic nature of the West is given in Yancey's description of how people arrived at the border on the day of "The Run": "As I got nearer the line it was like ants swarming on sugar. Over the hills they came, and out of the scrub-oak woods and across the prairie. They came from Texas, and Arkansas and Colorado and Missouri. They came on foot, by God, all the way from Iowa and Nebraska! They came in buggies and wagons and on horseback and muleback. In prairie schooners and ox carts and carriages. I saw a surrey, honey colored, with a fringe around the top, and two elegant bays drawing it, still stepping high along those rutted clay roads as if out for a drive in the Presidio."[109]

Such an eclectic crowd, though different in its particulars, is reminiscent of the groups gathered at the El station who inspired Charles Ives's *From Hanover Square North,* and of the "motley crowd" that John W. Osborn describes in his story "The Brand Burners of Cimarron." In all three instances it is hard to avoid the suggestion of America's diverse and accommodating society. In these readings, the young nation provides a level field for all players; in the plains of Oklahoma, the field takes on geographic reality as well.[110] When Yancey finally describes the actual moment of the run, he invokes both patriotic and religious images:

Well, the Border at last, and it was like a Fourth of July celebration on Judgment Day. The militia was lined up at the boundary. No one was allowed to set foot on the new land until noon next day, at the firing of the guns. Two million acres of land were to be given away for the grabbing. Noon was the time. They all knew it by heart. April twenty-second at noon. It takes generations of people hundreds of years to settle a new land. This was going to be made livable over night—was made—like a miracle out of the Old Testament. Compared to this, the Loaves and Fishes and the parting of the Red Sea were nothing—mere tricks. . . . A wilderness one day—except for an occasional wandering band of Indians—an empire the next. If that isn't a modern miracle . . .[111]

Drawing upon his skill and finesse as a seasoned storyteller, Ferber's Yancey Cravat dramatically takes his listeners through the last minutes before the shotgun blast that signals the run. Finally: "Twelve o'clock. There went up a roar that drowned the crack of the soldier's musketry as they fired in the air as the signal of noon and the start of the Run. You could see the puffs of smoke from their guns, but you couldn't hear a sound. The thousands surged over the Line. It was like water going over a broken dam. The rush had started, and it was devil take the hindmost. We swept across the prairie in a cloud of black and red dust that covered our faces and hands in a minute, so that we looked like black demons from hell."[112]

With such colorful characters and dramatic events, one can hardly blame Harris for wanting to claim the story as his own, even if he left the frontier and moved to California with his family when he was five. The San Gabriel Valley could hardly compare with Cimarron Country for its westernness.

Land rushes in the Oklahoma territory, like the one Ferber described in her fictional account, occurred five more times during the next six years. By 1893, when President Grover Cleveland announced the opening of the Cherokee strip for a land grab, the government had devised more sophisticated methods for dealing with the enormous crowds of people seeking land and registering their claims. On 16 September 1893 settlers raced across the northern border of Oklahoma—an area 226 miles east to west and 58 miles north to south.[113] One hundred thousand pioneers competed for 42,000 claims, a total of six million acres. The actual race lasted only about two hours, before those coming down from the Kansas border met up with those coming up from earlier settlements in Oklahoma. Stories abound of pioneers establishing a claim and within hours having entire towns grow around them. By the evening of 16 September 1893, after family members had arrived, the newly opened territory boasted a population well in excess of 100,000. While the

1890s land grabs were boons for white settlers, they were the final action in a series of events that destroyed Native Americans' sovereignty over their own lands. This was one of the legacies of the West that was seldom acknowledged.[114]

Cimarron, the Piece

Comments accompanying the score regarding the Cimarron land grab are strikingly similar to Ferber's. They are used to explain Harris's music:

> The work tells the story of the beginning of a sleeping, uncivilized land— nature undisturbed by man—gradually becoming intensified to an utmost height of excitement, at which point the percussion with the resounding staccato of a shotgun, lets loose a drum shot report, representing the firing of a ten-gauge shotgun, to release those men on horse-back, foot and wagons lined along the Cimarron banks at noontime prepared to make a dash for the land on which to build their homesteads.
>
> At this point the work changes suddenly into a galloping 6/8 rhythm of full band. Out of this will gradually come a steady, sonorous idealistic march representing the progress of pioneering toward an established civilization.[115]

A note at the bottom of the page advises, "If a ten-gauge shotgun is available for firing, this will immeasurably increase the pictorial and musical animation of the composition."[116] A number of aspects of this commentary are noteworthy: First, the absence of Native Americans in this land, "nature undisturbed by man," and the assumption that it was the pioneers who "established civilization" echo Turner's version of how the West was settled. What had in reality been a long series of violent confrontations is reduced to a sportslike event, complete with starting pistol and a race to the finish line. Second, placing this run "along the Cimarron banks" suggests that Harris is referring to the land grab within the Oklahoma panhandle, the one closest to the banks of the Cimarron River. If he was trying to suggest some kind of familial connection with this event, it was a significant stretch of the truth. This run could not have involved Harris's parents in any way, since their Chandler, Oklahoma, house was built hundreds of miles east of the panhandle.

Finally, the programmatic outline provided in the commentary, with its assertion "the work tells the story," and multiple references to representation culminating in the "sonorous idealistic march *representing* the progress of pioneering toward an established civilization" appear to contradict earlier sentiments expressed by the composer, especially those communicated in a 1931 letter to Arthur Farwell as the older musician was preparing his *Musical Quarterly* article. Harris reminded Farwell that he had "eschewed Programmatic tendencies from the first at a time out West when all the rage was Programmatic."[117] Farwell obliged and wrote: "for as a youth in the West, he eschewed programmaticism and its allied divagations at a time when these ideas were rampant in the musical life about him."[118] *Cimarron* suggests that Harris had a change of heart in the intervening years. There is nothing abstract about the shotgun blast.

In writing *Cimarron* for symphonic band, Harris composed for a medium free of a dominating string sound.[119] Although fiddling had already enjoyed a long tradition in American vernacular music, and fiddles certainly accompanied many settlers westward, stringed instruments were closely associated with refined European symphonic music, an evocation that Harris would have happily avoided when conjuring Cimarron Country. A band piece was perfect for a bold assertion of America, as John Philip Sousa's enormous success proved.

Harris's overture opens with a series of overlapping melodic fragments in the woodwinds. A gong and vibraphone struck on beat 1 and left to reverberate seven measures before being struck again create an otherworldly effect. The melody is long, sinewy, flexible, and wandering; seeming to grow from within, it does not easily parse into antecedent and consequence phrases.[120] It becomes apparent that Harris's stylistic traits are consistent: from symphony to chamber music to band overture, genre does not alter his dependable voice. He does not adopt a different compositional style to depict this colorful place. In discussing general characteristics of Harris's melodies, Dan Stehman observes, "His melodies owe in their contours, modal characteristics, and flexibility of phrase structure a debt to both monophonic chant and the lines of Renaissance vocal polyphony. They also reveal a kinship with Anglo-American folk music and early Protestant hymnody."[121] The end of the piece will bear out this last affinity.

When Harris describes the sound of the initial tenor sax solo that he wants as "sweet, lonesome—*poco vibrato*," intentionally or not, he suggests another character type of the West, the "lonesome cowboy." The saxophone sings suspended within a widely spaced, soft, sustained chord held by clarinets, basses, bass clarinets, and a single string bass. Once again the musical tradition of the bucolic duet heard in Charles Ives's *Housatonic*, and before that in Berlioz's *Symphonie fantastique,* is adapted by Harris when an oboe and, later, a muted trumpet, alto sax, horns, and English horn take up the melody and answer each other. It is as if they were calling to each over a vast distance.[122] There is no strong meter to push the music forward; a metronome marking of a quarter note at 64 restrains the tempo. A series of descending melodic fragments emerges within Harris's open soundscape. He succeeds in evoking a still environment, not all that different from the one portrayed in Frederick Dewey's 1883 dime novel "Cimarron Jack . . . A Tale of the Land of Silence."

The land, however, is not without life. A gently animated flute and piccolo line starting at measure 25 is taken over, modified, and speeded up by clarinets at measure 33, and then further accelerated and energized at measure 42. Here Harris introduces a rising and falling pattern that includes sixteenth notes for the first time in the piece. They energize the music and anticipate the drama that will unfold. The dynamic level increases as musical tension builds; it bursts open at measure 48 when timpani and large and small drums join in the fray. Brass instruments sing out fortissimo. The tempo accelerates more than twofold from the opening, and the once-falling melodic gesture now reverses direction in a series of repeating ascending figures.

If the opening impressionistic measures are characterized by lyrical lines and notes of long duration, the piece gradually changes character and picks up speed by increasing the surface rhythms and tempi. Harris's "sleeping, uncivilized land" prepares for the dash.[123] Here again, though the symphonic band genre might not be characteristic of Harris, his treatment of rhythm in *Cimarron* shows striking similarities to other, more typical pieces. Rather than modify his voice for this particular piece, he adapts *Cimarron* to his style. In summarizing the composer's approach to matters of rhythm, Dan Stehman observes: "Rhythmically, Harris's music is characterized by two principal features: 1) slow, lyrical passages generally begin with long notes and gradually introduce smaller values, which eventually prevail; 2) fast, aggressive music usually features a more even distribution of note-values within phrases. He also uses asymmetrical meters chiefly in highly rhythmic passages in fast tempo."[124] Stehman's description of Harris rhythms holds for *Cimarron:* the piece starts out slowly, lyrically, with long notes. At measure 48, common time changes to the asymmetrical 5/4. Sixteenth notes, first introduced at measure 42 in the highest instruments, dominate the moving parts by measure 55, where the quarter note moves at 132.

Harris's use of percussion at measure 48 indicates that he missed no opportunity to place his overture in "the West": he peopled his soundscape with Indians. Accented, pulsing drum beats in the timpani recall similar efforts by many composers with no western claims, who also evoked America's Indians in their music by means of "tom-tom" rhythms and sounds.[125] Because Harris had such close ties to Arthur Farwell, the nation's leading Indianist composer of the early twentieth century, listeners might have expected a more subtle reference to America's indigenous people from him. But Harris, like William

Grant Still, was not presenting an ethnomusicological study of the region. He was not celebrating Native American culture, but rather white culture's triumph over Indian territory. Authenticity was not required to convey the effect he sought.[126]

Like Yancey Cravat telling about the anxious moments leading up to "The Run," Harris builds tension in his musical version of the tale with pacing brass, fluttering woodwinds, and an eight-measure drum roll. Finally, at measure 63 Harris instructs his players: "At this point all percussion instruments combine to approximate a 10 gauge shot-gun report."[127] The meter changes from an asymmetrical 5/4 to a rocking 6/8. The uniformly notated meter, which continues until measure 101, disguises a jaunty and somewhat unsynchronized effect that Harris achieves by means of timbral contrasts. Horns and saxes play a two-note phrase that enters on beats four and one, while trumpets and trombones respond with their own galloping two-note gesture that begins on beats six and three. Marshals firing their rifles might have controlled the start of the land grabs, but the ensuing stampede across the open territory was just that—everyone for himself. When played up to tempo, Harris's overture achieves great energy and excitement.[128] Listeners hear settlers heading off at various paces in numerous directions: John Osborne's "motley crowd" is on the loose.[129]

At measure 102, Harris returns to the opening 4/4 meter and begins his "idealistic march representing the progress of pioneering." The solemn effort "toward an established civilization" is borne by clarinets, saxophones, cornet, and baritone horns in a lengthy, half- and quarter-note melody that Harris writes, should be played "*cantabile legato.*"[130] Brief dotted-note trumpet and trombone fanfare figures comment upon the pioneers' achievement and lend a martial air to the endeavor. Harris sanctifies their accomplishment with a chorale to close the overture; the full ensemble joins in. The reference to Protestant church music is not without resonance. *Forte* and *fortissimo* dynamics that characterized the musical land rush quiet down to a more reverent *mezzo forte.* Staid quarters and halves replace energetic eighth and sixteenth notes. Accents and staccato markings smooth out in Harris's "sustained *legato.*" A listener can almost imagine an "amen" after the final chord.

"Manifest Destiny," a phrase first coined in 1845, was alive and well in 1941 in Roy Harris's *Cimarron*. Nineteenth-century writers had portrayed the expansion of the nation across the continent as the natural fulfillment of God's plan for America, the required response to a divine command. In the same way, Harris's religious close to a piece about a land rush in the Oklahoma territory gave voice to that continuing belief. For reasons that went beyond mere patriotism, his investment in such thinking was complete.

FERDE GROFÉ:

Mississippi Suite, Grand Canyon Suite, Hudson River Suite, and
Niagara Falls Suite

Unlike his contemporary Roy Harris, Ferdinand Rudolph von Grofé (1892–1972), known as Ferde Grofé, spent little effort arguing his claim as spokesperson for American music, although he proudly identified himself as a composer of Americana.[131] Between 1920 and 1968, his most active years, Grofé was too busy pursuing multiple careers as pianist, arranger, composer, and conductor to devote much thought to shaping his image. Most famous, initially, for his work with Paul Whiteman's orchestra (1920–32) and his history-making arrangement of George Gershwin's raw two-piano score of *Rhapsody in Blue* (1924), which catapulted all three into the national spotlight, over the years Grofé became more closely associated with his own creations, *Mississippi Suite* (1925), and *Grand Canyon Suite* (1931) especially.[132] With the theme of "On the Trail" from the latter loping into millions of radio listeners' living rooms as the signature tune for the Philip Morris radio show for twenty years, Ferde Grofé became a household name. Radio announcers of the 1950s and 1960s introduced him simply as "one of America's greatest composers,"[133] and "a man who will live forever."[134]

Grofé was a New Yorker by birth but moved to California early in his life, which made him familiar with both coasts and much of the country between. During his active career his travels took him to Arizona, Chicago, up the Hudson, and all over Europe. Wherever he went, Grofé seems to have been especially receptive to natural scenes. In explaining his 1956 tone poem *Dawn at Lake Mead,* Grofé remembered the site of a fishing trip there: "I was inspired by the wild terrain and the absolute absence of vegetation, and the almost forbidden look of the mountains there. . . . dawn coming up [and] the magnificent colors in the sky, a near flotilla of clouds."[135] Such a poetic reaction to one's surroundings goes a long way toward explaining the number of place pieces that Grofé composed, especially those with a direct connection to the land. Grofé admitted to that particular affinity when he spoke about a commission to write a work for the 1964–65 New York World's Fair: "I considered the fact that my hand had always been best at composition more closely related to nature. In such as the *Grand Canyon Suite, Mississippi Suite,* and *Death Valley Suite,* I measured in music the sights, sounds and sensations, which seemed to spring so naturally from our land. A suite to depict a World's Fair, however, called for a harmonic yardstick of another kind. . . . Where to start?"[136]

But Grofé did not always need mountains and clouds to stir his creative juices, nor did he confine himself to such depictions. With the early compositions *Broadway at Night* (1924) and *Metropolis* (1927–28), he captured sounds of the more urban environment where he worked.[137] The 1938 ballet *Café Society,* named after the famous Manhattan nightclub, and plans for a *Madison Square Garden Suite* (1939) suggest a continuing connection with America's city of cities. Comfortable in both urban and rural environments, Grofé did not confine himself to a particular region of the country. A sampling of the more than twenty place pieces that Grofé composed reveals an ecumenical embrace of the United States: *Mississippi Suite* (1925), *Hollywood Ballet* (1936), *Kentucky Derby Suite* (1938), *Death Valley Suite* (1949), *Hudson River Suite* (1955), *San Francisco Suite* (1960), *Niagara Falls Suite* (1961), *Hawaiian Suite* (1965), *Virginia City: Requiem for a Ghost Town* (1968). From the original American icon to the last admitted state, Grofé commemorated American places with an enthusiastic thoroughness unequaled by any composer before or since.

What did Grofé say about so many places, and how did he say it? His music, even the canonical *Grand Canyon Suite,* was often criticized for its lack of depth, its too-immediate appeal, its reliance on numerous effects, its style—one presumes at the cost of substance—arguments that recall those leveled against the music of William Henry Fry a century earlier. Francis D. Perkins captured the tenor of such criticisms in a review that he wrote in 1937:

> Skillful and variously-colored instrumentation, coupled with equally skillful and colorful performance under the communicative leadership of Mr. Grofé, characterized the program in general. . . . The concert showed progress in a variety of rhythms, as compared with the Whitemanesque pioneering experiments of a dozen years ago. . . . But, as before, there was an impression of relatively few fertile musical ideas, despite the skill shown in their treatment; the various works, where they scored, did so through the use of their material rather than the material itself, which was not infrequently tenuous or conventional.[138]

No one questioned Grofé's skills as an orchestrator or his genius for musical characterization, but, as was true of Fry, when his music was measured against a standard that prized the absolute, abstract, and transcendent above all, it appeared to fall short; its appeal was (and is) its undoing.[139]

But achieving transcendence was not the goal that Grofé envisioned for his pieces. As is evident in numerous interviews, he was keenly aware of different types of music. He distinguished carefully between "hot" jazz and the concertized versions of it that characterized his arrangements and Whiteman's sound.

And he was very clear on that point: "I never wrote one note of jazz. I put jazz licks in [my music], but I never composed jazz." He also understood the uniqueness of his achievement: "It's an original type of music . . . a different kind of music."[140] Within this category Grofé made further distinctions, noting the differences between the short "dance pieces" he had arranged for Whiteman and his larger suites, first inspired by work with Gershwin's lengthy *Rhapsody*. Never intended to be jazz, it is not. Never striving to compete with Beethoven's symphonic standards, it does not. Conceived as light, descriptive concert music whose goal is to entertain broad audiences, Grofé's music continues to succeed. In a 1937 *Time* article, the composer explained his position: "I am not foolish enough to place myself in a class, for example, with Ravel or Sibelius, whom I admire tremendously, but there is a real place for my music. Sometime, when I get older I may try a strict symphony form, but in the meantime I am going on trying to describe America in my music."[141]

Even so, years later, when Toscanini programmed the *Grand Canyon Suite* for performance by his NBC Orchestra at a concert of all American music, Grofé considered it the apex of his professional career.[142] While not consciously striving to write "music of the highest class,"[143] Grofé was nonetheless honored when his music was welcomed into its ranks.

According to James Farrington's study, "two compositions stood out to [Grofé] as revealing 'an extraordinarily close kinship with [America]'—the *Grand Canyon Suite* and the *Hudson River Suite.*"[144] Here we will consider those works and two others, the *Mississippi Suite* (1925), which, along with the *Grand Canyon*, was among Grofé's most famous pieces; and the 1961 *Niagara Suite*, the last large symphonic work written to commemorate the famous falls.[145] These four works, created over the course of thirty-seven years, suggest the continuing appeal of the nation's places as musical inspiration for Grofé.

With the February 1924 success of *Rhapsody in Blue* resonating in the minds and ears of Whiteman and Grofé, the ambitious conductor encouraged his arranger to "compose something of [his] own."[146] Within nine months Grofé obliged with his first extended composition, *Broadway at Night*, dedicated "to my friend Paul Whiteman." A year later he completed *Mississippi: A Journey in Tones*, to be known as *Mississippi Suite*. The suite premiered in Chicago on 11 October 1925. It was perfomed again on 29 December 1925 at Carnegie Hall, as part of Whiteman's "Second Experiment in Modern Music."[147] In June 1926 the suite was played in the Netherlands, as Whiteman and his orchestra toured Europe. It quickly carved out a regular place for itself on Whiteman's concerts and, until *Grand Canyon* six years later, would be Grofé's signature piece.

Although Grofé distinguished between the short pieces, the "dance music" that he regularly arranged for Whiteman, and his "larger works like the suites," in reality *Mississippi Suite* is a series of very brief pieces culminating in the longest movement, "Mardi Gras," which, regardless of performance, comes in at just over four minutes. In the case of *Mississippi*, Grofé's "larger work" is not long.[148] The distinction is not in length so much as in conception and intent. In spite of the occasional syncopated passages and jazz licks, the four movements are intended for listening and not dancing. It is concert music. In *Mississippi* the tempi of the four movements suggest a modified classical symphonic order: fast, dancelike, slow, fast. The final movement ties together previous movements by recalling similar gestures, patterns, and harmonies that have come before as well as the playful theme heard in the second movement, "Huckleberry Finn." The first instance of counterpoint in the entire suite appears halfway through the final movement, contributing to a sense of a genuine culmination of activity. A listener is left with the impression that this is a unified, extended work. Grofé explained his four movements: "The titles of the various movements speak for themselves. 'Father of Waters' portrays the upper reaches of the river, 'Huckleberry Finn,' the haunts of the roguish boy of Mark Twain's famous story near the Mississippi. Then, 'Old Creole Days,' which is a lullaby and cradle song of the old negro [*sic*] mammy further down the river. The climax, 'Mardi Gras,' brings the tone journey to an end, depicting the carnival spirit of New Orleans and completing the musical portrait of the mighty river."[149]

In none of the hours of interviews that Grofé left behind does he hint at the impetus for the *Mississippi Suite* beyond Whiteman's encouragement to compose something of his own. With others of his extended works he related inspirational experiences or specific commissions, some explanation of *why* a particular place was commemorated in a composition. Of the four pieces discussed here, *Mississippi* remains an exception; Grofé appears not to have had a specific personal experience with the Mississippi, at least none that he chose to cite. But he would not have conjured an unknown locale; thanks to paintings, stories, the very real influence of New Orleans on the kinds of American music that Grofé was writing, and Mark Twain's 1884 masterpiece, *Huckleberry Finn,* the Mississippi was a vivid presence in the American consciousness, much as Niagara had been a century earlier.

The river and its culture would be celebrated in another way just two years later, with Jerome Kern's Broadway musical *Show Boat.* The two Mississippi tributes would share more than their subject matter. Whether by design or coincidence, the refrain to Kern's wildly popular song "Ol' Man River" used a melodic motto that recalled the opening to Grofé's first movement "Father of Waters," with its ascent of a fourth via a major second and a minor third.[150] If Kern was trying to evoke the earlier work, he succeeded. Without fore-thought, the two pieces reinforced the idea that this melodic gesture was synonymous with the Mississippi. Just as paintings had imagined Niagara Falls for viewers in the nineteenth century, Grofé's suite and Kern's Broadway musical helped to shape an aural concept of the Mississippi River in the first half of the twentieth century.

Mississippi Suite is Grofé's earliest effort in that genre, yet it reveals a com-poser's voice that is clear, sure, and distinctive. In numerous interviews dis-cussing musical preferences Grofé singled out "smooth" music, a style that featured lyrical, expressive lines. "I inaugurated a smooth style. This was my specialty," he said. He preferred quartet and quintet textures. For contrast, he noted, he used "very animated, lively, syncopated, jazzy [music] before a re-turn to the smooth section."[151] He was describing the arrangements he created for Whiteman, but this same pattern is evident in "Father of Waters." After a twelve-measure *mezzo forte* fanfare in the brass that is punctuated by dramatic fermatas, the piece continues with a long, prominent horn melody that glides over arpeggiated figures in the strings.[152] It is the fanfare melody, now parsed in two eight-measure phrases. The mostly pentatonic tune floats over rolling eighth-note triplets and shimmering cymbal work.[153] This is Grofé's smooth style.

By way of contrast, Grofé interjects a highly rhythmic section. Where le-gato articulations characterized the opening andante maestoso, now staccato takes over the animato. Percussion and syncopation reign where strings and brass and predictable accent patterns prevailed. Seventeen measures later the smooth music returns, but this time riding upon a slightly more complex rhythmic underpinning. Quarter-note triplets in upper woodwinds rub against the clear half-note melody. Without substantially altering the balance of voices, Grofé has intensified the music. The seventy-measure piece closes on a solid *pianissimo* major chord. The movement contains essential stylistic elements that will stamp much of Grofé's music: a definite preference for lyrical, tuneful lines, the reliance upon tonality—although it will be nuanced with chromatic ascents and descents—flatted thirds and sevenths, contrasting sections within a single movement, and extreme sensitivity to orchestration.

Like the rascal he is, Huckleberry Finn swaggers onto the scene in the guise of a playful bassoon solo in the second movement.[154] Pizzicato and staccato strings and woodwinds help set the light scherzando mood and recall the middle section of the previous movement. The use of flutter-tonguing (sug-gestive of some prankish escapade or the young hero actually wagging his tongue) reveals another of Grofé's stylistic traits. As will be observed in later suites, Grofé makes full use of a range of effects, and when traditional instruments cannot deliver the desired result, he does not hesitate to bring in whatever can. Grofé's "Huckleberry Finn" is free of the political controversies that have surrounded the character in more recent years. Here is a lighthearted look at childhood, complete with what sounds like young boys charging to imaginary cavalry calls (measures 37–40, 51–54, 80–83), tiptoeing around fantasized intrigues (measures 55–72), and doing all with a braggadocio synonymous with that innocent age. Grofé's interjection of a jazzy, syncopated transitional section as he gears up to a return of the opening theme (measures 73–94) reveals his experience with Whiteman's hybridized style. Moving beyond the short dance pieces that were at the heart of Whiteman's band repertoire, Grofé nonetheless employs some of the same vocabulary, and it fits seamlessly. A pair of muted trumpet "blats" at the penultimate measure stamp the piece as a playful romp.

The third movement again showcases Grofé's lyrical bent. Listeners return to a long-breathed melodic style originally heard in the first movement, but in "Old Creole Days" the music rocks back and forth more lazily than it did in the dramatically intense "Father of Waters." Grofé recalls the first movement's opening fanfare, with its initial descending major second and its rich seventh chords, in similar melodic and harmonic motions in the strings. A harp strums seventh chords and major triad arpeggios. Given Grofé's description of the movement, there is little need for a contrasting section in this brief, thirty-measure lullaby; and none is present. Variety is achieved with instruments calling back and forth to each other, and with a modified inversion of the simple opening descending melody starting at measure 17 and lasting until the a tempo at measure 21. Where in the first movement the return of the lyrical framing section was accompanied by increases in rhythmic complexity and surface activity, in "Old Creole Days" Grofé eliminates all distractions. The previously busy harp is reduced to octave chords that chime on the offbeats. A final ninth chord with an added sixth closes the triple-piano cradle song.

"Mardi Gras" is by far the longest and most complex of the four movements, and it is replete with memorable melodic bits. As "Father of Waters" included a motive similar to that found in Kern's *Show Boat*, one of the themes of "Mardi Gras" reminds listeners of George Gershwin's "I Got Rhythm" from *Girl Crazy* (1930).[155] So much crossover between Grofé's "concert music" and what was clearly popular music contributes to the difficulties that scholars experience when attempting to categorize his works.

Like the fanfare that introduced the suite, "Mardi Gras" has its own brass introduction; it is immediately apparent why this piece became so popular. A jaunty eight-measure theme and plucking pizzicatos keep the mood light.

Grofé plays with his tune, sending it to different instruments in different keys. When the idea is repeated a third time, a legato countermelody floats above it. The new tune, although flattened out in straight quarter notes and not particularly audible, sports the same rising major second and minor third that identified the original motive of the suite. Grofé prepares us for the more distinct counterpoint to come.

Consistent with his practice of composing a contrasting middle section, Grofé introduces an expressive andantino. The writing is full and lush, with divisi strings, dense harp arpeggios, and numerous instructions to swell the dynamics. Grofé clearly revels in a beautiful tune. When he joins the opening and lyrical themes together, both are clearly audible. A series of harp undulations and the fullest scoring yet heard in the entire suite propel the music forward through this contrapuntal section.

Little more than halfway through the movement, the composer focuses his listener's attention on a four-note ascending passage that blossoms into the proto–"I Got Rhythm" motive four measures later. This same motive contains the essential intervals that characterized the first motive of "Father of Waters." Not only are the intervals those that identify Gershwin's tune, but in six iterations Grofé subjects them to such rhythmic diminution and variation that he spotlights their temporal qualities to the exclusion of everything else. Grofé's got rhythm. All attention is on the brass choir as it sings out *fortissimo,* molto marcato. Given the fame of this particular movement, it is impossible to believe that Gershwin was unaware of this melodic gesture or that audiences hearing his 1930 song would not have made some connection between the two pieces.[156]

Grofé's mastery of the popular concert music idiom is most evident as he pushes to the finish. All instruments are playing either *fortissimo* or triple *forte.* A brass choir penetrates through the dense scoring with yet another iteration of the opening "Mardi Gras" music. A spirited (con spirito) return of the "Huckleberry Finn" theme by woodwinds, horns, and upper strings, and a return of the harp's arpeggiated triplet passage that first appeared in "Father of Waters," recalls earlier moments in the larger suite. Grofé bids good-bye to his Mississippi journey with a final animato based on the "I Got Rhythm" motive. Writing for a popular audience accustomed to flashy endings, Grofé "stings" a series of rising trilled chords that crescendo to the close. It is a finish sure to bring people to their feet.

While still part of a team, with the *Mississippi Suite* Grofé secured a reputation for himself separate from that which he had achieved as Paul Whiteman's arranger. Ferde Grofé emerged a recognized composer in his own right, and *Mississippi* became the first of a series of "geographical" pieces that would endear him to audiences around the world. Inspired by famous places and always working with "a definite subject in mind, a picture of what I write about," Grofé created resounding pictures of America. [157] His extraordinary success with this first soundscape encouraged later musical visualizations. Over the next forty years, Grofé immortalized a dozen other American places in his music.

No piece would bring him greater notice than the *Grand Canyon Suite,* composed, as was *Mississippi,* at the suggestion of Whiteman.[158] But this time Grofé had a rich reservoir of personal experiences upon which to draw. In an interview conducted in the early 1960s, he shared his impressions of the Grand Canyon the first time he saw it, in 1917: "It was summertime, August. We had camped at night. It was dawn, no clouds; I was spellbound. The silence. As it got lighter and brighter you could hear nature coming to life. I get chills right now just thinking about it. You feel awful close to God there. It just over-whelms. Words are inadequate. It made such an impression on me."[159] Grofé kept these pictures in his mind for more than a dozen years, nurturing them with additional visits out West. It was while he was working on the film *King of Jazz* that he put his first thoughts on paper. "Sunrise" was completed in fall 1929 in Santa Monica, California. Grofé finished what became the fourth movement, "Sunset," in the summer of 1930 while living in New Jersey.

For the second movement, "The Painted Desert," he recalled "the silence, the desolation, [the] wasteland, except for brightly colored rocks . . . lots of colors. . . . It's all about colors."[160] To achieve the palette he sought, Grofé turned to quartal and quintal harmonies made famous by Debussy.[161] The comparison with Debussy does not end with preferences for non-tertiary chords. Grofé also designed a fragmentary melodic gesture that recalls the opening of *L'Après-midi d'un faune.* Series of planed chords, static ostinato figures, and the prominent role given to woodwinds (especially the English horn) all evoke the Impressionist master. While there is no mistaking Grofé for Debussy, the influence of the Frenchman is heard. As in the music of "Sunrise," the second movement had its genesis in Grofé's powerful, personal experience of the place. For one so facile in musical expression, the logical outcome of the image imprinted on his mind was sound.

"On the Trail," the third and most famous movement of the suite, was written in a hotel in Chicago and had a less purely inspired genesis. Though Grofé had never been on the canyon trail himself, he had been to the top of it several times and seen hordes of tourists climbing up and down. Their accounts and his own vivid imagination were enough to provide him with the material he needed. Years later it became clear that Grofé took great pride in the accuracy and vividness of his musical likeness: "People who've never been on the trail can experience it in the music . . . the music portrays the trail so faithfully."[162]

As Kern and Gershwin appear to have been inspired by musical ideas from the *Mississippi Suite,* Grofé was not above "borrowing" ideas for the *Grand Canyon Suite.* With unabashed candor he later explained the source of his famous octave-leaping donkey theme: "I borrowed a song writer's theme . . . [set to the words] 'horses, horses,' although he'd set it in a steady four and I switched it to 6/8."[163]

By keeping the clip-clopping of the horse's hooves in a steady duple and overlaying the hee-haw theme in 6/8, Grofé created a lazy, loping gait. With careful attention to effects, the composer instructed his percussionist to use coconut shells muffled on leather to achieve the precise sound that he sought. A lullaby-like "cowboy song" first heard in the trombones at measure 130 was also composed in Chicago, far from the subject of the piece, but it rings true. Grofé recalled the tune coming to him while he pushed his son in a baby buggy.

Grofé's established role as an arranger and composer in the popular realm provided him with valuable creative freedom when he turned to the composition of more serious concert music. Worried less than many of his exclusively high-art contemporaries about aesthetic values that prized absolute music over programmatic music, Grofé publicly acknowledged his preference for composing descriptive pieces and enjoyed securing the precise effect he envisioned. He was driven to appeal to his audience: "The man in the street should understand my music."[164] In the early 1960s he described in detail the intricate connections between ideas and music in each of the movements of the *Grand Canyon Suite.* The effort exerted to create the perfect storm for the final movement, "Cloudburst," is indicative of Grofé's commitment to descriptive composition. In preparation, he studied earlier scores of storms: Strauss's *Eine Alpensinfonie,* Rossini's *William Tell,* and Beethoven's Pastoral Symphony. He noted the differences between their works and his: "They employed chromatics. I don't; I use augmented chords; different accents . . . no arpeggios going up and down. I employed the fewest notes possible to create a storm."[165]

The composer created the effect of pelting rain by instructing the strings to play double pizzicato, as fast as possible but not in sync with each other.[166] According to Grofé, the different speeds and "irregular" rhythms more accurately captured the sound of raindrops. The same kind of controlled freedom simulated the wind: slow glissandos in seconds, with no two instrumentalists playing at exactly the same pace.[167] At the climax of the storm, Grofé employed a wind machine. In recounting Toscanini's performance of the piece, the composer recalled the conductor's "very subtle" use of the machine: he employed "lots of discretion."[168] One can imagine lightning flashing in the jagged octaves of the piano.[169] Thunder rumbled from rolled timpani and heavy piano chords. Grofé evoked calm interludes using a large Chinese gong. Soft hammers rumbled a "soft roar" and, according to Grofé, painted a "barely perceptible" eerie atmosphere.[170] Recollections of sudden, drenching storms in Arizona provided Grofé with all the inspiration he needed to create his own musical maelstrom.

Appealing to a Depression-era audience that needed diversion, entertainment, and a reason to feel good about itself, Grofé singled out a natural American phenomenon, one that embodied the mythological West, and gave it a unique expression. Here was an American place and an American sound. Instrumentation that favored brass and percussion, jazzy syncopated rhythms, and cowboylike melodies stamped the piece as the product of a specific American time. Simultaneously, the five-movement suite competed with Beethoven's Sixth Symphony in program, number of movements, and overall dimensions; this was American music to be taken seriously. If there were moments of flash, dazzle, and humor in Grofé's work, there was also self-conscious nationalism. Both reflected broadly shared cultural values of the 1930s.[171] In an article written in 1938 for *The Etude* magazine, Grofé reflected on the condition of music and nationalism in America: "Musical creation in America is daily soaring to new heights; and more than this, it is becoming distinctly American, reflecting the dynamic industrial power of our country, our virile pioneer spirit, our inherent love of liberty, our sense of appreciation of the limitless beauty and grandeur of our country, our quaint humor, and our lofty ideals of life. Music in America surely has a magnificent future."[172]

Having taken over two years to compose, with less than a week of rehearsals the *Grand Canyon Suite* premiered in 1931, with Paul Whiteman conducting. In the composer's words, "The thing went over with a bang," and Whiteman "had to play an encore." He chose "On the Trail," the movement that would become the most oft-played piece by Ferde Grofé.[173] The thirty-three-minute suite remained Grofé's magnum opus; no other piece would approach it in magnitude of conception, ultimate dimension, or popularity. In the seven years since the premiere of *Rhapsody in Blue* in 1924, Grofé had evolved from a respected arranger into a celebrity composer in his own right. After twelve years with Whiteman's orchestra, in 1932 Grofé left the organization.[174]

During the next thirty years Grofé was in demand as an arranger, conductor, and composer. He became involved in the growing radio business and developed an interest in band music. Between *Grand Canyon* (1931) and the

Hudson River Suite (1955), he wrote five additional place-inspired pieces.[175] Perhaps the most unusual was *Death Valley Suite*, written over a ten-day period in 1949. The fifteen-minute work was the overture to a centennial pageant that reenacted the trek of the "forty-niners" through Death Valley; it was played in a natural amphitheater in the desert.[176] The *Hudson River Suite* returned Grofé to more bucolic climes and more traditional performance venues.

Sometime around 1939, Grofé met André Kostelanetz.[177] That would be the extent of their interaction for fifteen years. But in 1954, in anticipation of a trip to New York, Grofé wrote a letter to the conductor to request a meeting.[178] Over tea at the Plaza, Kostelanetz inquired about the possibility of Grofé composing something on "an American scene" and was surprised to learn that he had never written about the Hudson River.[179] As Grofé explained, the river was "very close to my heart."[180] When he had been about six months old, there had been a "terrific heat wave in New York City and a typhoid epidemic broke out." Grofé's mother knew a captain of one of the riverboats that steamed from the city to Albany. According to the composer, he and his mother "put upon that boat for about two weeks." Years later he credited the waterway with saving his life.[181]

Soon after their meeting Kostelanetz commissioned the work, although Grofé refused to take any payment for it beyond the assurance that all copy work went to his wife, Anne.[182] In lieu of payment Grofé did insist upon "all the publicity [he could] get."[183] The piece was written in about five months, from January to June 1955, and Kostelanetz premiered it in Washington, D.C. Making good on his promise to publicize the work, he took it on the road, went to Philadelphia, and then recorded it.[184]

The *Hudson River Suite* recalls a number of structural characteristics of Grofé's earlier famous waterway suite, the *Mississippi*. There are four movements:[185] "The River," "Hendrick Hudson," "Rip Van Winkle," and "Albany Night Boat—New York." As in the *Mississippi Suite,* the first movement of the *Hudson* is a broadly painted soundscape. The second and third movements are quasi–character studies that allow for significant contrast in style and mood, and the final movement, the longest in both works, moves from the waterway proper to the city at its mouth. The second movement of the *Hudson* is unique, however, in its reference to a historical figure, Henry (sometimes referred to—erroneously—as Hendrick) Hudson.

In 1609, while sailing for the Dutch East India Company, Hudson first navigated the waters of the river in search of a Northwest Passage. Although he did not find one, his explorations resulted in a large claim of land for the Dutch. He returned a year later, sailing for the English, and reached Hudson

Bay. Hudson's abandonment at sea by a mutinous crew and his probable death, were among many dramatic episodes that transpired in the settling of the New World and quickly became part of the lore of the Empire State.

Just as the second movement of the *Mississippi Suite* is named for Huckleberry Finn, the second movement of the *Hudson River Suite* is named for a character from American literature who is closely identified with that river, Washington Irving's Rip Van Winkle.[186] By pairing American authors and their characters with famous American places, Grofé commends both the nation's nature and its culture. As becomes evident in the next chapter, referencing other American artworks in musical pieces is a strategy shared by many twentieth-century composers. It is one way in which they imbued the nation's still-young culture with tradition, history, and value.

If multiple contrasting ideas within a brief movement were the norm in Grofé's earliest works, by 1955 he had become more adept at developing a single idea and having it suffice for an entire movement. This allowed the composer to give nuance to his musical images. As will be seen, a combination of vintage gestures and newly matured treatments coexist in the piece. "The River" opens with bells chiming a four-note ostinato while a bassoon traverses a brief ascending and descending run, which evolves into the primary theme of the movement and the piece. The opening music sparkles. Strings murmur underneath. Muted brass and woodwinds call back and forth to each other, evoking the sounds of nature.

An undulating, legato melody emerges in the low strings, revealing Grofé's continuing preference for a smooth, expressive style. It will be the only theme that he uses in the movement, and it will provide the primary thematic material for the second and fourth movements as well. As different instruments take turns singing the lyrical line, it changes and transforms. Where earlier works regularly concluded with a forceful, dazzling cadence, "The River" suggests no such inclinations. Not interested in wowing his listeners at this juncture, Grofé allows the musical image to linger and then fade from our hearing with an open ending.

The tragic demise of Henry Hudson seems to cast a pall over the second movement. Months at sea under the leadership of a difficult and often abusive captain had taken its toll on the sailors. In June 1611 they set Henry Hudson and a group of eight, including his son John, adrift in a small boat in the cold waters of what is now known as Hudson Bay. Although Hudson's fate was never documented, his almost certain death ended the career of one of the most successful explorers of the seventeenth century. He has been immortalized in a bay, a river, a valley, and a town, all of which bear his name. Grofé's theme of "Hendrick Hudson" is derived from that of the first movement, now transposed and modified rhythmically, yet its appearance in a mellow brass choir against plucked strings casts it in a whole new light and renders it more somber and reflective. Swaying triplets hint at a slow sea-chantey style, while the four-part writing suggests a hymn. The pealing of chimes that interrupt the fragmented theme twice reinforces allusions to church music. A full brass choir sings an augmented statement of the theme, with subdued snare drum rolls in the background that bring the second movement to a conclusive ending. As the explorer met his death in the waterway that took his name, Grofé uses a single melodic idea for the first and second movements, merging "Hendrick Hudson" with "The River."

A whistling piccolo and a barking dog introduce "Rip Van Winkle" and provide an effective foil for the preceding movement. By referring to Washington Irving's legend set in the magical Kaatskill (Catskill) Mountains along the Hudson River, Grofé moves forward in the nation's history as he moves forward through his suite, from seventeenth-century explorers to the eighteenth-century Revolution and beyond. In this story, Rip heads up into the mountains as a subject of King George. When he returns from his twenty-year torpor he is a U.S. citizen in a not-too-subtle parable of the sudden transformation from a European colony into an independent nation. Irving's numerous references to the untrammeled beauty of the region that surrounds the Hudson—the mountains, the effects of light on the trees and cliffs—reflect the deep pride that nineteenth-century Americans felt in the physical attributes of their country.[187] Capturing that story and making it music suggests Grofé's similar feelings.

Using those aspects of Irving's story most easily captured in sound, the barking of Rip's faithful dog Wolf and the rumbling of the thunderous game of ninepins, Grofé concentrates on the lighter side of the story and the effects he can marshal to tell the tale.[188] There is no suggestion of the marital discord that caused a beleaguered Rip to retreat to the mountains in the first place: in keeping with the denouement of the story the music is upbeat, even sprightly. The contrast that Grofé formerly sought within a single short piece is now accomplished through the juxtaposition of movements of distinctly different qualities.

Grofé relies upon traditional instrumental characterizations when he employs a bassoon to portray the strange old man who lures Rip away in his dream. The unanswered whistle as the newly awakened Rip beckons for his dog accurately depicts Irving's story line, in which, after a twenty-year slumber, Wolf is no more. With these obvious references, Grofé speaks directly to his audience. Just as "Hendrick Hudson" concluded with an unequivocal, if somber, final cadence, "Rip Van Winkle" exits the soundstage with a rousing *fortissimo* gesture that recalls the upward slide of the initial whistling idea and Rip's irrepressible spirit.

"Albany Night Boat—New York" follows a leisurely evening riverboat ride from deep in the pastoral river valley to the Forty-second Street Pier.[189] An ostinato based upon the undulating theme of the first two movements is treated by alternating woodwinds, and recalls the timbral palette first heard in *Grand Canyon*'s "Painted Desert." Tying together the larger work, Grofé subtly recollects the whistling idea from the beginning of "Rip Van Winkle," while melodic fragments that vacillate between minor and major reflect the shifting moods of the river. In addition to his mastery of orchestration, Grofé's lyrical gifts are showcased in a new, tuneful string melody; here is vintage "smooth" music. The rising minor third that characterizes this tune recalls the rising major third that identified the whistling motif; the four movements are of a piece. A muted trumpet picks up the theme and prepares listeners for the introduction of a jazzy Dixieland section: trumpet, clarinet, tuba, and drums swing the tune. The new treatment reveals the protean potential of Grofé's line; one can hear the seasoned jazz arranger at work. He concludes the night boat journey as the strings take back their melody; the trip is over. This is the ending that Grofé sought.

Kostelanetz, however, had other ideas.[190] According to the composer, Kostelanetz wanted an ending that would capture the din of New York (and, most likely, the wild applause of his audience). Against his better judgment, Grofé obliged and created the noisy one-minute "New York" tag on the end of an otherwise predominantly lyrical soundscape. Screeching trumpets and strings take on the fourth-movement theme. A slide whistle evokes the circuslike atmosphere of the city, as a final crescendo involving the entire orchestra belts out an emboldened version of the tune, bringing the suite to its flashy close. Grofé's dissatisfaction with the final movement appears justified, even if the reasons for which he acquiesced remain unclear. The final minute of the work has little in common with the rest of the suite beyond the recycled theme of the final movement. The closing has little to do with the Hudson River that Grofé depicted in his historically informed suite, and little to do with the paean to the historic river that Grofé created, even if it did reflect an updated place.

Ferde Grofé's final suite turned once again to America's original natural icon, Niagara Falls, but now from a new perspective. In 1961, sixty-eight years after George Bristow wrote his *Niagara: Symphony for Grand Orchestra and Chorus*, Grofé accepted a commission from Robert Moses and the New York State Power Authority to compose a work celebrating the opening of the nation's then-largest power plant, the Robert Moses Power Plant.[191] The transformation of the country's premier *natural* wonder into an industrial resource was complete: what had been a ready symbol of God's presence in the New Found Land now emblematized American ingenuity and might. Grofé, however, did not ignore the history or the changing significance of the waterway. In the four-movement *Niagara Falls Suite,* he explored aspects of the Falls prior to their industrial conversion; he depicted historic events that had transpired there, and he luxuriated in the romantic stage the Falls had supplied for honeymoon couples. In keeping with his preference for "the sights, sounds and sensations which seemed to spring so naturally from our land,"[192] Grofé started with the feature of the Falls that had captured Anthony Philip Heinrich in the 1840s, and that lent itself so readily to musical depictions, "The Thunder of the Waters."[193]

Heinrich had approached the waters as if from a distance, soft rumbling only gradually swelling to an engulfing din; Grofé's thundering waters confront auditors immediately. Four measures of hard-hammered *fortissimo* timpani rolls introduce an equally aggressive trumpet choir that blares out the first half of an eight-measure pentatonic tune molto marcato. Woodwinds respond in kind to finish the phrase. The Falls pound away at listeners in brief ostinato figures, frantically swirling scalar passages, and continuous snare drum rolls that hiss underneath cyclical cymbal crashes. The sound, like that of the Falls, is relentless.

Grofé also pays homage to the earliest painted images of the Falls, which included colorfully dressed natives. His tune, doubled at the octave and filled with fourths and fifths, represents Hollywood notions of American Indian music rather than authentic Native American sounds.[194] Pairing the Falls with musical evocations of America's native people (regardless of how hackneyed) is an honest gesture. Just as eighteenth-century paintings of the Falls regularly featured America's first inhabitants on the ledges surrounding the waters, Grofé's suite includes music intended to suggest their presence. By placing Indians at the Falls in the first movement, Grofé not only refers to an earlier time, but he also prepares listeners for the second movement, "Devil's Hole Massacre," a title that refers to a real event in Niagara history.

Through the early 1760s, Seneca Indians had provided valuable assistance to French and then British explorers and soldiers, by carrying supplies and cargo over the Niagara Portage, a strip of land that connected the Niagara region to the upper Great Lakes. But Conestoga wagons soon replaced the Senecas, and what had been a mutually beneficial collaboration ceased to exist. On 14 September 1763, as John Stedman led a supply convoy through the Portage, the Senecas ambushed the British, and killed eighty, although Stedman escaped. When British troops arrived they found no survivors. The massacre became a bloody reminder of the price of colonization.

Grofé creates a hushed, intense atmosphere, with upper strings playing repeated sul ponticello chords while cellos execute narrow chromatic runs over continuously sustained pedal octaves in the bass. The mood is completely different from that of the first movement; power is replaced by perturbation. A contained, chantlike melody played by a solo English horn creates a restless soundscape; the extended, exposed solo seems to portend danger. The initial mood prevails for close to three minutes of the four-and-a-half-minute piece, before it is broken by a timpani glissando and a *forte* explosion of woodwinds and horns. Brass belt out a new quasi-Indian melody as drums and staccato strings lash out; clearly the musical ambush has begun. Fighting escalates in increasingly louder, higher, and more rhythmically intense music. An animato (beginning at measure 187) signals a new level of intensity, which continues until eight measures from the end. A final dissonant chord echoes through the orchestra, as the volume diminishes to *pianissimo*. The Senecas wiped out their enemy in this particular encounter, but relationships between the settlers and natives were not over. The lingering dissonance aptly captures the situation. Many encounters later, it will be the Native Americans who suffer the ultimate removal.

From early in the nineteenth century, Niagara Falls was a destination for tourists from all over seeking *the* New World experience on their grand tours. More specifically, by the last quarter of the century, wedding trips to the Falls had become cliché. Hotels, tours, and photography studios sprouted in response to the starry-eyed clientele. Later, Hollywood did its part to reinforce the image of Niagara as the ideal romantic setting, with its use of the Falls in numerous films.[195] Grofé captured this aspect of the cataract's history in his sweetly expressive third movement, "Honeymooners."[196]

Here the composer draws upon his experience as an arranger of melodic band music, although for the first sixteen measures Grofé shuns woodwind and brass for an exclusively string timbre. The theme is gentle, predictable, and tuneful. One can imagine hand-holding honeymooners humming along as they sway to the regular 4/4. A second theme at measure 17 introduces mellow horns and woodwinds, and a softly struck "church" bell, a reference perhaps to the numerous weddings for which Niagara is famous. At measure 33, Grofé combines fragments of both themes and trades them between celli and upper woodwinds. The soft-spoken conversation between instrumentalists is just what one might imagine occurring between two young lovers, at least in the Hollywood version. Listening to the mellifluous "Honeymooners" one can't help wondering, however, if Grofé intended to suggest that Niagara as a honeymoon resort had itself become hackneyed. The music is too simple, too easy, and too transparent; it doesn't offset the physical first movement or the anxious second movement, nor does it set the stage for the cacophony of what is to come, "The Power of Niagara—1961."

The fourth movement is Grofé's musical realization of a power plant, and to that end it includes the sounds of sirens, factory whistles, and all the jarring, clanking noises that might be associated with modern, industrial America. Here is the perfect forum for a master of effects, and Grofé goes all out. Given the composer's displeasure at being asked to supply a brief "noisy" tag for the ending of the *Hudson River Suite* and his numerous explicit declarations of a preference for "smooth" lyrical composition, one can only imagine his thinking regarding this movement. While it does contain melodic moments, especially the brass choir section at the andante molto and its reprise near the end at the andante molto e maestoso, what is most memorable about the almost-ten-minute movement is the sheer quantity of sound. This is extremely loud music that stays loud a long time; the effect is overpowering, and perhaps that is Grofé's intent.

If early visitors to Niagara were awed by the deafening sound of millions of gallons of water cascading over the precipice, modern-day pilgrims are confronted with a new man-made thunder every bit as overwhelming. In the case of the din emanating from the power plant, though, one would be hard pressed to hear such sounds as "the sublimest music on earth," as Eugene Thayer characterized the Falls in 1881.[197] Here Niagara the natural phenomenon has been completely subsumed by Niagara the industrial helpmate. If nineteenth-century paintings, photographs, and prose consciously manipulated the way visitors perceived the Falls, by the mid-twentieth century impressions of the Falls were engineered more thoroughly than any Hudson River School painter could have imagined. Whether it was obvious to the average visitor, by the mid-twentieth century the entire Niagara experience was packaged. Glimpses of the beautiful waterfall and its environs were restricted to those calculated to deliver maximum effect, by Frederick Law Olmsted in his parklike reconstruction of the site. Water flow and divergence was strictly controlled and timed to be at maximum strength during those hours tourists were most likely to be in attendance. Sophisticated lighting effects changed the colors of the water to make it more dramatic and camera friendly. In its relentless clangor, Grofé's fourth movement recognized the utter capitulation of nature to mankind at Niagara. The music may not be his most moving or appealing, but it is perhaps his most honest. By 1961, Niagara had become a power plant.

Grofé's picturesque depictions of American places raise a host of questions.

How successful are the geographical suites as music? As commemorations of specific places? Without the aid of a program or a descriptive title, would listeners be able to distinguish the Mississippi from the Hudson, or Huckleberry Finn from Rip Van Winkle? Would the uninitiated connect the fictional characters with their respective places at all? And would popular audiences intuit the reasons for chimes in "Hendrick Hudson" or those in "Honeymooners"? How are the Debussyian coloristic effects of "The Painted Desert" especially depictive of a western American scene?

It is not necessary to enumerate the many specific place-music correspondences that exist to appreciate the extent of Grofé's memorialization of America's landscapes. While he was inspired by the sights and sounds of particular places, Grofé often used widely understood musical symbols for his depictions: undulating arpeggios for water, brass choirs for majestic or serious moments, woodwinds for bucolic settings, bassoons for humorous characterizations. He also went beyond inherited conventions, however, to achieve the precise effect that he was after by employing state bowling champions, barking dogs, coconut shells, factory whistles, sirens, and wind machines. Perhaps this was a sign of Yankee ingenuity, doing whatever was necessary to achieve a desired result. Never aspiring to documentary truth, Grofé claimed only to "try to describe America in my music."[198] From canyon trails to power plants, sylvan scenes to the Forty-second Street Pier, there was no hierarchy of appropriate materials. Everything was suited for musical treatment. Like Charles Ives's hymn tunes and Civil War songs, classical references and ragtime dances, Grofé's music embraced the high and the low, the cultivated and the popular, the rarified and the raucous; it was all America.

chapter five

Return to Nature:
Recent Reconsiderations

———

ROBERT STARER
Hudson Valley Suite

AT the end of a century that had witnessed unparalleled urban growth, suburban sprawl, the wholesale destruction of natural estuaries and wilderness lands, government-backed policies of clear-cutting that ravaged old-growth timber stands, water contamination that threatened entire species of fish and plants and the nation's drinking supplies, and the production of toxic wastes with no long-term strategies for their containment, U.S. citizens mobilized by the tens of thousands to save what remained of their country's natural bounty.[1] The early efforts of Olmsted and Church to salvage Niagara and protect western wilderness lands pointed the way for generations to come.

Late-nineteenth-century conservationism evolved into late-twentieth-century environmentalism. The Sierra Club, founded by John Muir with 182 charter members in 1892 (the year of Grofé's birth), grew to 2,537 members by 1930, 33,000 by 1965, and more than 325,000 by the early 1980s.[2] As of February 2003, the Sierra Club included 738,000 members. Political activism on behalf of the environment was invigorated by romantic images of nature, which many sought out and embraced. In one instance, residents of a picturesque town situated along the Hudson River Valley and immortalized in thousands of paintings organized to reconcile industry and environment with the artistic legacy.[3] At the same time, renewed interest in the work of the Hudson River School painters manifested itself in broadly disseminated feature articles and museum exhibits. Nineteenth-century landscapes could be seen in shows hung from New England to the Pacific Northwest.[4] In 2001 the *New York Times* devoted a ten-part series to an art-historical study of the Hudson River Valley. As Americans from all strata of society reawakened to the early promise of the nation's natural places, and as scholars once again considered the contributions of the country's first distinctive school of artists, a number of American composers also turned to nature for comfort and inspiration.[5] This chapter considers three of them and what their compositions say about American places and identity at the beginning of the new millennium.

If, as Perry Miller observed, place is one way in which Americans have recognized themselves throughout the nation's history, then musical works by Robert Starer (1924–2001), Ellen Taaffe Zwilich (b. 1939), and Dana Paul Perna (b. 1958) tell us something about the effectiveness and endurance of that idea. Collectively, they reflect a variety of contemporary attitudes toward America's natural places.[6] In *Hudson Valley Suite* (1983), Starer conjures music from the same promontory that inspired Frederic Edwin Church more than a century earlier, when he painted his misty landscapes of the river valley. Starer's program notes refer specifically to that nineteenth-century painter and his works; the composer is unabashed in his romantic revisioning of this oft-captured natural place.

Perna too memorializes places in the picturesque Northeast and, like Starer, has been animated by other artists. *Prout's Neck* (1991–92) is an orchestral essay he wrote in response to viewing Winslow Homer's paintings of Prouts Neck, Maine. In another work, trading on the title of Charles Ives's much beloved *Three Places in New England,* Perna presents his own *Three Places on Long Island* (1991, 1997), although he insists he is "alluding to [the Ives piece] in name and spirit only."[7] As a native of "the Island," Perna is most at home with the historic sites and natural beauty of that tract of land. He also frequents Manhattan with some regularity, as do many Long Islanders. Perna captures one upscale block in the city with the third of his *Three Locations for Guitar,* titled "164 East 74th Street," the final Manhattan address of Charles and Harmony Ives.[8] In still another piece, *Oswego Set,* the composer creates a sonic tour of an upstate New York college campus, including musical snapshots of distinctive buildings, sculptures, and landmarks. For Perna, the places he visits and inhabits are steady sources of musical inspiration.

If Perna regularly succumbs to a meaningful place, Ellen Taaffe Zwilich does not. Her fourth symphony, *The Gardens* (1999), is her only large-scale work to suggest any connection with a place. Nonetheless, it clearly manifests an important strain of late-twentieth-century thinking in its sung pledges to "protect our heritage" and "leave a verdant earth." Commissioned to celebrate the gardens at Michigan State University, Symphony No. 4 is as much a product of its time as were the urban-focused paintings, photographs, and musical compositions of the early twentieth century. They too reflected one aspect of their cultural milieu. Embedded deeply, if unconsciously, within *The Gardens* are nineteenth-century assumptions about the unique natural laboratory provided by the American place, along with twentieth-century attitudes toward environmentalism.[9]

The idea of the "palliative effects" of nature, nature as "a tonic for the ailments of civilization,"[10] successfully marketed with hydrotherapy and rest cures in the closing years of the nineteenth century, has been modified, updated, and injected with new urgency, as environmental groups mobilize to save what remains of America's natural places.[11] Zwilich's symphony captures this most modern concern and more. The works of these three composers provide yet another glimpse into our continually changing sense of self and how that is tied to the land we inhabit.

Any who doubt the vitality of place as a source of inspiration for late-twentieth-century American composers, should have spoken with Robert Starer.[12] A composer, teacher, pianist, harpist, holder of MacDowell and Yaddo residencies, winner of multiple Guggenheims and NEA awards, and member of the American Academy of Arts, Starer was an eloquent and persuasive spokesman on the topic of place. He was born in Vienna in 1924; a series of political acts and personal choices took him from his native Austria to Israel, to England, and finally to the United States in 1947. He became an American citizen a decade later. His early, more itinerant life made Starer especially aware and appreciative of place.

In 1999, speaking from his home overlooking the Hudson River, Starer explained: "I was born an Austrian, became a German when they took over, went to Israel to study music, was a member of the Royal Air Force of England in World War II, but *this* is my home."[13] He felt very strongly about place—and not just the generous, pastoral acreage in Woodstock, New York, that afforded him the serene environment in which to compose; he felt strongly about the larger idea of place as a source of inspiration. For Starer, "place . . . meets my intention."[14] Like Ives, he was motivated by the human associations with places. It was his connection to place that enabled him to write the sensitive and heartfelt *Hudson Valley Suite* in 1983.

Starer's Woodstock home was close to the fabled Olana, the Moorish-style mansion of the nineteenth century's most famous Hudson River School painter, Frederic Edwin Church. The two houses both sit high above the river and share similar views from different angles. Tamed gardens surround the houses, while lush greenery forms a ruffled collar around the larger properties. Each house looks down on the Hudson River Valley. Three hours north of New York City, relatively little has changed at this particular point along the river to interrupt the contemplative scene. Starer's second movement, "The View from Olana," honors the painter and the larger place in a single gesture. One indeed feels as if Starer's music and Church's numerous Olana sketches and paintings were inspired by the same spirit. Starer's appreciation of

Church's work and his own deep attachment to the lyrical landscape that surrounds his home invest the *Hudson Valley Suite* with an integrity that speaks volumes about the importance of place to the man and his music. Commissioned by the Hudson Valley Philharmonic, the suite is also a testament to the power of the fabled American place over this foreign-born citizen.[15]

The suite has five movements, "Sources," "The View from Olana," "Dances on a Terrace," "A Glimpse of West Point," and "Past Gotham and on to the Sea." Each celebrates the river or valley from a different vantage point with music of a distinctive mood. A recurring theme, however, unites the suite in much the same way as the river unites the perspectives. In addition, a rich assortment of percussion timbres lend their colors to all the movements, creating an integrated tone-color palette.[16] Starer takes listeners on a guided tour down the waterway, starting somewhere upstream of his home.

The first movement, "Sources," portrays the numerous tributaries that combine to form the Hudson. As Starer explained, the Hudson is not like the Nile, with a single source; many small streams and rivers come together. According to the composer, the multiple sources gave him his initial musical structure, one that gradually coalesced as if from a series of individual sound tributaries. Different instrument families in different registers depict the distinct sources. Starer's transparent counterpoint is the perfect vehicle for this physical phenomenon; we hear discrete rivulets join together. Woodwinds, long associated with pastoral scenes, are initially spotlighted, but before long percussion, brass and strings join forces.

Like the Housatonic memorialized in Ives's musical paean, the small sources that are at the head of the Hudson barely hint at their latent power. But the hidden potential that lies in Starer's musical rivulets becomes clear as excited, fluttering trills cascade through piccolos, flutes, and clarinets in a series of momentum-building arpeggios. Diminished sonorities pulsate with pent-up energy. In contrast to this lively gesture, a muted trumpet sings a more somber melodic fragment. This brief introspective melody, confined to the compass of a minor third, will be recalled in all subsequent movements. It will inject a mood of seriousness to even the most lighthearted moments of the piece. Though the river's sources may be playful, Starer insists that his listeners be reflective. The trumpet heralds something more weighty.

Ex. 5.1: Robert Starer, *Hudson Valley Suite,* First Movement, "Sources," trumpet melody, mm 9–10. © 1983 by MCA Music.

If the early arpeggios started and stopped and started up again, seeming to prevent momentum from gathering, the introduction of swirling string music launches the piece forward. Ultimately the entire movement pulses with momentum that is irresistible; we are drawn along with the river current. Starer clearly takes great joy in the different rhythms of the waterway as he juxtaposes measures of two, three, four, and five beats. Unable to contain the driving waters in neat symmetrical patterns, the music breaks into an extended passage in alternating 10/8 and 8/8 meters. Woodwinds, brass, and drums start the molto allegro passage, which is taken over by strings.

Ex. 5.2: Robert Starer, *Hudson Valley Suite,* First Movement, "Sources," mm 58–61. © 1983 by MCA Music.

The passage gathers forces and intensity over the course of fifty-two measures before the return of the opening theme. What was a somber, muted tune in the trumpet is now a victorious, *fortissimo* announcement made jointly by woodwinds and strings. What started as delicate *pianissimo* quiverings in woodwinds ends as thumping, hieratic triple *forte* unisons for the entire orchestra. Starer has established the vitality of this iconic river. As he coaxes the river from its sources to its widest spot, he summons images of the waterway from the recesses of our collective memories to the present moment.

Reverberations from a vibraphone doubled by glockenspiel against shimmering string harmonics paint a magical opening to the second movement, "The View from Olana." Starer's distinctive timbral preferences (woodwinds, glockenspiel, vibraphone) connect this movement to the first, even though what were sparkling, almost dazzling sounds in the opening moderato now appear more introspective in the andante. With its subdued instrumental colors and relaxed tempo, the second movement provides a sharp contrast to the rhythmically driving first and third movements; this is music of quiet moods and unhurried contemplation. A lyrical line floats deliberately from one instrument to another, with little suggestion of drama or purpose. Starer considers the view from Olana to be "uniquely beautiful, absolutely pastoral,"[17] and we hear the musical manifestation of that idyll in soft, gentle woodwinds and muted strings. Starer's oboe solo is a model of simplicity. *Pianissimo* strings sway in an effortless 6/8, while the soloist hovers on top. About this movement Starer wrote: "Olana was the home of Frederic E. Church, one of the Hudson River School of painters. It is situated a few miles south of the village of Hudson and the river valley is at its most lyrically beautiful there. There is a painting of this scene by Church with the sun breaking through a haze that engulfs the Catskill Mountains. That painting directly inspired this music."[18]

Ex. 5.3: Robert Starer, *Hudson Valley Suite*, Second Movement, "The View from Olana," mm 21–26. © 1983 by MCA Music.

Just as the Hudson River School painters idealized their subjects, a hundred years later Starer also does so with his second movement's romantic soundscape. Overlooking this quintessentially American river, Starer finds unique beauty: nature at her most serene, powerful, and perhaps even divine. This music captures one attitude toward America's natural places at the end of the twentieth century.

But Starer is not so trapped in a nineteenth-century vision of the Hudson that he doesn't acknowledge other, more modern associations; movements 3, 4, and 5 offer additional perspectives, ones that update the sacred iconic place. The third movement, "Dances on a Terrace," is pure fantasy. No equivalent to Church's Olana paintings anchors this particular musical postcard. Starer notes: "If you were going down the river in the evening past Kingston and Poughkeepsie, you might hear snatches of dance music from the various terraces of the estates that line the river. These dances are all imagined, of course."[19] "Dances" provides another venue for a rhythmic romp, as well as the first evidence that Starer's Hudson River Valley is peopled, albeit with an imaginary cast.[20]

True to his program, none of the dances is fully realized; we hear assorted "snatches" of rhythmic music, just enough to glean that the valley residents are spirited and energetic. The third movement is as carefree as the second was contemplative. Measures of five beats are juxtaposed with measures of four, three, and two, and suggest a melange of ballroom dances and quadrilles. There is something vaguely comic about this movement, with its opening faux-serious fanfare and gimpy clarinet solo. One senses that Starer doesn't take these cliff-side revelers all that seriously, or perhaps he just feels outside their milieu. As in the first movement, disengaged rhythms and fragments of tunes waft freely through the intervening atmosphere before an extended section midway through recalls a Latin-inspired dance; at this point the music settles down. Here Starer adjoins measures of 2/4, 2/4, and 3/4. Bongos, timpani, and then tom-toms pound out the rhythm; horns and trombones add their voices. Twenty measures into the syncopated passage, Starer overlays a sweeping melody in woodwinds and strings. As the entire orchestra becomes involved and crescendos to a climax, the effect is pure Hollywood.

Does Starer intend to portray the well-heeled estate dwellers as actors in some kind of big-screen extravaganza? The suggestion of film music is powerful. Before the evening balls are over, Starer captures a halfhearted waltz, recirculates earlier materials from the movement, and recalls the circumspect first-movement trumpet theme. He may not take the revelers completely seriously, but he does the river. The decorative terrace dancers are noteworthy only in relation to Starer's beloved river valley; the return of the trumpet theme reminds listeners of that.

West Point, just twenty miles south of Poughkeepsie, inspired Starer's fourth movement. Although he never attended the academy, the composer used its position along the Hudson to reflect upon his own experiences with military life, "its excitement, its difficulties and ironies."[21] "A Glimpse of West Point" is the shortest of all five movements and uses expected tone colors and gestures to evoke military images. Trumpets call back and forth to each other, while flutes and piccolo conjure the sounds of a fife. One wonders if the bassoons, which make a three-measure appearance starting at measure 25, are meant to suggest some kind of blowhard officer, an instance of the "ironies" of military life. The only lyrical gesture in the entire two-and-a-half-minute movement is given to the strings as they interpret the unifying trumpet theme of the previous movements, and then once again to strings accompanied by flute and piccolo as they play a fragment of that same tune. Starer uses one other gesture to unite this movement with the preceding three: just six measures from the end of the piece, he briefly showcases the vibraphone. As noted earlier, the instrument suggests something magical or imaginary. And perhaps this is an apt mood for a fantasy voyage down a mythical river past a spot where people train to be soldiers.

Though Grofé regretted Kostelanetz's imposition of a noisy, urban finish

Ex. 5.4: Robert Starer, *Hudson Valley Suite,* Third Movement, "Dances on a Terrace," mm 90–96. © 1983 by MCA Music.

on his otherwise pastoral *Hudson River Suite,* Starer showed no resistance to such a tag for his own work. As a composer whose "first impulse [was] often rhythmic," the city provided him with exciting subject matter.[22] The final movement, "Past Gotham and on to the Sea," is musically and programmatically a summation of all that has transpired, as the composer explains: "Gotham is one of the nicest names I know for New York City. This last movement is vigorous and lively and is in Rondo form. Just before the Coda, motives from all the preceding movements reoccur as though the river, just before it flows into the sea, re-experiences its entire past life."[23]

Like Ives, Starer harbored mixed feelings toward the city. Each man spent a major portion of his professional career in the metropolis, Starer as a teacher of composition and Ives as a businessman, but both preferred life away from the maelstrom of activity and sought refuge in rural retreats. The country gave each the space he needed to think, see, and hear. In the *Hudson Valley Suite* and *The Housatonic at Stockbridge,* each composer also associated what were initially small, apparently inconsequential rivulets and streams with great waters that lay beyond. In this way, both connected America's own rivers with the oceans of the world: the personally meaningful with the universally resonant. Ives's *Housatonic* portrayed a quiet pastoral waterway wending its way toward "the adventurous sea!"[24] As Starer's piece moves toward the sea, it recalls themes from each of the preceding movements "as though the river . . . re-experiences its entire past life." Like Starer, Ives also recalled the opening motive of the generative hymn tune of his piece in its very last sounds. But there the similarities end. Save for "The View from Olana," Starer's work was outgoing and assertive; this was a public statement written in response to a public request. Ives's piece, even at its most climactic, remained intensely personal; it was written for no one but Harmony and himself.

Starer launches his concluding movement, with a nimble 6/8 meter and presto leggiero tempo. The meter provides a flexible rhythmic template, one that easily accommodates passages of strict walking bass, brief syncopated forays, or sustained sections of swing, each of which makes an appearance in this final movement. Early on, Starer introduces a march theme in the strings that will reappear in the oboe and clarinet and again later, played by the flute and piccolo. The introspective trumpet melody heard first in "Sources" returns in a spirited string fughetta. One is reminded of Berlioz's idée fixe and its numerous distorting reincarnations.

Starer draws upon a distinct musical style to evoke "Gotham" itself when, like Grofé, he inserts a jazzy break. A slinky clarinet solo accompanied by string bass and brushed snare drums leaves its modern, urban imprint on the suite. No sooner does the *pianissimo* jazz moment get started, however, than brass interrupts with a *forte* fanfare version of the opening trumpet theme. The bassoon reasserts the jazz tune, this time accompanied by string bass and brushed suspended cymbals; the reference is unmistakable (see Ex. 5.5).

It too is overtaken, this time by a quiet return of the rondo march theme that gradually crescendoes to *fortissimo.* The march is fragmented and melds into a dignified, full-voiced recall of the trumpet theme in woodwinds and strings.

Starer is none too subtle in recalling the former lives of the river. Descending diminished arpeggios reminiscent of those that announced the opening of "Sources" and swirling string motions like those that energized the first movement both return. The Hudson meets the sea in a last gush that moves the

224

Ex. 5.5: Robert Starer, *Hudson Valley Suite,* Fifth Movement, "Past Gotham and on to the Sea," mm 145–151. © 1983 by MCA Music.

entire orchestra from *pianissimo* to *fortissimo* in the final three measures. It is a triumphant marriage of waters, one in keeping with Starer's belief in the river as an exalted American place. A brief, picturesque, musical tour, *Hudson Valley Suite* does not aspire to transcendence; neither does it chart a new course, nor express its ideas in a particularly distinctive or different voice. What it does do is confirm the vitality and importance of its subject as a continuing source of inspiration, especially for those who live within its realm. As the works of the Hudson River School painters enjoyed a renaissance of interest, as residents of small upstate New York towns faced off against insensitive purveyors of an increasingly homogenized culture to preserve their unique environs, Robert Starer contributed an homage of his own to his adopted place.

DANA PAUL PERNA

Prout's Neck and *Three Places on Long Island*

Other nineteenth-century artists have inspired contemporary U.S. composers, as Dana Paul Perna's *Prout's Neck* (1991–92) attests; it is based on two paintings by Winslow Homer. Perna was born in New Hyde Park, Long Island, N.Y., in 1958, and brought up just a few miles east, in Syosset. He was educated at C. W. Post College of Long Island University and at Northwestern University; he is a poet, painter, composer, arranger, teacher, mastering engineer, audio-editor, writer, music copyist, music editor, and conductor. His compositions have been heard from Rochester to Moscow, from Arkansas to Utah, from his native Long Island to Latvia. In March 1998, in anticipation of the premiere of *Three Places on Long Island,* Perna was the subject of a story in the *New York Times.*[25] Although he enjoys less name recognition than perhaps any other composer treated in this study, Perna invites consideration because of his ongoing memorialization of American places in music that is played around the country and the globe.

225

A regular traveler, over the years Perna has often visited relatives in Rochester, New York. On one such occasion in August 1990, the composer took in the Memorial Art Gallery of the University of Rochester, and a show entitled "Winslow Homer in the 1890s: Prout's Neck." That exhibit and a subsequent one in New York were the beginning of *Prout's Neck*. As Perna explained it: "Since I had always been interested in Homer's work, I found the exhibition moving and, as it turned out, musically inspiring. The paintings Homer produced in Prout's Neck afforded him with many opportunities to examine the colors and the interplay of the ocean waves as they hit land in different light and weather conditions. The sense of land and sky are not unrelated to his paintings either and it was the total impact of Homer's vision that allowed me to hear his work as well as to enjoy them visually."[26]

Two of Homer's works in particular caught Perna's attention: *The Artist's Studio in an Afternoon Fog* (1894) and *Right and Left* (1908–9). Both were created at Homer's studio-home in Prout's Neck, Maine. Although he had been born in Boston, Homer's deep attachment to this rugged place, his twenty-seven-year residence there, and his numerous paintings of its inlets and vistas have made his name synonymous with coastal Maine. As William Howe Downes observed in 1911, "the place, the time, and the man were well met."[27]

By the 1870s, Prout's Neck had become an established summer destination for many well-heeled urban dwellers seeking a retreat from the heat and grime of the city. As larger numbers of Americans were able to afford extended holidays, Prout's Neck attracted an increasingly diverse population. Access by railroad and steamer made it a convenient getaway "at the edge of modern society."[28] Soon after the extended Homer family started vacationing there in 1875, they began acquiring land and building their own homes to accommodate the growing family.[29] Through their purchases, activism, and influence, the Homer clan was largely responsible for the development of Prout's Neck, including the placement and types of houses that could be built—and, hence, the class of people who could afford to build them.[30]

Prout's Neck became the exclusive place it is today in no small measure because of the efforts of the Homers. According to Patricia Junker, the area quickly grew into a haven for the highly educated and affluent, "the social equivalent of the Century Club in New York or the North Woods Club in the Adirondacks."[31] Although Homer's brother's house, El Rancho, built in 1881, and his parents' house, "The Ark," completed in 1883, remained summer residences exclusively, Winslow Homer's studio-home did not. Originally a small carriage house close to The Ark, it was moved a bit farther north and renovated in 1884, under the guidance of the Portland architect John Calvin

Stevens. This became the year-round residence for the artist. Whereas The Ark was a gathering place for the summer social set, Homer's simple, rustic studio remained a workplace first and foremost.[32]

Winslow Homer's move to Prout's Neck was in keeping with the nineteenth-century trend of painters, starting with Thomas Cole and continuing with Church, Cropsey, Bierstadt, and Inness, among others, who sought inspiring retreats in picturesque locales.[33] Many built enormous showplaces, yet Homer sought only a space in which to do his work. Although he was often accused of being antisocial and reclusive, Winslow Homer actually forged close relationships with his family and grew to know many of the locals, who were his only company for much of the year. They respected his need for solitude and gave him the space he required. Homer's personal identification with the place, the organic relationship of his studio to the topography, and their collective manifestation in his painting *The Artist's Studio in an Afternoon Fog* are all present in Perna's piece (see color plate facing page 51).

The composer is careful to explain the nature of his music and its association with the painting: "I regard 'Prout's Neck' as an essay as opposed to a tone poem or an overture. Just as an essay forms logical patterns out of the material with which it opens in its first paragraph, here too is where I wanted 'Prout's Neck' to be formed; from literary models and not musical ones. Homer's visual world gave me the direction to take the orchestral colors from—that the instruments were the hues and not oils on canvas."[34]

In other comments, Perna distinguishes his work from more literally programmatic pieces: "This painting is only 'depicted' through this music in non-literal terms; that the mood of Homer's work and the tone of its visual fabric and vocabulary was [sic] to be evoked musically."[35] Clearly auditors are not to listen for craggy shores or lapping water, but rather for Homer's "visual world": its mood, tone, colors, and some larger, all-encompassing atmosphere.

Although Maine's coast looks out directly onto the Atlantic Ocean, hundreds of bays, coves, islands, and inlets suggest more intimate settings. In town after town, residents can walk directly to the shore and collect rocks; they can watch loons diving and hear their plaintive call. There is something personal and immediate about the Maine coast. Homer captures that sense of scale and intimacy in a painting that is relatively modest in dimensions, 24 by 30 inches.[36] He controls the sense of drama by using muted shades: mossy green, silvery gray, purple-black. Everything is subdued. Overly theatrical displays would ring untrue to both the landscape and the people who inhabit it. A luminous sky lifts a viewer's eyes upward from the dark foreground of the painting. Befitting the title, Homer's studio is the focal point of the canvas, but perhaps only reluctantly so; it is one of a set of buildings whose fuzzy outlines form the middle-ground horizontal. Given their lack of distinction, The Ark, the stable, and the studio are less *buildings* than they are additional land forms, so complete is their integration within the topography of the shoreline. What sets off the studio from the others is a fog-shrouded sun that hangs in the sky just above and to the right of the building, whose light glows through the balcony windows, suggesting that light emanates from within. Like firelight glowing from a hearth, the sunlight softly glowing through the studio makes viewers aware of a human presence: the artist is at work.

The painting is, in Perna's words, "a masterpiece of sustained mood."[37] Nothing, not even the thick, heavy daubs of white that suggest waves hitting the rocks, disturbs the sense of quiet containment that Homer creates. We are looking not at a passive or inert landscape, but at one whose power is momentarily subdued. All elements are in accord; they are all under the spell of the fog. This pervasive atmosphere, according to the composer, "influenced the final third" of the equally small-scale, ten-minute orchestral essay.[38]

If the final third of *Prout's Neck* responds to this mood, so too does the opening of the piece. Like Homer's painting, Perna's music is a unified vision. All the melodic ideas present at the close have grown from those found in the opening measures. And these, like the light that glows in the painting, are evanescent in character. Just a few notes that suggest a melodic shape are plucked in the harp, then picked up in the bassoon and expanded upon by a French horn before finding their fullest expression in the violins. But even here the soft, smooth, unobtrusive string treatment keeps the idea from dominating the larger soundscape; it is a part of the whole effect (see Ex. 5.6).

As fog shrouds everything in the painting, a misty palette of orchestral colors bathes the larger piece. Low woodwinds and muted brass anchor the sound; Perna asks bass clarinet and bassoon to play "supportively."[39] A variety of percussion instruments contribute their unique sounds to the atmosphere: orchestral bells, triangles, *crotales,* vibraphones, chimes, and gongs, struck with every kind of soft and hard mallet, take turns reverberating throughout the piece. Their lingering resonances permeate the soundscape. The contrasting middle section is more clearly inspired by the Homer painting *Right and Left,* which captures two ducks shot out of the air plunging to their deaths. Here Perna enlists the piccolo for "bird-like" effects, and whips, and rim shots on snare drums to evoke the sounds of hunters' guns.[40] While eschewing literalism, his score is replete with verbal cues to guide instrumentalists toward the exact effects he seeks: "splash," "floating," "singingly," "snarl," "shriek," "splat," "explode," "seamlessly," "desolately." It was Homer's attention to myriad details, although not as obvious as they might be in an overly fussy painting, that allowed the artist to create the precise, suggestive atmosphere he sought. The same is true of Perna's work: the music flows naturally, even while he coaxes and tweaks every utterance.

One hears Homer's soft shades and fuzzy edges in slowly moving music that prefers the understated *pianissimo* to *piano* range.[41] A total of twenty incremental tempo changes traverse a narrow compass, from a slow of a quarter note at 44 to the most energetic pace, a quarter note at 80. A preponderance of quarter and half notes, especially in the framing outer thirds of the piece, preserves the unhurried atmosphere. When numerous small tempo changes occur within a few measures of each other, one wonders how audible they really are. But the goal is not obsessive accuracy, although that is necessary. The goal is *effect:* undulation, wavering, a musical manifestation of the blurry, out-of-focus image produced by fog, and Perna achieves that.

As is true of any composer living in a post-Debussy world, the imprint of the master colorist is evident throughout Perna's score, but especially in the framing outer sections. Appropriate to Perna's (and Homer's) subject, *La Mer* is never far away. A preference for woodwinds supported by strings, whiffs of whole tone scales, rocking non-tertiary harmonies, arpeggios that softly undulate, all these combine to contain musical momentum and evoke *being* somewhere rather than going somewhere. Dramatic events might occur at this locale, but they are not the focus of the music at this time; as the composer insists, this is not a narrative.[42]

Another composer's influence is also audible. Given the many references to Charles Ives in other place pieces by Dana Paul Perna, it is not surprising to hear echoes of *The Housatonic at Stockbridge* in *Prout's Neck*. These are most evident in the opening measures of the work, where Perna, like Ives, lays in a sonic background of sustained notes in the lowest strings that anchor the music and the momentum. Increasingly active lines are assigned to higher instruments. As Ives did in *The Housatonic,* Perna has a simple melody emerge from the soundscape: where Ives had the defining hymn tune waft into the atmosphere in a gentle French horn passage, Perna has a harp softly introduce a melody that is doubled by the cello. Within two measures the bassoon and then the French horn join in. Ives's *Housatonic* and Perna's *Prout's Neck* share three qualities: first, both evoke a "dreamy realm"—inspired for Ives by Robert Underwood Johnson's poetry, for Perna by Homer's foggy seascape; second, both attempt to capture a place at a particular moment in time; and third, at some level both pieces are responses to the creative efforts of others Americans.

This last quality connects Perna with a number of other American composers who have found and continue to find inspiration in their own nation's artists and writers who have also celebrated the American place. It connects

Ex. 5.6: Dana Paul Perna, *Prout's Neck*, mm 1–10. © 1998 by Pernaskopy Music. Used by permission.

him with William Henry Fry, who could easily have been influenced by the 1840 moving diorama or the Niagara panoramas of Friend and Frankenstein that circulated widely and concurrently with the composition of his *Niagara Symphony* in the 1850s. It connects him with Ives, and with Copland, whose *Quiet City* was composed as incidental music to Irwin Shaw's play of the same name. It connects him with Grofé, who reached into American history and

literature and used real events and fictional characters as sources of inspiration. It connects him with Starer, who made a painting by Frederic Edwin Church a focal point of his own tribute to the Hudson River Valley; and with Steve Reich, a composer to be discussed in the following chapter who turned to the poetry of William Carlos Williams. Music inspired by art inspired by place has become a national tradition. It is one way in which reverent attitudes toward America's places have persisted to the present.

Three Places on Long Island, Perna's own musical triptych of places, is another of these tributes. The sixteen-minute orchestral work has three continuous movements that, according to the composer, were named "to honor three Long Island locations that have deep meaning to me, the Walt Whitman Birthplace in Huntington, Theodore Roosevelt's home Sagamore Hill in Oyster Bay, and the lighthouse at Montauk Point."[43] As in *Prout's Neck,* rather than attempt to depict anything literally, Perna sought to capture the larger mood at each of these very different places. *Three Places* came together over a number of years as music and images coalesced. The work began as Perna was returning home after a trip to Europe in 1989: "I was flying back from Amsterdam when the pilot announced that [because of heavy clouds that had formed over the Atlantic] we were going to drop below the clouds. When we broke through the thick white cover at first all I saw was ocean, then a little spit of land, and all at once the Montauk Point Lighthouse filled my vision. I was so moved by the sight that it planted a seed in my brain, a musical seed."[44]

At a later date Perna visited Walt Whitman's birthplace in Huntington, Long Island. In an area dotted with dozens of three-hundred-year-old landmarks and towns incorporated in the 1600s, where history is a part of the fish-shaped landmass, Whitman's residence regularly elicits special reverence.[45] A native son, Whitman listened to America and spoke for an entire nation, and his words resonated with Perna. "I had always loved the opening line of *Leaves of Grass,* 'From Paumanok it begins.' As a Long Islander I felt he was writing about my life, too, using the Indian name for our home. And I felt the idea for a composition about landmarks begin to grow."[46]

A third site of inspiration was close by. Just northeast of Huntington, on the north shore, is Oyster Bay, the quietly picturesque town where Theodore Roosevelt had a home he called Sagamore Hill. It became familiar to hosts of Americans as the summer White House. With its placement deep within a thicket of trees, its dark brick and frame construction, and the prominent north room's mahogany and black walnut paneling decorated with flags, paintings, and trophies from numerous hunting trips, the sturdy, sprawling twenty-three-room house was a fitting symbol for the cigar-smoking, horseback-riding leader of the Rough Riders. Given this larger effect, it is all the more touching to come upon an outdoor memorial to the twenty-year-old son of the president, Quentin Roosevelt, who was killed in a dogfight with German planes over France in World War I. It is this aspect of Sagamore Hill that touched Perna, and he immediately began work on "an appropriately elegiac orchestral movement."[47] With this third place, his concept was complete.

In the "majestic and commanding" first movement, "Fanfare: Walt Whitman House, Huntington," Perna came face to face with the poet who regularly found inspiration in music: "I remember standing in front of the Walt Whitman Birthplace and thinking how this one poet's voice changed the course of literature. That triumphant feeling made me think of the sound of trumpets, and the orchestral piece began to take shape in my mind."[48]

One wonders about the extent to which the composer also "heard" the poem "The Mystic Trumpeter" emanating from the walls of Whitman's home: "HARK, Some wild trumpeter, some strange musician,/Hovering unseen in air, vibrates capricious tunes to-night./I hear thee trumpeter, listening, alert, I catch thy notes,/Now pouring, whirling like a tempest round me,/Now low, subdued, now in the distance lost."[49] As a trumpeter himself, Perna could feel a personal bond with, perhaps even "catch the notes" of, the poet who on numerous occasions sought the imagery of trumpets and bugles for his verses.[50] Befitting a fanfare, brass and percussion timbres dominate the three-minute movement, with woodwinds joining in only to segue into the following elegy. The fanfare is emphatic and enjoining, outspoken in its *forte* declamations and clashing dissonances, regal in its rhythms. This is the confident, optimistic poet, the author of a "glad, exulting, culminating song!"[51] Though Perna did not consciously seek to be nationalistic, by summoning the spirit of Walt Whitman to announce his musical essay, he inevitably stamped the piece and the place he memorialized as American.[52]

With "Elegy: Sagamore Hill, Oyster Bay," Perna commemorates another place ripe with associations for Americans. Of Teddy Roosevelt's six children, none captured the attention of his father or the fancy of the nation more than Quentin, his youngest. As a three-year-old when his father assumed the presidency, the always-mischievous leader of the "White House Gang," as Roosevelt referred to Quentin and his friends, grew up beloved.[53] His charmed progress through childhood, adolescence, and entry into Harvard was followed by a national press eager to chronicle the antics of the golden boy. With his father's blessing, Quentin left college to follow his three older brothers to war; Americans cheered his patriotism and bravery. But in July 1918, a member of the press delivered the news to the former president at Sagamore Hill that Quentin had been shot down and was presumed dead. The nation grieved, his family most of all. "To feel that one has inspired a boy to conduct that has resulted in his death, has a pretty serious side for a father," acknowledged the president.[54] On 14 August, one month to the day after his son died, Theodore Roosevelt wrote, "He died at the crest of life, in the glory of the dawn."[55] Never recovering from the shock of losing his boy, within six months he too was dead. The spirit that had so animated Sagamore Hill was gone. Millions of parents lost millions of sons in the "war to end all wars," but Quentin Roosevelt's death carried symbolic weight, for he had been the nation's darling.

Perna's second movement captures this larger sadness. Ives's spirit first makes its presence known here, informing this new set of *Three Places*. Ives conjured the fallen Civil War soldiers of the 54th Massachusetts Regiment and a nation's grief in *The "St. Gaudens" in Boston Common (Colonel Robert Gould Shaw and His Colored Regiment)*; similarly, Perna creates his own atmospheric tribute to another war's martyr in "Elegy: Sagamore Hill, Oyster Bay."[56] With time separating both composers from the wars they commemorate, each approaches his subject as if from a distance. In "Elegy," slow, muted, *pianissimo* strings set a somber tone before they are overtaken by even slower woodwinds. When horns enter, the pace slows down more. Moments after a dissonant chord rattles through the entire orchestra, taps wafts in from an offstage trumpet. Snare drums accompany with their cadence. What could be a superficial gesture, a gimmick, is not.[57] Numerous brief, expressive melodies weave their way into the musical lamentation, but, like Quentin himself, none develops beyond its initial promise. Though Sagamore Hill will forever be a place of national historic significance because of its associations with the twenty-sixth president of the United States, it also will remain the home of a family who lost one of their own. At Sagamore Hill, the personally meaningful and the nationally significant are thoroughly entwined. Perna is at his best capturing places of thoughtful reflection.

The third movement, "Evocation: Montauk Point, 'The Lighthouse,'" gives the composer another chance to commemorate a significant landmark familiar to all Long Islanders. Standing sentry at the easternmost tip of the isle, it rises from sandy soil to announce where the land and the Atlantic meet. It warns ships and guides planes, and it inspires reflection as well. Surrounded on three sides by chilly waters, a visitor is immediately aware of the vulnerability of this narrow point. At the same time there is something powerful and expansive about the site. When one looks out over the ocean, nothing restrains the imagination, nothing confines one's thoughts. There is a welcoming unknown. Such spots encourage dreaming, and the Montauk lighthouse symbolizes that state of mind.

Perna sees all that and more in the beacon: "There's so much history here on Long Island. George Washington signed the construction papers that allowed the Montauk Lighthouse to be built. And Teddy Roosevelt led his Rough Riders there after they returned from the Spanish-American War. I really wanted to capture some of that drama and significance in my music."[58]

He accomplishes this in music that starts introspective and ends victorious. Along the way, we hear evocations of the surrounding water in rippling clarinet passages and tremolo strings, and memories of the moods and music of the two earlier movements. The timbre of a choir of French horns recalls a similar choralelike moment in "Elegy,"[59] while the music they play comes directly from the opening "Fanfare" movement. The soft, slow-moving string choir that opens "Evocation" reminds listeners of a similar palette of sounds that introduced the second movement. A descending melodic passage, which connected "Fanfare" to "Elegy" and then reappeared in a modified graceful reincarnation later in the second movement, returns for a third time, now in a newly altered and augmented version in "Evocation." Here the presence of tritones in the melodic line suggests an ambiguity that didn't exist before, perhaps an apt sonic representation of the phrase "toward the unknown region," which Perna includes in his score minutes later in the music.[60] With this phrase, Perna alludes one last time to Walt Whitman: "Darest thou now, O soul,/Walk out with me toward the unknown region,/Where neither ground is for the feet, nor any path to follow?"[61] As the final movement recalls earlier aspects of the piece, it celebrates all of Long Island. For Perna, art, literature, history, and place are thoroughly entwined as symbol and reality.

ELLEN TAAFFE ZWILICH
Symphony No. 4, *The Gardens*

Unlike Starer and Perna, whose attachments to places have manifested themselves in numerous programmatic works, Ellen Taaffe Zwilich has concentrated on writing predominantly abstract instrumental pieces in the classical tradition—symphonies, concerti, and chamber music in particular. Aside from Symphony No. 4, *The Gardens*, written in 1999, there is little musical evidence that place has mattered much at all to the Pulitzer Prize–winning composer. In this unique instance Zwilich reveals a profound, if subliminal, contemporary attitude toward America's natural places.[62] By composing a paean and pledge to the Earth, Zwilich reflects not only modern-day notions of environmental stewardship but also one aspect of America's historic relationship to its natural bounty.

Born in Miami, Florida, and educated at Florida State University and the Juilliard School of Music in New York, Zwilich has made homes in both East Coast states and, to date, divides her time between them. Such continuous identification with the East makes Zwilich's authorship of a work celebrating a Midwest site initially perplexing. But there is an explanation. When John and Dortha Withrow of Michigan State University commissioned Zwilich to write a major work in honor of their alma mater and its gardens, the place was little known to the composer except by name; it did not hold any particular meaning for Zwilich. Unique among the composers discussed in this book, Zwilich had no extended experience or investment in the place she eventually memorialized in sound. It was only in the process of visiting the East Lansing campus, getting to know the Withrows, and writing her Symphony No. 4 that Zwilich became genuinely attached to the gardens and paused to consider the lessons they had to offer.

The William James Beal Botanical Garden at Michigan State University was established in 1873 and is "the oldest continuously operating botanical garden of its kind in the United States."[63] Here students, scholars, and visitors can enjoy more than five thousand kinds of plants and trees, as well as demonstration gardens and exhibits. Individual beds devoted to perfume plants, fiber plants, food plants, flavoring plants, and medicinal plants, among others, introduce observers to the idea of nature as an essential resource. From its inception the Beal Garden was "an outdoor laboratory for the study and appreciation of plants by students in botany, horticulture, forestry, agriculture, biology, pharmacology, natural science, veterinary science, landscape architecture, anthropology, and art."[64] And so it is today. The garden is part of Michigan State's collection that includes horticulture gardens, a 4-H Children's Garden, and exhibits focused upon forest communities and landscape and economic plants.[65]

Tucked in the northern corner of the five-acre site is an exhibit dedicated to endangered and threatened species; this spot in particular caught Zwilich's attention. In the composer's words, the visit to the gardens of threatened and endangered plants "profoundly effected me. Here we are destroying species while contemporaneously finding pharmaceutical uses for those same plants; destroying species that potentially hold something essential and life-saving. We don't know what they might do for the world." Zwilich focused on the "tragedy of losing plants."[66] This became the impetus for the first movement, "Introduction: Litany of Endangered Plants."

Zwilich asked for a list of Latin names of the endangered species, selected nine with names that possessed especially sonorous qualities, and created a modern-day hymn to nature.[67] Despite having chosen the word "litany" for her catalog, Zwilich denied religious associations: "Rather than suggest religion specifically, the Latin conjures something ceremonial, something more generally spiritual."[68]

Yet her urge to identify specific plants by their Latin names ties her thinking and her piece to the very earliest history of the nation in completely unintentional ways. The first movement begins with repeated chanting of *Castenea dentata,* more commonly known as the American chestnut. Although

Zwilich exerted no particular effort to identify her Symphony No. 4 as an American work, she could hardly have chosen an endangered plant more closely tied to the nation's early history than the chestnut. Here was a tree revered for its majestic beauty, whose overall size and strength also made it the perfect tree for railroad ties and telegraph poles. Its handsome wood endeared it to furniture builders and instrument makers. Its fruit appealed to humans and animals alike.

Thoreau spoke affectionately of the tree in 1854 in a passage in *Walden:* "When chestnuts were ripe I laid up half a bushel for winter. It was very exciting at that season to roam the then boundless chestnut woods of Lincoln,—they now sleep their long sleep under the railroad." He talked of climbing the trees to shake loose their fruit, and of the "bouquet which scented the whole neighborhood" when it was in flower.[69] Fifteen years earlier, the tree's place in American mythology had been secured in the opening lines of Henry Wadsworth Longfellow's poem "The Village Blacksmith": "Under the spreading chestnut-tree/The village smithy stands." Many a schoolchild would be required to recite the eight-stanza poem by heart. Thoreau returned to a discussion of the American chestnut in his last natural history writings, in which the prescient poet warned of the "special pains" that would be necessary to "secure and encourage" this tree and others that were threatened.[70] It was as if he anticipated the blight, first detected in New York in 1904, that nearly wiped out the entire species.

Barbara Novak shows the confluence of art, science, and nature with religion in the earliest American explorations. She recounts an English explorer's experiences in drawing images of fresh plants and traces the resonance of his efforts: "This interaction of the empirical eye with the categories of natural history became a major theme of the nineteenth-century artist. The early urge to label, with its emphasis on classification, persisted longer in America than abroad, as Americans held tenaciously to the 'artificial' system of Linnaeus. Since this was bound to absolute fixity of species, the American devotion to this concept and to its religious implications is easily understood."[71] Although such thinking was complicated by equally persuasive arguments for an organic reading of nature, the idea of nature as a mirror in which human beings were reflected and deified was essential to Emerson's vision of Transcendentalism. Natural history became meaningful to the degree that it expressed human history, and vice versa.

A similar close kinship with nature is everywhere in the writings of Thoreau, but perhaps most succinctly stated in a journal entry dated 23 October 1855. Here the Concord woodsman observes, "Old trees are our parents and our parents' parents."[72] This mid-nineteenth-century reading survived into the twentieth century and made its way into *The Gardens*. The theme of mankind as nature's progeny reappears in the opening text of Zwilich's final movement, where the children's chorus resolutely promises, "We will protect our heritage." It is a small leap to suggest that protecting and nurturing plants, trees, and flowers is closely tied to the survival of humanity itself. And here is a recurring theme of the modern environmentalist movement.

Tying one's heritage to nature was a goal for both individuals and the young nation in the nineteenth century, and science offered a way to do this. Pointing to the work of botanists, biologists, and geologists, advocates of scientific inquiry presented America's vast wildernesses as a pristine laboratory in which to observe the Earth's ancient geological past. Here was something that Europe's civilization and culture had destroyed. Regular references in the W. J. Beal Botanical Garden literature to the site as an "outdoor laboratory" maintain this vision of nature and the nation. Rereading America's potentially frightening and primitive territories as untouched examples of God's handiwork helped the nation reinterpret itself to the world. What could have been a deficit was now a unique and divine asset.[73]

In addition to recalling nineteenth-century thinking about nature as it was manifest in art and literature, Zwilich's opening movement, "Introduction: Litany of Endangered Plants," conjures an earlier, more generally spiritual twentieth-century musical work: Igor Stravinsky's 1930 *Symphony of Psalms*, for orchestra and chorus. Whether Zwilich had this piece in mind as she set out to create her own is not really the issue. What is important is that *The Gardens* evokes this previous unequivocally spiritual work and connects nature and spirituality, a not-unimportant theme in American history.

Large-scale comparisons between Zwilich's and Stravinsky's works go beyond performing forces, the use of Latin, and overall mood. Both works include not only choruses but children's choruses. Basic musical elements and procedures show a kinship. Pulsing rhythms undergird extremely legato vocal lines in the first movements of Symphony No. 4 and *Symphony of Psalms*. Voices enter in unison in both works and within a few measures expand to four parts. Where Stravinsky uses solo voices or parts singing in octaves to contrast with the multipart choral sound, Zwilich alternates octave chant sections with punctuating fuller chords. Both composers use fourths and fifths, intervals rich with early polyphonic sacred music connotations. And both movements build similarly to *fortissimo* closes. Whereas *Symphony of Psalms* was composed "to the glory of GOD,"[74] Zwilich's *Gardens* was composed to "celebrate" what some might argue to be the handiwork of the Creator.[75]

Symphony No. 4 starts out majestically and confidently. String basses sustain a pedal tone A, while brass and percussion deliver a sharply articulated fanfare figure. The bright sounding glockenspiel, one of the bell-like instruments so important to Zwilich's timbral palette, signals the ultimately positive message that the composer is about to deliver. But it is not a wholly happy work. There is much of the tragic in the opening movement, and this is a reflection of Zwilich's immediate message. She interleaves her very serious modern environmental concerns in numerous subtle ways. One of the more seamless is in her manipulation of the text. This might seem difficult when a text is no more than a listing of plant names in Latin, but Zwilich works with the roots of words to make her point: one such example is *Uniola latifolia,* more commonly known as wild oats or spangle grass. As the composer explains, to underscore the "folly" of our past attitudes toward nature, she redivided and reaccented the Latin word *folia* (leaves or foliage), which in its initial appearances she had set as a two-syllable word "folia." Starting at measure 47, however, and three times thereafter, the chorus chides FOL I a, FOL I a, FOL I a, diminishing from *fortissimo* to *forte* to *piano*.[76] Anger and outrage subside to grief.[77] Zwilich maintains this new accentuation in every subsequent appearance of the word (see Ex. 5.7).

But Zwilich is not one to wallow. She and her music move beyond despair. As the music recalls the opening unison chant materials and approaches what might typically be regarded as the recapitulation, the composer lifts the pitch level at which the chorus sings. What started out darkly now sounds determined. Without pulling back from the overall serious tone of the "Litany," Zwilich allows for hope.

The final plant named is *Opuntia fragilis,* commonly known as the fragile or brittle prickly pear. As she did with *folia,* Zwilich zeros in on that part of the name that will allow her to convey her concerns. With the zeal of a new convert, she impresses upon her listeners the urgency of her cause. We need to be nature's stewards; it is dependent upon us; it is fragile. Seven times the chorus reminds us, "Fragilis!" with the final warning *fortissimo* (see Ex. 5.8).

If Zwilich's first reaction upon visiting the Endangered and Threatened Species Garden was one of overwhelming sadness, it is clear that she has now moved on. Her determination is clear. As all instruments join together on a final fortissimo F♯ minor chord, listeners feel her resolve. There is no ambiguity about the ending, no fading into the distance. Musicians count out their two full beats of music and all sound stops. Zwilich has laid down the gauntlet.

The second movement, "Meditation on Living Fossils," is a purely instrumental reflection on a different exhibit at the botanical garden. Zwilich refers to the mystery of "the living continuity with the deep past" that she experienced there.[78] And she captures that mystery in music that seemingly emerges

Ex. 5.7: Ellen Taaffe Zwilich, Symphony No. 4, *The Gardens,* "Litany of Endangered Plants," mm 34–48. © 1999 by Merion Music, Inc. Used with permission.

241

Ex. 5.8: Ellen Taaffe Zwilich, Symphony No. 4, *The Gardens*, "Litany of Endangered Plants," mm 84–94. © 1999 by Merion Music, Inc. Used by permission.

from nowhere and everywhere simultaneously. Soft tam-tams and *pianissimo* celli augur a magical world. Picking up on the same F♯ that ended the first movement, Zwilich immediately connects the movements to each other. Throughout the "Meditation," the composer refers to melodic and rhythmic gestures that characterized the "Litany." In so doing she insists upon the steadfastness of her earlier concerns in this untexted second section. As public and outspoken as the first movement was, however, this one is personal and introspective.

Starting at measure 6, a single string bass softly sings a plaintive song. Over the course of eight measures, it rises up from a low F♯ to C♯ above middle C, before sinking down two octaves and coming to rest on C. Similar arpeggiated motions in low instruments are ubiquitous in Beethoven's symphonies.

Ex. 5.9: Ellen Taaffe Zwilich, Symphony No. 4, *The Gardens,* "Meditation on Living Fossils," mm 6–13. © 1999 by Merion Music, Inc. Used by permission.

Murmuring flutes recall a prominent melodic fragment heard initially in the "Litany," while sizzle cymbals and muted violins and violas comment. At measure 21, celli try on the opening string bass solo. A more introspective mood permeates the "Meditation" in subdued sounds of all kinds: muted strings, various types of brass mutes—straight mutes and harmon mutes—and woodwinds that softly mutter extended, low, trill-like figures. Zwilich conjures the voices of the ancient trees that populate the living fossils garden, but they speak from ages past, as if from a great distance.

Although F♯ returns to a place of prominence at measure 56 in the string bass, the overall pitch motion first observed in the opening string bass solo portends the overall harmonic motion of the entire movement: the second movement ends on C.[79] "Meditation" fades from our hearing *pianissimo,* amid ever-softening tam-tams and bass drum strokes; its close is as fuzzy as the first movement's was decisive. While the C ending does not call attention to itself in a forceful way, its tritone relationship to the pitch that had opened the movement and closed the previous one does speak of large-scale harmonic ambiguity that may well mirror the problematic issues Zwilich is addressing.

244

Reconciling the needs of mankind with those of nature is not accomplished easily. The harmonic tension inherent in the traditionally problematic interval of the tritone may be a musical reflection of the basic tensions that Zwilich feels so keenly.

"A Pastoral Journey" is, according to the composer, a musical analogue of a spiritual journey. But unlike other artistic pilgrimages, which often focus upon the reflective and meditative moments of the trek, Zwilich's third movement focuses more on the movement along the way. In this regard the composer works within the norms of traditional symphonic structure where the third movement is typically highly rhythmic, even dancelike, thus providing contrast to the conventionally quieter and more lyrical second movement. For the third movement Zwilich reenlists her vocalists, and they muse on two verses from the Bible (Matthew 6:28–29) that she adapted. "Behold the lilies of the fields. They toil not, they spin not, but Solomon in all his glory was not adorned like one of these." For Zwilich, "the text serves as an integral part of the musical exploration."[80]

In notes to the movement, the composer makes clear that she is not after a literal "depiction of the many gardens," but rather that she intends "simply . . . a musical celebration of them."[81] A celebratory mood is everywhere in this highly atmospheric soundscape; the music alternately shivers with delight, bounces weightlessly, struts, stands back in awe, and rings out. Zwilich clearly revels in the beauty and richness of the Beal gardens. As a composer drawn to more traditional musical genres and structures than are many of her contemporaries, she feels a special kinship with the form, evolution, and organic growth at work in nature. Zwilich hears the music of the gardens and captures it in various effects: string harmonics, slow and quick glissandi, instructions to the brass and later the violas to play "bell-like,"[82] directions to the singers to "hum."[83] She is precise in her goals. At one point the composer tells the brass to play "into [their] stands,"[84] and at another for instrumentalists to "keep ringing through fermata."[85] Zwilich uses all sorts of percussion instruments to create shivering and shimmering effects—an assortment of cymbals, tubular bells, and handbells, which are played by the children. In "A Pastoral Journey" Zwilich allows herself to be immersed in and swept away by nature as it is revealed in the gardens.

The "Pastoral Journey" begins with the outline of a C-major arpeggio that connects it to the final C of the second movement, and with a brass fanfare that recalls the opening mood of the first movement. Dotted rhythms that dominated the "Litany" become background commentary in the "Pastoral Journey." Glissandi that behaved in a purely accompanimental role in the second movement are now a featured effect, and they reappear at prominent places throughout the third movement.[86] An entire melody first heard in the "Litany" at the introduction of the supercharged phrase *Uniola latifolia* (measure 34) is augmented and hummed by a unison chorus in "A Pastoral Journey." The third movement recollects all that has been experienced in the gardens.

"Behold the lilies of the fields" rings out in *forte* octaves sung by the four-part chorus at measure 56; their announcement heralds the newly important pitch E.[87] The remainder of the text is declaimed in similar octaves until the biblical text "was not adorned," at measure 92, which compares the beauty of the lily to King Solomon. At this point Zwilich *adorns* what had been a simple declarative delivery with imitative, overlapping vocal entrances. With each iteration the composer reconsiders the eloquent, understated beauty of the lily, a common flower. When the same text reappears (at measure 219) the contrapuntal texture returns as well, but these are the only instances of any but the simplest unison choral writing.

Zwilich is not above employing tried-and-true techniques to communicate her text, including word painting. This device, first used during the Renaissance, pairs musical activity with the meaning of the word being sung. When overused it becomes little more than a gimmick, but when applied thoughtfully it has the power to bind music and text intimately, and to supercharge the meaning of the sounds. Immediately after the imitative passage describing Solomon's adornment, Zwilich moves to an *a cappella* unison on the line "like one of these." Without any instrumental accompaniment, the unison chorus becomes a single entity, alone in the vast soundscape. We are made to hear the abundant beauty of a single, common flower. Throughout the movement voices and instruments alternate a number of similar gestures; this creates an effortless weave of text and music. Among the most effective instances of shared materials is a descending scalar passage that first appeared accompanying the words "Solomon in all his glory" (see Ex. 5.10).

A second time the descending scale leads out of the counterpoint on the word "adorned" (measure 97). And a third time, "Behold the lilies of the fields" (measure 117) closes with the descending scale starting on high A. At measure 198, tubular bells ring out an augmented version of this same descending pattern, again starting on A, and this time sounding very much like church bells heard from a distance. The bells repeat the passage another four times and reinforce, deliberately or not, the connection of nature, as contemplated in these gardens, with religion.

Zwilich also commands "Behold!" in voices and instruments alike. Immediately after the initial vocal entrance, handbells and brass imitate the voices with their own assertive repeated E. At measure 151 horns are instructed to

Ex. 5.10: Ellen Taaffe Zwilich, Symphony No. 4, *The Gardens,* "A Pastoral Journey," mm 87–89. © 1999 by Merion Music, Inc. Used by permission.

play their two chords "bell-like"; as they do, we hear the echo of the vocalists' admonition to "Behold." A similar instance of instrumental ventriloquism occurs at measure 167, when tubular bells strike out two consecutive octaves. The composer speaking through her music insists that listeners look around them: "Behold!" Zwilich is clear in her desire to integrate voices and instruments. At measure 189, the unison chorus hums a melody based upon one heard for the first time in the "Litany." While in both appearances instruments accompany the vocal melody, in the third movement the instrumentalists are directed to "blend into [the] chorus."[88] The same holds true for the next joint appearance at measure 203. Zwilich's programmatic note "the text serves as an integral part of the musical exploration" is made clear before our very ears.[89] As if to take advantage of the last opportunity to impress upon her listeners her desire that they heed nature, Zwilich ends her movement with trumpets, handbells, tubular bells, and strings all singing out two iterations of the chorus's initial pitch E, the one where they first commanded listeners to "Behold!" The message has transcended words and become pure music.

"The Children's Promise," the fourth movement, is Zwilich's clearest statement of her hope for this symphony. Using a text by Erik LaMont that is made up entirely of simple declarations, Zwilich has her children's chorus pledge, "We will protect our heritage; nourish our plants and trees; nourish from root to bough; leave a verdant earth; gather our corn and herbs; gather from forest to plow." The chorus ends with repetitions of promises to "leave a verdant earth." This fourth movement was directly inspired by Zwilich's experiences at the 4-H Children's Garden on the Michigan State campus. She was "moved by the care given to helping children understand their need to cherish and preserve the natural world they inherit."[90] Thus Zwilich has the children lead the way.

The pairing of children and adult choruses, with the children drawing the adults to their concerns and convincing the adults to join them in their pledge, suggests another biblical verse, "and a little child shall lead them," although the composer does not mention any reference to it.[91] Zwilich recalls the first movement litany with adult voices chanting Latin plant names, but they are overwhelmed by the pure intensity of the children's pledge and enthusiastically join in the simple declarations. By the end, all involved have committed themselves to being nature's stewards.

If the text resolves the moral dilemma first apparent in the "Litany of Endangered Plants," the music resolves harmonic tensions that motivated, connected, and propelled the four movements forward. The initial A that anchored the opening of the first movement returns to close the symphony. A consummate craftsperson, Zwilich revisits melodies, rhythms, timbres, and gestures that characterized the previous three movements. The music is formally tight and unified, growing out of materials first introduced in the opening movement. As the composer's thinking about nature coalesces, so too does the symphony. Here is the "wonderful organic form" that Zwilich sees everywhere in the gardens; she has made it music.[92]

A Word on Gardens

In a recent book entitled *What Gardens Mean,* the author-philosopher Stephanie Ross considers a "unique garden style [that] evolved in eighteenth-century England" and the concomitant elevation of gardening to the status of a bona fide art. While her book concentrates on that moment, place, and style, her motivating question regarding the meaning of gardens resonates across ages, cultures, and continents. She sees the garden as "a springboard for investigating important and enduring philosophical issues." Perhaps most important for this present study, Ross looks at the connections between gardens and art and asks a series of questions, among them: "How are gardens experienced by those who view them or walk through them? How does imagination enter in? What sorts of messages can they convey? Can they have moral force? What artistic tasks can they perform?" These questions lead to a final one: "What is art and what does it do for us?"[93] Although it is not the goal of this study to take on this last "fundamental question of aesthetics," as Ross characterizes it, it is useful to briefly consider her concerns, especially as they relate to Zwilich's symphony.

According to the composer, when she was commissioned to write a piece about the gardens and prior to her visit to campus, she "began thinking along the line of natural processes: the scientific side of nature." Such a response seems fully in character with the thoughtful, well-read, and pragmatic composer. Science, however, took a backseat to celebration when Zwilich got to Michigan State. Her experience among the acres of flowers, plants, and trees shifted her focus away from a purely intellectual investigation toward one that acknowledged her visceral response. Something changed when the empathetic and imaginative artist partook of the sensorially explosive sights and smells of the Beal gardens. Zwilich spoke of "a spiritual experience writing the symphony."[94] What powers did the gardens possess to so move this seasoned, creative soul?

Ross observes: "Gardens yield prodigal pleasures. Their bounty includes not only fruits and flowers, vegetables and herbs, but also beauty, respite, and reflection."[95] The opportunity for respite and reflection is especially significant to busy twenty-first-century urbanites, such as Zwilich, whose daily contact with nature is limited and whose dependence upon nature is not always apparent. Our routine distance from nature allows us to separate it from ourselves, to see it only as it is portrayed in photographs, and paintings, and television programs. But to be in the midst of it, to see a hundred shades of green, to smell the complex perfume, to hear it crunch under one's feet, to be dwarfed by eighty-foot-tall trees, to feel its power is a wholly different experience. And this is just what Professor William James Beal intended in 1873, when he planted a garden where students could "observe for themselves." For Beal the garden was a place where one confronted life; and this is what it became for Zwilich.

In *Gardens of the Heartland,* Laura C. Martin devotes eleven pages to the Michigan State University gardens, including a lengthy discussion of their founder. "Beal . . . wanted a place where his students could study nature firsthand." That place didn't need to be fancy or large, just real, and so "instead of waiting for funds that would allow him to create a grand garden, Beal simply found a spot of land on campus and began planting grasses and clovers." Martin quotes Beal's son-in-law: "I learned from him the one thing I needed most of all to know. This was to look at life before I talked about it; *not to look at it second-hand,* by the way of books, but so far as possible to examine the thing itself, and form my own conclusions about it."[96] In the case of Ellen Zwilich, her firsthand examination of the gardens changed her sense of what she was going to compose. Her experience spawned a symphony of moral force.

How do the gardens at Michigan State transcend their didactic origins and yet continue to serve their initial function? How does a twenty-first-century observer interact with a nineteenth-century vision? Have worldwide recognition and thousands of visitors altered their essence? Have the gardens become more an artwork than a lab, and Zwilich's symphony another example of art inspired by art, another analogue to Ives's *Housatonic at Stockbridge,* Starer's *Hudson Valley Suite,* or Perna's *Prout's Neck*? Are art and science distinct from one another?

In an effort to raise eighteenth-century English gardens to the status accorded the sister arts of poetry and painting, Ross asked the twin questions: "What can gardens do, and what can they be?"[97] Ross sought to define art in a way that allowed gardens to be construed as such, at least eighteenth-century English gardens. To that end she considered numerous philosophers and aestheticians, among them Plato, Aristotle, Tolstoy, Benedetto Croce, Suzanne Langer, and Clive Bell. She surveyed their thoughts on the requirements of "art" and fashioned a definition, concluding that "there is no one single task which all works of art perform," and no set of criteria that captures "our rich interactions with works of art."[98]

Ross found a definition in *Ars poetica* by Horace, the nature-loving Latin poet. After negotiating other philosophers' exhortations for art to imitate life, to communicate feelings, to express intuition and emotion, and to exhibit significant form, Ross embraced Horace's view "that art ought to instruct and delight." She observed that "all manner of functions fit between these two poles. Works of art can offer clear-cut moral exhortation, exhibit truths about human nature, amuse, provide mere sensory surface."[99] It is the flexibility and breadth of this view that appeals to Ross, and that best reveals the power of the gardens at Michigan State.

In a way unimagined by Professor Beal in 1873, the botanical gardens have continued to teach, to provide a firsthand encounter with nature, to function as a living laboratory, and to inspire. In their enduring meaningfulness they achieve that which the best art does. And in their preservation of what is unique to American nature, they guarantee its continuation for generations. In Symphony No. 4, Zwilich contributes her own art inspired by art inspired by nature, and in so doing becomes part of the American musical tradition that celebrates place.

[*chapter six*]

A Sounding Place:
America Redefined

STEVE REICH

Vermont Counterpoint, The Desert Music,
New York Counterpoint, and *City Life*

As relations to the natural environment have changed, so has the nation's sense of itself. Gardens large and small and government-
protected wildlife preserves and parks now safeguard nature, although
they cannot duplicate the raw wilderness that greeted explorers. Packaged
nature differs significantly from what originally existed, as Olmsted's prettified
Niagara differed from the cataract described in Father Hennepin's 1697 travelogue, but it is the only course if nature is to survive at all.

As the idea of America as a place has continued to evolve, the music it has
inspired has changed too. More than a single iconic waterfall, mountain range,
canyon, river, or any other natural phenomenon, the country has increasingly
become identified with its people.[1] Simultaneously with other contemporary
composers' tributes to America's natural endowments, Steve Reich (b. 1936 in
New York) has captured the pace of millennial America using the speech
rhythms and cadences of its people. Among the most thoughtful, facile, and
articulate spokespersons for contemporary musical culture, Reich, unsurpris-
ingly, finds inspiration in the verbal arts. Prior to his university studies in
composition at Mills College, Reich earned a bachelor's degree in philosophy
from Cornell, where he wrote his senior thesis on Ludwig Wittgenstein. His
broad interests and wide reading inform the composer as much as do purely
musical influences.

In many ways Reich draws upon the works of the poet William Carlos
Williams (1883–1963), who commandeered American English, with its percus-
sive attacks and short bursts of sound, and chiseled them into a unique
"American idiom." Williams was determined to let "the colloquial language,

my own language, set the pace."[2] A fan of Williams since he was sixteen years old and first read the poem "Paterson," Reich absorbed the poet's commitment to real American culture: not the high-blown rhetoric of the academy, but spoken speech as Williams heard it in the streets of his native New Jersey.[3] Reich's use of "speech melody," which refers to the pitch, rhythm, and timbre of speech, creates a musical analogue to Williams's vernacular voice.[4] Rich with musical influences as well, ranging from Bach, Bartók, Stravinsky, Debussy, and Coltrane, to Balinese gamelan and African drumming, Reich's boundary-defying music is modern America made sound.[5]

Within Reich's varied oeuvre are pieces that focus upon solving complex musical problems (the "phase" pieces), and others that chronicle personal experiences or specific moments in contemporary culture. *It's Gonna Rain* and *Come Out* are two of his most famous works of the latter type; they also draw upon Williams's ideas regarding vernacular speech.[6] Reich's music is, in Edward Strickland's words, "unrepentantly premeditative," yet many of his works are also super–emotionally charged, and palpably so.[7] *Different Trains* was inspired by regularly recurring trips from New York to Los Angeles in the late 1930s and early 1940s, when Reich was a young child visiting his divorced parents.[8] In numerous interviews Reich has spoken of these train rides with Virginia Mitchell, his governess, as they crossed the country every six months. A reflective Reich observes today that if he had been a little Jewish boy taking a train at the same time in Germany, "I would have been taking very different trains, and I wouldn't be writing any pieces of music."[9] Working on the piece, Reich searched out and taped the voices of the Governess; Lawrence Davis, a long-retired Pullman porter; and Holocaust survivors, choosing people and phrases for their particular speech melody. *Different Trains* is a virtuosic achievement of acoustic music *cum* technology, yet it is also a heartfelt comment upon a personal experience; it is musical autobiography. Assessments of Reich's music that focus exclusively upon its systemization, method, precision, and formal balance tell only part of the story. Perhaps more affecting and enduring is the deeply *human* quality that inspires and permeates many of Reich's works. If his music endures, this is why.

Among fifty works composed over forty years, Reich has written four pieces whose titles refer to specific American places: *Vermont Counterpoint* (1982), *The Desert Music* (1984), *New York Counterpoint* (1985), and *City Life* (1995). Though all are commissioned works and hence responses to outside requests, place plays a role in the concept of each piece. At the very least, Reich has a personal connection to each of the places named; he writes only about that which he knows.[10]

Although Reich is associated almost exclusively with New York City, a summer home in Vermont has provided him with a retreat from the city scene for more than thirty years. Parts of *New York Counterpoint* and *The Desert Music* were written there. His knowledge of the Green Mountain State informs *Vermont Counterpoint,* although, as the composer points out, "being in Vermont doesn't translate into slow movements of images of clouds."[11] The composer has been to deserts too: during his four years in San Francisco, 1961–65, Reich drove through the Mojave. "Sometimes I'd begin to feel very strange there because I'd get so dehydrated, I'd have to drink enormous amounts of fluids just to keep going and keep my mind functioning normally."[12] But perhaps more important than that fleeting experience of the desert, Reich spent a summer in New Mexico prior to getting the place in Vermont. While there he visited the deserts of White Sands, home to the National Missile Range, "where weapons of the most intense and sophisticated sort are constantly being developed and tested."[13] The composer seized upon the contradiction between how things appeared and how they really were: "It's creepy. So pure . . . so delightful . . . I'm running the hell out of here. What you see is *not* what you get."[14] According to the composer, images of deserts are confined to the last movement in *The Desert Music;* mostly he drew on his White Sands experience. His instinctive reaction to the desert, coupled with its rich metaphoric history and William Carlos Williams's volume of poetry entitled *The Desert Music* (1954), came together in his own piece.[15]

More than paying tribute to particular places, *Vermont Counterpoint* and *New York Counterpoint* are Reich's "way of dealing with soloists."[16] Opposed to the concerto form, with its dependence upon established musical structures and the need for extraordinarily large performing forces, Reich solved the problem of writing solo works that reflected his unique interest in the musical process by composing pieces built upon layers of taped individual lines against which a soloist played.[17] Although designed to require only a single live musician and a tape, Reich allows for the taped lines to be played by ensembles of players instead, thus leaving open the possibility of a fully acoustic performance.[18] The strategy has proven successful, as the *Counterpoint* pieces are among his most performed.[19] *Vermont Counterpoint,* the first of the series, provides one example of the varied roles that place plays in Reich's thinking. Each of the others pieces suggests a unique relationship with place.

Initially Reich was concerned that a rural New England setting might prove too different from his natural urban habitat to allow him to work there. At the very least, the tempo of Vermont speech and life would appear foreign to a New Yorker. Today, the composer sees the slower environment as providing "a kind of equilibrium" to his high-energy self. A "nature lover and nature neeter," a person who "can sit on the porch and watch clouds move," he is now comfortable in both worlds.[20] Though *Vermont Counterpoint* does indeed bear the imprint of the setting in which it was composed, the place has not compromised his voice. The music bounces and drives in Reich's characteristically intense way, with no loss of edge, energy, or vitality.

The nine-minute work was commissioned by the flutist Ransom Wilson, who eventually went to Vermont to work with Reich on some technically difficult passages. Born as it was in a bucolic setting, the piece is nonetheless tightly woven and demanding. According to Reich: "In that comparatively short time four sections in four different keys . . . are presented. . . . the relatively fast rate of change . . . , metric modulation into and out of a slower tempo, and relatively rapid changes of key may well create a more concentrated and concise impression."[21] The comparatively limited timbre of the flute, even when one adds the extended range and color of the alto flute, also contributes to a sensation of concision and concentration, perhaps even of limitation. There is a sameness to the sound, no doubt exacerbated by motoric rhythms. But there are other features that suggest something else. The flute itself, long associated with depictions of the outdoors, phrasing that makes audible the instrumentalist's breathing, a prevailing triple meter, and a slower third section combine to suggest a more bucolic inspiration than one hears in the jazz-inspired *New York Counterpoint.* That said, this is hardly a relaxing work.[22] While Reich asserts that *Vermont Counterpoint* "is certainly a more pastoral piece" than its city counterpart,[23] anyone familiar with the tranquillity of Lake Bomoseen or the Green Mountains will be hard pressed to hear their evocation, and perhaps one should not.

Understanding the genesis of the title goes a long way toward clarifying just how much Vermont there is in *Vermont Counterpoint.* Reich explains that he had a problem with the title. He knew that he wanted to call it "something" *Counterpoint,* but "didn't know what the first word should be."[24] Wilson suggested "Vermont" to honor the place of its composition, and it was named. But, as such a story makes clear, the place was not the motivating force behind the work. While it may be present in some unconscious way, it is neither the focal point nor an integral aspect of the soundscape.

With its jazzy riffs and kinetic motion, *New York Counterpoint,* on the other hand, enthusiastically evokes the place named in its title; Reich needed no help here. The composer explained, "*New York Counterpoint* is an allusion to my image of an earlier New York."[25] Richard Stoltzman, a jazz aficionado and occasional player, commissioned the work through the Fromm Music Foundation. Reich's own love of the clarinet timbre and early jazz, along with the inspiration of a virtuosic instrumentalist, combined to produce an intense but lighthearted creation.[26] According to the composer, "it's Boogie Woogie and Cootie Williams. It's the jazz of the 1920s and 30s."[27] K. Robert Schwarz described it as "the most exuberant, unbuttoned, and rhythmically ingenious" of the counterpoint series.[28] Here is an example of music referring to a place by conjuring the sounds of that place. For a composer who admits to having limited visual images, Reich's reliance on the *sounds* of an era and a locale are his truest source of inspiration.[29] Reich hears New York.

New York Counterpoint is an example of Reich's "process music," music that evolves from a relatively brief subject that is then played against itself in a series of staggered, varied entrances. Such a technique describes imitative contrapuntal behavior in general, but what distinguishes Reich's music is his desire that the process should emerge slowly, gradually, and audibly. It is as if a dozen balls were being juggled in slow motion. We see individual objects, but always against the moving scenery of the others, and none is ever dropped. The patterns are stimulating and hypnotic at the same time. Although the music that results from such preordained processes runs the risk of sounding mechanical, sterile, and devoid of the human touch (criticisms Reich had leveled against the music of the serialists, which he had rejected), Reich avoids such a fate for *New York Counterpoint* by fashioning a subject that contains seemingly infinite facets. As each line is heard in relief against the others, new perspectives reveal themselves. A kind of self-sustaining energy field is created. Many pieces of this type appear to have no natural ending and hence simply stop, but *New York Counterpoint* pushes to a fully convincing, rousing close: the process has run its course.

The continuous, eleven-minute, three-movement work gradually moves toward its Goodman-esque denouement. A single soloist plays with and against an ensemble of ten taped clarinets, which include three bass clarinets. Reich was especially interested in working with a greater pitch and timbral range beyond that which he was able to explore in *Vermont Counterpoint,* and he did so by employing the highest possible note on the B-flat clarinet and the lowest possible note on the B-flat bass clarinet. As he explained it, "I wanted to have a bottom on this." With the addition of the bass clarinet, "you've got a whole quasi-orchestral sonority."[30] Reich establishes the clarinet timbre with a choralelike pulse. The ambiguous harmonic opening sonority smacks of Debussy and jazz, not unrelated sounds in Reich's thinking.[31] As instruments fade in and out with their relentlessly repeated eighth notes, listeners are unsure of a specific meter or direction; there is only continuous, fluid pulse. The collective pulse becomes a unifying sound for long stretches of the first two movements.[32] When a single clarinet breaks away with a repeated syncopated riff in the first movement (first clarinet of the taped ensemble, measure 45), Reich sets a process in motion. The live soloist responds, joined by clarinet 2, then 3, 4, 5, and 6. Clarinets 7, 8, 9, and 10 enter with pulsing eighth notes like those that introduced the work.

Ex. 6.1: Steve Reich, *New York Counterpoint,* first movement, m 45, clarinet 1. © 1986 by Hendon Music, Inc., a Boosey and Hawkes company. Reprinted by permission.

In the opening movement, Reich explores the clarinet sound first as a collective sonority, then as a solo timbre, and then a group of individual lines against that collective sonority. The jazzy break and the playful banter of instrumentalists set the tone for the rest of the piece, where the interactions of individual lines gradually dominate any collective pulsing sound mass. Reich moves from the larger, more orchestral sound mass to a smaller, more intimate combination, perhaps reflective of a move toward a smaller, more intimate jazzlike ensemble, one of the sounds heard in New York.

If the first movement established the parameters of "clarinet-ness," the second, "Slow," confirms Reich's roots in jazz. Key, tempo, texture, and meter shift from the resolute first movement into a sweet, swinging duet in a gentle 3/4. As the music elides from one movement to the next, downbeats become hard to ascertain as notes drop in on the "ands" of beats and the final gruppeti of the two-measure pattern are slurred to the beginning of the repetition. A downward-swooping, melodic fragment similar to the one that appeared a third of the way through the first movement opens the second movement. Reich the percussionist creates a rhythmic pattern that is ripe with possibilities, revealing the malleability of his materials in the evolving unity of the larger work.

Ex. 6.2: Steve Reich, *New York Counterpoint,* second movement, rehearsal 44, clarinets 7 and 8. © 1986 by Hendon Music, Inc., a Boosey and Hawkes company. Reprinted by permission.

In each of the first two movements, Reich worked within a single key signature: the first movement in four flats, the second in five sharps. By contrast the third movement, "Fast," vacillates ten times among four flats and four and five sharps, all within three and a half minutes. The tempo returns to that of the first movement, as does the 6/4 = 3/2 meter, at least initially. Reich's preference for flexible meters, those that can be divided into duple and triple groupings that contain within themselves subdivisions, is fully evident as the final movement bounces back and forth, hemiola-fashion, between 6/4 and 12/8.[33] This ambiguity is something Reich consciously seeks; he sees it as "the rhythmic life-blood of [his] music."[34] The music trips along. Numerous meter changes first coincide with and then move away from key changes, thus creating a kaleidoscopic effect of shifting accents and pitches. While every element is the product of a carefully calculated process, the music sounds instinctive, spontaneous, and spirited, "unbuttoned." As in real jazz, where instrumentalists revel in testing their chops and stretching the boundaries, in the final movement limits are literally pushed. The bass clarinet sinks to its lowest possible note, D-flat (rehearsal 67), and the soloist soars to F♯, the extreme upper range of the B-flat clarinet (rehearsal 90). With the soloist pressing to the close, Reich's music climbs higher and higher. It takes little imagination to hear Benny Goodman wailing.

New York is a place Reich knows well, and early jazz is a musical style that speaks directly to this native son; both are in his bones. Perhaps the success of *New York Counterpoint* lies in Reich's intuitive understanding of the riffs and rhythms of this milieu. Perhaps, as did William Carlos Williams, Reich found his vernacular American idiom.

In 1984, a year prior to writing *New York Counterpoint,* Reich completed *The Desert Music,* a large work for orchestra and amplified chorus requiring up to 116 musicians and lasting approximately fifty minutes.[35] Using lines from three poems by Williams, "The Orchestra," "Theocritus: Idyll—A Version from the Greek," and "Asphodel, That Greeny Flower," Reich infused his music with William's moral urgency. In setting his lines, Reich paid tribute to the poet whose ideas about language and national identity had shaped his own thinking.

To the same degree that Reich claims to be without visual imagery, Williams is dependent upon it, perhaps because he harbored "a strong inclination . . . to be a painter."[36] Regular references to "the picture" crop up in his speech. In describing the evolution of his volume of poems *The Desert Music,* for instance, Williams explained: "I had just returned from a trip to the West and the picture of the desert country around El Paso was fresh in my mind.

I'd crossed the desert and *seen* the desert. It is always important to me to be familiar with what I am writing about."[37]

Long before Williams used the image or Reich composed his work of the same title, however, the desert was a rich metaphor. It was a mainstay of Puritanism. Biblical references alone number in the dozens.[38] As a medical doctor, and more specifically as an obstetrician, Williams spent his life coaxing and preserving life. The harsh, apparently desolate desert must have left a powerful imprint on the imagination of the doctor-poet. Reich's own awareness of the contradiction between what his eye saw in the deserts of White Sands and what he knew existed beneath the pristine surface made Williams's already moving verses even more poignant to the composer.

In Reich's texted pieces, composition begins with the words. As he explains it: "In *The Desert Music,* I went to William Carlos Williams's poetry. No music in mind. I knew it was going to be built on the text. . . . I then sat down and started composing harmonic cycles that seemed to match the tone and meaning of each text/movement. . . . The nature of the harmony reflected the meaning of the words."[39] In "The Orchestra," the poem from which Reich quotes the greatest number of lines, Williams compares nature waking to an orchestra tuning, the purpose of which is to "organize those sounds and hold them to an assembled order in spite of the 'wrong note.' "[40] Reich quotes the text that follows: "Well, shall we/think or listen? Is there a sound addressed/not wholly to the ear?/We half close/our eyes. We do not/hear it through our eyes./It is not/a flute note either, it is the relation/of a flute note/to a drum. I am wide/awake. The mind is listening."[41] This excerpt becomes the text of the second and fourth movements of the archlike five-movement piece, and it plays a large role in setting the questioning tone of Reich's work.[42]

Reich was attracted to Williams's late poems and drew from those written "after the bombs were dropped on Hiroshima and Nagasaki." As he explained in the notes to his score: "Dr. Williams was acutely aware of the bomb, and his words about it, in a poem about music entitled *The Orchestra,* struck me as to the point: 'Say to them:/"Man has survived hitherto because he was too ignorant/to know how to realize his wishes. Now that he can realize/them, he must either change them or perish." ' "[43] Nowhere in "The Orchestra" does Williams directly mention the bomb, although the lines that Reich quotes do refer to the annihilation of the species via a weapon of mass destruction. In "The Orchestra" it is all allusion. Williams does, however, refer to the bomb many times in Book 2 and the coda of "Asphodel, That Greeny Flower," another poem that Reich quotes. The combination of oblique and direct references, the ambiguity of what is stated and what is implied, make these two poems naturally valuable sources for Reich. The middle section of the third movement uses a Williams text that must have spoken immediately to a composer known for his repetitive musical processes: "it is a principle of music/to repeat the theme. Repeat/and repeat again,/as the pace mounts. The/theme is difficult/but no more difficult/than the facts to be/resolved."[44] Reich responds with a feverish, frenzied canon.

Remaining excerpts come from "Asphodel" and a second poem, "Theocritus: Idyll—A Version from the Greek." A brief, cautionary passage from the latter emerges halfway through the first movement. The poet, having spoken to the composer, now speaks to us: "Begin, my friend/for you cannot,/you may be sure,/take your song,/which drives all things out of mind,/with you to the other world." With such lines, the poet appears to invite Reich's collaboration. And finally, for his fifth movement text Reich quotes from two separate passages in the coda of "Asphodel": "Inseparable from the fire/its light/takes precedence over it," and "who most shall advance the light—/call it what you may!"[45] The optimistic last line comes from a much longer passage, which Reich does not include. It begins: "So let us love/confident as is the light in its struggle with darkness . . ."[46]

In program notes to the score, CD liner notes, and numerous interviews and essays (many repeating the same information), Reich has spoken often and at great length about *The Desert Music*. The fullest discussions appear in Reich's notes to the Nonesuch recording and in his essay "The Desert Music (1984)" in *Writings on Music, 1965–2000*, his most recent prose collection.[47] Always the composer mentions Williams's role in inspiring the work, and his process of working from the words. Reich also explains the larger structure of the five-part piece and its unifying harmonic cycles, which are "more chromatic and 'darker' . . . to suit the text."[48] Ambiguity, so evident in his preference for flexible meters, also colors cadential activity in *The Desert Music*. As the following lengthy explanation reveals, Reich takes great pains to guarantee ambiguity, an idea to which he refers five times:

> This ambiguity resides in the fact that a prominent A altered dominant chord follows the D but an F altered dominant precedes it. The cycle of the second and fourth movements does not clearly cadence on any center, although it, too, contains a prominent altered A dominant chord. The cycle for the large third movement is the most ambiguous of all, since all the chords are altered dominants, with their roots moving in major and minor thirds, making a clear V-I or IV-I cadence impossible. Thus, the overall harmonic movement of *The Desert Music* is from the possibility of a D dorian minor center to more and more ambiguity, until in the third move-

ment, where the text would seem to suggest it, there is no clear harmonic center at all. This ambiguity more or less remains until well into the fifth movement when, just before the chorus enters, there is a large orchestral cadence—albeit coming from the F altered dominant—to D dorian minor. The only chord present in all movements is the A altered dominant. This chord is then used to move from one movement to the other at each change of tempo. The piece ends with the women's voices, violins, and mallet instruments pulsing the notes (reading up) G, C, F, A, which are the common tones to the A altered dominant, the D dorian minor, and the possible F major. The piece therefore ends with a certain harmonic ambiguity, partially, but not fully, resolved.[49]

But to what extent is the spacious desolation and eerie beauty of the desert *in* the music? Reich responded to this question in a 1984 conversation with Jonathan Cott: "Well, there's no portrayal of the desert in my piece as there is in, say, the *Grand Canyon Suite*—no picturesque evocation of sand dunes! I don't think there's any direct correlation between the title and the music, except as regards the setting of the text."

In the next breath, Reich revised his assessment. "Now that I think of it, though, the last movement has a very long opening orchestral section. And when I first played a taped version of that section to David Drew—from my publisher, Boosey & Hawkes—I remember turning to him and saying, 'Out on the plain, running like hell.' And that's the image—it's as if you're in the desert and you're running as fast as you can."

In the process of discussing his music, Reich discovered aspects of *The Desert Music* that had been hidden from even himself. He acknowledged the presence of the desert.

There are these very large clouds of harmony that seem to tilt the entire rhythmic structure in different directions until rehearsal number 318 of the score, when, finally, after about 40 minutes, we return to the tonal center of the piece. For me, this is an extremely emotional moment. And the chorus enters and sings, "Inseparable from the fire/its light/takes precedence over it./ Who most shall advance the light—/call it what you may!" That last line is just thrown out, and then you return to the pulse. . . . So, yes, in a sense, at least for me, there is a desert in this piece; and it's in the opening of the last movement, where there are no words at all.[50]

Perhaps the greatest ambiguity of the piece goes beyond chameleon-like meters and harmonies, beyond revelations of meanings that eluded the composer, and relates to Reich's larger experience at White Sands Desert. Like the pure and beautiful landscape that hid nuclear missile silos, Reich's rich, luminous, shimmering sound mass appears to be at odds with the ominous text. Poetry warning of mankind's self-annihilation is woven into a lush, sensuous, and exquisite musical texture. As Reich observed, if one listens only to the sounds of the words and not to their meaning, this most essential ambiguity is lost. Reich, fully appreciating the richness of ambiguity, recognizes the possibility: "That constant flickering of attention between what words mean and how they sound when set to music is one main focus of *The Desert Music*."[51]

Many musical behaviors apparent in *New York Counterpoint* are present in the earlier *Desert Music;* they are, in fact, characteristics of Reich's style. Supercharged, repeating pulses open both works, but in *Desert Music,* dissonant, percussive piano chords go far beyond providing a sonic background as they do in the *Counterpoint* series. In *The Desert Music,* the tight, agitated clusters are a portent.[52] (Similar dissonant, sharp attacks announce the openings of movements 2, 3, and 4 as well.) In both works, Reich introduces a syncopated melodic fragment approximately a third of the way through the first movement. *The Desert Music* fragment shares a descending profile and similar stresses on beats 1 and 3 with *New York Counterpoint.* In both works the melody serves as a larger unifying agent.

Ex. 6.3: Steve Reich, *The Desert Music,* first movement, rehearsal 21. © 1984 by Hendon Music, Inc., a Boosey and Hawkes company. Reprinted by permission.

Extremely flexible meters and numerous fast-paced metrical changes are present in both works as well, but whereas they conjure playfulness in *New York Counterpoint,* they suggest uncertainty, even anxiety in *The Desert Music.* The presence of voices in *Desert Music* provides additional opportunities for uncertainty. When voices enter pulsing "De De De De" at measure 5, they are doubled by woodwinds and both are amplified and mixed together. The resultant timbre is not immediately identifiable; it is ambiguous. This quality is essential to the piece, as the composer explains: "The chorus begins wordlessly. You know, a voice can sing words—but does one hear the voice or the words? At certain points in *The Desert Music,* there's no more to be said—there are things that can only be said musically. So the voices continue, without words, as part of the orchestra. The text emerges out of a completely nonverbal, totally abstract sound into something that says 'Begin, my friend.' Maybe it's fitting that the piece begins *and* ends with a totally abstract use of the voice, going into a text and then out of it again."[53]

As in *New York Counterpoint,* swelling crescendos and decrescendos supply momentum in a relatively static environment; the sound surges and retreats in waves while not necessarily moving forward. And both pieces demonstrate a mastery of large-scale form. Where the clarinet piece reaches its climax at the very end with the last note, an arch form is an appropriate structure for the weighty question addressed in *The Desert Music,* a question that won't go away.[54] It also allows the composer to weight the work toward the most disturbing text, that which focuses upon mankind's self-created dilemma: "Now that he can realize [his wishes], he must either change them or perish," and "The theme is difficult, but no more difficult than the facts to be resolved."

The urgency of mankind's dilemma is brought home starting in the third movement. As Reich explains: "The very center of the piece is canons on the word 'difficult.' There's something self-referential about the repeating—it refers to the music itself, but it also refers to the persistence of the whole set of the piece as well as its problems. That's the fulcrum . . ."[55] A single maraca shaken in a series of four groups of four sixteenth notes introduced the second movement. Now a xylophone struck with hard rubber mallets "ticks" time on a metaphorical Doomsday clock, while a vibraphone chord locks the music in place with a dissonant pedal. At rehearsal 117, the second violin enters with an ostinato pattern that gradually consumes the entire string ensemble. Contrabasses lay in long, low pitches that swell and fade while the chorus enters softly with its own undulating dissonance. A similar pulsing heartbeat introduces the third section of the movement. Here it is made even darker by its tritone interval and accompanying strokes on bass drums. And if listeners still haven't understood the issues at stake, sirenlike viola glissandi starting at rehearsal 228 and then again at 235 wail the point home. Reich guarantees they are heard by instructing his players: "Microphones are turned up so as to be heard over entire chorus and orchestra."[56] The fourth movement starts up with maracas shaking even more agitatedly than in the second movement, and now against an accompaniment of pulsing, clicking sticks. Reich often claims that he could do without most music of the nineteenth century, but his debt to Berlioz and that composer's sensitivity to instrumental effects is clear. Were this the only Reich work to survive, it is doubtful the word "minimalist" would ever be applied to the composer; this is "pure sensuous sound," and lots of it.[57]

In 1984, a year imbued with special significance thanks to George Orwell's prophetic novel *1984,* Reich was not ready to give up on humanity. This becomes evident in the final movement.[58] The arch form is complete, with a return to the tempo and harmonic cycle of the first movement and the reprise of the melodic fragment introduced forty-four minutes earlier (see Ex. 6.3). But much is different. Where hammering, dissonant chords opened the work, Reich begins movement five with the melodic material.[59] The initial *forte* dynamic level relaxes to *mezzo forte* and *mezzo piano.* Vibraphones and ma-rimbas pulse *mezzo piano* eighth notes throughout the movement, with two notable exceptions: When voices appear for the first time in the movement singing "Inseparable from the fire" at rehearsal 324, they are doubled by strings and woodwinds, but there is nothing else. The absence of the pulse directs all attention to the human presence. A second moment of pulse-free sound occurs at rehearsal 349, as vocalists carefully enunciate the words "the light, the light." Here Reich once again focuses attention on the singers and their words by eliminating all other instruments but those that double them. As the vocalists return to their wordless incantation, shimmering, swelling chords lift the music. Mildly dissonant intervals, select timbres, a high tessi-tura, swelling dynamics, quick pulsing rhythms, and sharp-edged articulations create a musical analogue to emanating light.[60] By closing with these final transcendent sounds, Reich suggests that light can overtake darkness. Perhaps there is hope in the desert after all, if we listen.

During the eleven years separating *The Desert Music* and *City Life,* Reich's stature as an internationally recognized composer solidified. In addition to the popular *New York Counterpoint,* he composed about a dozen works, including *Electric Counterpoint* (1987), *Different Trains* (1988), and *The Cave* (1993), a documentary video-music theater work in three acts written in collaboration with his wife, Beryl Korot.[61] Although *New York Counterpoint* alluded to the sound of that city's jazz, *City Life* captures a different kind of music, that of the people themselves. *City Life* was commissioned by the Ensemble Modern, the London Sinfonietta, and the Ensemble InterContemporain; it was first performed in March 1995 at Arsenal de Metz in France, before it was heard in Germany, Great Britain, and finally New York in February 1996. It was a curious chronology for the New York–inspired piece. In contrast to the Mah-lerian forces required for *The Desert Music,* the chamber-size ensemble of pairs of woodwinds, pianos, and samplers, along with three or four percussion, a string quartet, and a contrabass, provided Reich with the flexible palette he needed to create the cityscape.[62] Of course, the two sampling keyboards con-tain a wealth of sounds to be released at the press of a key.

City Life is also an arch-form work, this one framed by the regionally specific voices of Reich's fellow New Yorkers. Vocalists may have achieved transcendence in *The Desert Music,* but they remain firmly grounded in this response to New York in 1995, a time, as the composer explains, of great tension. "*City Life* was written at a time I found New York City a very difficult place to live in; it's not *An American in Paris.* In 1995 New York was very full of a lot of racial tension, the Fundamentalist Muslin extremists were making themselves known, and it was a bleak time. Certainly the character of the piece was definitely cautionary."[63] Different though it may be in tone, *City Life* manifests Reich's same, singular, personal voice.

The work is a culmination of techniques, and in a way a metaphor for the variety of influences that work upon the composer and the city. With sampled sounds Reich recalls earlier tape loop pieces and the power of technology; canonic structures invoke the densely polyphonic layers of Bach's counterpoint as well as Reich's own *Clapping,* his violin and piano phase pieces, African rhythmic influences, and *Drumming.* Incorporating horns, whistles, car alarms, and everyday industrial sounds as integral aspects of his music ties Reich to Edgard Varèse, George Antheil, and John Cage. Beginning with the speech melody of New York City street vendors and then echoing the patterns of civil rights rally speakers and city firefighters, Reich pays homage once again to Williams, Janáček, and Bartók. His use of human voices negotiating tragedy reveals his ongoing involvement with the human condition. If *City Life* is not an autobiographical work, it is most assuredly a personal one offering a twenty-four-minute aural glimpse into Reich's world.

As he did in *The Desert Music,* Reich starts from the text and then creates harmonic cycles. But whereas in the earlier work he quoted the words of a poet imitating the rhythms of American speech, in *City Life* Reich captures the authentic voices, records them, and uses them as the basis of what unfolds.[64] In its realism, *City Life* resembles *It's Gonna Rain* and *Come Out.* But this work is perhaps more reflective than assertive. A restrained twenty-four-measure introduction prepares listeners for this snapshot of New York, circa 1995. The music processes in long-note-value block chords that wend from 2/4 to 3/4 to 4/4, perhaps an unconscious manifestation of the "flexible foot" that Williams heard in American speech or, more directly, a reference to the counterpoint of paces that inhabits the city. The sound is completely unhurried, matter-of-fact, even dignified, although laced with ominous dissonances. One gets the sense that Reich is aurally panning the city from a great distance, perhaps even from his memory.[65]

That all changes, however, at the downbeat of measure 25, where listeners are thrust onto the street and confronted with the sounds of a street vendor barking, "Check it out."[66] The first movement becomes the incarnation of New York speech melody. We are surrounded by the actual sounds of the place. One can almost hear the subtly thrust chin that accompanies so many New York utterances. With its nudged first phoneme, elided second to third syllables, and swallowed final consonant, the brief three-word phrase is a microcosm of city dialect. But the three-syllable phrase appears first as an *instrumental* motive, and only six measures later with the actual text.

Ex. 6.4: Steve Reich, *City Life*, "Check it out," mm 25–30. © 1995 by Hendon Music, Inc., a Boosey and Hawkes company. Reprinted by permission.

The interplay between generative speech and instrumental gesture is so intimate that one loses track of which is the cause and which is the effect. Speech grows out of the environment, while the musical environment grows from the cadences of speech. The union is seamless. As "Check it out" repeats it becomes the rhythm of the movement and eventually an essential generating source for the entire piece. The same rhythm appears in the non-texted second movement, and it is picked up again in the first speech sample of the fifth movement, "Heavy smoke," another three-syllable phrase.

The third movement uses a different speech melody sample: "It's been a honeymoon—Can't take no mo'," which was recorded "at a mostly African American political rally near City Hall."[67] Here Reich seizes upon fragments of those words and develops a complex, pounding counterpoint of threes against twos. As the words repeat and repeat, many listeners "can't take no mo'" either. The position of this intense rhythmic activity in *City Life* recalls Reich's similar placement of his most complex polyphony in *The Desert Music*. In both pieces he works up to these densest textures, and in both cases the third movements grow naturally from music that precedes them. The rhythmic rivalry in "It's been a honeymoon" is forecast in the introduction to the first movement, where duple and triple rhythms, albeit juxtaposed rather than simultaneous, and gentle rather than aggressive, tug against one another. Relentlessly repeated, brief rhythmic patterns hammer us. Dissonance increases and thickens the texture. Tension is palpable. Listeners are forced into the fray. Fifty-six measures into the movement, a black male voice explodes, "It's been a honeymoon." Once again instrumental music and generating speech are of a piece; the angry energy present in the speaker's ironic assertion becomes the pounding music that follows. If this is New York in 1995, we understand Reich's characterization of the city as "a very difficult place to live in."[68]

The non-texted fourth movement, "Heartbeats/boats & buoys," with its calming boat horns and buoy bells, provides relief from the previous sonic assault. Beyond people and machines, harbor sounds are part of the city too. But what might provide a meditative moment for Reich does not materialize. Behind the soft sounds of distant boats lies a throbbing heartbeat. Thumping first at a dotted-quarter at 68, over the course of the piece the pace increases to 78 (measure 610), 88 (measure 637), 98 (measure 671), and finally 102 (measure 687). One might like to imagine a jogger running along the water's edge as explanation for the increased pulse rate, but dissonant droning harmonies disallow such a cheery read. Reich's "bleak time" seems to be in the water as well as in the air. There are no hopeful messages here.

A consummate craftsman as well as a sensitive observer, Reich attends to the musical requirements of his five-part form by balancing this movement with the second. As the composer explains, "both start slow and increase in speed," and "both are harmonically based on the same cycle of four dominant chords."[69] In addition, each is just under four minutes in length, creating a temporal symmetry. Having achieved the apex of his musical arch in the third movement, the composer creates a pulsing heartbeat in the fourth movement that recalls the thudding pile drivers of the second movement. This time the quickening heartbeat leads to Reich's final movement, a work built upon "actual field communications of the New York City Fire Department on February 26, 1993, the day the World Trade Center was [first] bombed."[70] In the fifth movement we glimpse what New York has become.

A powerful musical response to the first attack by terrorists on the iconic towers of the World Trade Center in 1993, "Heavy smoke" takes on additional meaning in the wake of their complete destruction eight years later. Once again Reich draws upon American vernacular speech to generate the rhythms and cadences of his music. We hear men's and women's voices, all with their New York accents, in eleven sampled phrases spoken by firefighters who responded to the attack: "Heavy smoke," "Stand by, stand by," "It's full a' smoke," "Urgent!" "Guns, knives, or weapons on ya?" "Wha' were ya doin'?" "Be careful," "Where you go," "Careful," "Stand by." Again Reich recalls rhythms heard earlier in the piece. In the fifth movement, the punchy two-pulse "Urgent!" "Careful," and "Stand by" echo a similarly accented "take mo'," from a fragment of the phrase "Can't take no mo'" in the third movement. At other times Reich introduces wholly new patterns. The relatively lengthy questions "Guns, knives, or weapons on ya?" and "Wha' were ya doin'?" emerge as fully formed musical phrases in the clarinets, first piano players, and cello. While rhythmic fragments of the larger phrase appear throughout the work's twenty-four minutes, no earlier gesture approaches these paired questions in length. Reich's limited pitch contour captures the flat range of the speakers. This is American speech melody (see Ex. 6.5).

Reich's cautionary tale ends with appropriately cautionary words. Sampled voices of firefighters warn each other to "Stand by" and "Be careful." But their professional communications go well beyond providing interesting rhythms or patterns for the speech-sensitive composer. Using their voices and his music, Reich seems to warn us of the same; stand by and be careful. As the piece draws to a close, flexible 2/4 and 3/4 meters, recalling those that opened the work, return. A droning, all-encompassing dissonance fades from *mezzo forte* to *mezzo piano*, *piano*, and *pianissimo* and then stops. There is no closure here, no logical end. The city captured by Ives, Varèse, Copland, and Ellington has become synonymous with the term "ground zero," and in place of gleaming glass towers we are left with questions.

As did Charles Ives in *From Hanover Square North, at the End of a Tragic Day, the Voice of the People Again Arose,* Reich hears the sounds of people and the city as one; here is a man-made place. But the eighty years between the two compositions tell of a different New York and a different America. Whereas Ives laid in the background music of his city with soft ostinato patterns and chanting choirs, Reich establishes the sonic range of his late-twentieth-century urban landscape with door slams, bus and subway air, car horns, popping manhole covers, subway chimes, harbor sounds, tire skids, and people's voices. Flexible meters and flattened-out melodic contours grow out of the speech of modern America. These sounds interweave their music as naturally as did Ives's chugging train. Where Ives offered the comfort of a hymn to speed commuters on their way, Reich offers only a warning.

Ex. 6.5: Steve Reich, *City Life,* "Heavy smoke," mm 807–8. © 1995 by Hendon Music, Inc., a Boosey and Hawkes company. Reprinted by permission.

Conclusions: Where We Are

ONSIDERED as a group, the pieces explored in this book reveal a changing sense of what distinguishes America, both to the world and to itself. It is a tale of increasing complication and, Steve Reich might say, ambiguity. But it did not seem so at first. Faced with an entire continent whose size and variety were unlike any that European explorers had experienced elsewhere, the earliest among them sent back descriptions of the new world that extolled the natural wonders they encountered. In the early years of the nineteenth century, Anthony Philip Heinrich would do the same with musical works that celebrated the woods of Kentucky. America was synonymous with waterfalls and wilds, unspoiled beauty, unlimited opportunity. As the nation evolved from a colonial outpost to a powerful political entity, for many years its identity remained closely intertwined with the most obvious of its endowments: its seemingly endless nature. In stories, paintings, and pieces, writers, artists, and eventually composers helped create and then perpetuate the association of nation with nature. This pairing fueled national pride, Manifest Destiny thinking, and westward expansion. It provided the foundation for many a myth; it served the fledgling nation well.

When the United States moved to the forefront of the world stage in a newly industrialized Western culture, however, its identity changed; its symbols changed to urban ones. Man-made structures, institutions, and environments edged out agrarian images of America. And literature, art, and music responded. When Heinrich and William Henry Fry commemorated Niagara, their soundscapes were musical evocations of the Falls: the natural place was the subject. But starting with Charles Ives—and evident in this study through Aaron Copland, Edgard Varèse, Duke Ellington, and Steve Reich—people became essential players in the landscape. This was not merely to provide a sense of scale, as they had in many early paintings. Whether pieces celebrated natural or urban sites, deserts or elevated train stations, the Mississippi River or the Oklahoma plains, cities or gardens, people interacted with and altered places in basic ways. While it never had been the complete story, place alone no longer sufficed to symbolize America.

This trajectory was forecast in an unsuspecting source more than two hundred years ago. In 1782, one year after Heinrich was born, Davies and Davis of London published Hector St. John de Crèvecoeur's *Letters from an American Farmer*. It was an immediate success, appeared in Ireland, Holland, and Germany, and in 1784 was issued in a French edition.[1] For many, the book provided a dispassionate documentary on life an ocean away, an account of America as it evolved from a British colony to an independent nation. But more than that, it was a cautionary tale. Crèvecoeur foresaw the tensions inherent in a country founded upon the individual pursuit of wealth and happiness, and he was not optimistic. In addition, *Letters* reflected numerous late eighteenth-century inclinations, not the least of which was a growing scientific interest in agriculture.[2] It is no coincidence that Crèvecoeur made his observations of the American "laboratory" as a man of the soil, an insider at home in the new world. As Heinrich understood in the 1840s and Roy Harris calculated a hundred years later, a connection with the land could be useful in validating one's role as spokesperson for America.

Crèvecoeur wrote his letters as Farmer James from Pennsylvania, and he addressed them to an unidentified "F. B." He drew upon real-life experiences at Pine Hill, his farm in Chester County, New York, a rich store of folk legends,[3] and an earlier work written by Abbé Raynal, to whom he dedicated his book.[4] Only recently have the more allegorical messages and artistic intentions of Crèvecoeur's *Letters* captured the spotlight. As Susan Manning notes, "the *Letters* are at once a celebration of America, and its tragedy."[5] But it is a tragedy that unfolds slowly. Two centuries after Crèvecoeur, we hear those messages resonate in the music of Zwilich and Reich.

The twelve letters take readers on a tour of the colonies by focusing upon three representative areas: the New England seacoast at Nantucket and Martha's Vineyard; the farm communities of the mid-Atlantic colonies; and the city of Charleston, South Carolina, using it as an exemplar of southern culture. But beyond describing the physical place that was America and the impact it had on the people that inhabited those regions, Crèvecoeur commented upon the religious, political, and economic institutions that made American society unique. These features, he decided, more than any natural attributes, would determine the nation's fate. In the early letters Crèvecoeur sang rhapsodically of the land, whose size amazed him, but by the final message he had come to appreciate the dangers inherent in abundance. Brief excerpts from three letters reveal his changing perceptions.

In Letter 2, "On the Situation, Feelings, and Pleasures, of an American Farmer," Crèvecoeur's Farmer James extols life in the ideal agrarian society. "Where is that station which can confer a more substantial system of felicity than that of an American farmer. . . . The instant I enter on my own land, the bright idea of property, of exclusive right, of independence, exalt my mind. Precious soil, I say to myself . . . What should we American farmers be without the distinct possession of that soil?"[6] In 1820 Heinrich offered a similarly romantic perspective, even if he was less concerned with possessing land. In the dedication of his opus 1, *The Dawning of Music in Kentucky,* Heinrich explained the genesis of his music. It was "drawn up in the wilds of America, where the minstrelsy of nature, the songsters of the air, next to other Virtuosos of the woods, have been my greatest inspirers of melody, harmony, and composition."[7] Heinrich too was taken with the agrarian ideal.

If the soil itself was the focus of Crèvecoeur's second letter, by the third people had caught his attention. In Letter 3, "What Is an American?" Crève-coeur suggests connections between the different geographical regions and the types of people who live there. "Men are like plants. The goodness and flavour of the fruit proceeds from the peculiar soil and exposition in which they grow. . . . Whoever traverses the continent must easily observe those strong differences which will grow more evident in time."[8] In the 1930s Roy Harris would make much of the peculiarly American qualities that were his alone because of his roots in the Oklahoma plains. Threatened by the energy and success of numerous urban composers, Harris claimed his distinctiveness by rooting himself in the western soil—a more American place, he would argue, than were the concrete canyons of New York. During the course of his remaining letters, Crèvecoeur's optimistic outlook fades. The natural place seems to have less power over Americans as their power over it grows.

In Letter 12, "Distresses of a Frontier-Man," Farmer James recalls an earlier time, one when an agrarian utopia seemed possible: "Once happiness was our portion; now it is gone from us, and I am afraid not to be enjoyed again by the present generation. . . . what is man when no longer connected with society; or when he finds himself surrounded by a convulsed and half-dissolved one?"[9] From Crèvecoeur's perspective, the potential for unlimited individual growth that he valued so much in Letter 2 undermined communal responsibility. Accumulation of wealth resulted in consolidation of power. Greed and personal gain became the engine of a society in which people acted inhumanely toward each other. The possibilities that America had promised, and that had been symbolized so completely in the beauty and vastness of the continent, in the soil itself, turned on themselves.[10]

Crèvecoeur's gloomy, if prescient, observations were not shared by Americans happy to shake off the yoke of British rule, or by Heinrich, Fry, and others who were determined to embrace, realize, and propagate the American dream.[11] In the closing days of the nineteenth century, confronted with incontestable change, Bristow clung to a transcendent vision of America as it manifested itself at Niagara Falls. At the turn of the century, Ives kept one foot firmly planted in the countryside of western Connecticut. Always reluctant to let go completely of a more pastoral notion of America, Ives would spend half of every year in New York City and the other half at his home in West Redding, Connecticut. In the fourth decade of the twentieth century, Harris participated in a different manifestation of the dream when he followed mythologized pioneers out West and rooted himself in the open plains. And at the end of the twentieth century, Robert Starer and Dana Paul Perna still found much to celebrate in purely natural sites, although both composers peopled their places.

At the opening of the twenty-first century, Americans relate to their places in less self-conscious ways than did Heinrich or Fry. There is no unified effort to present America to the world via its natural endowments, as there was with the Hudson River School painters—unless one believes that local and state chamber of commerce literature showing peaceful mountain vistas and glassy lakes is a latter-day manifestation of an organized effort to keep such a perspective alive. Americans are less inclined than they once were to seek the cachet of topographical uniqueness to shape an identity. Works by Ellen Taaffe Zwilich and Steve Reich embody this new relationship to place. Without setting out to commemorate the idea of place per se, both composers nevertheless have. In a symphony inspired by a botanical garden, Zwilich acknowledges the natural history of the nation and the importance of our stewardship of that inheritance. In pieces whose very rhythms and cadences are born of American speech patterns, Reich consciously stamps his works "Made in the USA." Less chauvinistic about place now than they were years ago, perhaps most Americans feel more at home.

In her introduction to Crèvecoeur's *Letters,* Susan Manning makes an observation that has particular resonance in a study that closes with the music of Reich. "With hindsight," she notes, "we may see the *Letters'* concern with 'process' rather than outcome as typically American: its structure reflects the open-ended experience of becoming, not the meditated accomplishment of being."[12] If Manning is correct, Reich's essential concern with process underscores his Americanism. His naming particular places in the titles of his works and his use of vernacular speech only locate that identity more specifically.

At the beginning of a new century, we live in a convulsed wilderness of our own making, one that harbors unimaginable dangers. But it is one that also houses the same natural wonders that first captured the imagination of explorers more than three hundred years ago. If the majority of Americans are, indeed, more comfortable with where we are, then perhaps we can turn to who we are and what we want to become.

NOTES

NOTES TO INTRODUCTION

1.   I am grateful for numerous conversations with Stuart Feder, M.D., a practicing psychiatrist and musicologist, and for his insights into the essential importance of place in the human psyche.

2.   Robert Hughes, *American Visions: The Epic History of Art in America* (New York: Alfred A. Knopf), 1997.

3.   The French painter Claude Lorrain (1600–1682) was the most important landscape painter of his time. Barbara Novak explained American painters' reliance on his style: "Perhaps it was inevitable that the American artists seeking grandeur through general effect should refer instinctively to the European convention that most blatantly signified the 'ideal' in landscape. Thus they looked to Claude for a compositional structure which, once adapted, remained little more than a superficial imposition of a worn-out structural cliché." See Barbara Novak, *Nature and Culture: American Landscape and Painting, 1825–1875* (New York: Oxford University Press, 1995), 25.

4.   For the most complete survey of this artistic headquarters, see Annette Blaugrund, *The Tenth Street Studio Building: Artist Entrepreneurs, from the Hudson River School to the American Impressionists* (Southampton, N.Y.: Parrish Art Museum), 1997.

5.   Ibid., 30

6.   The word "studio" appeared in relief on the lintel over the front door. In addition to the untold benefits accruing to artists immersed in a cooperative atmosphere, Blaugrund observes that Frederic E. Church and Albert Bierstadt were "masters of self-promotion [who] used their Tenth Street Studios to great advantage" by hosting well-publicized shows in their elegantly decorated work spaces. Each became rich and famous, spurred on by the other's achievements. (Blaugrund, *Tenth Street Studio Building*, 70). "Their studios became showrooms that were testaments to their success" (57). The cooperative spirit of the studio, however, did not prevent extreme rivalries from developing. Church and Bierstadt were regularly engaged in professional competition with each other.

7.   See Louis Legrand Noble, *The Life and Works of Thomas Cole,* ed. by Elliot S. Vesell (Hensonville, N.Y.: Black Dome Press, 1997). In his introductory remarks, Vesell notes the unique achievements of the Hudson River School: "Their achievement was to present a new view of nature and of man's relationship to nature which had widespread ramifications in American literature as well as in other aspects of American culture. The work of the Hudson River School represents the first, and perhaps the last, systematic attempt to depict on canvas a unified vision of the American landscape" (xxvii).

8.   Blaugrund, *Tenth Street Studio Building*, 35.

9.   This observation is not intended to discount the worthy contributions of hymn composers, who wrote in a circumscribed idiom for specific purposes. Their efforts, however, were not directed at creating a national style in the ways American writers and artists consciously set out to do.

10.   Given the low esteem in which programmatic music was held by many of America's

most influential music critics in the nineteenth century, there were real penalties rather than rewards for too closely capturing the imagery of a place in music or suggesting the connection. Prejudices against programmatic music will be discussed in connection with the compositions of Anthony Philip Heinrich, William Henry Fry, and Ferde Grofé in particular.

11. Assaults on theater orchestra musicians for not playing tunes the audience requested were known to occur in the early Federal period.

12. Anyone who has contemplated the position of the camera in dozens of Carleton Watkins's photographs will immediately recognize the inherent difficulties and dangers. Watkins (1829–1916) used large and heavy cameras with wet plates (as compared with the lightweight and portable 35-mm. and digital cameras of today). His equipment was so cumbersome it required transportation by a train car. Nonetheless, Watkins created some of the first photographs of Yosemite Valley and in so doing shaped a nation's sense of the American West. Abraham Lincoln declared the Yosemite area a national preserve in large measure because of Watkins's work.

13. Quoted in Michael Broyles, *"Music of the Highest Class": Elitism and Populism in Antebellum Boston* (New Haven: Yale University Press, 1992), 162; originally in "The Euterpeiad—No. 10," *Boston Intelligencer,* 11 April 1818.

14. See John Sullivan Dwight as quoted in William Treat Upton, *Anthony Philip Heinrich: A Nineteenth-Century Composer in America* (New York: Columbia University Press, 1939), 199–200.

15. Quoted in Broyles, *"Music of the Highest Class,"* 254; originally in "Concerts of the Past Winter," *The Dial 1* (July 1840): 124.

16. Quoted in Nicholas Tawa, *High-Minded and Low-Down: Music in the Lives of Americans, 1800–1861* (Boston: Northeastern University Press, 2000), 18; the original quote is attributed to "A Young Gent," *Squints through an Opera Glass* (New York: Merchant's Day-Book, 1850), 43.

17. The painters used European presentation techniques, but their subjects were undeniably American. The phrase "manifest destiny" was coined by a close friend of Walt Whitman's, John L. O'Sullivan, editor of the *Democratic Review,* in 1845. The thinking represented by the phrase had been popular for a long time before that date.

18. Although none of the composers discussed in this book refers to these works as "place pieces," I have labeled musical compositions that identify specific locations in their titles in this way.

19. Miller addressed a conference on the topic of "Values in the American Tradition," 12 October 1954. This address was later published as an article entitled "The Shaping of the American Character" in the *New England Quarterly* 28, no. 4 (December 1955), 435–454.

20. Perry Miller, *Nature's Nation* (Cambridge, Mass.: Harvard University Press, 1967). Miller died in 1963.

21. Miller does not insist that the nation's nature alone determined American identity. It is one of a number of themes, including the idea of a religious covenant, unusual reliance upon common sense, and the sheer willfulness of its people. These themes and others are woven throughout Miller's collection of essays.

22. "Pivotal utterance" is a phrase that Perry Miller used to describe Emerson's 1836 essay

"Nature." See *The Transcendentalists: An Anthology,* ed. by Perry Miller (Cambridge, Mass.: Harvard University Press, 1950), 5.

23.   The Presidential Medal of Freedom is the highest honor given to civilians in the United States. For additional remarks by the president at the Twenty-fifth Anniversary of Earth Day, see http://www.ecomall.com/activism/pres.htm (4 September 2002).

24.   There are numerous instances of pieces whose titles suggest the importance of place but whose composers deny the significance of such. Correspondence with John Harbison clarified the lack of importance of any specific place in his *Three City Blocks* (John Harbison to author, 26 January 1999). Francis Thorne dismissed the importance of place in his Symphony No. 7, "Along the Hudson": "My 7th would indicate that I have strong tendencies in that direction. I'm afraid the opposite is true. To me, music is an abstract art, and the only reason I had the Walt Whitman finale was that the conductor asked me to refer to the Hudson river, and my friend the poet J. D. McClatchy looked up the Whitman texts for me to set" (Francis Thorne to author, 15 November 1998). As much as could be determined, all pieces discussed in this study were intended as tributes of some kind to the places named in their titles.

25.   As the Francis Eppes Professor of Composition at Florida State University, Zwilich is on campus part of each semester to work with students and visit music classes. The first woman to win a Pulitzer Prize for composition is asked on a regular basis some variation on the question "What is it like being a woman composer?" In every instance she has made clear that she does not think of herself as a "woman composer," although she acknowledges being both. She is puzzled and amused by discussions of her music that point to its masculine qualities, and wonders aloud how these two seemingly contradictory descriptions are to be reconciled. In rejecting the tendency to categorize people, Zwilich shares a basic attitude with William Grant Still, who saw himself as an American composer who happened to be black.

26.   The United States is also identified with its exported culture and thus associated with Mickey Mouse and any number of logos, products, and businesses. Over the course of the twentieth century, the nation became the symbol of economic and political power. It was the iconic significance of the Pentagon and the World Trade Center Towers, two man-made symbols of American military and financial might, that made them such attractive targets for terrorism in September 2001.

NOTES TO CHAPTER ONE

1.   The Falls had been referred to even earlier in the seventeenth century, although they were unnamed. Samuel de Champlain's *Voyages,* published in 1604, mentioned "Falls at the extremity of [Lake Ontario], very high, where many fish come down and are stunned." Samuel de Champlain, *Voyages,* trans. Charles Pomeroy Otis (Boston, 1880; reprint, New York: Burt Franklin, 1966), 301.

2.   See Jeremy Elwell Adamson, "Nature's Grandest Scene in Art," in Adamson, ed., *Niagara: Two Centuries of Changing Attitudes, 1697–1901* (Washington, D.C.: Corcoran Gallery of Art, 1985), 17–18.

3.   The other two were an engraving of a bison and a map of the territory that LaSalle had explored.

4.   "Sublime" is a term that itself underwent changes of meaning in the early nineteenth

century. The *Oxford English Dictionary* quotes from an 1806 gazeteer in which the term connotes terror: "This fall of water is indeed awful and sublime, but has too much of the terrible in its appearance." By 1820, Washington Irving uses it to mean something quite different: "Never need an American look beyond his own country for the sublime and beautiful of natural scenery."

5. A 1985 show mounted by Washington, D.C.,'s Corcoran Gallery of Art entitled "Niagara: Two Centuries of Changing Attitudes, 1697–1901" paid homage to the morphing icon with more than 250 paintings and objects culled from thousands that were available. The Corcoran was the perfect place for such a nationally important artistic subject. Founded in 1869 as Washington's first art museum, it is today the largest private one in the capitol city and, with Boston's Museum of Fine Arts and New York's Metropolitan Museum of Art, one of the nation's three oldest.

6. Elizabeth McKinsey, "An American Icon," in Adamson, ed., *Niagara: Two Centuries of Changing Attitudes,* 88.

7. Quoted in Charles Mason Dow, LL.D., *Anthology and Bibliography of Niagara Falls,* 2 vols. (Albany: State of New York, 1921), 1:230–231.

8. Ibid., 233–234; originally taken from John Quincy Adams's "Speech on Niagara." Adams's pairing of America's nature with a pledge from God is a reminder that the 1840s was the decade that recorded the first usage of the phrase "Manifest Destiny."

9. Edward T. Taylor, *Father Taylor, the Sailor Preacher. Incidents and Anecdotes of Rev. Edward T. Taylor, for over Forty Years Pastor of the Seaman's Bethel, Boston* (Boston: B. B. Russell, 1872), 214–215.

10. According to Adamson, "the term [Niagaraized] was coined by [the artist John F.] Kensett's friend, the editor of *Harper's Monthly,* G. W. Curtis, in *Lotus-Eating,* 1852, 81." See Adamson, ed., *Niagara: Two Centuries of Changing Attitudes,* 79. The full title of Curtis's collection is *Lotus-Eating: A Summer Book* (New York: Dix, Edwards and Co.). The title pages shows an 1856 date; the dedication page shows June 1852. Adamson asserts that Kensett (1816–72) "was one of the first [artists] to become thoroughly 'Niagaraized.'" Adamson, *Niagara,* 51.

11. Dow, *Anthology,* 2.

12. See Einar Haugen and Camilla Cai, *Ole Bull: Norway's Romantic Musician and Cosmopolitan Patriot* (Madison: University of Wisconsin Press, 1993), 85–87, 303. Attempts by Cai to locate a manuscript or score to *Niagara* have thus far been unsuccessful. I am grateful to Ms. Cai for sharing this information. Cai hypothesizes that "if there is or was a manuscript, it would be just a sketch because improvisation in concert was one of [Bull's] virtuoso attractions as a performer. The piece was probably different to some degree every time." Camilla Cai, e-mail to author, 21 June 2001.

13. Quoted in Vera Brodsky Lawrence, *Strong on Music: The New York Music Scene in the Days of George Templeton Strong, 1836–1875,* vol. 1, *Resonances* (New York: Oxford University Press, 1988), 289–290.

14. Ibid., 201.

15. Dow, *Anthology,* 2: 784–785.

16. Eugene Thayer, "Music of Niagara," *Scribner's Magazine,* February 1881, 583.

17. Ibid., 584.

18. Ibid., 583.

19. Ibid., 586.

20. Ibid., 586. All italics are original to Thayer's article.

21. Hermann Helmholtz's seminal work on acoustics, *On the Sensations of Tone,* was first published in 1863 and translated into English for the first time in 1875. That same year, *Century Magazine* published an article by two German geologists in which they explained that rushing water always sounded the pitches C, E, G, and F. Clearly there was widespread interest in providing scientific explanations for acoustical events, and Thayer would contribute his own observations to the effort.

22. Henry James, *Portraits of Places* (Boston: James R. Osgood, 1884), 366–367, 369.

23. John F. Sears, "Doing Niagara Falls in the Nineteenth Century" in Adamson, ed., *Niagara: Two Centuries of Changing Attitudes,* 115.

24. Ten years earlier Henry James had noted aural qualities of the Falls, but just in passing: "it melts and shifts and changes, all with the sound as of millions of bass-voices; and yet its outline never varies, never moves with a different pulse." James, *Portraits of Places,* 371.

25. *Funk and Wagnalls Standard College Dictionary,* 1966 edition, defines "roar" as "a full, deep, resonant cry, as of a beast, or of a human being in pain, grief, or anger."

26. Most likely Thayer didn't know these works, as they were all unpublished at the time and only one may have received a public performance.

27. Quoted in F. E. Church, *F. E. Church's Painting of Nature's Grandest Scene; The Great Fall, Niagara. Painted by F. E. Church* (New York: Williams, Stevens, Williams and Co., 1857), 7.

28. According to Elizabeth McKinsey, "Church's massive canvas was the culmination of all [previous] images . . . it was lionized. Thousands paid their twenty-five cents and stood in line to see it. Reviewers hailed it as the first painting to do the impossible; 'the eye that could command the hand has seen [the cataract] at last." McKinsey, "An American Icon," 97.

29. Henry James noted the multiformity of the place when he described his impressions as he came upon the American cliff: "This is the first act of the drama of Niagara; for it is, I believe, one of the commonplaces of description that you instinctively convert it into a series of 'situations.'" James, *Portraits of Places,* 365.

30. This is especially true in the case of Fry, whose piece, while containing two distinctly different sections, was nonetheless a single-movement descriptive work along the lines of a symphonic poem, overture, or tone poem.

31. The July 1846 concert contained at least two instrumental works by Heinrich of an overtly programmatic (and nationalistic) nature, the above-mentioned piece and *Ouverture,—"To the Pilgrims,"* for full orchestra. Heinrich provided a description for each of the four sections of the ouverture: "Adagio Primo—The Genius of Freedom slumbering in the forest shades of America"; "Adagio Secondo—She is awakened into life by those moving melodies, with which nature regales her votaries in her primeval solitude"; "Marcia—The efforts of power to clip the young eagle of liberty"; "Allegretto Pollacca—The joyous reign of universal freedom and universal intelligence." The remainder of the program included a variety of songs by Heinrich, as well as "Una Voce poco fa," by Rossini; "I Dearly Love the Sea," a song by G. F. Hayter; and the overture to von Weber's *Der Freischütz.* For a

copy of the program, see Upton's *Anthony Philip Heinrich*, unnumbered pages following page 196. Also found in A. P. Heinrich Scrapbook, Library of Congress, Music 1877 Reel 11, pages 514–515.

32.   Dwight chose not to comment upon Beethoven's Ninth Symphony, whose choral finale begged the question of abstraction.

33.   Upton, *Anthony Philip Heinrich*, 200–201. Dwight did not single out Heinrich's programmatic music for special criticism. In 1852 he blasted Ole Bull's music for being "disjointed, fragmentary, confusing, and oftentimes of a tendency . . . to attempt descriptions, pictures, narratives of historical scenes and events through tones." See *Dwight's Journal of Music* 1, no. 9 (5 June 1852): 69. Still later he would hold the music of Louis Moreau Gottschalk to a similar standard and find it wanting. In the case of Gottschalk, Dwight would also criticize the flamboyance of the pianist's performances, a manifestation of the growing cult of virtuosity. For an introduction to other issues that might have informed Dwight's reception of Gottschalk, see Laura Moore, "Bombastic Bamboolas and Boston Brahmans: L. M. Gottschalk and J. S. Dwight, and Their Viewpoints on American Music," master's thesis, Florida State University, 2000.

34.   A. P. Heinrich Scrapbook, page 1027. Quoted in Upton, *Anthony Philip Heinrich*, 4.

35.   Surprisingly, such trips were not all that unusual in the first decade of the nineteenth century.

36.   See Upton, *Anthony Philip Heinrich*, 66–67n81.

37.   A. P. Heinrich, Scrapbook, 1060.

38.   *Boston Euterpeiad*, November 1822, 133; quoted in Upton, *Anthony Philip Heinrich*, 76n11.

39.   See Betty E. Chmaj, "Father Heinrich as Kindred Spirit; or, How the Log-House Composer of Kentucky Became the Beethoven of America," in *American Studies* 24, no. 2 (fall 1983): 42. Almost one hundred years later another composer, Roy Harris, sought to identify himself as a genuine American by referring to his log-cabin roots. By then Harris hoped to benefit from the connection of Abraham Lincoln with that humble style of wooden house. Harris is considered in depth in a later chapter.

40.   This must have created some awkward moments, as Heinrich spoke English with a very thick German accent.

41.   Quoted in Adamson, "Nature's Grandest Scene in Art," 14.

42.   Andrew Stiller, ed., *The War of the Elements and the Thundering of Niagara: Capriccio Grande for a Full Orchestra* (Philadelphia: Kallisti Music Press, 1994). A beautifully preserved copyist's manuscript is located at the Library of Congress. It is oblong in shape, consists of fifty-four pages, and is written in an elegant, precise hand. (There is no page 16 to the score, although there is no music missing.) One can see Heinrich's own hand in metronome markings that were added later.

43.   Hewitt gave music lessons to James Tyler's daughter Alice and so had access to the president.

44.   John Tasker Howard, *Our American Music: Three Hundred Years of It* (New York: Thomas Y. Crowell, 1931), 237.

45.   It is possible that *The War of the Elements* was intended to form some part of the larger *Jubilee*, as Heinrich was not at all opposed to reusing his own earlier works in later creations.

46. Howard, *Our American Music*, 238.

47. It is unfortunate that to date no commercial recording exists of this work, as its large and unusual orchestration would distinguish what otherwise appears to be a rather unexceptional composition. As Andrew Stiller explains: "The first modern performance (and probable world premiere) took place on 18 January 1976, with the Buffalo Philharmonic Orchestra under the direction of Michael Tilson Thomas." It is possible that an in-house recording was made of this performance; however, extensive efforts to locate it have been unsuccessful. See Anthony Philip Heinrich, in Stiller, ed., *The War of the Elements*, prefatory remarks, unnumbered page.

48. This was only one type of problem facing visual artists. They also struggled to capture the particular colors that characterized the waters of Niagara, especially green. See James, *Portraits of Places*, 368–370, for a writer's thoughts on "the world-famous green."

49. See Adamson, ed., *Niagara: Two Centuries of Changing Attitudes*, 15. The quoted passage originally appeared in *Home Journal*, 9 May 1857, 2. Italics original to the article.

50. Dwight's standard was appropriate, perhaps, for abstract instrumental works. This piece made no pretense at being abstract; it was dramatic and programmatic and so adhered to a different criterion, one closer to the overtures being written by Mendelssohn around the same time. Upton records that Heinrich "had met and dined with Mendelssohn on his visit to London in 1829," and that "Mendelssohn had visited Heinrich at his lodgings." See Upton, *Anthony Philip Heinrich*, 116. I am grateful to Michael Broyles, who helped to clarify Heinrich's models of musical form. See Broyles, *Mavericks and Other Traditions In American Music* (New Haven: Yale University Press, forthcoming).

51. Upton, *Anthony Philip Heinrich*, 240–244.

52. Ibid., 240.

53. Ibid.

54. Heinrich's experience as a theater orchestra musician provided ample opportunity for him to play this repertoire.

55. The entire coda has only two fermatas: one at measure 445 and the second on the final chord.

56. Henry James had observed, "to look is to be immersed," *Portraits of Places*, 373.

57. Andrew Stiller clarifies: "Cymbals in Heinrich's day were much smaller on the average than they are now . . . requir[ing] plates of an appropriate diameter—30 cm. or less—to achieve adequate balance and clarity. The cymbal rolls are performed by rubbing the two plates together." Stiller, ed., *The War of the Elements*, preface, unnumbered page.

58. See Upton, *Anthony Philip Heinrich*, 216, for a reference to Heinrich's involvement in the establishment of the New York Philharmonic Society.

59. Quoted in Irving Lowens, *Music and Musicians in Early America* (New York: Norton, 1964), 217–218.

60. Ralph Waldo Emerson, *Ralph Waldo Emerson: Essays and Lectures* (New York: Literary Classics of the United States, 1983), 53.

61. For discussions of art and architecture in the early decades of nineteenth-century America, see Thomas Flexner, *That Wilder Image: The Painting of America's Native School, from Thomas Cole to Winslow Homer* (Boston: Little, Brown, 1962); and William H. Pierson

Jr., *American Buildings and Their Architects: The Colonial and Neo-Classical Styles* (Garden City, N.Y.: Anchor Press/Doubleday, 1976).

62. See William Treat Upton, *William Henry Fry: American Journalist and Composer-Critic* (New York: Crowell, 1954), 5, for an explanation of the Fry family history based upon discussions with Thomas Ridgway, a grandnephew of William Henry Fry.

63. Kile Smith has observed: "[Fry] was the first native-born American to write for large symphonic forces, and the first to write a grand opera. He was the first music critic for a major newspaper, and the first vociferously to insist that Americans support the music created on their own soil." See liner notes to Naxos recording American Classics 8.559057, William Henry Fry, *Santa Claus* Symphony, Royal Scottish National Orchestra, Tony Rowe, conductor, 2000. Smith is the curator of the Edwin A. Fleisher Collection of Orchestral Music at the Free Library of Philadelphia and an expert on the Fry manuscripts collected there.

64. Lowens, *Music and Musicians*, 222.

65. Quoted in Upton, *William Henry Fry*, 128. The series consisted of ten lectures (with an eleventh added) that covered the entire history and fundamentals of music. It was first announced in *Dwight's Journal of Music* 1, no. 3 (24 April 1852): 22. An outline of its syllabus appeared a few months later in *Dwight's Journal* (24 July 1852): 126. The lectures covered everything from acoustics to the orchestra, church, oratorio, and chamber music. Two sessions were devoted to "The Lyrical Drama," Fry's phrase for opera, and the series concluded with a free-wheeling talk that covered American music and the future of the art.

66. Fry's vocal abilities took many by surprise when he accompanied himself at one of his lectures.

67. Fry's sojourn in Europe, 1846–52, included numerous attempts to secure a European production of *Leonora*.

68. Lecture series were ubiquitous in the mid-nineteenth century. As Upton put it in *William Henry Fry*, "a veritable epidemic of learning swept over New York at the time" (122). It should be noted, however, that such lectures were not limited to New York; they could be found taking place throughout the growing nation.

69. As quoted in Upton, *William Henry Fry*, 123. It has been estimated that Fry lost close to four thousand dollars on the series.

70. None of the reviewers doubted Fry's enthusiasm or passion for his subject, but there seemed to be consensus that he lacked the necessary organizational skills. Others questioned the degree to which the series appeared to be an excuse for Fry to promote his own works, which he used liberally to demonstrate various points that he made. No transcript of the lectures exists, although this may be because none was ever created. According to observers, Fry appeared to talk extemporaneously most of the time, making only brief references to small cards. The two-hour-long lectures probably required more than a few notes for the composer-critic to hold them together; this might account for the feeling of disorganization sensed by reviewers.

71. "Mr. Fry's Letter to Mr. Willis," *Dwight's Journal of Music* 4, no. 18 (4 February 1854): 138.

72. The synopsis is reprinted as appendix 3 in Upton's *William Henry Fry*, 335–338.

73. Upton, *William Henry Fry*, 140. My emphasis.

74. Ibid., 336.

75. Ibid., 240. In addition to Fry's music, Jullien's manner would have attracted criticism from the Dwights and Willises of the world. When performing Beethoven, the gloved maestro was presented his jeweled baton on a velvet-covered tray brought to him at the podium.

76. Two other pieces, the "Metropolitan Hall March" for band, composed and performed in February 1853, and a choral work written for the reopening of the Crystal Palace in New York in May 1854, the "Crystal Palace Ode," are the only others among Fry's oeuvre that name specific places in their titles.

77. There is some question regarding the performance of this piece. In the *New Grove Dictionary of Music and Musicians,* David E. Campbell and John Graziano list the work as having been performed in New York on 15 June 1854. But Baker's dictionary lists a performance of the work in the same city on 4 May 1854. According to Vera Brodsky Lawrence, during the 15 June concert the piece appears not to have been performed. Lawrence bases this upon a review by Strong that discusses pieces played at that event. See Lawrence, *Strong on Music,* 2:465–466. It is possible, of course, that Strong so disliked the piece he never even mentioned it, but this would most certainly have resulted in a response from Fry. The caption accompanying the work, "Niagara—A Symphony composed for the Musical Congress at the Crystal Palace of New York, 15 June 1854," may be responsible for assumptions about a performance. It most certainly couldn't have been performed in May of that year, as it had not been finished at that time. At the foot of page 5 of the holograph it reads: "W. H. Fry, New York, Saturday, 10 June 1854." See Upton, *William Henry Fry,* 317.

78. Kile Smith has explained that the work was finished "only five days before the concert." William Henry Fry, *Niagara Symphony,* Royal Scottish National Orchestra, Tony Rowe, conductor, Naxos CD 8.559057.

79. A recording of *Niagara* has recently been released by Naxos. In addition to this work, the Royal Scottish National Orchestra, conducted by Tony Rowe, performs Fry's *Santa Claus, Christmas Symphony, Overture to Macbeth,* and *The Breaking Heart* on CD 8.559057. Rowe follows exactly the twenty-two-page full score housed at the Philadelphia Free Library.

80. Upton discusses the piece in *William Henry Fry,* 245, 248.

81. *Philadelphia Public Ledger,* 24 February 1840, 3. Jeremy Elwell Adamson explained: "According to a Philadelphia press announcement, Lindsay's construction represented 'the Rapids and falling sheets of water in actual motion." See Adamson, "Frederic Edwin Church's 'Niagara': The sublime as Transcendence," Ph.D. diss., University of Michigan, 1981, 258–272.

82. Fredericka Bremer, *The Homes of the New World,* 2 vols. (London: Hall, Virtue, 1853), 2: 588; quoted by Adamson in "Nature's Grandest Scene in Art," 51.

83. Ibid.

84. While these were not the first moving tableaus dedicated to Niagara, Frankenstein's was surely the most spectacular and famous. It was responsible for his international reputation. An earlier work entitled *The Cataract of Niagara Falls in North America,* by Philip James de Loutherbourg, was shown in 1782. See Adamson, ed., *Niagara: Two Centuries of Changing Attitudes,* 79n177.

85. See John Zeaman, "Birth of the Box-Office Blockbuster," *The [Bergen] Record On-*

line, 5 February 1999, for a discussion of John Banvard's 1,300-by-12-foot panorama of the Mississippi River from the mouth of the Ohio to New Orleans.

86. An exception to this is the recently discovered *Panorama of Bunyan's Pilgrim's Progress* of 1850–51. It had languished in the basement of the York Institute Museum in Saco, Maine, for nearly one hundred years before its discovery in 1996. The 850-by-8-foot panorama, painted by Joseph Kyle and Jacob Dallas, is believed to have been viewed by more than 100,000 people in its first year. Many of its designs were based upon compositions by Frederic Edwin Church, Jasper Cropsey, and Daniel Huntington. A restoration project was undertaken, and major sections were recently exhibited at the Portland Museum of Art in Portland, Maine. See the museum's Web site, *http://www.portlandmuseum.org* (19 July 2001).

87. See David E. Nye, *American Technological Sublime* (Cambridge, Mass.: MIT Press, 1994), 42.

88. See an article by A. H. Guernsey entitled "Niagara" in the August 1853 issue of *Harper's Monthly,* 289–305, for reproductions of wood-engraved images of Frankenstein's studies for the panorama; and Frederick H. Johnson's *Guide for Every Visitor to Niagara Falls* (Rochester, N.Y.: D. M. Dewey, 1852) for additional reproductions of Frankenstein's portrayals of the Falls.

89. *National Democrat,* 22 July 1853. See Adamson, ed., *Niagara: Two Centuries of Changing Attitudes,* 79n179.

90. Adamson is quoting from *Literary World* 13 (23 July 1853): 589.

91. Savannah, Ga., *News,* 5 June 1854. See Adamson, ed., *Niagara: Two Centuries of Changing Attitudes,* 79n181.

92. The ophicleide is an obsolete bass bugle with nine to twelve keys that produces an especially full sound; it was popular in the nineteenth century and used by Schumann, Verdi, and Wagner. Berlioz wrote for ophicleide in his *Symphonie fantastique,* and Mendelssohn, the composer whose works were most performed through 1851 by the New York Philharmonic Society, used the instrument in the *Midsummer Night's Dream* Overture. The bombardon is a tuba-type instrument in twelve-foot and fourteen-foot lengths, favored by bands.

93. One wonders if Fry had access to eleven timpani and five timpanists in New York in 1854, or whether this might have posed another problem in getting the piece ready for performance.

94. A brindisi is a drinking song, examples of which can be found in Donizetti's *Lucrezia Borgia* and Verdi's *La Traviata* and *Otello.* Fry's second section has characteristics of this genre, in combination with a choral-aria style exemplified by Verdi's "Va pensiero" from *Nabucco.*

95. See *Niagara Symphony,* page 17. A copy of the score is in the Fleisher Collection of the Free Library of Philadelphia. I am grateful to Mr. Kile Smith, curator of this collection, for sharing this score me and answering numerous questions regarding the work.

96. This structural downbeat is dramatically approached. Starting at C major in measure 13, Fry quickly traverses D-flat major (measure 15) and E major (measure 17) before arriving at the dominant G major (measure 19).

97. Haydn's oratorio "Die Schöpfung" (The Creation) was, along with Handel's oratorio "Messiah," the most popular choral work in the American repertoire. It was a staple of the

Handel and Haydn Society (founded in Boston in 1815), as well as of many smaller and lesser-known choral societies throughout the nineteenth century. Fry would have known this work.

98. Upton, *William Henry Fry*, 116, 299.

99. Ibid., 277–278. *Harold en Italie* was written in 1834.

100. As in the rest of the piece, it is impossible to know Fry's programmatic intentions for this lyrical interlude. Perhaps the section is Fry's musical nod to Niagara as a tourist destination. Certainly by mid-century, the Falls were the most popular natural attraction the country possessed.

101. This work may be the only symphony in the nineteenth-century repertoire to end on a triple *piano* diminished chord.

102. It is possible that Fry had heard Heinrich's piece in some other guise. As far as is known, *The War of the Elements and the Thundering of Niagara* was not performed in the nineteenth century. Heinrich, however, like the best European composers, regularly recycled works and parts of his works, incorporating sections of one piece within another. That Fry knew of Heinrich is clear from preconcert comments that he wrote in 1853: "There will be five original pieces, vocal and instrumental, composed by Mr. Heinrich, the merit of which we cannot speak of from personal knowledge, but for anything the public knows to the contrary they may be first rate and worthy of any composer." Upton, *William Henry Fry*, 137. Heinrich's fame would have precluded Fry's not knowing of him.

103. Broyles, *Mavericks and Other Traditions*.

104. See Delmer Dalzell Rogers, "Nineteenth-Century Music in New York City as Reflected in the Career of George Frederick Bristow," Ph.D. diss., University of Michigan, 1967. Rogers observes, "The work included vocal solos and choral numbers so labeling it as an orchestral work is arbitrary," 182. H. Wiley Hitchcock refers to this work as a cantata in *Music in the United States: A Historical Introduction* (Englewood Cliffs, N.J.: Prentice-Hall, 1988), 96. Rogers's 1967 dissertation remains the only book-length study dedicated exclusively to George Frederick Bristow.

105. Quoted in Gilbert Chase, *America's Music: From the Pilgrims to the Present*, rev. 3d ed. (Urbana: University of Illinois Press, 1987), 309. The quotation originally appeared in *Musical World* (4 March 1854): 100.

106. According to Rogers, Bristow and Timm formed a close relationship, "and in 1845 [Bristow] dedicated one of his piano compositions to Timm, the *Grand Waltz de Bravura*, Opus 6." Rogers, "Nineteenth-Century Music in New York," 67.

107. There was a brief period in the spring of 1854 when Bristow resigned from the New York Philharmonic Society. His participation in the Fry-Willis debate referred to earlier, and his protest of what he saw as the programming of nearly exclusively European composers by the Philharmonic Society caused him to leave his post for the remainder of the season. He was back in the fall.

108. Bristow performed as a violin and piano soloist in 1848, 1850, and 1851. See Rogers, "Nineteenth-Century Music in New York," 74–75.

109. The Crystal Palace in New York was the mid-century equivalent of a modern-day convention center, housing large festivals and industrial and commercial exhibitions of the time.

110. For a list of seven American composers whose works Bristow performed, see Rogers,

"Nineteenth-Century Music in New York," 93. Bristow's first oratorio, *Praise to God,* was premiered by the Harmonic Society on 19 February 1861 (ibid., 100).

111. Ibid., 161. See Rogers's appendix A for a chronological list of Bristow's works.

112. Ibid, 188–198. Rogers provides performance information for each of Bristow's works. Starting in 1852, there is a marked increase in the number of vocal works being composed and performed.

113. According to Rogers, "The published libretto included the statement that 'the manuscript has been submitted to Mr. Irving, and the deviation from, or rather addition to, the legend as related by him, met with his approval.'" "Nineteenth-Century Music in New York," 164–165.

114. Ibid., 165.

115. Ibid., 139, 182.

116. *Harper's Weekly* 17 (9 August 1873): 698. See McKinsey, "An American Icon," for an insightful discussion of the meaning of this work.

117. McKinsey, "An American Icon," 98.

118. Alfred Runte, "The Role of Niagara in America's Scenic Preservation," in Adamson, ed., *Niagara: Two Centuries of Changing Attitudes,* 117.

119. Ibid., 125.

120. Ibid., 122.

121. That the Falls are shared with Canada and the preferred view of them is from the Canadian side has never inhibited Americans from broadly claiming them as their own.

122. Frederick Law Olmsted, "Notes by Mr. Olmsted," in *Special Report of the Commissioners of the New York State Survey of 1879* (Albany, N.Y.: C. Van Benthuysen, 1880), 27–28.

123. John F. Sears, "Doing Niagara Falls in the Nineteenth Century," in Adamson, ed., *Niagara: Two Centuries of Changing Attitudes,* 115.

124. The earlier centennial celebration held in Philadelphia in 1876 proved to be much less successful than hoped. While U.S. industrial progress was everywhere in evidence, cultural achievements were just as obviously lacking. The centennial celebration became a source of embarrassment for America's cultural community.

125. This was actually the second piece that Twain wrote on the Falls. An earlier one, titled simply "Niagara" (c. 1871), challenged the sacred meaning of the waterfall and exposed the hypocrisy of the commercial tourist trap. Both works are discussed in McKinsey, "An American Icon," 98.

126. McKinsey, "An American Icon," 98.

127. Ibid., 98–99. Originally found in Mark Twain, "The First Authentic Mention of Niagara Falls: Extracts from Adam's Diary," in William Dean Howells, *The Niagara Book* (New York: Doubleday, Page, 1901), 215, 221.

128. Musical works were presented throughout the run of the exposition, and so it is possible that Bristow wrote the work with the hope of a performance at the Chicago event.

129. See "The Manuscript Society," *New York Times,* 28 January 1890, 3. The name was suggested by Addison F. Andrews, the first recording secretary of the society, and it reflected the practice of member musicians bringing their new, unpublished works to meetings still in manuscript form, from which performances were given. See Sumner Salter,

"Early Encouragements to American Composers," *Musical Quarterly* 18 (1932): 84–105, for the most thorough discussion of this society.

130. Salter, "Early Encouragements," 93, 96.

131. Given the self-consciousness of the society, it is troubling that "all of its official records and accumulations, including the library of autograph manuscript compositions contributed by members, have disappeared." Salter, "Early Encouragements," 84.

132. Ibid., 97–98.

133. Ibid., 98.

134. David Joel Metzer, "The Ascendency of Musical Modernism in New York City, 1915–1929," Ph.D. diss., Yale University, 1993, 155–157.

135. Rogers, "'Nineteenth-Century Music in New York," 136.

136. Ibid., 135. Rogers quotes from the *Bulletin of the Manuscript Society of New York,* January 1898, 2; and March 1898, 1.

137. To get a sense of Seidl's popularity and prominence and the calamity of his death for New York's music patrons, one need only read the prelude, "A Gilded Age Funeral," to Joseph Horowitz's *Wagner Nights* (Berkeley and Los Angeles: University of California Press, 1994), 11–17.

138. The valved horn was invented in 1813 and was in common use by the middle of the nineteenth century. Bristow's use of the natural horn is somewhat anachronistic in 1898.

139. A microfilm of the holograph shows the timpani to have been tuned originally to C and G, with D and A written over the original pitches. New York Public Library microfilms ZZ-2935, Reel 3. I am grateful to George Boziwick and the personnel at this library for locating these materials and making them available to me.

140. Fifteen measures into the maestoso there is a brief move away from the choral Cs, but it is temporary and only serves to strengthen the return to the tonic at the twenty-third measure of the movement. One wonders to what degree Bristow gave his singers a rest from C in order to assure that they sing in tune. Most choir directors have discovered that as choruses repeat a unison note, it often slides down in pitch. Bristow's built-in retuning would have avoided this problem and assured that the pitch stayed in place for the climactic final text.

141. Eugene Thayer, "Music of Niagara," *Scribner's Magazine,* February 1881, 584.

142. J. Horace McFarland, "Shall We Make a Coal-Pile of Niagara?" *Ladies' Home Journal* 23 (October 1906): 39. In 1906 the first measures were enacted to protect the Falls against unchecked development in the region. It took until 1950 for details of water-diversion policies to be completed.

NOTES TO CHAPTER TWO

1.   See Michael Broyles's article "Charles Ives and the American Democratic Tradition," in *Charles Ives and His World,* ed. J. Peter Burkholder (Princeton: Princeton University Press, 1996), 118–160, for a discussion of the Colonial Revival movement, which thrived from c. 1890 to 1940, and its impact on Ives. Evidence of the ubiquity of the movement can be seen in the Sears, Roebuck catalog from which customers could order Colonial Revival–style houses. The Society for the Preservation of New England Antiquities (SPNEA), officially founded in 1910, was one manifestation of heightened interest in the

past. Although numerous efforts to preserve building and monuments associated with important historical events and persons had been made for a few decades, the society brought many of these activities together. SPNEA's mission was to protect New England's cultural and architectural heritage, which many old-family New Englanders felt was under siege by increasing numbers of immigrant populations.

2.   This is seen again and again in Ives's music: the most traditional genres—string quartets, sonatas, and symphonies—embrace unexpected sources (popular tunes, marches, hymns, Civil War songs) and rhythmic and harmonic complexities.

3.   Broyles ranks these industry-rocking investigations among "the most important shaping factors in Ives's life." See Broyles, "Charles Ives and the American Democratic Tradition," 135–136, 140.

4.   In 1933 Henry Bellamann quoted Ives: "I have experienced a great fullness of life in business. The fabric of existence weaves itself whole. You cannot set an art off in the corner and hope for it to have vitality, reality, and substance. There can be nothing exclusive about a substantial art. It comes directly out of the heart of experience of life and thinking about life and living life." See Bellamann, "Charles Ives: The Man and His Music," *Musical Quarterly* 19 (1933): 45–58.

5.   He is also an international figure, as is demonstrated by the serious consideration given his work by European scholars such as David Nicholls in Great Britain and Wolfgang Rathert in Germany, and by the presence of his music on numerous concert programs throughout the world. Among them: Richard Trythall performed Ives's Second Piano Sonata in Torino, Italy, in June 1973; *The Unanswered Question* was performed as part of the Belgian-European benefit concerts held in Brussels in June 1994; the Canadian Brass Ensemble played Ives's *Variations on America* at the Schleswig-Holstein Musik Festival in August 2000; and *The Housatonic at Stockbridge* was performed in Newcastle in November 2001. These are just four of hundreds of performances and broadcasts of Ives's music that have occurred outside the United States.

6.   This does not mean, however, that he was unacquainted with European musical traditions. He knew them well. Ives's identification as an American composer was not limiting or shortsighted. In the tradition of Emerson, Thoreau, and Whitman, Ives valued the unique opportunities that the United States afforded, in the arts and otherwise. As a result, his music operates on multiple levels simultaneously: personal, national, universal. Ives saw the universal in the personal and the local, and he used his music to make that point. His personal American experience was a universal one.

7.   See Denise Von Glahn, "Charles Ives, Cowboys, and Indians: Aspects of 'The Other Side of Pioneering,'" *American Music* 19, no. 3 (fall 2001): 291–314.

8.   An article by Leo Rubinfien entitled "The Poetry of Plain Seeing," in *Art in America* (December 2000): 74–85, 132–133, 135, discusses the complex issue of documentary and what it might mean in the photographic works of Walker Evans. Rubinfien observes, "The distortion of natural seeing that occurs in the best photographs makes it hard to say that they are very faithful to their subjects at all, and often makes the photograph more vital than its subject ever was in life. A superb photographer may brush up against the momentous concerns of his age, but the sum of his distortive choices—what, borrowing from Wallace Stevens, we might call 'the fiction that results from feeling'—is what we will value him for when his age has become as dull to us as a textbook" (79).

9.   In *Tom Sails Away*, Ives's lyrics conjure an imaginary family, in an imaginary setting, but the European theater of World War I to which he refers via *Over There* is real. Similarly, in *The Things Our Fathers Loved*, references to "a place in the soul" require that listeners acknowledge the existence of places that can't be seen. In an age just growing accustomed to the concept of "the unconscious" and the power of memory and dreams to affect behavior, such lyrics represent an awareness and acceptance of the subjectivity of experience.

10.   Larry Starr discusses Ives's songs *The Things Our Fathers Loved*, and *Tom Sails Away* as two examples of a category he calls "Mental Journeys." See Starr, *A Union of Diversities* (New York: Schirmer Books, 1992), 57–79.

11.   For discussions of both these pieces, including their functions as journeys, see Denise Von Glahn Cooney, "A Sense of Place: Charles Ives and 'Putnam's Camp, Redding, Connecticut,'" *American Music* 14, no. 3 (fall 1996): 276–312; and Von Glahn Cooney, "New Sources for 'The St. Gaudens' in Boston Common (Colonel Robert Gould Shaw and His Colored Regiment)," *Musical Quarterly* 81, no. 1 (spring 1997): 13–50.

12.   The *First Orchestral Set*, otherwise known as *Three Places in New England*, is made up of three movements: *The "St. Gaudens" in Boston Common (Colonel Robert Gould Shaw and His Colored Regiment), Putnam's Camp, Redding, Connecticut,* and *The Housatonic at Stockbridge*. All musical references will be to James B. Sinclair's edition of Charles Ives, *A New England Symphony: Three Places in New England* (Bryn Mawr, Pa.: Mercury Music Corporation, 1976).

13.   People were often included in American landscape paintings of the nineteenth century to provide a sense of scale. Proud of the size of America's natural endowments, from its waterfalls to its mountains, lakes, rivers, and gorges, artists regularly included a proportionately small figure or groups of figures. The emphasis was not on the people, but on the natural phenomenon that surrounded or eclipsed them.

14.   Charles E. Ives, *Memos,* ed. John Kirkpatrick (New York: W. W. Norton, 1972), 87. Ives dictated *Memos* in 1931 and 1932; it was eventually published forty years later. Ives's portrayal of this scene resembles the scene from Henry David Thoreau's *Walden* that the composer summarized in his song *Thoreau,* number 48 of *114 Songs:* "His meditations are interrupted only by the faint sound of the Concord bell, 'A melody, as it were, imported into the wilderness. At a distance over the woods the sound acquires a certain vibratory hum as if the pine needles in the horizon were the strings of a harp which it swept . . . a vibration of the universal lyre, just as the intervening atmosphere makes a distant ridge of earth, interesting to the eyes by the azure tint it imparts.'" Charles E. Ives, *114 Songs,* (self-published in Redding, Conn., 1922; reprint, New York: Peer International, Associated Music Publishers, and Theodore Presser, 1975), 103.

15.   Ives, *Memos,* 87.

16.   See Ives, *Memos.* He could trace his family's interest in Emerson to his grandmother Sarah Hotchkiss Wilcox Ives, "a schoolteacher and Emerson-enthusiast from Killingworth, Conn." (245). For a nuanced discussion of the role that Transcendentalism played within the Ives family, see J. Peter Burkholder, *Charles Ives: The Ideas Behind the Music* (New Haven: Yale University Press, 1985), especially chapters 3, "Ives and Transcendentalism," and 4, "The Philosophical Tradition of the Ives Family." I am grateful to Peter Burkholder for reading through this chapter and making numerous suggestions.

17. For extended discussions of the significance of Thoreau to Ives, see especially the work of Stuart Feder, a musicologist and medical doctor: "Charles Ives and Henry David Thoreau: 'A Transcendental Tune of Concord,'" in *Ives Studies,* ed. Philip Lambert (New York: Cambridge University Press, 1997), 163–176; and "Thoreau Was Somewhere Near: The Ives-Thoreau Connection," in *Thoreau's World and Ours,* ed. Edmund A. Schofield and Robert C. Baron (Golden, Colo.: North American Press, 1993), 93–98.

18. See Philip Van Doren Stern, *The Annotated Walden,* (New York: Clarkson N. Potter, 1970), 311.

19. Ibid., 319–320.

20. Ibid., 406.

21. Additional encounters with nature à la Thoreau might have occurred at Pine Mountain on land owned by his Uncle Lyman and Aunt Amelia, where Ives had built himself a small shack, and at Elk Lake in the Adirondacks. See Mark Tucker, "Of Men and Mountains: Ives in the Adirondacks," in *Charles Ives and His World,* ed. J. Peter Burkholder (Princeton: Princeton University Press, 1996), 161–196.

22. "Nature," in *The Portable Emerson,* ed. Carl Bode in collaboration with Malcolm Cowley (New York: Viking Press, 1981), 11.

23. Cited in Barbara Novak's *Nature and Culture,* 39, 279nn11, 12.

24. Quoted in Novak, *Nature and Culture,* 151. Originally in Heinrich Baldwin Möllhausen, *Diary of a Journey from the Mississippi to the Coasts of the Pacific* (1858; reprint, 2 vols., New York and London: Johnson Reprint Co., 1969).

25. The poetry of Robert Underwood Johnson was a frequent source of ideas for the composer; in fact, Ives set more poems by Johnson than by anyone else, except Harmony Ives. Four of the *114 Songs* were composed to Johnson texts: "At Sea" (number 4), "Luck and Work" (number 21), "Premonitions" (number 24), and "The Housatonic at Stockbridge" (number 15). See Ives, *114 Songs.*

26. Robert Underwood Johnson, *Songs of Liberty, and Other Poems* (New York: Century, 1897). It would appear that Johnson viewed the river, the subject of one of the poems in this collection, as a source of patriotic pride as well as religious inspiration. A later collection entitled *Poems,* whose second edition was published by Century in 1908, is likely where Ives first encountered "To the Housatonic at Stockbridge." See Johnson, *Songs of Liberty,* 105–107.

27. It is beyond the scope of this study to address details of the poems. For more extensive treatment, see Denise Von Glahn Cooney, "Reconciliations: Time, Space, and the American Place in the Music of Charles Ives," Ph.D. diss., University of Washington, 1995, 178.

28. William Cullen Bryant, ed., *Picturesque America; or, The Land We Live In. A Delineation by Pen and Pencil of the Mountains, Rivers, Lakes, Forests, Water-falls, Shores, Canons, Valleys, Cities, and Other Picturesque Features of Our Country. With Illustrations on Steel and Wood by Eminent American Artists,* 2 vol. (New York: D. Appleton, 1872, 1874). See especially 2:288–317, for a chapter entitled "Valley of the Housatonic."

29. Ives, *Memos,* 87.

30. Bryant, *Picturesque America,* 289–291.

31. Ibid., 304.

32. Photostats of Emil Hanke's full score housed in the Ives Collection at Yale show the

excerpted lines from Robert Underwood Johnson's poem attached to the last page. In this position they function more as a postface than as a preface, allowing, as Debussy did with his *Préludes,* where titles followed pieces, for the music to create an impression without the composer's suggestion. Without commentary from the composer it is difficult to ascertain whether anterior or posterior positioning of the poetic source was a matter of concern for Ives. The texts to accompany each of the earlier movements of *Three Places in New England* are typed on separate sheets, and so their intended positions in relation to the music are not established.

33.   There are subtle differences between Ives's uses of Johnson's text in the Hanke score, which became the 1935 Mercury edition, and the 1976 Sinclair score, which is no doubt informed by the text as it appears in Ives's song version. Line 19 of the 1935 version of text stops with an exclamation point after the word "away," reading: "Wouldst thou away!" In the same edition, the word "tomorrow" does not appear in line 21.

34.   See Robert Morgan, "Spatial Form in Ives," in *An Ives Celebration,* ed. H. Wiley Hitchcock and Vivian Perlis (Urbana: University of Illinois Press, 1977), 145–158.

35.   The parts of the poem that Ives set influence the music whether the words are sung or not.

36.   A half-cadence at the end of measure 4 leads directly into the beginning of measure 5.

37.   The hymn tune "Dorrnance" is often set with different texts. As J. Peter Burkholder has pointed out, we do not know which text Ives might have had in mind, if any at all. In the case of *The Housatonic at Stockbridge,* a particular text is not as important as the hymnlike sound of the piece, whether or not listeners are aware of a text. See Burkholder, *All Made of Tunes: Charles Ives and the Uses of Musical Borrowing* (New Haven: Yale University Press, 1995), 333.

38.   Basic points of this analysis, including the framing notion of background, middleground, and foreground layers of sound and Ives's lining out of the last phrase of the hymn as introduction to the longer movement, are discussed in Von Glahn Cooney, "Reconciliations," 166–226. In *All Made of Tunes,* especially 330, 380, and 483n52, Burkholder makes many similar observations.

39.   See celli measures 1–2, horns measure 6, English horn measure 8, and oboe, clarinet and harps at measure 21.

40.   I am grateful for a conversation with J. Peter Burkholder, 15 November 2001, when he called my attention to dynamic stratification accompanying the rhythmic one.

41.   The second appearance of the pitch pattern begins on the final third of beat 4 in measure 1. The third appearance of the pitch pattern begins directly on beat 4 of measure 2. The fourth through thirteenth recurrences alternate entering one-third and two-thirds beats earlier through the second half of measure 12.

42.   The start of the second iteration begins in measure 1, on the last eighth note of the final triplet of beat 4, one-third beat earlier than the first pattern. The start of the third iteration begins on beat 4 of the second measure, two-thirds earlier than the second pattern.

43.   Variations of the cyclic patterns found in the violas occur starting at measure 21 in the music of the flute and oboe.

44.   The presence of E also provides minor-chord flavoring to the C♯-major chord that is heard here. I appreciate Peter Burkholder's calling my attention to this dual function.

45. The horn assumes a foreground position until the strings enter and take over, at which time it retreats into a middle ground.

46. See note at the bottom of score, p. 68.

47. Both English horn and brass move in quarter and eighth notes against the more agitated smaller note values of the upper strings.

48. During our conversation of 15 November 2001, Burkholder observed that this is the hymn-paraphrase's opening four notes.

49. In his essay "Of Men and Mountains," Mark Tucker discussed Ives's many trips to upstate New York between the years 1896 and 1915, specifically to Keene Valley, Saranac Lake, and Elk Lake. While the Adirondacks provided Ives with a somewhat wilder version of nature than he was accustomed to in the environs of Danbury, it was nonetheless another rural setting. See Burkholder, ed., *Charles Ives and His World*, 161–196. The present chapter explores Ives's responses to a completely different type of physical and cultural environment, the city.

50. Ives's grandniece Sally Ives Wilkes told me the following story when we met on 21 May 1994. In the 1940s seventeen-year-old Sally left Danbury, Connecticut, for her first visit to New York City. She visited with her Aunt Harmony and Uncle Charlie, and over dinner one evening, Charlie asked his niece what she thought of the city. According to Sally's recollection, she went on at great length about the wonders of New York, and how much more exciting it was than her hometown. After a meaningful silence, her uncle leaned toward her and said, "It's a H O A H." Aunt Harmony looked disapprovingly at her husband while the young niece waited for enlightenment. "It's a hell of a hole," Uncle Charlie explained.

51. In 1926 Charles and Harmony Ives purchased the brownstone at 164 East Seventy-fourth Street in New York. They had already been spending nearly equal amounts of time in their West Redding and New York homes, a pattern they continued. Usually they headed to New York in November or December and stayed through April or May, then went back to West Redding for the remainder of the year. See Ives, *Memos,* 325–337, for John Kirkpatrick's "Chronological Index of Dates."

52. Leon Botstein points out that "Ives shared with Emerson and Thoreau their well-known mistrust of the city. Ives knew that Emerson contrasted the rural landscape as the proper place for the cultivation of spiritual clarity with the city as the location of falsity, betrayal, and artificiality." See Botstein, "Innovation and Nostalgia: Ives, Mahler, and the Origins of Twentieth-Century Modernism," in *Charles Ives and His World,* ed. Burkholder. 51.

53. The Historian Herbert Janick suggests that Ives's two-world existence was in keeping with a nineteenth-century regional trend that saw increasing numbers of people working in New York and commuting to their Connecticut homes. Rather than being unusual behavior, Ives's retreat to the country was typical of an entire class of people: "The suburbanization of America began in the middle of the nineteenth century when the railroad enabled an affluent elite to escape the dangers and ugliness of the growing city. Rural towns located on the railroad corridors leading into and out of every metropolis were transformed into bedroom communities for wealthy urban commuters. Charles Ives was one of those who led this dual life." Herbert Janick, " 'Connecticut' the Suburban State," *Connecticut Humanities Council News* (fall 1993): 7.

54. For an extended discussion of this work see Von Glahn Cooney, "Reconciliations," 228–264.

55. See James B Sinclair, *A Descriptive Catalogue of the Music of Charles Ives* (New Haven: Yale University Press, 1999), 45, for the most thorough compilation of materials related to sources and dates.

56. The *Second Orchestral Set,* like the first, is made up of three movements: *An Elegy to Our Forefathers* (originally called "An Elegy for Stephen Foster"), *The Rockstrewn Hills Join in the People's Outdoor Meeting,* and *From Hanover Square North, at the End of a Tragic Day, the Voice of the People Again Arose.*

57. The British Cunard Line passenger ship *Lusitania* sailed from New York Harbor and was torpedoed by the Germans on 7 May 1915. Of the 1,198 passengers who died, 128 were Americans. This event was one of a series that eventually galvanized American public opinion against Germany. Two years later, the United States entered the war.

58. Ives, *Memos,* 92–93. Ives's enumeration of various "types" at the El station recalls an analogous recitation by Walt Whitman in his poem "I Hear America Singing." See Whitman, *Poetry and Prose* (New York: Literary Classics of the United States, 1982), 174. Whitman's types included a mechanic, carpenter, mason, boatman, shoemaker, woodcutter, and mother, all "singing with open mouths their strong melodious songs."

59. *From Hanover Square North* shares with *The Housatonic at Stockbridge* an important reference to water. However, though the river in *The Housatonic* is a source of calm, wonder, power, and universal connection, the ocean obliquely referred to in *From Hanover Square North* is a grave for hundreds of victims of the torpedoed ship who never make it to "the beautiful shore." Burkholder makes a similar point about *From Hanover Square* in *All Made of Tunes,* 264.

60. Burkholder hears the opening as a Te Deum from a religious service, an invocation before the incident. See *All Made of Tunes,* 264.

61. Both *Central Park in the Dark* and *The Unanswered Question,* the second of Ives's *Two Contemplations,* exhibit this quality, as do *The 'St. Gaudens' in Boston Common (Colonel Robert Gould Shaw and His Colored Regiment)* and *The Housatonic at Stockbridge.* Another place piece, *The Pond,* also begins in the middle of an ostinato pattern, suggesting that a listener comes upon music already under way.

62. Jan Swafford refers to the "tangle of individual voices" in *Hanover Square.* See Swafford, *Charles Ives: A Life with Music* (New York: W. W. Norton, 1996), 270. J. Peter Burkholder notes that Ives's "multi-layered background . . . can only be described as muddy," and then explains the necessity for such sounds and how the mud "helps to communicate the experience Ives intends to convey." Burkholder, *All Made of Tunes,* 379–380.

63. Ives, *Memos,* 93.

64. Ibid.

65. The chanted tune is actually a variant of a Gregorian psalm tone, one of a group of medieval formulas used to recite psalm verses. These melodies are among the oldest in the Western church tradition and may actually have been adapted from Hebrew melodies. Whether consciously choosing to do so, by using this tune Ives borrows a melody that transcends time and tradition and so speaks for a variety of people living in New York and elsewhere. Perhaps Ives is speaking for all humanity.

66. For comments on the correspondences between Ives's and Emerson's thinking, see Botstein, "Innovation and Nostalgia," 56. Beethoven's music also manifested such unities. It might have been more a function of nineteenth-century thought in general than of Emerson in particular.

67. For the original presentation of the major analytical points, see Von Glahn Cooney, "Reconciliations," 265–295. Major-minor third tensions are an aspect of the largest harmonic motions of the piece as well, though they are not necessarily audible either. These large-scale thirds are present in pedal tones. Note especially the D pedal that begins at measure 20, the A pedal that starts up at measure 56, and the F pedal that establishes itself at measure 83. The F will be interrupted at measure 96 by a C pedal, but reaffirmed by the V to I motion from C to F at measure 102. The F pedal continues to the end, supporting a return to the pitch that was most prominent at the outset, and outlining a large minor third motion from D to F over the course of the piece.

68. The opening viola and violin series share similar pitches and sequencing, although they have different starting points. The series are: viola: A–B-flat–C♯–D–F–A; violin: F♯–A–B-flat–C♯ (over A)–D (over B-flat). As in *The Housatonic*, there is a blurring of minor and major. Here it is D minor and major. The violins repeat their ostinato pattern throughout the piece, finally coming to rest in measure 199 on the harmonically challenging C♯.

Even though D to F♯ is prominently positioned at the end of the violin series, and the F♯ seems purposely set off by a registral leap and an adjustment in phrasing, the major third interval is surrounded by a pair of minor thirds (augmented seconds): the obvious B-flat to C♯ and the less prominent F♯ to A that results as the series repeats itself. This string pattern, like the piano pattern, is rich with possibilities for blurring pitch and interval distinctions. Its ambiguity rests in part on the C♯, which acts as the axis of this series. The tensions produced by a C♯ and the open fifth on D and A in the opening music are echoed in the harp drone, which persists for 108 continuous measures, as well as in the evolving piano part, where C♯ becomes an important fixture starting at measure 40 and continues unabated until the final measure.

Near the end of the piece, the harp drops the C♯ drone for a brief recitation of F major triads, at measures 108–113, before it recalls the C♯. The importance of F major was recently solidified by the accordion in measures 102–108. From this point until the end, the harp alternates C♯ with a series of polychords—D7/F, G7/B-flat, D7/F, A7/C—the roots of which are all separated by the distance of a minor third. This activity is an extension of the minor-major juxtaposition present in the hymn.

69. This results in an aural image that is similar to many futurist and cubist paintings in which multiple perspectives are presented simultaneously. Overlapping visual planes suggest movement within the canvas.

70. Ives, *Memos*, 93.

71. One might even argue that shared characteristics should *not* be heard at this point. Given Ives's account of the events that inspired the work, these common elements should come to life (become audible) only when coaxed by extraordinary circumstances. As *Hanover Square* unfolds, this becomes the case.

72. Burkholder, *All Made of Tunes*, 137. See his chapter 5, "Cumulative Settings," for a thorough discussion of this compositional approach. In a later chapter, Burkholder observes that even though "this movement directly represents a series of events and evokes in

both sound and structure the way in which the hymn was actually performed . . . the shape of the movement is determined by musical factors . . . the piece is not a literal rendition of the sounds [that Ives] heard" (266). Short of recording the events themselves, no musical interpretation would be "a literal rendition" of the sounds heard. And this is not what Ives sought. All composers, artists, and photographers *re*-present their subjects by the mere act of interpretation. See Rubinfien, "The Poetry of Plain Seeing," 79 especially, for a discussion of the unavoidable distorting influence of the creative artist.

73. These observations have taken on even greater significance in the wake of the events of 11 September 2001.

74. See Von Glahn Cooney, "Reconciliations," 285; and Burkholder, *All Made of Tunes,* 264.

75. A similar condition exists in the beginning and ending of *The 'St. Gaudens' in Boston Common (Colonel Robert Gould Shaw and His Colored Regiment),* another work memorializing an event of tremendous political consequence.

76. T. W. Timreck, *Charles Ives: A Good Dissonance Like a Man* (Metropolitan Museum of Art Home Video Collection, Home Vision 412–9055, 1977).

77. See Von Glahn, "Charles Ives, Cowboys, and Indians."

78. See Dominic Ricciotti, "City Railways/Modernist Visions," in *The Railroad in American Art: Representations of Technological Change,* ed. Susan Danly and Leo Marx (Cambridge: MIT Press, 1988), 127–146, for a discussion of the ubiquity of railroad imagery in the works of early-twentieth-century painters. Ricciotti observes, "Their paintings of subways, elevated trains, and trolleys remind us how thoroughly the city was replacing the wilderness in the imagination of American artists, modernists and others alike. . . . Not surprisingly, the increase in images of the city railways, in a variety of styles, toward 1920 accorded with the population shift toward the city at the same time" (127). Twentieth-century composers also found the railroad a source of inspiration. In 1923 the Swiss composer Arthur Honneger immortalized train imagery in *Pacific 231.* The jazz historian Gunther Schuller has observed the "well-established tradition among the orchestras that played the so-called symphonic jazz." "Entire train rides were depicted musically, evidently with considerable realism." Here, Schuller notes, train sounds were often evoked nostalgically. "Take the A Train" and "Day Break Express" are only among the more famous of jazzy train pieces. See Gunther Schuller, *The History of Jazz,* vol. 1, *Early Jazz: Its Roots and Musical Development* (New York: Oxford University Press, 1968), 321. In 1988 Steve Reich captured another aspect of trains when he focused upon their hypnotic effect in his piece for string quartet and tape entitled *Different Trains.* Reich's music will be discussed in a later chapter.

79. The title alone of Leo Marx's landmark study, *The Machine in the Garden: Technology and the Pastoral Ideal in America* (New York: Oxford University Press, 1964), is only the first indication of the discord that surrounded the unstoppable entry of the railroad into American culture.

80. Henry D. Thoreau, *Walden,* ed. J. Lyndon Shanley, introduction by Joyce Carol Oates (Princeton: Princeton University Press, 1971), 119.

81. Early in the *Walden* chapter "Sounds," Thoreau recounts sitting at his window during a summer's afternoon listening to the wild pigeons and watching fishhawks and minks against a background of "the rattle of railroad cars" (114). A few paragraphs later, he

describes the whistle of the locomotive that "penetrates my woods summer and winter, sounding like the scream of a hawk sailing over some farmer's yard" (115). See also 116, 117–118.

82. Ives had read *Walden* on multiple occasions and knew it well. He paraphrased lines from the book and incorporated them into his own *Essays before a Sonata* in the section addressing the fourth movement, *Thoreau*. Ives also arranged a song from this movement and entitled it "Thoreau," which was prefaced by similar paraphrases from *Walden*.

83. See Walt Whitman, "To a Locomotive in Winter," originally published in the *New York Tribune*, 19 February 1876. In Whitman, *Complete Poetry and Collected Prose* (New York: Literary Classics of the United States, 1982), 583. In line 13 Whitman honors the national iconographic status achieved by the train in the last quarter of the nineteenth century: "Type of the modern—emblem of motion and power—pulse of the continent."

84. David S. Reynolds, *Walt Whitman's America: A Cultural Biography* (New York: Vintage Books, 1996), 532.

85. Ibid., 531.

86. Ibid., 499.

87. In "The Return of the Heroes," see stanza 8. In "Song of the Exposition," see ibid., pages 343 and 347, stanzas 3 and 7.

88. Reynolds, *Walt Whitman's America*, 499.

89. See Frank P. Donovan Jr. *The Railroad in Literature: A Brief Survey of Railroad Fiction, Poetry, Songs, Biography, Essays, Travel and Drama in the English Language, Particularly Emphasizing Its Place in American Literature* (Boston: Railway and Locomotive Historical Society, 1940).

90. Ibid., viii, 59.

91. I am not alone in seeing an equivalence between these icons. Perry Miller observes: "The force of Nature, the majesty of Niagara, were transmuted into machinery and locomotives by passing through the brain of man." See Miller, *The Life of the Mind in America from the Revolution to the Civil War* (New York: Harcourt, Brace and World, 1965), 30.

92. Novak, *Nature and Culture*, 177.

93. Ibid., 170.

94. For a thoughtful discussion of multiple interpretations of this particular work, see ibid., 169–172.

95. See Danly and Marx, eds. *The Railroad in American Art*, 13.

96. Ives, *Memos*, appendix 13, 247.

97. See Thomas M. Brodhead, "Ives's Celestial Railroad and His Fourth Symphony," in *American Music* 12, no. 4 (winter 1994): 389–424.

98. Those familiar with the geography of lower Manhattan will appreciate that Hanover Square is located just south of Wall Street in one of the oldest parts of the city. As trains headed north out of the dark, narrow, canyonlike streets that distinguished this section of the city, they would be moving to decidedly more residential and friendlier-looking terrain.

99. One could argue that none of the events inspiring *From Hanover Square North* would have occurred without technological advances, and that the city dwellers were victims of their own dependence on technology, but this seems beyond the thoughts Ives had for the piece. While *From Hanover Square North* recalls a profoundly moving and tragic event,

Ives's piece is not about condemnation; it is about redemption. Here the El station makes community and transcendence possible in the city.

NOTES TO CHAPTER THREE

1.　Aaron Copland, "One Hundred and Fourteen Songs," *Modern Music* 11, no. 2 (January–February 1934).

2.　For the text of Ives's letter and the context of Copland's remark see Vivian Perlis, *Charles Ives Remembered: An Oral History* (New Haven: Yale University Press, 1974), xii.

3.　A 206-page, typed, revised copy (12 January 1939) of Irwin Shaw's original manuscript to *Quiet City* is in the Mugar Memorial Library of Boston University. It contains numerous emendations and instances where lengthy sections of dialogue are vigorously crossed out, as well as handwritten additions to the dialogue. There are parts for twenty-one characters and a chorus. Whether Shaw intended to involve a majority of the Group Theatre ensemble in his production, or whether multiple parts were to be taken by the same actor, is not clear. I am grateful to Howard Pollack for his assistance in locating this manuscript, and for his many helpful suggestions regarding this chapter.

4.　See David Mellinkoff's line on page 182 of Irwin Shaw's revised manuscript.

5.　See Howard Pollack, *Aaron Copland: The Life and Work of an Uncommon Man* (New York: Henry Holt, 1999), 258–259. The pals were the writer and director Elia Kazin, the actors Robert Lewis and Sanford Meisner, and the American social-protest playwright Clifford Odets, who, Pollack points out, began his career as an actor.

6.　*Music for the Theatre,* composed in 1925, celebrated one aspect of New York City's culture, its theater scene.

7.　See Wendy Smith, *Real Life Drama: The Group Theatre and America, 1931–1940* (New York: Alfred A. Knopf, 1990), 9.

8.　In the case of composers such as Charles Seeger and Ruth Crawford Seeger, this meant turning to folk music as a source of study and inspiration. Charles eventually turned away from composition altogether, and Ruth would begin a return to her earlier, more dissonant ways. Her premature death prevented her from realizing this course.

9.　Smith, *Real Life Drama, 66.*

10.　Harold Clurman was the brother-in-law of Copland's cousin Elsie Abrams, who heard of Aaron's planned trip to Europe and suggested that the two young men might like to go together. While their beliefs—especially political—and interests often took them in somewhat different directions, they remained warm, devoted supporters of each other until Clurman's death in 1980.

11.　A political environment rife with anti-German feelings made postwar France an appealing destination for American composers seeking European training in the arts.

12.　Copland did not confine himself to musical studies. He attended classes in French literature and history at the Sorbonne, and he accompanied Clurman to numerous plays. The composer became a disciple of the author André Gide, a friend of Nadia Boulanger, and a collaborator with Igor Stravinsky. Though Copland often bemoaned his lack of a college education, he more than made up for it with voracious reading, the company of the world's leading artists and intellectuals, and attendance at myriad cultural events throughout his life.

13. Harold Clurman, *The Fervent Years: The Story of the Group Theatre and the Thirties* (New York: Alfred A. Knopf, 1945), 6.

14. Harold Clurman interview recounted in Aaron Copland and Vivian Perlis, *Copland: 1900 through 1942* (New York: St. Martin's/Marek, 1984), 60.

15. The Copland-Sessions concerts lasted three years, from 1928 to 1931. This series was one of a number of efforts to promote contemporary music of young composers in the United States. For a discussion of this particular series see Carol J. Oja, "The Copland-Sessions Concerts and Their Reception in the Contemporary Press," *Musical Quarterly* 65 (1979): 212–229. Additional "official" efforts by Copland to encourage music in America included his active role in the League of Composers, founded in 1923, and in the two Yaddo Festivals; he also oversaw the Young Composers' Group in 1932 and 1933, organized concerts at the New School for Social Research in 1935, and cofounded Cos Cob Press in 1929 and Arrow Press and the American Composers' Alliance in 1937. Notwithstanding these organized efforts, Copland's greatest legacy in promoting American music may be in his support and nurture, both formally and informally, of dozens of young composers. For an overview of his influence, see especially chapters 11 and 12 of Howard Pollack's *Aaron Copland*. For a history of the Group Theatre, see Wendy Smith's *Real Life Drama*. An early model for Group Theatre may have been the Provincetown Players. This group of Greenwich Villagers who summered on the Massachusetts coast in 1915 was in the vanguard of the New Theatre movement in the decade and would have provided a prototype of a socially conscious ensemble. The Provincetown Players, like Group Theatre, was committed to reform. As a result, it came under the watchful eye of the Bureau of Investigation (later the Federal Bureau of Investigation, FBI) "for their subversive ideas." Both groups believed "in the power of cultural expression as a transformative agent in society." See Adele Heller and Lois Rudnick, eds., *1915 the Cultural Moment: The New Politics, the New Woman, the New Psychology, the New Art, and the New Theatre in America* (New Brunswick, N.J.: Rutgers University Press, 1991), 8, 10.

16. Having outgrown Clurman's rooms and then Cheryl Crawford's larger apartment as organizational meeting places, Copland made his own studio at Steinway Hall on West Fifty-seventh Street available to Clurman and the nascent group rent-free. As one indication of the breadth of Copland's contacts in 1931, among those who contributed money to support the initial summer residency of the group was Alfred Stieglitz, the acknowledged leader of the modernist art movement in New York in the Teens and Twenties.

17. Clurman, *The Fervent Years*, 33–34. Emphasis mine.

18. Ibid., 35. Emphasis mine.

19. For a list of the original Group Theatre members, see Smith, *Real Life Drama*, 30.

20. The *House of Connelly* opened 29 September 1931 at the Martin Beck Theatre.

21. For a sensitive assessment of the pressures placed upon the Group Theatre to provide an entire social order for its members, see Clurman, *The Fervent Years*, especially 211–212.

22. There is disagreement regarding exactly how many performances *Quiet City* received before it closed. Harold Clurman recalls two, but the play's director, Elia Kazan, recalls six. All concur that the play was performed in front of scenery for another play, and without full costuming. See Pollack, *Aaron Copland*, 630n38.

23. See Clurman, *The Fervent Years*, 247.

24. Pollack, *Aaron Copland*, 330–331. The play contains additional subplots: David Mel-

linkoff's sexual frustration with his unyielding girlfriend, Israel and Lenora Mellinkoff's (Gabe and David's parents) difficulties with a Gentile-Jewish marriage, action-packed encounters between the senior Mellinkoffs and a threatening pro-Nazi thug at gunpoint, and the rekindling of an old romance between Gabe Mellon and Sara Geyer, the woman to whom Gabe had dedicated his book *Fifty Poems* ten years earlier. The play may have been too riddled with distracting subplots to carry any single message powerfully.

25. Pollack, *Aaron Copland,* 329. While the U.S. premieres of *El Salón México* and *Billy the Kid* in 1938 brought Copland widespread fame, and he was relatively better off than many of his impoverished actor friends, he was also financially squeezed at the time. He might very well have chosen to write incidental music knowing that he could extract it for his own remunerative purposes regardless of the success of the theatrical venture. As it was, Copland had a less-than-stellar history writing music for the theater. Music written for the 1931 Theatre Guild production *Miracle at Verdun* was never published and the play never made it to Broadway, and his score for the Mercury Theatre's *Five Kings* (February 1939), starring Orson Welles, also remained unpublished when the play failed. From the beginning, production problems plagued *Quiet City,* and it never achieved a single complete performance. Copland observed: "My career in the theatre has been a flop—through no fault of my own I hasten to add." See Copland and Perlis, *Copland: 1900 through 1942,* 287.

26. Tempting as it might be to suggest that Copland identified with the characters and situation, prudence dictates against making any such claims. He did, however, appear to be drawn to topics that enabled him to objectify experiences similar to his own.

27. Early in the play, Gabe Mellon asks his wife, "Belong, where do I belong? Who knows where I belong?" See Irwin Shaw manuscript, 56. The degree to which Copland read these lines as expressing his own frustration as a homosexual male in a heterosexual world should not be exaggerated. These were Shaw's lines. On page 62, in lines the author crossed out, Gabe's wife, Evelyn, suggests he might need to see a psychoanalyst to cure his anxieties. Gabe jests, "Be careful. He may find out that the trouble with me is I really like young boys." This too seems to be not a suggestion of a homosexual theme in the play, or evidence that Gabe suffers from a conflicted sexual identity, but an off-the-cuff remark. Gabe may well have been referring to a group of people he understood felt outside the culture, and not himself.

28. I am grateful to Larry Starr for sharing his article "The Voice of Solitary Contemplation: Copland's *Music for the Theatre* Viewed as a Journey of Self-Discovery" prior to its publication. See *American Music* 20, no. 3 (fall 2002): 297–315.

29. Harold Clurman alluded to Copland's autonomy in his recollection of an exchange between the two men. Clurman explained: "Everything was done in the name of the theatre and its art, but our conception of this art made almost nothing foreign to it. From consideration of acting and plays we were plunged into a chaos of life questions, with the desire and hope of making possible some new order and integration. From an experiment in the theatre we were in some way impelled to an experiment in living. . . . In the early days of our formation Aaron Copland had asked me if, in dealing so intimately with our actors, I wasn't afraid of the well-known fruits of familiarity. I asked Strasberg what he thought of the question. Strasberg answered that we were making a group not hiring a company." Clurman, *The Fervent Years,* 42. See also Pollack, *Aaron Copland,* chapter 14, "Personal Affairs," 234–256, for recollections of numerous intimates.

30. In one sense Gabe Mellon doesn't yield either, since he ultimately is not lured by his

brother's memory-laden trumpet playing. But Gabe Mellon arrives at his painful decision in public, whereas Copland avoided all such displays.

31. Louis Biancolli, *The Concert Companion: A Comprehensive Guide to Symphonic Music* (New York and London: McGraw-Hill, 1947), 193.

32. Copland and Perlis, *Copland: 1900 through 1942,* 287.

33. An example of one such specific cue can be found on page 7 of the rough sketch, where Copland wrote: "To true men everywhere, Play, play Brother David." The instruments enter with a tune that Howard Pollack has labeled Gabe's "nostalgia" music. See Pollack, *Aaron Copland,* 331. For numerous other examples, see *The Quiet City* Incidental Music, rough sketch, pages 7–18 in particular, in the Aaron Copland Collection ca. 1900–1990, Music Division, Library of Congress.

34. I am grateful to conversations with Howard Pollack (1–2 February 2001) that helped sharpen my thinking regarding Copland's musical personae: the socially conscious declamatory composer, the romantic personality, and the satirical commentator. Pollack sees nascent expressions of these personae in his piano work *Three Moods:* "Embittered," "Wistful," and "Jazzy."

35. In a 1973 videotaped interview, Agnes de Mille discussed Copland's music for the 1942 ballet *Rodeo:* "He struck certain cold, rather penetrating, and evocative intervals that suggest space to us." In his biography of Copland, Howard Pollack observes, "working together, de Mille, Copland, and [the designer Oliver] Smith successfully conjured an ambience strongly suggestive of a vast and sparsely settled land." Pollack, *Aaron Copland,* 372.

36. Wilfrid Mellers hears similarities between *Quiet City* and the elegiac music in Copland's 1938 ballet, *Billy the Kid.* He also speaks of "the basic identity between Copland's . . . rural and . . . urban manners." Hellers, *Music in a New Found Land: Themes and Developments in the History of American Music* (New York: Oxford University Press, 1987), 90–91. Pollack observes that "Samuel Lipman noted Copland 'catches the emptiness of the city and the quiet of the land' as if, perhaps, they were the same thing." Pollack, *Aaron Copland,* 529. For the original statement, see Samuel Lipman, "Copland as American Composer," *Commentary* 61 (1976): 72.

37. Copland comments on the usefulness of the arts to express what one might otherwise not: "The arts offer the opportunity to do something that cannot be done anywhere else. It is the only place one can express in public feelings ordinarily regarded as private. It is the place where a man or woman can be completely honest, where we can say whatever is in our hearts or minds, where we never need to hide from ourselves or from others." See Aaron Copland and Vivian Perlis, *Copland: Since 1943* (New York: St. Martin's Press, 1990), 423.

38. Ives often compounds a listener's sense of directionlessness by denying any harmonic center as well. See *The "St. Gaudens" in Boston Common (Colonel Robert Gould Shaw and His Colored Regiment), The Housatonic at Stockbridge, Central Park in the Dark,* and *From Hanover Square North, at the End of a Tragic Day, the Voice of the People Again Arose* as examples of harmonically ambiguous openings to Ives's place pieces.

39. Comparisons with another Ives piece, *The Unanswered Question,* are obvious. The dominant meditative mood of both works and their similar stratification of strings, brass, and woodwinds invite conjecture. And we know that *The Unanswered Question* became a

favorite Ives piece for Copland to conduct in his later years. But where Ives's work contemplates a philosophical question on a cosmic scale—Ives did subtitle the work "A Cosmic Landscape"—Copland's work confines itself to the world within, both within the city and within the auditor.

40. I have found no sources suggesting that Copland conferred with Irwin Shaw prior to the author's writing his play, and so I must assume that Copland inherited a trumpet-playing character from the playwright without consultation.

41. In his music for the film *Of Mice and Men*, written within months of that for *Quiet City*, Copland uses repeated notes to suggest tension. According to Pollack: "In the killing of Candy's dog, Copland juxtaposes a dirge with high repeated notes, thereby vividly denoting the scene's poignance along with its tension" (*Aaron Copland*, 343).

42. In one scene David auditions for a possible place in a band. He wants nothing more than to play his horn in a club band. But he is not good enough and doesn't win the job. David fails at that as he fails at keeping any job, at convincing Gabe to lend him two thousand dollars, at coercing his girlfriend to go to bed with him, and at pressuring his brother to give up his middle-class ways.

43. See verso of the title page, Aaron Copland, *Music for the Theatre: Suite in Five Parts for Small Orchestra* (New York: Boosey and Hawkes, 1960).

44. *Quiet City* was originally scored for two clarinets (doubling on bass clarinet and saxophone), trumpet, and piano. It would seem that Copland quickly set about his goal of integrating American culture and theater, even if *Music for the Theatre* was written for no play in particular. Although debates continue over the success of Copland's assimilation of jazz into symphonic works and, more basically, whether the idiom is assimilateable at all without becoming something else entirely, the belief that jazz-inspired sounds became a regular aspect of Copland's musical parlance is broadly accepted.

45. The "nervous" trumpet in *Music for the Theatre* might indicate something completely different from what it does in *Quiet City*. The 1925 piece, the result of a commission from the League of Composers, was among Copland's very first completed works after his return to the United States. It was preceded only by Organ Symphony and *Cortège Macabre*, both of which had been started in Paris. Perhaps the young composer, for all his energy, confidence, and support from influential people, felt somewhat hesitant and projected this onto his soloist. Or perhaps, in a move reminiscent of Charles Ives, Copland captured the rough edges of real pit orchestra musicians, complete with their nervousness. His own comments on the piece deny that "the composer had [any] play or literary idea in mind." Rather, Copland insists, "the title simply implies that, at times, this music has a quality which is suggestive of the theater." Liner notes, *Bernstein Conducts Copland*, Columbia Masterworks, ML 6098.

46. See Pollack, *Aaron Copland*, 523.

47. Wilfrid Mellers heard "Negroid" influences "in its blue notes." *Music in a New Found Land*, 91.

48. See composer's note, Aaron Copland, *Quiet City* (New York: Hawkes and Son, 1941), 2.

49. If Copland had only been after breathing space for his trumpeter, the original clarinets or saxophone would have sufficed.

50. The saxophone's reed is clarinet-like, its bore is conical like that of an oboe, and its

body is most often made of brass. While such characteristics give the instrument a great deal of timbral flexibility, the same combination also works against its being considered a pure representative of either the woodwind or the brass families.

51. It is unlikely that Copland knew Ives's piece. Although it was written in 1906, it was not premiered until 11 May 1946 in New York. See Sinclair, *A Descriptive Catalogue of the Music of Charles Ives*, 129, for the history and source materials related to this work.

52. As one well-known example, Verdi uses trumpets and a hieratic rhythm in *Aida* to depict the march of the priests. He collapses religion and the military in a single musical association.

53. Beethoven's Sixth Symphony, third movement, "Lustiges Zusammensein der Land-leute," features the oboe in extended passages; Berlioz's *Symphonie Fantastique*, "Scène aux champs," showcases both the oboe and English horn in a pastoral duet; and Ives's *Housatonic at Stockbridge* has a prominent role for English horn. All three pieces, among others, call upon the woody-sounding double-reed family to evoke rural scenes.

54. See Pollack, *Aaron Copland*, 331. See also measures 33 and following for the first melody, and measures 74 and following for the second. Israel Mellinkoff owns a hardware store. He too is married to a non-Jew. In addition to struggling with his own demons, the father is tortured by his son's rejection of his family name and capitulation to modern American values.

55. Irwin Shaw manuscript, 206.

56. See notes by Aaron Copland to Columbia recording M 30374, *Aaron Copland Conducts Music for a Great City*.

57. Pollack, *Aaron Copland*, 495.

58. See Copland and Perlis, *Copland: Since 1943*, 333, 335. Also quoted in Pollack, *Aaron Copland*, 495.

59. Copland and Perlis, *Copland: Since 1943*, 335.

60. See *Aaron Copland Conducts*, Columbia recording M 30374.

61. The variety of drums, blocks, bells, maracas, and ratchets recalls similar setups manned by the great drummers in jazz and dance bands (Sonny Greer, Chick Webb, and Buddy Rich come to mind). These instruments evoke sounds closely associated with the United States in general and the New York jazz scene in particular.

62. Copland quoted in Pollack, *Aaron Copland*, 530.

63. Rehearsal is a standard indication in a musical score to refer to a specific spot in the piece. It is used instead of referring to a particular measure by number, and it often denotes a new section within the music.

64. See one measure after rehearsal 68, two measures before rehearsal 75, and four measures after rehearsal 75.

65. Howard Pollack to author, 14 January 2001.

66. To be fair, the limited forces required by *Quiet City* might make it a more attractive choice for symphony programmers. Financial concerns do have a way of determining what gets heard.

67. Paul Rosenfeld, "Edgard Varèse," in *An Hour with American Music* (Philadelphia and London: J. B. Lippincott, 1929), 163.

68. Louise Varèse, *A Looking Glass Diary*, vol. 1, 1883–1928 (W. W. Norton, 1972,) 119.

The war in Europe put severe strains on the French film industry, and production was severely curtailed. American films filled the void.

69. Olivia Mattis, "Edgard Varèse and the Visual Arts." Ph.D. diss., Stanford University, 1992, 96–97.

70. Varèse quickly found a congenial group that included Marcel Duchamp, Francis Picabia, Gabrielle Buffet, Albert Gleizes, Juliette Roche, and Henri Martin Barzun, among the most prominent members. He became extremely close to Carlos Salzedo and Joseph Stella. According to Louise Varèse, "Stella and Varèse had a kindred—a creative—passion for New York, and Stella's five paintings . . . are its magnificent portrait." Varèse, *A Looking Glass Diary*, 158.

71. Rosenfeld, *An Hour with American Music*, 167. Rosenfeld's use of the plural is noteworthy given Varèse's use of the plural in *Amériques*.

72. Fernand Ouellette refers to the "natural-artificial environment, that new nature produced by the hands of man: the twentieth century city." See Ouellette, *Edgard Varèse*, trans. Derek Coltman (New York: Orion Press, 1968), 39.

73. Another Stieglitz photograph that juxtaposes the United States' two natures is *The Flatiron*. Once again, a foreground tree and a background skyscraper define the boundaries of the picture. This time, however, the middle ground of trees and benches brings man and nature together.

74. Although the photographer Alfred Stieglitz is often credited with single-handedly starting the modernist movement in the United States with his Gallery 291, painters of New York's pre–World War I Ash Can School, including perhaps most importantly Robert Henri and later George Bellows, also signaled the swing toward modernism in paintings that focused upon urban scenes and captured urban energy. Stieglitz did more than perhaps anyone else to nurture and sustain modernist artists of all disciplines. But it was not until the Armory Show of 1913 that modernism took a strong foothold in the larger public's awareness.

75. Frederick Lewis Allen, *Only Yesterday: An Informal History of the 1920s* (New York: John Wiley and Sons, 1997), 133.

76. Varèse's inclination to title his work after his newly adopted homeland is reminiscent of Anthony Philip Heinrich's earlier efforts to associate himself with America. The Bohemian composer sought to create closely programmatic works, but Varèse eschewed such practices.

77. Varèse was not alone in this belief, as earlier chapters have explained. Most American composers striving to create a distinctive American music shared his sentiments.

78. Allen, *Only Yesterday*, 182.

79. Elliott Carter, "France-America Ltd." (1977), trans. Jonathan Bernard, in *Composers on Modern Musical Culture: An Anthology of Readings on Twentieth-Century Music* (New York: Schirmer Books, 1999), 231.

80. Carol Oja, "Creating a God: The Reception of Edgard Varèse," from a paper read at the Modernist Studies Association conference, Pennsylvania State University, October 1999.

81. Allen, *Only Yesterday*, 16.

82. Ibid., 22. Varèse was not the only composer to benefit from a particular political

climate. For another example, see Howard Pollack's article "Samuel Barber, Jean Sibelius, and the Making of an American Romantic," in *Musical Quarterly* 84, no. 2 (summer 2000): 175–205. Sibelius, a Finnish composer, benefited from his nationality during the 1930s, according to Pollack a time of "growing alienation from an increasingly totalitarian Europe careening toward catastrophe," 183.

83.   Ouellette, *Edgard Varèse,* 56.

84.   Louise Varèse, *A Looking Glass Diary,* 235.

85.   Ouellette, *Edgard Varèse,* 55–56.

86.   Ibid., 85.

87.   In truth, none of the composers studied thus far simply depicted scenes with their music. But this argument was a common one among modernist composers, who strove to separate themselves from the programmatic tendencies that they observed in the works of the late romantics. Varèse's adamancy on this issue makes him a perfect subject for this study, which is interested more in the ways in which composers were inspired by places than in tracking specific manifestations of places in music.

88.   Quoted by Jonathan Bernard in *The Music of Edgard Varèse* (New Haven: Yale University Press, 1987), 8. Originally the quotation appeared in an article by Winthrop P. Tryon entitled "A New Edifice from Mr. Varèse," *Christian Science Monitor,* 28 August 1926.

89.   Quoted in Ouellette, *Edgard Varèse,* 46.

90.   Quoted in ibid., 38–39.

91.   Quoted in Mattis, "Edgard Varèse," 122; originally from a letter to Thomas H. Greer, 15 August 1965, Otto Luening Collection (New York Public Library).

92.   Quoted in Elaine de Kooning, *The Spirit of Abstract Expressionism: Selected Writings* (New York: George Braziller, 1994), 13.

93.   For a thoughtful treatment of these artistic positions, see Bernard, *The Music of Edgard Varèse,* especially chapter 1, "Varèse's Aesthetic Background."

94.   Mattis, "Edgard Varèse," 123. That being the case, one is left to wonder about Varèse's instruction to trombone players to "laugh Ha! Ha! Ha! Ha! Ha!" at measures 283–284 of *Amériques* (one measure after rehearsal 27). Could this be an instance of a "frivolous" Varèse? Or is it simply an attempt to get his players to attack their notes a particular way? Jonathan Bernard has noted a similar laughing direction in *Hyperprism,* although in a letter to the author dated 11 November 2000 he was quick to point out, "Sure it is humorous, but an anomaly in his work. Anyway, one laugh does not a Dadaist make. Or even two, for that matter."

95.   Between 1913 and 1921, Italian Futurist Luigi Russolo created a family of "noise intoner" instruments he named *intonarumori,* which were used in a number of his works. George Antheil's *Ballet mécanique* (1925) included the sounds of small and large airplane propellers and electric bells in its orchestra.

96.   Linton Martin, "Catcalls Greet Orchestra Work," *Philadelphia Inquirer,* 10 April 1926, 10.

97.   In her article, "Subject: What, How, or Who?" Elaine de Kooning observed: "Dadaism, in the hands of the artists who directly utilize its forms and techniques today, has become a classical style, completely shorn of its original bitterness, as respectable as any

other and more graceful than most. New esthetic values have swallowed the old anti-social, anti-art motivations." *Art News,* April 1955, 62.

98. I am grateful to Jonathan Bernard for helping me clarify this idea.

99. From Varèse's 1959 lecture delivered at Sarah Lawrence College, entitled "Spatial Music." The lecture is excerpted in Elliott Schwartz and Barney Childs, eds., *Contemporary Composers on Contemporary Music* (New York: Da Capo Press, 1998), 204.

100. Bernard, *The Music of Edgard Varèse,* 137.

101. I mention these three painters because of their contemporaneity with Varèse and their obvious rejection of traditional notions of perspective. The weightiness of *Amériques* has little in common with many of the wispier creations of Miró or Klee.

102. From Wassily Kandinsky, "Reminiscences/Three Pictures," Berlin, 1913, reprinted in Robert L. Herbert, *Modern Artists on Art: Ten Unabridged Essays* (Englewood Cliffs, N.J.: Prentice-Hall, 1964), 35.

103. See as examples: Three measures before rehearsal 4, where 4/4 continues for ten measures; four measures after rehearsal 6, where a 4/4 meter persists for fifteen measures; at rehearsal 33, where a 2/8 meter holds for thirteen measures. One measure before rehearsal 38, 2/8 is introduced and holds for thirty measures. This may be as close as Varèse comes to an audible pulse in the piece, but even here ties, triplets, and tremolos reduce a strong sense of pulse.

104. See continuous measures of presto at measures 68–99, 159–185, 355–440, and 510–535.

105. Taken from a lecture that Varèse gave at Princeton University in 1959, entitled "Rhythm, Form and Content." See Schwartz and Childs, eds., *Contemporary Composers,* 202.

106. It is worth noting that Copland cites rhythm as being the most characteristic element of "American" music.

107. In his letter dated 11 November 2000, Jonathan Bernard suggested that Varèse might be "simply expressing the overwhelming effect of America's racket, its newness, its sheer size on him[self]." Others might point to Varèse's dominating personality revealing itself in his music. His need to control relationships and situations became problematic as he attempted to work with American colleagues in the International Composers' Guild; they were unaccustomed to such dictatorial practices. Ultimately his preferences for total control over all aspects of the guild, both its administration and its music, resulted in the splintering of the group and the formation of the League of Composers. See Carol J. Oja, *Making Music Modern* (New York: Oxford University Press, 2000), chapters 11 and 12 especially, for a summary of these events.

108. Emphasis mine.

109. John Cage addressed the issue of Varèse and control in an article that appeared in 1958. Regarding "those who are interested in sounds just as they are," Cage opined, "This is not found in the character of his imagination, which has to do with *him*—not with sound itself." Emphasis mine. Later in the same article, Cage concluded: "In these respects Varèse is an artist of the past. Rather than dealing with sounds as sounds, he deals with them as Varèse." See Cage, *Silence: Lectures and Writings by John Cage* (Middletown, Conn.: Wesleyan University Press, 1961), 83–84.

110. It is tempting to concur with John Cage, who observed, "Analytical studies of his work are somehow not relevant to one's experience of it." Analytical illumination, however,

depends a great deal upon the methodology employed. In this regard, Jonathan Bernard's 1987 study, *The Music of Edgard Varèse,* provides a useful and "relevant" model. For Cage's remarks, see *Silence,* 84.

111. Varèse does rely upon the most general concepts of continuity and contrast to structure his piece, but he avoids all suggestion of traditional forms. His goal would have been to create a piece whose structure grew out of his unconventional vision; and that he accomplished.

112. See Edgard Varèse, *Amériques,* rev. and ed. Chou Wen-Chung (New York: Colfranc Music Publishing, 1973), x. The original 1921 version of the piece, published in 1925 by Curwen and Sons of London and premiered by Leopold Stokowski and the Philadelphia Orchestra in 1926, had additional percussion instruments. These included a steamboat whistle, a cyclone whistle, and a crow call. The steamboat whistle would have been a sound Varèse heard in his New World home. In 1995 Steve Reich made reference to the sounds of boat horns and harbor noises in his piece *City Life,* to be discussed in a later chapter. The city changed dramatically in the intervening years, but many of the identifying sounds remained the same.

113. Martin, "Catcalls Greet Orchestra Work," 10.

114. In *Parade* Satie was referring to all things American, including John Philip Sousa, typewriters, train whistles, and ragtime. At the end of the section of *Parade* entitled "Ragtime on the Titanic," when waves overwhelm the ship, Satie uses *sirène graves* to recall the distress signal of the sinking cruise ship. A 1968 recording of *Parade* uses what sounds like a foghorn rather than the wailing continuous pitch that is more commonly associated with the word "siren" in American usage. The Paris Conservatoire Orchestra, conducted by Louis Auriacombe, 1968, Angel S36486.

115. In order to create a new music for a New World, Varèse recast the instrument family most closely associated with old-world symphonic literature by downplaying the role of bowed strings in *Amériques.* Percussion, woodwinds and especially brass convey the bulk of the musical material. Brass included eight horns, six trumpets, three tenor, one bass, and one contrabass trombone, a tuba, and a contrabass tuba.

116. Quoted in Ouellette, *Edgard Varèse,* 57.

117. Helmholtz's treatise was first published as *Die lehre von den Tonempfindungen als physiologische Grundlage für die Theorie der Musik* in 1862. *On the Sensations of Tone as a Physiological Basis for the Theory of Music* was translated by Alexander John Ellis and first published in London by Longmans, Green in 1875.

118. Edgard Varèse, "Spatial Music," Schwartz and Childs, eds., *Contemporary Composers,* 205.

119. Ibid.

120. Claire R. Reis, *Composers, Conductors, and Critics* (New York: Oxford University Press, 1955), 9.

121. Ibid.

122. Or perhaps Varèse misremembered the timing of his earlier interest.

123. This could also have been what Alejo Carpentier was referring to when he wrote about *Amériques* in 1929: "Encouraged by the possibilities for its realization, Varèse conceives the work on a vast scale." Ouellette, *Edgard Varèse,* 55–56.

124. Professor Chou Wen-Chung studied and then collaborated with Varèse from 1949 until the composer's death in 1965, and eventually he became the literary executor of the Varèse estate. Chou Wen-Chung has edited numerous works of Varèse and maintains tight control over manuscripts and materials belonging to the composer.

125. In notes accompanying the most recent recording of Varèse's works Professor Chou explains: "The original version contains some different material from the better-known revision. The difference is mostly in the orchestration, employing considerably more woodwind and brass. Among the percussion—aside from the siren in both versions—there are also such additions as the steamboat whistle, cyclone whistle and the crow call." *Varèse Complete Works*, Royal Concertgebouw Orchestra, Asko Ensemble, conducted by Riccardo Chailly, London 289 460 208–2 LH 2. Additional remarks regarding the general history of editions are provided by Professor Chou Wen-Chung in the preface to his revised and edited version of *Amériques*.

126. Through the Teens and into the early Twenties, many emergency vehicles in New York still used large brass bells that were rung by hand or fitted with spring-loaded clappers. Sirens gradually came into use throughout the Twenties. At the time Varèse was composing *Amériques*, factories and ships employed a combination of steam whistles, foghorns, and sirens that he could also have used without intending any specific program for his work. I am grateful to Kevin O'Connell, a businessman, writer, and collector of sirens and warning signals, for sharing his knowledge of the history of sirens and emergency vehicles. Phone interview, 19 April 2001.

127. Edward Kennedy "Duke" Ellington, *Music Is My Mistress* (Garden City, N.Y.: Doubleday, 1973), 65–66.

128. In comments accompanying his piece *Harlem*, Ellington insisted that contrary to popular impressions of the place, Harlem had more churches than dance halls and clubs. This might always have been true, but it was especially apparent in 1949, when he composed his work. Ellington's comments will be considered in more depth as part of the discussion of the music.

129. A recent New York City travel guide defined Harlem as follows: "Harlem is really two areas. Harlem proper stretches from river to river, beginning at 125th Street on the West Side and 96th Street on the East Side. Spanish Harlem (El Barrio), an enclave east of Fifth Avenue, runs between East 100th and East 125th streets." See Cheryl Farr Leas, *Frommer's 2000 New York City* (New York: Macmillan, 1999), 65. A description of some of the architecture underscores the variety of buildings that existed: "Some houses date back to a time when the area was something of a country retreat, and represent some of the best brownstone mansions in the city. On Sugar Hill . . . are a significant number of fine town houses" (66). In Duke Ellington's poetic commentary to *Harlem*, he referred to Harlem as that section of the city between 110th and 145th streets. See Decca Records DL 710176, accompanying small disk.

130. In a pattern similar to Ives's, Ellington made a series of moves within the city that reflected his improving financial position and growing fame. After his arrival in Harlem in 1923, Ellington lived in various humble apartments. At another point later on, he lived with his sister in the Sugar Hill section of Harlem. In the 1950s Ellington moved to 400 Central Park West. His last residence was at 140 West End Avenue, between Sixty-sixth and Sixty-seventh Streets. In this Upper West Side location, he lived on the twenty-second floor of the Lincoln Towers. For information on Duke Ellington's addresses see Stephen

W. Plumb, *The Streets Where They Lived: A Walking Guide to the Residences of Famous New Yorkers* (St. Paul, Minn.: Marlor Press, 1989), 99, 106, 110. Ellington devotes a chapter to New York in his autobiography.

131. Mark Tucker, *Ellington: The Early Years* (Urbana and Chicago: University of Illinois Press, 1995), 84–85.

132. This work is known variously as *Harlem, Harlem Suite, Harlem Symphony,* and *A Tone Parallel to Harlem.* Throughout this chapter, I will refer to it as *Harlem.*

133. Upon marrying in 1908, the Iveses settled in a house at 70 West Eleventh Street in the Greenwich Village section of the city. In 1911 they moved a few blocks to 118 Waverly Place, and three years later to 27 West Eleventh. In 1916 the Iveses moved to the East Side, first to 142 East Fortieth Street just south of Midtown East, and then, in 1917, to 120 East Twenty-second Street, a section known as Gramercy Park. Finally, in 1926 the couple moved permanently to 164 East Seventy-fourth Street, on the Upper East Side. This area is bordered by Central Park on the west and the East River on the east, and it lies about two and a half miles north of lower Manhattan's Financial District. This was Ives's address at the time of his death in May 1954.

134. *Central Park in the Dark* is another piece in which Ives allows for a positive consideration of an urban place. Central Park, however, was a bucolic retreat from the surrounding city life, and so in many ways the piece celebrates this bit of nature (even if man-made) nestled deep with Manhattan.

135. As has been discussed, his urban upbringing did not preclude Copland from turning to the West and commemorating it in works that are among his most popular: *Billy the Kid* (1940), *Rodeo* (1942), and, celebrating Latin American culture in his 1936 work, *El Salón México.* It might be that Copland's New York upbringing allowed him to embrace diverse cultures easily.

136. Ouellette, *Edgard Varèse,* 6.

137. Copland acknowledged Ellington as the master of the jazz musicians in his lectures at the New School for Social Research as early as 1936. See Pollack, *Aaron Copland,* 116. Years later, Copland and Ellington shared the experience of having FBI files kept on them by the Special Congressional Committee on Un-American Activities. In championing the causes of people or ideas outside mainstream America, each man became suspect. Copland's outlook and career were little affected by the congressional interrogation, but Ellington, because of this and a dispute with the NAACP stemming from his willingness to play for segregated audiences, became much more circumspect about his participation in any kind of social or political action. See Stuart Nicholson, *Reminiscing in Tempo: A Portrait of Duke Ellington* (Boston: Northeastern University Press, 1999), 280–281, for comments by Ellington's son Mercer regarding his father's Cold War political activism.

138. See Tucker, *Ellington,* 5. Tucker quotes Washington's former chief historian Constance McLaughlin Green in *Washington: Capital City, 1879–1950* (Princeton: Princeton University Press, 1963), vii–viii.

139. Ellington dropped out just months shy of his graduation from Armstrong Technical High School after a not-stellar career. He was offered an art scholarship to Pratt Institute in Brooklyn, but declined it to pursue music instead. Early in his career, Ellington set up business as a sign and poster designer and painter. He often found clients for his budding instrumental ensembles by informing his poster customers of his availability as a musician

for their future events. In this way, Ellington used his visual art talents to advance his musical art career. If privately he bemoaned his lack of additional formal education, like Copland he more than made up for it by a lifetime of voracious reading. Among Ellington's many awards was an Honorary Diploma of Graduation issued by Armstrong High School, Washington, D.C., on 17 June 1971.

140. See Tucker, *Ellington,* 22 for details of Duke Ellington's attendance at churches as a youth.

141. Ellington's sacred concerts in San Francisco (1965), New York (1968), and London (1973) are manifestations of his continued interest in the spiritual life. For many blacks who had migrated from the South, religious traditions were among the few welcome memories they brought with them. The church also provided a central social and educational institution. As such, religion assumed even greater importance in their lives.

142. Nicholson, *Reminiscing in Tempo,* 192. Ellington and commentators of the time regularly used the words "Negro" and "colored." Although both terms are considered pejorative and undesirable by today's standards, their inclusion in this book is dictated by the use of the terms at the time under consideration.

143. The phrase "the New Negro" comes from Alain Locke's book of the same title, *The New Negro: An Interpretation* (New York: A. and C. Boni, 1925).

144. Duke Ellington, *Black, Brown and Beige: Tone Parallel to the American Negro* (1943); *Creole Rhapsody* (1944); *New World a-Comin'* (1945); *The Liberian Suite* (1947); and *My People* (1963), among others.

145. See Jervis Anderson, *This Was Harlem: A Cultural Portrait 1900–1950* (New York: Farrar, Straus and Giroux, 1982), 105. Thirty-three years later, on 30 January 1950, all white schools in East St. Louis were finally integrated and an eighty-five-year policy of segregation was ended. See *The Crisis,* April 1950, 209.

146. James "Bubber" Miley (1903–1932) was a cornetist known for his growling "hot" style of playing. The title *East St. Louis Toodle-O* may or may not have been the result of Ellington or Miley's inspiration. Mark Tucker reports that "the name of the piece . . . may have emerged during the record session. Apparently Vocalion wanted to increase sales in the largely black section of East St. Louis, Illinois, hence the place name in the title." Tucker, *Ellington,* 250. Bubber Miley "imagined 'East St. Louis Toodle-O' to be about an old, tired man limping home after a day's work." Ibid., 231. The same work was "Sonny Greer's favorite piece in the early days because it established the band's identity so strongly. 'People heard it and said, 'Here they come!' Indeed, 'East St. Louis Toodle-O' served as the band's theme song until about 1940 and stayed in the repertory for the rest of Ellington's life," 243. Tucker believes that the piece "represents Ellington's highest compositional achievement from the early years," 248. It is important to this study not only for its musical sophistication and accomplishment, but also for its social and political associations.

147. Marcus Garvey was among the most public and powerful black leaders to emerge in the United States in the Teens and Twenties. In 1914 he founded the Universal Negro Improvement Association (UNIA), headquartered in Harlem, and later proclaimed himself the provisional president of Africa. W. E. B. Du Bois outspokenly rejected Garvey's actions, which he saw as self-aggrandizing, and focused his efforts instead upon the National Association for the Advancement of Colored People, which he helped found in 1909 as an outgrowth of the Niagara Movement, and upon *The Crisis,* the NAACP journal. The

NAACP was also headquartered in Harlem. Like the more conservative black leaders and especially black clergy, Du Bois rejected ragtime, blues, and jazz, seeing them as perpetuating unwelcome racial stereotypes and debasing African Americans. Du Bois valued spirituals, as his book *The Souls of Black Folk* (1903; rept., New York: Penguin, 1995) makes plain. As long as jazz was seen as something "outside" of mainstream culture, it was difficult for black leaders striving for assimilation to be enthusiastic supporters of the music. See Anderson, *This Was Harlem,* 22.

148. In a BBC interview in 1973, Ellington recalled: "We stopped using the word jazz in 1943, that was the point when we didn't believe in categories." See Nicholson, *Reminiscing in Tempo,* 247, quoted from Michael Parkinson interview on *The Parkinson Show,* BBC-TV, 1973. Ellington began his annual concerts at Carnegie Hall in January 1943. In 1956, after decades of declaring that he disapproved of any categorization of music, Ellington concluded: "[The term jazz] drives people away, I don't see the necessity of using it." This remark, which first appeared in the *Christian Science Monitor,* 2 April 1956, is quoted in Nicholson's *Reminiscing in Tempo,* 302. Ellington's rejection of the term may have had as much to do with an awareness of marketing strategies as it did with deeply held aesthetic principles.

149. These policies were enforced at concerts given by the black artists Marian Anderson, Duke Ellington, and later Sarah Vaughn.

150. "Echoes of Citizens Boycott against Anderson Recital Still Ring in Richmond," *The Afro-American,* 28 January 1951, 8.

151. "Ellington Cancels Richmond Concert," *The Afro-American,* 3 February 1951, 8.

152. See Nicholson, *Reminiscing in Tempo,* 290–302, for excerpts from *The Afro-American* and numerous comments regarding this issue.

153. Tucker, *Ellington,* 94–95.

154. Oja, *Making Music Modern,* 332.

155. See Lisa Barg, "Black Voices/White Sounds: Race and Representation in Virgil Thomson's *Four Saints in Three Acts,*" *American Music* 18, no. 2 (summer 2000): 147, for a reproduction of the advertisement containing this text. It is impossible to know exactly which "best exponents of modern music" Ziegfeld had in mind, although he does distinguish this group from the Tin Pan Alley composer Irving Berlin. The ad is reproduced in Klaus Stratemann, *Duke Ellington Day by Day and Film by Film* (Copenhagen, Denmark: JazzMedia, 1992), 4.

156. In 1913 Stravinsky pounded his way into music history with the primitive dances of *Le Sacre du printemps.* In the same year, the composer-pianist Leo Ornstein's *Danse Sauvage* assaulted polite sensibilities with noisy, dissonant, spasmodic chords that were struck repeatedly. In 1924 George Antheil focused upon mechanistic rhythms and modern sound sources in his *Ballet mécanique.* Rhythm was embraced as an alternative organizational element for high-art music at the same time as it was a defining feature of the newly emerging jazz style.

157. "Jungle music" was a phrase used by Duke Ellington and his band members to describe certain of their more sensuous and evocative pieces. Gunther Schuller has defined it as "A term applied to certain pieces (and a style derived therefrom) by the Duke Ellington band in the late 1920s; named after the jungle-like sounds and imitations particularly

of the brass instruments." Schuller, *Early Jazz,* 379. The part of Harlem that was home to a number of fashionable nightclubs was known as Jungle Alley. Barg, "Black Voices," 138.

158. Some might suggest that America had succumbed to the European hierarchy of culture over nature. See Novak, *Nature and Culture,* for a thoroughgoing and elegant discussion of this oppositional pair.

159. See Oja, *Making Music Modern,* 295. Oja chronicles numerous European composers, from Stravinsky to Bartók to Milhaud to Ravel, who arrived in the United States already smitten by jazz and advising Americans to recognize its importance in their own musical culture.

160. The titles and dates come from Ellington's book *Music Is My Mistress.* The dates represent copyright, not composition. There are, of course, other pieces that refer to Harlem without using the place name in the title, works such as *Savoy Strut* (1943), a reference to the Savoy Ballroom on Lenox Avenue, and *Sugar Hill Penthouse,* a tribute to the most elite section of Harlem, from 145th to 155th Streets. These are only two obvious examples. For background on the Savoy Ballroom see Anderson, *This Was Harlem,* 307–314.

161. Description was a basic element of all of Ellington's music. Mark Tucker addresses the importance of programmatic associations for Ellington and his band members: "Looking back at the twenties, Ellington recalled in his memoirs how musicians attempted to depict scenes or describe states of feeling in their solos: 'Painting a picture, or having a story to go with what you were going to play, was of vital importance in those days. The audience didn't know anything about it, but the cats in the band did.'" Tucker summarizes the role that such thinking played in Ellington's music: "Whatever their source, these mood or character pieces became Ellington's trademark. As Mercer Ellington has written, his father always tried to 'make the listener *feel* experiences with the sound, almost as though he were creating apparitions within the music.'" Tucker, *Ellington,* 231–232.

162. In *Duke Ellington: A Listener's Guide* (Metuchen, N.J.: Scarecrow Press, 1999), Eddie Lambert questions the integrity of the title and the program that Ellington offered. He explains: "at the time of recording, the piece was known as 'Rumpus in Richmond,' suggesting that Duke's famous program was something of an afterthought" (90). Regardless of its original title, Ellington ultimately decided upon *Harlem Air Shaft* and publicized the detailed program as an aid to understanding what was happening in the music. The program has become popularly identified with the work. Given the congenial nature of the piece, it is hard to imagine it as the musical manifestation of a rumpus anywhere.

163. My own memories of Brooklyn and Queens air shafts include being told not to listen to conversations from neighboring houses that could easily be overheard. As it turned out, if you didn't listen to the precise words, the sounds became a kind of background music to your own activities: a human white noise to your life.

164. Quoted in Nat Hentoff and Nat Shapiro, eds., *Hear Me Talkin' to Ya: The Story of Jazz as Told by the Men Who Made It* (London: Peter Davies, 1955), 203.

165. James Lincoln Collier, *Duke Ellington* (New York: Oxford University Press, 1987), 231. Nanton is Joseph "Tricky Sam" Nanton (1904–46), a trombonist who joined Ellington's band in 1926 and remained with him until he died. See Rex Stewart, *Jazz Masters of the Thirties* (1972; rept., New York: Da Capo, 1982), 104–107, for more on this erudite West Indian instrumentalist. Cootie Williams (1908–85) was a trumpeter who replaced Bubber Miley in 1929 and stayed with the band until 1940. He then went to play with

Benny Goodman and later fronted the house band at the Savoy Ballroom. Williams eventually went back to Ellington's band.

166. Gunther Schuller observes that the "separation of reeds and brass . . . marks the entire early Ellington period." Schuller, *Early Jazz,* 321. While 1940 was well beyond his "early period," Ellington continued to pit these two tone colors against each other as a way of creating timbral contrast and heightening dramatic tension and effect. A second characteristic, early Ellington sound that stayed with the band was growling brass using a plunger mute. Ellington credited Bubber Miley with originating this technique in the mid-Twenties. Cootie Williams and Ray Nance maintained the tradition. See Ellington, *Music Is My Mistress,* 106.

167. Irwin Shaw's use of the trumpet as David Mellincoff's alter ego in *Quiet City* gains in significance as one appreciates the degree to which the instrument was associated with America's urban culture in general and jazz more particularly. Copland's *Quiet City* and Ellington's *Harlem Air Shaft* were composed one year apart.

168. See *Duke Ellington 1940,* RCA recording DPM 20351, liner notes by Larry Gushee.

169. *Sounding* good was Ellington's criterion for determining if the music *was* good.

170. Wilberforce College awarded Duke Ellington an Honorary Doctorate of Music in 1949.

171. Unfortunately, while Ellington moved on to better times personally, by the late 1940s and early 1950s, Harlem had begun its descent into a city whose name was synonymous with poverty and crime. Recent efforts have been made to revitalize Harlem by bringing in upscale retail chains and offering luxury office space, which former president Bill Clinton has rented, but the northern enclave of Manhattan island has not yet returned to its 1920s–30s glamour or glory.

172. Given Ellington's curiosity about music of all types, it is hard to believe he would not have known this work. In *Making Music Modern,* Carol Oja suggests similarities between Still's *From the Land of Dreams* (1925) and Ellington's *Creole Love Song* (1927), 332–333.

173. For background on this piece, including its genesis from an earlier work entitled "Central Avenue," see Verna Arvey's essay "William Grant Still," in Catherine Parsons Smith's *William Grant Still: A Study in Contradictions* (Berkeley and Los Angeles: University of California Press, 2000), especially 332–334. Still and Arvey were married in 1939. See also Wayne Shirley's paper "Central Avenue and Lenox Avenue," presented at the conference "A Tribute to WGS," Flagstaff, Arizona, 26 June 1998. I am grateful to Wayne Shirley for sharing his unpublished paper with me. For a thorough discussion and analysis of *Lenox Avenue* see Gayle Minetta Murchsion, "Nationalism in William Grant Still and Aaron Copland between the Wars: Style and Ideology," Ph.D. diss., Yale University, 1998.

174. By referring to these four specific streets, Still includes various regions of the United States: Beale Street, Memphis; Decatur Street, New Orleans; State Street, Chicago; and Central Avenue, Los Angeles. In a 1967 interview, William Grant Still referred to a great jazz club he visited several times on Central Avenue, the Club Alabam or The Alabam. See "William Grant Still: An Oral History," California State University–Fullerton, Oral History Program, California Black History Project, interview of William Grant Still by R. Donald Brown, 13 November 1967. At the time Brown explained: "Located on Central Avenue in the section of Los Angeles most densely populated by Negroes (Watts), 'The

Alabam' or 'Club Alabam' was one of the two great jazz clubs in the City in the 1940s. In New York at the time, there were two dozen great jazz clubs." Later in this same interview, Still commented that he had never visited the Cotton Club in New York. See transcripts of this interview, Judith Anne Still, ed., *William Grant Still: An Oral History* (Flagstaff, Ariz.: the Master-Player Library, 1998), 25–26.

175. Text introducing the section entitled "The Philosopher" provides another instance of Arvey and Still's preference for the simple explanation: "But Lenox Avenue is not all gaiety, look at that fine old man daydreaming in that doorway. . . . maybe he's thinking of the strides his race has made since slavery, and smiling proudly to himself as he remembers all the colored men and women who have brought honor to their people." All text is transcribed from the 1938 recording by the CBS Orchestra, conducted by Howard Barlow, Bay Cities BCD 1019.

176. During the 1930s, Still moved permanently to Los Angeles and developed his "universal" style, leaving his more racially focused idiom. For a discussion of his various periods, see Gayle Murchison's essay "'Dean of Afro-American Composers' or 'Harlem Renaissance Man,'" in Parsons Smith, ed., *William Grant Still*, 39–65.

177. See the Arvey essay in Parsons Smith, *William Grant Still*, 333. For excerpts from selected letters see Verna Arvey, *Studies of Contemporary American Composers: William Grant Still* (New York: J. Fischer and Bro., 1939), 40–42.

178. It is noteworthy that among Still's ten musical vignettes, none portrays a Harlem club specifically. In the late 1930s, dance and music clubs were still a powerful presence in Harlem's culture. It could be that Still felt he covered this particular soundscape in the section entitled "The House Rent Party," or perhaps he wanted to downplay this aspect of Harlem, as it might be associated with what many considered to be a seamier side.

179. Anderson, *This Was Harlem*, 106. When the drama critic John Anderson reviewed Rapp and Thurman's Broadway play *Harlem*, he too singled out 135th Street: "Most of it is untamed and broad-gauged stuff, full of rowdy jokes and gestures which do somehow catch an authentic jungle note in the brownstone wastelands of One Hundred and Thirty-fifth street." *New York Evening Journal*, 21 February 1929, quoted in Parsons Smith, ed., *William Grant Still*, 6–7.

180. The church had originally been situated in downtown Manhattan on Worth Street, then moved to Waverly Place, and then to West Fortieth Street between Seventh and Eighth Avenues, a section of town known for prostitution. In the 1920s it was moved one last time to its current location to keep up with its congregation, who had migrated northward to Harlem. For information on the Abyssinian Baptist Church see Anderson, *This Was Harlem*, 254–261.

181. Given earlier works such as *Africa* (1930), *Afro-American Symphony* (1931), and the Symphony in G Minor subtitled *Song of a New Race* (1937), it is hard to believe that Still really accepted this simple characterization of Harlem's black population. It is also inappropriate to assume that the text reflected Verna Arvey's attitude toward black Americans. As a white, Jewish woman who was vilified for appearing to break up Still's twenty-three-year marriage to Grace Bundy in 1938 (Bundy and Still had four children together), Arvey would have been extremely sensitive to the complexities of racial and ethnic stereotyping. It is hard to imagine her being unaware of the ramifications of the text.

182. Oja, *Making Music Modern*, 332.

183. Anderson, *This Was Harlem,* 347–349.

184. Langston Hughes's extraordinarily powerful poem is a series of six questions: "What happens to a dream deferred?/Does it dry up/Like a raisin in the sun?/Or fester like a sore—/And then run?/Does it stink like rotten meat?/Or crust and sugar over—/Like a syrupy sweet?/Maybe it just sags/Like a heavy load./Or does it explode?" Arnold Rampersad and David Roessel, eds., *The Collected Poems of Langston Hughes* (New York: Alfred A. Knopf, 1994).

185. The commentary fleshes out the episodes of the piece outlined by Ellington as: (1) Pronouncing the word "Harlem," itemizing its many facets—from downtown to uptown, true and false; (2) 110th Street, heading north through the Spanish neighborhood; (3) Intersection further uptown—cats shucking and stiffing; (4) Upbeat parade; (5) Jazz spoken in a thousand languages; (6) Floor show; (7) Girls out of step, but kicking like crazy; (8) Fanfare for Sunday; (9) On the way to church; (10) Church—we're even represented in Congress by our man of the church; (11) The sermon; (12) Funeral; (13) Counterpoint of tears; (14) Chic chick; (15) Stopping traffic; (16) After church promenade; (17) Agreement a cappella; (18) Civil Rights demandments; (19) March onward and upward; (20) Summary—contributions coda. See *Four Symphonic Works by Duke Ellington,* American Composers Orchestra, conducted by Maurice Peress, Music Masters MMD 60176L; *Harlem* for Jazz Band and Orchestra, orchestrated by Luther Henderson and Maurice Peress, notes by Maurice Peress.

186. This is a transcription of Ellington's commentary as recorded on the small disk accompanying *Duke Ellington: New World A'Coming, Harlem, The Golden Broom and the Green Apple,* Duke Ellington, piano, Cincinnati Symphony Orchestra, conducted by Erich Kunzel. Decca Records DL 710176.

187. Adam Clayton Powell Jr. (1908–72) was the pastor of Harlem's Abyssinian Baptist Church starting in 1937, and a U.S. congressman from 1945 to 1970. He was known for his passionate stands on African American issues.

188. In *Music Is My Mistress,* 106–109, Ellington talks about his trombonist Joe "Tricky Sam" Nanton and Nanton's West Indian legacy and his involvement in the Marcus Garvey movement. With Nanton, Juan Tizol, and Paul Gonsalves in his band, Ellington was personally acquainted with different ethnic groups who combined to make New York's culture rich.

189. Ellington's Carnegie Hall concerts of the 1940s were pathbreaking events.

190. Jazz would undergo additional hybridization in the 1960s, perhaps most notably with the jazz-rock fusions of Miles Davis.

191. *Four Symphonic Works by Duke Ellington,* American Composers Orchestra, conducted by Maurice Peress, Music Masters recording MMD 6000176L, notes by Maurice Peress. Peress and Luther Henderson orchestrated the version of *Harlem* that is performed on this album.

192. All remarks about the piece are based upon this version as recorded on Music Masters MMD 60176L, with Maurice Peress conducting. Ellington did record *Harlem* in an arrangement for band alone in 1954.

193. This quotation appears in the Henderson-Peress edition of the score.

NOTES TO CHAPTER FOUR

1.   This is not to suggest that these men wrote pieces celebrating rural places exclusively, but only that in comparison with composers such as Varèse and Ellington, Still, Harris, and Grofé were more interested in nonurban locales and commemorated them more often in their music.

2.   Grofé initially established himself as an arranger of popular music, and so responded to different demands than did the exclusively art-music composers William Grant Still and Roy Harris.

3.   When Heinrich promoted himself as American, it was a personal campaign to solidify his own identity. When Still and, especially, Harris promoted themselves as American, they sought to align themselves with larger ideological positions. Their Americanism took on a moral tone. Living through the interwar years and then the McCarthy era no doubt reinforced such thinking.

4.   Many writings by Still and Harris, as well as articles written on their behalf, exist to explicate their thinking. Grofé left numerous taped interviews as well as written comments. These are cited throughout the chapter.

5.   Aaron Copland could be described in many of the same terms. His ballets *Billy the Kid* (1938), *Rodeo* (1942), and *Appalachian Spring* (1944), as well as a host of other pieces, celebrate places and cultures beyond the city and avoid the more dissonant idiom of some of his earlier works. Copland, however, identified himself as a boy from Brooklyn, a child of the city.

6.   The other piece was *Dismal Swamp*.

7.   William Grant Still senior had formed a brass band in Woodville and showed other musical inclinations. In a speech entitled "A Composer's Viewpoint," the composer took great pride in his father's cultural achievements in this otherwise unprogressive town. Knowing this about his father might have provided Still with the courage he needed to pursue his own musical ambitions in a dominantly white high-art world. See "A Composer's Viewpoint," reprinted in Jon Michael Specer, ed., *The William Grant Still Reader: Essays on American Music* (Durham, N.C.: Duke University Press, 1992), 216.

8.   Willard B. Gatewood, "The Formative Years of William Grant Still: Little Rock, Arkansas, 1895–1911," in Parsons Smith, ed. *William Grant Still*, 22.

9.   Robert Bartlett Haas, *William Grant Still and the Fusion of Cultures in American Music* (Los Angeles: Black Sparrow Press, 1972), 10.

10.   Gatewood, "The Formative Years," 32.

11.   Parsons Smith, ed., *William Grant Still*, 70.

12.   For a discussion of how blues structures inform Still's *Afro-American Symphony*, see Catherine Parsons Smith's essay "The Afro-American Symphony and its Scherzo," in Parsons Smith, ed., *William Grant Still*, 114–151.

13.   According to Tammy Kernodle, Carrie Still's "conservative and elitist ideals" suggest that she could have been a "race woman." She concludes that if this was so it "would greatly influence [William Grant] Still's ideals and beliefs." Personal conversation, 9 May 2002.

14.   Parsons Smith notes that there is no formal record of Still's studies with Chadwick,

although this would not be unusual if Still worked with Chadwick privately, outside the confines of the New England Conservatory. See Parsons Smith, ed., *William Grant Still,* 88n13. See also Verna Arvey's essay "William Grant Still" in the same book for another explanation of Still's interactions with the New England Conservatory (310).

15. The ICG premiered three Still works in the mid-Twenties: *From the Land of Dreams* in 1925, and *Levee Land* and *Darker America* in 1926. Developing alternative musical structures was important to Varèse for his own music as well.

16. "Double-consciousness" is W. E. B. Du Bois's concept at the heart of his 1903 book *Souls of Black Folk.* The phrase refers to the need for America's blacks to operate within two worlds: that of the larger and dominantly white American culture and that of the smaller but perhaps more personally meaningful black culture. I am using the phrase in this context to refer to the awareness of white reviewers that Still was a black composer operating in a white modernist musical culture.

17. Paul Rosenfeld, "Musical Chronicle," *Dial,* April 1925, 352.

18. Still's title, *Darker America,* raises the question to what extent, if any, the composer was influenced by the monthly journal published by the NAACP and edited by W. E. B. Du Bois. Its full title was *The Crisis: A Record of the Darker Races.* There is no question that Still was aware of Du Bois and the journal, and he would not have minded the association. Still subscribed to the integrationist tenets of both the man and the organization, although he was significantly more broad-minded than was Du Bois when it came to which types of black music might be valuable or appropriate. While Du Bois championed spirituals exclusively, Still saw the blues as being freest from European influences. For a very early view on the value of different black music (including the evils of ragtime), see an editorial by J. Hillary Taylor, "Our Musical Condition" in *Negro Music Journal,* 1, no. 7 (March 1903): 137.

19. *Musical Courier* 93, no. 23 (2 December 1926): 20. The ICG concert of 28 November 1926 included works by Carlos Chávez, Colin McPhee, Ildebrando Pizzetti, and Anton Webern. It is hard to imagine Webern's "Fünf geistliche Lieder" sounding like "muddy grime."

20. Hanson initiated this series in 1925. Gayle Murchison quotes Still as saying, "After this period, I felt for a while that I wanted to devote myself to writing racial music," in her essay "'Dean of Afro-American Composers' or 'Harlem Renaissance Man': The New Negro and the Musical Poetics of William Grant Still," in Parsons Smith, ed., *William Grant Still,* 39–65. Here Murchison discusses Still's participation in three twentieth-century "trends": musical modernism, musical nationalism, and the Harlem Renaissance, which resulted in Still's racial idiom.

21. According to the festival bulletin commemorating the tenth anniversary of the Eastman School American Composers' Concerts, Hanson premiered a total of eight works by William Grant Still: *Darker America* (1927–28 season); *From the Journal of the Wanderer* (1928–29 season); *Africa* and *Sahdji* (1930–31 season); the *Afro-American Symphony* (1931–32 season); *La Guiablesse* and *From the Black Belt* (1932–33 season); and *Blue Steel,* performed at the tenth-anniversary concerts in 1935. See "The Digital Scriptorium, Special Collections Library, Duke University, http://scriptorium.lib.duke.edu/sgo/ (17 July 2002). The *Musical Courier* of 2 December 1926 calls into question the claim that Hanson premiered *Darker America.* According to an article in that journal, *Darker America* received its premiere at

an ICG concert conducted by Eugene Goossens at Aeolian Hall, 28 November 1926. See "New York Concerts," *Musical Courier* 93, no. 23 (2 December 1926): 20.

22. Murchison, "Dean of Afro-American Composers," 54–56. As Murchison's essay shows, Still would be referred to as the "Dean of Afro-American Composers." Parsons Smith observed, "Still rejected 'black' but used 'colored,' 'Negro,' and 'Afro-American' pretty much interchangeably." Parsons Smith, e-mail to author, 1 October 2001.

23. This is quoted in Haas, *William Grant Still,* 271.

24. Phone conversation with Judith Anne Still, 18 April 2001.

25. In a 1967 interview with William Grant Still, conducted by R. Donald Brown of the Oral History Program at California State University–Fullerton, the composer mused over the mysterious pull that California had exerted on him in the 1930s: "Prior to coming here, I thought that I would only be satisfied living in the East, but after coming here, . . . California did something to me. . . . And I can't tell you what it was. There was just something about this section of the country that seemed to satisfy me, more so than any [other part of the country]. I had never been anywhere [else] that felt like home. When I came here, it was like coming home. Now don't ask me why, because I don't know. But I was perfectly well satisfied here." See Judith Anne Still, ed., *William Grant Still: An Oral History,* 22.

26. Phone conversation with Judith Anne Still, 18 April, 2001. It seems that William Grant Still was particularly fond of driving along California Route 1, which hugs the coast. His daughter recalls being quite frightened of the road, which in places had no guardrails. In contrast, William found the experience of speeding along the open road exhilarating.

27. Ibid.

28. In an e-mail of 1 October 2001, Catherine Parsons Smith observed that according to Wayne Shirley's report of the William Grant Still scores in the Music Division of the Library of Congress, the opera *Highway 1, USA* "is, almost note for note . . . the same as *A Southern Interlude* from 1942. There is no known commission or request for it from that time." In reference to *Highway 1, USA,* Parsons Smith concluded, "I think they chose the new title as more universally American, not as a geographical reference." This may in fact be the exception that proves the rule. In renaming the work for a well-known highway that traverses the entire East Coast, Still tapped into the proud postwar mood of the victorious United States. Americans were encouraged to see their own country, to enjoy their place. The stories that unfolded on the road would be viewed as quintessentially American. I am grateful to Catherine Parsons Smith and Tammy Kernodle for their work on William Grant Still, their reading of an earlier version of this chapter, and their help in refining ideas. If *Highway 1, USA* was indeed a later manifestation of *A Southern Interlude,* the practice of renaming and relocating place titles would have followed a pattern that Still established when he adapted *Central Avenue* into *Lenox Avenue* years earlier. In a paper entitled "Central Avenue and Lenox Avenue," originally presented at the William Grant Still conference in Flagstaff, Arizona, in 1998, Wayne Shirley referred to the former as "a sort of first-draft version of *Lenox Avenue*."

29. Verna Arvey, *In One Lifetime* (Fayetteville: University of Arkansas Press, 1984) 173.

30. Phone conversation with Judith Anne Still, 16 April 2001.

31. This modern music organization was formed, in large part, by disgruntled members of Varèse's ICG. It is a testament to Still's broad appeal (and the power of some of his

advocates, including Hanson, Stokowski, and Goossens) that he should have been so closely associated with Varèse, maintain that warm friendship, and still be commissioned by the League.

32. Parsons Smith, ed., *William Grant Still*, 91n44.

33. Anne K. Simpson describes *Kaintuck'* as "a hauntingly beautiful tonal piece, shimmering as it depicts misty sunlight on Kentucky blue grass," in Haas, ed., *William Grant Still*, 90. Mitchell Patton's notes that accompany the Cincinnati Philharmonia Orchestra recording of the work state, "This short work for piano and orchestra is Still's reaction to moonlight on the bluegrass of Kentucky" (Centaur CRC 2331).

34. Frederick Yeiser, "Blue Grass," *Cincinnati Enquirer,* 22 March 1936. This article was written as a preview of the premiere.

35. Twelve-measure blues structure may have informed Still's thinking in this piece. Numerous ninth chords might also bespeak Still's attempt to assimilate both black and European musical cultures.

36. It is first heard in measures 7 and 8 in the right-hand piano music: D–E-flat. In both cases, a G at the top of the chord on beat 4 provides an important closing motion.

37. Minor seconds are heard throughout the piece. Particularly obvious occurrences are at measure 8; seven measures after rehearsal 2; three measures before rehearsal 9; and three measures before rehearsal 19.

38. Beethoven's *Choral Fantasy,* opus 80 (1808), is an example of a piano, orchestral, and choral work in which the piano has a lengthy introduction prior to the orchestra's initial entrance. Here the piano introduction is so long that a first-time listener might actually be surprised when the orchestra enters, having been led to believe the work was a solo piano piece.

39. Paul Whiteman commissioned George Gershwin to write a piece in January 1924. With significant help from Ferde Grofé, *Rhapsody in Blue* premiered on 12 February 1924. Whiteman was so pleased with its reception that he immediately arranged for another six performances. It made Gershwin, Whiteman, and Grofé famous. Still would have been in New York at that time working with Varèse, writing his own compositions, and having them performed in ICG concerts. Whether Still's rurally-inspired *Kaintuck'* is in any way influenced by or derivative of Gershwin's urban *Rhapsody* is not an issue in this discussion. Given the popularity of Gershwin's piece, it would have been impossible for Still not to have known of the work and absorbed its lessons. Additional discussion of *Rhapsody in Blue* appears in the section on Ferde Grofé.

40. Still indicated that this work was not intended to be a literal picture, but an evocation of the mood at this scene. But Judith Anne Still's assertion that her father composed the sounds of the train *into* the music would seem to leave room for this expanded interpretation. Conversation with Judith Anne Still, 18 April 2001.

41. See Judith Anne Still, Michael J. Dabrishus, and Carolyn L. Quin, *William Grant Still: A Bio-Bibliography* (Westport, Conn.: Greenwood Press, 1996), 30.

42. Parsons Smith, ed., *William Grant Still*, 117.

43. As quoted in Parsons Smith, ed., *William Grant Still*, 169: "they, Verna and Billy."

44. Including Cowell among those listed is most disturbing. According to Judith Anne Still, her father and mother remained loyal friends of Henry Cowell throughout his incarceration. Perhaps Still named Cowell only to suggest the ways in which innocent Ameri-

cans could be unknowingly used by the Soviets for their own purposes. However, it is not clear whether this was Still's intention.

45.   All quotations are transcribed directly from the audiotape of the speech "Communism in Music." The tape is available through William Grant Still Music, Flagstaff, Arizona.

46.   Catherine Parsons Smith, " 'Harlem Renaissance Man Revisited: The Politics of Race and Class in Still's Late Career," in Parsons Smith, ed., *William Grant Still*, 182–212. Still referred to himself and those of his race as Negroes. See Judith Still, *William Grant Still: An Oral History*, especially 13–45.

47.   Still contributed an article to *The Crisis* in January 1944. "The Men behind American Music," 12–15, 29, tells of the impact that black American composers had on numerous other composers and arrangers, often without being given any credit. He mentions Paul Whiteman playing Still's arrangements, and Benny Goodman doing the same with Fletcher Henderson's, and then he talks of the ways in which African American music had a direct impact on composers as diverse as Dvořák, Debussy, Delius, Ravel, Brahms, and George Gershwin.

48.   A regular feature of the monthly magazine was a list of recent university graduates, often with their photos.

49.   See the *Crisis* articles "Jim Crow in Prison" (March 1946), "Still a Jim Crow Army" (April 1946), "Jim Crow Rents a Pew" (June 1946), "Metropolitan Opera Policy Not to Engage Negro Singers" (February 1948).

50.   "Keep an Eye on the Communists," *Crisis*, April 1948, 105; "Error," *Crisis*, June 1948, 169. The editor is Roy Wilkins.

51.   "Robeson Speaks for Robeson," *Crisis*, May 1949, 137.

52.   Walter White, "The Negro and the Communists," *Crisis*, August–September 1950, 502–506, 537, 538.

53.   Ibid., 538.

54.   Herbert Hill, "Communist Party, Enemy of Negro Equality. An Examination of the Record Exposes the American Communist Party as the Enemy of Negro Aspirations," *Crisis*, June–July 1951, 365.

55.   Ibid., 367.

56.   Roy Wilkins, "Undergirding the Democratic Ideal," *Crisis*, December 1951, 647. That phrase comes from a longer statement: "America needs more than normal might in her fight against godless Communism."

57.   Throughout the Fifties, Still wrote a number of songs for music textbooks. The conservative world of this type of publishing found a safe proponent of traditional American values in Still's works. Textbooks of the era show a decided lack of more experimental works. See "Twentieth-Century Music in the Fourth and Fifth Grade Textbooks of Silver Burdett, 1960–1990," unpublished paper by Sarah Meredith, Florida State University, December 2000.

58.   This was the theme of an article that Still published in *The Crisis*, January 1944, "The Men behind American Music."

59.   In his 1953 speech "Communism in Music," Still mentioned Charles Wakefield Cadman among four composers he believed were loyal Americans. I am grateful to Catherine

Parsons Smith for Illuminating Chadwick's role in nurturing Still's interest in American aspects of music. Parsons Smith, e-mail to author, 1 October, 2001.

60. If these movements do not depict the melodies or rhythms of these cultures in ethno-musicologically accurate ways, they do make use of conventional gestures and sounds that would have been associated with those cultures by a general public. Once again, Still's desire was to write music accessible to that audience. In keeping with his integrationist beliefs, his emphasis would have been on the fusion of these musical cultures, not on the preservation of their distinctive qualities.

61. Gayle Murchison, "Dean of Afro-American Composers," 50. In a quirk of history, Still clung to such aesthetic values at a time when the most respected music was often that which was decidedly inaccessible and unlyrical. While lay audiences would continue to prefer music like Still's, increasingly powerful university composers championed a more esoteric music that was in many cases completely free of what would be considered a traditional melody. Much as Still wanted to believe that his rejection by the musical establishment resulted from political and racial differences exclusively, there were equally strong aesthetic explanations for the turn against his work, as there would be for that of Roy Harris and Ferde Grofé.

62. See Michael Beckerman, "The Dance of Pau-Puk-Keewis, the Song of Chibiabos, and the Story of Iagoo: Reflections on Dvořák's 'New World' Scherzo," in *Dvořák in America, 1892–1895,* ed. John C. Tibbetts (Portland, Oreg.: Amadeus Press, 1993), 210–227. Here Beckerman cites "the incessant rhythm, pounding drum beats, and the exotic 'minor drone' harmony" as "those elements identified as 'Indian' by the composer." See also Von Glahn, "Charles Ives, Cowboys, and Indians," 291–314.

63. Roy Harris, as quoted by Dan Stehman in notes to Harris's Symphony No. 6, "Gettysburg." Andante Records, AD 72402.

64. "Log Cabin Composer," *Time,* 11 November 1935, 36–37.

65. Virgil Thomson, *A Virgil Thomson Reader* (New York: E. P. Dutton, 1981), 198. Dan Stehman noted some of the consequences of Harris's attitude: "With Copland, his relationship moved from fairly close comradeship during the 1920s and 30s through friendly rivalry during the 1940s to open hostility from the 1950s on (a feeling that was not shared by Copland). Harris felt that his colleague had attempted, in such works as *Appalachian Spring, Billy the Kid,* and *Rodeo,* to cash in on the folk idiom and other Americanist elements that he apparently regarded as his birthright." See Stehman, *Roy Harris: A Bio-Bibliography* (Westport, Conn.: Greenwood Press), 1991, 9. William Grant Still felt toward Harris the same way that Harris felt toward Copland. Both Still and Harris wrote pieces about Kentucky, although Still clearly had the stronger claim to personal investment in that state. And Harris's multiple uses of two spirituals, "Li'l Boy Named David" and "De Trumpet Sounds It in My Soul," raised questions of usurping repertoire that more properly belonged to African Americans such as Still. According to Stehman, Harris came upon spirituals while doing research at the Library of Congress in the 1930s (*Roy Harris,* 295). Later on, William Grant Still would make much of Harris's claims to patriotism and then his 1942 efforts to reach out to the Soviets in his fifth symphony, followed by trips to that republic in the 1950s.

66. Harris's program notes for an orchestral work entitled "Kentucky Spring" (1949) reveal his attachment to one such place: "The word 'Kentucky' means springtime to me for the very simple reason that I have always been in Kentucky in the springtime. Whenever

we have visited Kentucky the air has been soft and fragrant and filled with bird song. The earth has been clothed in a riot of colors and time seemed to belong to the people instead of people belonging to time. Our recollections of Kentucky are filled with gaiety, good spirits and large margins for living. And so, I have written a piece called 'Kentucky Spring' hoping to recapture some of the colorful memories in music." See Roy Harris, *Kentucky Spring,* recording by Louisville Orchestra, Robert Whitney, conductor, 1960, LOU 602.

67. The composer makes no mention of the book or the movie in discussions of his piece, although he would almost certainly have been aware of their existence; each was enormously successful.

68. See Roy Harris, *Cimarron: Symphonic Overture* (New York: Mills Music, 1941). Given Harris's use of this story to connect his family to the West, it is noteworthy that he refers to the land rush as one of the most stirring "tales." Land rushes did occur, but one wonders if this is a subtle acknowledgment of the folkloric quality of his personal story.

69. Oklahoma was settled by whites as a territory in 1889 but not admitted to the union until 1907. Harris was born in Lincoln County, then in the Oklahoma Territory. His family moved to California in 1905, before Oklahoma became a state. Statehood was granted not long after oil was discovered in Osage Indian territory.

70. Often the simplest facts of the Harris biography are difficult to pin down. He is said to have been born in Lincoln County, in the center of the state, about forty miles northeast of Oklahoma City. Yet the *New Grove* (2001) entry on Harris describes his childhood "on land claimed in one of the rushes on the Oklahoma Panhandle." See Dan Stehman, "Harris, Roy," *New Grove,* vol. 11, 55. Even the easternmost corner of the panhandle is more than two hundred miles to the west of Lincoln County. Given the territorial status of the region at the time, many documents that we have come to assume are a matter of public record and accessible are in fact simply not available. It is difficult to corroborate data regarding Harris's early life.

71. All Oklahoma pioneers came from somewhere else, and so in that regard Harris's parents were no different. What is noteworthy about Harris's heritage, however, is the degree to which any information connecting him with places other than "the West" is minimized in early literature about the composer. Harris spent twenty-three of his first twenty-eight years in southern California. Given his efforts to identify himself with Oklahoma, it is somewhat ironic that a current list of 234 famous Oklahomans posted by the State of Oklahoma's Department of Commerce does not include Roy Harris. See "Famous Oklahomans," www.odoc.state.ok.us.oknet (updated April 2001; accessed 15 May 2001). While this list may not include people who moved away before statehood, it is noteworthy that Harris does not make such a distinction.

72. See, among others, John Tasker Howard, *Our Contemporary Composers: American Music in the Twentieth Century* (New York: Thomas Y. Crowell, 1941), 145.

73. Among the most insightful and eloquent "new" western historians is Donald Worster. In his book *Under Western Skies: Nature and History in the American West* (New York: Oxford University Press, 1992), Worster refers to Henry Nash Smith's book *Virgin Land: The American West as Symbol and Myth* (Cambridge: Harvard University Press, 1950) as among the very first expressions of a new vision of the West. Worster makes an essential point about the fuzziness of myth and reality when he notes: "In later years Smith admitted he had been a little too quick to dismiss myth as simple falsehood when in truth popular

belief and historical reality are joined together in a continuous dialogue, moving back and forth in a halting, jerky interplay." Worster, *Under Western Skies,* 6.

74.   See Beth E. Levy, "'The White Hope of American Music': Or, How Roy Harris Became Western," *American Music* 19, no. 2 (summer 2001): 131–167, especially 140–141. The Rosenfeld remarks appeared in his book *An Hour with American Music,* 117–119, 123–124. I am extremely grateful to Ms. Levy for sharing her work with me prior to its publication. It has informed much of my thinking about Roy Harris and his connection with the American place.

75.   The single published work was the Piano Sonata, written in 1928. Other works written to that date included his symphony (1928–29); string quartet (1929); concerto for piano, clarinet, and strings (1928–31), sextet for woodwinds (1931); and toccata for orchestra (1931). Farwell included examples from the manuscripts of the Piano Sonata, string quartet, woodwind sextet, and toccata for orchestra in his article.

76.   Arthur Farwell, "Roy Harris," *Musical Quarterly* 18 (1932): 30–31. Emphasis mine.

77.   See Stehman, *Roy Harris: A Bio-Bibliography,* 19. Stehman explains Harris's concept: "In this, a melody or harmonic design flowers from a seed motive, each phrase following the first often either launching itself from a figure in the last measure of its immediate predecessor or referring back to the seed, the aim being to produce an effect of gradual, organic growth. His music thus often unfolds in additive fashion in autogenetically-generated blocks of texture, each gradually preparing, in Beethovenian fashion, for the following through anticipation of one or more elements of the new material. Although some of his livelier music contains sharp contrasts, Harris had difficulty assimilating these into his idiosyncratic process, and they sometimes seem awkward" (19–20).

78.   See Evelyn David Culbertson's study *He Heard America Singing: Arthur Farwell, Composer and Crusading Music Educator* (Metuchen, N.J.: Scarecrow, 1992) 263. The emphasis is original to Farwell's 9 January 1931 letter.

79.   Culbertson, *He Heard America Singing,* 272. It is not clear whether Harris intended the words "Eastern" and "European" as references to East Coast American influences and European influences, or to "Eastern European" influences, thinking of a composer such as Stravinsky, of whom he would have learned during his study with Nadia Boulanger in Paris.

80.   Howard, *Our American Music,* 572.

81.   Farwell, "Roy Harris," 31–32. Harris might have stayed longer in Paris had not a serious back injury caused him to return to the United States for treatment.

82.   Howard, *Our Contemporary Composers,* 133. For a discussion of the racial and ethnic implications inherent in Howard's remarks, see Levy, "The White Hope of American Music."

83.   In a very brief article entitled "Folksong—American Big Business," which appeared in *Modern Music,* in 1940, Harris "recalled" a cowboy reunion and then chided the many "folksong vendors" who exploited a repertoire that didn't belong to them (whereas it did, apparently, belong to Harris.) Separating himself from the urban crowd, Harris noted: "Some city boys may take a short motor trip through our land and return to write the Song of the Prairies—others will be folksong authorities after reading in a public library for a few weeks. . . . We'll have Folk Song Hot and Cold and in the Pot with whiskers on it." *Modern Music* 18 (November–December 1940): 11.

84. In 1998 the western novelist Gary McCarthy wrote his own tribute to the history-rich river and trail with his book *Rivers West: The Cimarron River* (New York: Bantam Books, 1998).

85. The January 1889 skirmish was still fresh in the mind of George Bolds sixty-seven years later, when *Across the Cimarron: The Adventures of "Cimarron" George Bolds, Last of the Frontiersmen* was published (New York: Crown Books, 1956). An aged Bolds told his story to James D. Horan, who recorded the account of this frontier deputy complete with shoot-outs and narrow escapes on horseback. For a detailed description of the confrontation, see the chapter entitled "Battle of Cimarron," 271–281.

86. According to *Webster's Unabridged Dictionary* (2d ed.), other definitions for "cimarron" include: (1) the Rocky Mountain sheep; the bighorn; (2) a runaway slave. There is a similar word among the Mexican-Apache peoples that means "wanderer." See www.odoc.state.ok.us/oknet/commprof (15 May 2001).

87. With various nineteenth-century relocation efforts by the U.S. government, many Indian tribes were moved to Oklahoma and the plains, although culturally they were not "Plains Indians."

88. The *Concise Columbia Desk Encyclopedia,* 3d ed. See entries for "Comanche" and "North America, Indigenous peoples of." The Society of American Indians was formed in October 1911. Over the course of the following years, numerous meetings between tribal representatives and government officials took place in Washington, D.C. Throughout the period, newspapers chronicled the vicissitudes of America's indigenous peoples: their internal debates over assimilation versus self-identity; their ongoing battles with disease; their victimization by land grabbers and lawyers; and their continual struggles for cultural survival.

89. Harris was a restless man. He taught at Mills College, Westminster Choir School, Juilliard, Cornell, Colorado College, Utah State Agricultural College, Peabody, the Pennsylvania College for Women, Southern Illinois University, Indiana University, the Universidad Interamerican de Puerto Rico, the University of the Pacific, and California State University at Los Angeles. Change seemed to be essential to his survival.

90. This concept was articulated in 1893 by Frederick Jackson Turner, who hypothesized: "Moving westward, the frontier *became more and more American.* As successive terminal moraines result from successive glaciations, so each frontier leaves its traces behind it, and when it becomes a settled area the region still partakes of the frontier characteristics. Thus the advance of the frontier has meant a steady movement away from the influence of Europe, a steady growth of independence on American lines." See "The Significance of the Frontier in American History," in Frederick Jackson Turner, *Rereading Frederick Jackson Turner: The Significance of the Frontier in American History, and Other Essays,* commentary by John Mack Faragher (New York: Henry Holt, 1994), 34. Emphasis mine.

91. Turner's epoch-making paper was delivered at the annual conference of the American Historical Association in 1893. Since 1950 many historians have argued with Turner's sanitized explanation of American expansion and identity, not only the aforementioned Donald Worster and Henry Nash Smith, but also Richard Hofstader, George Anderson, and Gerald D. Nash, among others. Even so, his thesis has continued to affect students and scholars of American history to the present day. See Worster, *Under Western Skies,* chapter 1, "Beyond the Agrarian Myth," for a discussion of the context.

92. Turner's failure to acknowledge the presence of Native Americans or the prevalence of violence in the nation's westward expansion has been a source of great distress for many modern historians.

93. Buffalo Bill was the stage name of Wyoming-born William F. Cody (1845–1917).

94. It was this same version of the West that would form the bases of numerous western-inspired television programs of the 1950s, 1960s, and 1970s.

95. See Smith, *Virgin Land,* 90–120, "The Western Hero in the Dime Novel" and "Dime Novel Heroine." Smith characterized Seth Jones as the "Dime-Novel Descendant of Leatherstocking" (92–93).

96. See the Beadle and Adams Dime Novel Digitization Project, a project of the Northern Illinois University Libraries, DeKalb, http://libws66.lib.niu.edu (4 April 2003).

97. John T. McIntyre, foreword to the Beadle and Adams Dime Novel Digitization Project.

98. Buffalo Bill appears to have been among the very earliest promoters of "tie-in" products. Where today's movies generate dozens of spin-off products to boost interest in films—everything ranging from T-shirts, to mugs, lunchboxes, hair clips, and action figures—Buffalo Bill's Wild West Extravaganza took advantage of the dime-novel press to create and reach an enlarged audience. The Wild West could be brought into the refined eastern parlor via the novel.

99. See http://xroads.virginia.edu/~HYPER/HNS/BuffaloBill/realbill.html (accessed 2 July 2002).

100. John W. Osborn, The Brand Burners of Cimarron" (New York: Beadle and Adams, 1897), Microfilm 8509, reel 43:31, Beadle's Dime-Store Novels, Florida State University.

101. Ibid., reel 43:32.

102. Among characteristics of the dime and half-dime novels are multipart titles; this one is typical.

103. The Gila River runs from southwestern New Mexico across Arizona and the Gila River Indian Reservation south of Phoenix. Frederick Dewey, "Cimarron Jack, the King-Pin of Rifle-Shots; or, The Phantom Tracker, A Tale of the Land of Silence" (Beadle's Half-Dime Library, 24 July 1883), 1. Florida State University, Microfilm 8509, reel 60:58.

104. Edna Ferber, *Cimarron* (New York: Doubleday, 1931), ix–x.

105. Ferber's father was a Hungarian Jew and her mother a native of Milwaukee, Wisconsin. In her youth Edna Ferber lived in Ottumwa, Iowa (about a hundred miles from the Missouri border); Chicago, Illinois; and Appleton, Wisconsin. She died at her Park Avenue home in New York City. The Algonquin Hotel at Forty-fourth Street was the meeting place of a group of writers and critics in the 1920s. Dorothy Parker, Harold Ross, Robert Benchley, Alexander Woollcott, Edna Ferber, and an assortment of other literary tastemakers met daily for lunch and animated discussions. People dined at the hotel in the hopes of catching a glimpse of the quick-witted and acerbic group, which Ferber dubbed the Poison Squad. The Algonquin Club remains one of the most important informal artists' communities in American history.

106. "Edna Ferber, Novelist, 82, Dies," *New York Times,* 17 April 1968, 32.

107. The 1931 version of *Cimarron* is available on video. While it suffers from primitive sound technology, which makes much of the dialogue difficult to understand, many mod-

ern viewers will find its stereotypical portrayals of blacks, Jews, and American Indians much more problematic. Feminist viewers might also take issue with the ostensibly passive role of the lead character's wife. Sabra waits on Yancey and is subject to his whims. Her strength and independence, however, are powerful if quiet statements about the essential role that women played in settling and civilizing the West. In the novel, Sabra eventually runs for political office in the state of Oklahoma and wins.

108. Ferber, *Cimarron*, 11. Cravat's unknown heritage makes him simultaneously an exotic and an Everyman, a character who appeals broadly.

109. Ibid., 14–15.

110. Such readings overlook certain realities, including the degree to which westward expansion often resulted in one group of people overtaking and conquering another.

111. Ferber, *Cimarron*, 16.

112. Ibid., 24–25.

113. This area includes the northern part of Oklahoma that is not in the panhandle.

114. An article that appeared in the *New York Times*, 27 May 2001, 1, chronicled the return of Native Americans and bison to the territory 130 years after they were driven out: Timothy Egan, "As Others Abandon Plains, Indians and Bison Come Back." Seen from this perspective, one might conclude that the land grabs were even more gratuitous than they initially appeared.

115. Harris, *Cimarron: Symphonic Overture*, front matter.

116. Ibid. It is not clear who wrote these remarks, although Harris regularly provided his own commentaries. Whether he wrote these specific comments, he would almost certainly have had to approve of their inclusion within his score.

117. Quoted in Culbertson, *He Heard America Singing*, 273.

118. Farwell, "Roy Harris," 24. *Cimarron* is not unique in its programmatic content. A large number of Harris's pieces contain descriptions of events or places that inspired them and are portrayed in the music, although *Cimarron* is among the most obvious in its attempt to depict specific events. See *Kentucky Spring* as another example.

119. In both the full and symphonic band arrangements of this piece, Harris includes a single string bass. *Cimarron* is "Dedicated to the State of Oklahoma," yet the motivation for writing the piece is not completely clear. As Dan Stehman explains: "Although *Cimarron* was commissioned by the University of Chicago Band [for the fiftieth anniversary of the university] . . . in an article based on an interview with the composer published just before [the 23 February 1941 performance in Chicago], Harris is quoted as stating that was merely a 'dress rehearsal' and that *Cimarron* had actually been written for the Enid Festival." This was a Tri-State Band Festival held in Enid, Oklahoma, 19 April 1941. See Stehman, *Roy Harris*, 48–49.

120. This is consistent with Harris's ideas regarding musical autogenesis.

121. Stehman, *Roy Harris*, 18.

122. As in much music by Aaron Copland, Harris often employs open-spaced chords that some listeners equate with the wide open spaces of the American landscape. Harris's admiration of medieval chant and organum might also explain his preference for open textures.

123. Harris, *Cimarron*. See program note preceding the score, front matter.

124. Stehman, *Roy Harris,* 19.

125. Charles Ives, in his song "The Indians," groups notes in patterns of four sixteenth notes set off from each other by recurring accents. See Von Glahn, "Charles Ives, Cowboys, and Indians." William Grant Still in "Navaho Country" employs actual tom-tom drums, although his rhythm is grouped in a most uncharacteristic triple meter.

126. It may be that the pretense of authenticity is more important.

127. Roy Harris, *Cimarron,* 12.

128. It is unfortunate that the only commercial recording of *Cimarron* is consistently under tempo. Any suggestion of the wild scene created by thousands of people blazing across the open land on horseback and in bouncing covered wagons is lost in the studied and labored performance. SRV 347SD Bay Cities BCD-1002, Stereo Classical.

129. See Osborn, "The Brand Burners of Cimarron," 1.

130. Roy Harris, *Cimarron,* front matter.

131. Florida State University, Allen Music Library, Ferde Grofé Tape Archive 114. The Grofé Tape Archive consists of 152 reel-to-reel tapes, a number of cassette copies, and three binders of cataloging information containing dozens of hours of interviews, radio broadcasts, and recorded music. The collection was donated to the library by Ferde Grofé's son Ferdinand. Tape 114 is a ninety-minute-long interview, conducted by an anonymous interviewer, and covers various aspects of Grofé's musical life. In this session Grofé attempts to clarify the type of music he wrote. Rejecting the phrase "symphonic jazz," although he acknowledged its ubiquity by critics, Grofé preferred the term "concert music." "I'm a composer of concert music, Americana, light music. I couldn't write anything heavy."

132. Grofé Tape Archive 114. In this interview, recorded in the early 1960s, Grofé explained the significance of *Rhapsody in Blue.* "It took me out of the realm of dance music arranger and into the concert field. It took all three of us [Gershwin, Whiteman, and Grofé] to a higher plane." In another interview, Grofé observed that *Rhapsody in Blue* "stamped the American School of Music." See Ferde Grofé Tape Archive 55, interview conducted 27 July 1940 by Joe O'Brien at the New York World's Fair.

133. Ferde Grofé Tape Archive 72. Interview conducted with Bruce Wendell at Radio KCBH-FM, Beverly Hills, Calif., 7 July 1957.

134. Ferde Grofé Tape Archive 95. Radio interview conducted 14 October 1966 in Laguna Beach, Calif., by an unidentified announcer. That music history texts have regularly given Grofé little attention is an issue for another study.

135. Ferde Grofé Tape Archive 72. Lake Mead is near Las Vegas. Tape 82 includes a recording of the work.

136. Quoted in James Farrington, "Ferde Grofé: An Investigation into His Musical Activities and Works." Master's thesis, Florida State University, 1985, 154.

137. *Broadway at Night* was premiered by Paul Whiteman at Carnegie Hall, 15 November 1924. An excerpt of *Metropolis: A Fantasie in Blue* can be heard on Ferde Grofé Tape Archive 10.

138. Francis D. Perkins, "Grofé Presents Modern Music in Pool Benefit," *New York Herald Tribune,* 20 January 1937, 12. As James Farrington points out, "most of the works on the program were written or arranged by Grofé, including premier performances of his *Hollywood Suite* and *Symphony in Steel.*" Farrington, "Ferde Grofé," 115. As an indication

of Grofé's inclination for effects, the composer had percussionists use shoes rather than drumsticks on their instruments in an effort to simulate a tap-dance routine.

139. In a 1940 interview, Grofé acknowledged that his "hobby was always orchestration." Ferde Grofé Tape Archive 55. Between 1922 and 1925, while in New York, Grofé formally studied orchestration with Pietro Floridia (1860–1932), an Italian-born composer who had immigrated to the United States. Prior to that he had studied much on his own. After his work with Floridia, Grofé consulted Arthur E. Heacox's *Project Lessons in Orchestration.* See Florida State University, Ferde Grofé Tape Archive 118 and Farrington, "Ferde Grofé," 32.

140. Ferde Grofé Tape Archive 114.

141. "Grofé's America," *Time* 24, no. 5 (1 February 1937): 38.

142. Ibid. Regarding the *Grand Canyon Suite,* Grofé recollected Toscanini's claim, "There are two kinds of music—good and bad, and this is good." This was also Ellington's claim.

143. The phrase comes from John Rowe Parker, *Euterpeiad* 1 (29 July 1820): 70.

144. Farrington, "Ferde Grofé," 133.

145. The relative fame of these works was stated matter-of-factly in a radio interview with Grofé conducted by Mary Proal Lindeke 22 July 1940. Grofé easily assented. Ferde Grofé Tape Archive 55.

146. Ferde Grofé Tape Archive 95.

147. Whiteman's use of the phrase "experimental music" for his series of concerts requires twenty-first-century readers to adjust their notion of what can only be considered tame and traditional music. At the time, this was music unlike traditional European concert music. In Whiteman's mind, the blending of jazz and popular sounds with classical instrumentation made it "experimental."

148. Ferde Grofé Tape Archive 114.

149. Ferde Grofé, jacket notes for Grofé, *Grand Canyon Suite* and *Mississippi Suite,* Capitol P8347, quoted in Farrington, "Ferde Grofé," 73.

150. Grofé actually starts with a note a major second higher than the lowest note and then ascends the major second and minor third through the fourth. Kern simply repeats the first note before ascending the major second and minor third. In addition, Grofé's movement begins in three and eventually moves to common time, where the similar melody is most prominent; Kern's song is wholly in duple.

151. Ferde Grofé Tape Archive 114.

152. The recording, to which all comments refer, is by the New York Philharmonic with André Kostelanetz conducting (MYK 37759). Kostelanetz was a close friend of Grofé and the person who encouraged Grofé to write the *Hudson River Suite* in 1955.

153. Any suggestion that Grofé had American Indian tunes in mind must be considered carefully. Since folk music from many cultures features pentatonic scales, without commentary from Grofé, the idea that the composer was specifically evoking Native Americans must be considered purely speculative. To date no such reference has been found.

154. In 1936 Prokofiev used the bassoon for another playful characterization in his narrated orchestral work *Peter and the Wolf.*

155. Both Grofé and Gershwin might actually have heard the famous ascending motif in the Eubie Blake and Noble Sissle musical *Shuffle Along,* a work that enjoyed a long run

starting in 1921. See http://scriptorium.lib.duke.edu/sgo/exhibit/captions/caption6.html (14 July 2002).

156. As evidence of the popularity of the "Mardi Gras" movement, consider the number of times the work was mentioned or played on tapes in the Florida State University Ferde Grofé Tape Archive. Of the twenty references to the *Mississippi Suite,* twelve referred to "Mardi Gras." Another five tapes referred exclusively to the "Huckleberry Finn" movement. Another tape is a recording of the entire suite, and two others make general remarks about the work.

157. Ferde Grofé Tape Archive 116. In this tape, Grofé explains to an unidentified interviewer that when composing, "[I] always have a definite subject in mind. I have a picture of what I write about. Whether it is a geographical piece or an industrial piece." Grofé mentions the idea of "geographical" pieces again, in the continuation of this interview. Ferde Grofé Tape Archive 117.

158. Grofé insists that regardless of Whiteman's suggestion, he had "always had the idea" of writing something about the Grand Canyon. Ferde Grofé Tape Archive 116.

159. Ibid.

160. Ibid.

161. Ibid. Grofé was quick to point out that Debussy was not the first to use fifths. He cited Bach's chorales, "my musical Bible," as replete with augmented fifths.

162. Ibid.

163. Ibid.

164. Ibid.

165. Ibid. In this same interview, Grofé claimed that Toscanini declared his "Cloudburst" to contain "the greatest storm effect ever created in music." If Grofé didn't use many arpeggiated figures in this movement, he did use numerous glissandi.

166. See measures 65–89.

167. See measures 45–64.

168. See measures 89–143.

169. The score indicates a lightning machine at measure 157, although Grofé made no reference to it in the interview. See Ferde Grofé, *Grand Canyon Suite* (New York: Robbins Music Corporation, 1943), 150.

170. See measures 31–64.

171. This remark is not meant to suggest that 1930s culture was characterized exclusively by light diversionary works. On the contrary, an equally powerful effort was exerted to heighten awareness and involve large numbers of people in social organizations whose goals were political activism directed at correcting what were considered to be rampant social ills. Howard Clurman's "Group Theatre" is an example of this type of artistic effort.

172. Grofé's remark refers to aspects of America and Americans that had been cited over the years as characteristic features of the country: the size and beauty of the place, the virility of pioneers who settled it, and the power of its industrial might. All of these qualities have inspired pieces in this study. See " 'Carve Out Your Own Career,' from a conference with the Well-Known Composer, Orchestral Arranger and Radio Conductor Ferde Grofé. Secured expressly for *The Etude* Music Magazine by William Roberts Tilford." *The Etude* 56, no. 7 (July 1938): 425–426, 474. The quoted passage is the final paragraph of the article.

173. Ferde Grofé Tape Archive 117.

174. The reasons for Grofé's departure were numerous and complex and, according to the composer, included Mrs. Whiteman's interference in the daily management of the organization, her demands that Grofé "grind out a piece a week," and a clause in his new contract that gave all the rights to his arrangements and pieces to Paul Whiteman and, after him, to his heirs. On the advice of his lawyer, Grofé refused to sign the contract. He gave Whiteman four weeks' notice and left in January 1932. See Grofé Tape Archive 117. The economic climate had also hit Whiteman hard. Within a year he halved the size of his orchestra and cut pay among the remaining instrumentalists. Fresh from the success of *Grand Canyon,* Grofé must have felt some confidence that he could go it alone. Regardless of the cause of the rupture, over the years Grofé continued to supply Whiteman with arrangements from time to time, and he regularly took the opportunity to cite Paul Whiteman as among the greatest influences upon his career.

175. *Hollywood Ballet* (1936), *Café Society* (1938), *Kentucky Derby Suite* (1938), *Tin Pan Alley* (1939), and *Death Valley Suite* (1949). Given the nonexistence of an actual place Tin Pan Alley, it can be argued that this piece is not about a place at all, but rather about the music that was produced.

176. In an extended interview, Grofé spends much time discussing this event, including the number of people who attended (100,000), Jimmy Stewart's narration of the pageant, the traffic jam and resulting stalled cars in the desert, and many other aspects of the spectacle. See Ferde Grofé Tape Archive 117.

177. Grofé recalled a concert organized by Meredith Willson in which Kostelanetz was in attendance. The men were introduced at that time but did not keep up with each other in the intervening years. See Ferde Grofé Tape Archive 117.

178. Ibid. "I wrote a letter to Kostelanetz hoping something might come out of it."

179. Ibid.

180. Ferde Grofé Tape Archive 72.

181. Ibid. Whether or not this is true, it only matters that Grofé believed it to be.

182. Anne Grofé was an accomplished pianist and musician on her own. Grofé trusted her completely to oversee all editing and proofreading of the score.

183. Ferde Grofé Tape Archive 117.

184. Kostelanetz also recorded the *Mississippi Suite* and the *Grand Canyon Suite.*

185. There is some confusion regarding the number of movements of the suite. In an interview Grofé referred to a fifth movement, "New York." This "movement," however, because of its brevity, is most often combined with the fourth and follows immediately. Its title reads "Albany Night Boat—New York."

186. Juxtaposing movements about the sober Henry Hudson and the playful "Rip" allows Grofé to transfer character contrast to the music. Grofé might be dedicated to writing descriptive geographic pieces, but at the largest level he is guided by the exigencies of traditional musical form. This includes a relatively conventional approach to continuities and contrasts.

187. *The Sketch Book,* by Washington Irving, was published in 1820, at the beginning of the decade that saw the emergence of the Hudson River School of painters. Thomas Cole's oil painting *From the Top of Kaaterskill Falls* was completed in 1826. In the years that

followed, the Hudson River and its environs were captured in thousands of paintings. The place became associated with the nation's first artistic and literary traditions. Its continuing allure is attested to in Grofé's suite and one by Robert Starer, a composer who will be discussed in the following chapter.

188. Grofé offers extensive commentary on the composition of this work and, in particular, on the difficulties he experienced getting a dog to bark on cue. See Ferde Grofé Tape Archive, 117. He was always interested in the most realistic effects possible. According to Grofé, when Kostelanetz performed the work in Philadelphia, a set of bowling pins was positioned on stage and the state women's bowling champion enlisted to bowl on cue to recreate that part of the story in which Rip encounters the strange mountain people playing ninepins.

189. For an extended discussion of Grofé's dissatisfaction with this final movement, see Ferde Grofé Tape Archive 117. According to the composer, he originally wanted a "honeymoon couple accompanied by a jazz band. Kostelanetz wanted a Debussy beginning . . . and a percussion holiday at the end . . . just a lot of noise." Rather than argue with him, Grofé capitulated to Kostelanetz's suggestions.

190. Ferde Grofé Tape Archive 117.

191. As director of the 1939–40 New York World's Fair, Robert Moses had commissioned Grofé to write a work for that event. He obliged with the tone poem *Trylon and Perisphere*, in keeping with the theme of the fair. With very minor revisions, Grofé retitled this piece *Black Gold* and dedicated it to the Standard Oil Company of California. It premiered April 1945 on the *Standard Hour Concerts* series. Given their earlier history, it is not surprising that Moses should turn once again to Grofé.

192. See Farrington, "Ferde Grofé," 154.

193. Heinrich titled his coda "The Thunders of Niagara."

194. In none of the taped interviews does Grofé refer to this suite or his preparations for its composition. Given the way he worked on other suites, however, it is unlikely that he spent any time studying Native American music. Preparations most likely included a lengthy visit to the site, absorbing the sounds he heard, and reading up on the history of the Falls.

195. The Internet Movie Database, www.imdb.com (4 April 2003), lists many films, TV movies, and shorts that feature Niagara Falls as a setting. Among the most famous perhaps are *Niagara Falls*, a romantic comedy of 1941; *Niagara*, the Marilyn Monroe star maker of 1953; and *Superman II* of 1980, in which Lois Lane and Clark Kent declare their love to each other at the Falls.

196. Grofé indicates that the movement is to be played "dolce e espressivo." See *Niagara Falls Suite* manuscript score (New York: Robbins Music Corporation, 1961), 13.

197. See Eugene Thayer, "The Music of Niagara," *Scribner's Magazine*, February 1881, 586.

198. See "Grofé's America," *Time*, 38.

NOTES TO CHAPTER FIVE

1. These efforts were not restricted to the United States, but U.S. initiatives led the way throughout the world.

2.   See http://www.sierraclub.org/history/timeline.asp for statistics. The Sierra Club, one of many such groups, was, along with George Bird Grinnell's Audubon Society, among the very first. Grinnell organized his group in 1886 and within three months had 38,000 members. It disbanded briefly and reemerged as a preeminent group, beginning again in 1905. In 1951 the Nature Conservancy was organized. In 1970 the Environmental Protection Agency and the Natural Resources Defense Council were established, and the celebration of the first Earth Day took place. A whole spate of organizations emerged soon after, including Greenpeace in 1971 and Friends of the Earth in 1973.

3.   Kirk Johnson, "Town Immortalized by Art Is Divided over Industry," *New York Times,* 30 June 2001, B-1.

4.   Between 1997 and 1999, an exhibition entitled "All That Is Glorious Around Us: Paintings from the Hudson River School" toured throughout the Northeast and ended with a two-month show at the National Academy. At the same time, a show entitled "Landscapes in America, 1850–1890," appeared three thousand miles away in Tacoma, Washington. It included works by Church, Bierstadt, Homer, Inness, Kensett, and others. In July 1999 a story entitled "The Enduring Landscape" appeared in the *Chronicle of Higher Education.* With photos and text it presented the "unparalleled" tradition of paintings inspired by the Hudson River Valley, from the nineteenth century to the present. In the summer of 2001, the *New York Times* ran a series of ten articles on the landscape paintings of the Hudson River School. After decades of disfavor, landscape paintings enjoyed a renaissance of popularity.

5.   In art scholarship, the work of Barbara Novak is among the best known. Starting with *American Painting of the Nineteenth Century: Realism, Idealism, and the American Experience,* 2d ed. (Boulder, Colo.: Westview Press, 1979,) first published in 1969; and *Nature and Culture: American Landscape and Painting, 1825–1875* (published in 1980 and reprinted in 1995), Novak has systematically investigated the interactions between America's natural places and the nation's identity. *The Making of the American Landscape,* ed. Michael P. Conzen (New York and London: Routledge, 1994), looks at U.S. places with a geographer's eye and offers additional perspectives on the country's cultural landscape. These are just three among dozens of books that appeared in the closing decades of the twentieth century.

6.   The word "variety" is here, of course, restricted to responses by three composers of high-art music, a rarefied sampling of attitudes to be sure.

7.   Personal interview with the composer, 24 July 1999.

8.   Revealing most Long Islanders' preferred mode of travel into the city, the first movement is entitled "Mass Transit." The second movement, "'Hometown'—Syosset, USA," identifies the station where Perna would catch the Long Island Rail Road (LIRR).

9.   Personal interview with Ellen Taaffe Zwilich, 25 October 2001. While claiming no conscious effort to make this piece particularly American, Zwilich acknowledged that cultural values can be absorbed unconsciously and most likely have informed her attitudes regarding nature and place. For a discussion of the complex relationship between art and nature as a scientific laboratory, see Novak, *Nature and Culture,* part 2, "The Geological Timetable: Rocks," "The Meteorological Vision: Clouds," "The Organic Foreground: Plants," 47–134. For a discussion of America as a laboratory, see Thomas Philbrick, *St. John de Crèvecoeur* (New York: Twayne Publishers, 1970), 56.

10. See Kirk Johnson, "Artful Echoes, in Parks and Porches," *New York Times,* 2 September 2001, 24.

11. See Joyce Henri Robinson's essay "'Hi Honey, I'm Home': Weary (Neurasthenic) Businessmen and the Formulation of a Serenely Modern Aesthetic," in *Not at Home: The Suppression of Domesticity in Modern Art and Architecture* (London: Thames and Hudson, 1996), 98–112, for a discussion of how the idea of nature's palliative effects informed early modernist artists and manifested itself in their works. The quest for serenity that Robinson identifies as being important to the late-nineteenth-century domestic art scene is not unrelated to the search for retreat from urban chaos that has impelled many late-twentieth-century corporate types to drop out and seek solitude in the far reaches of the Rocky Mountain states. Each group has sought a therapeutic release in nature: the former in nature-inspired artworks that hung within the home; the latter by changing the entire environment and putting the home inside the more serene, natural environment. But nature, of course, is not always serene, as many of the modern-day Thoreaus soon learn.

12. Personal interview with Robert Starer, 14 July 1999, at his home in Woodstock, New York.

13. Ibid. Emphasis Starer's. The composer became a U.S. citizen in 1957.

14. In discussing the scope of this project with Robert Starer, we considered a number of potential composer subjects. As each came up, Starer observed, "I think you should concentrate on people to whom [place] meant something." It clearly did to him. Personal interview, 14 July 1999.

15. *Hudson Valley Suite* was premiered 14–15 October 1983. Imre Pallo conducted the Hudson Valley Philharmonic.

16. In his book *Continuo: A Life in Music* (New York: Random House, 1987), Robert Starer explains, "My first impulse is often rhythmic and only later do I shape the initial rhythmic idea melodically." His interest in rhythm is certainly borne out in the percussion arsenal of the *Hudson Valley Suite,* which includes four timpani, bass drum, tenor drum, two snare drums, four tom-toms, bongo drum, three suspended cymbals of varying sizes, three temple blocks, wood block, triangle, large gong, glockenspiel, and vibraphone. See Starer, *Continuo: A Life in Music,* 132.

17. Personal interview with Starer, 14 July 1999.

18. Robert Starer supplied a copy of composer's notes that appeared with the first performances. These are also reprinted in Robert Starer, *Hudson Valley Suite* (New York: Belwin-Mills, 1983), ii.

19. Ibid.

20. To this point the suite has concentrated on the natural environment exclusively.

21. Starer, *Hudson Valley Suite,* ii.

22. Starer, *Continuo,* 132.

23. Starer, *Hudson Valley Suite,* ii.

24. The phrase comes from the last line of Robert Underwood Johnson's poem "The Housatonic at Stockbridge." See chapter 2 on this Ives work.

25. Linda F. Burghardt, "Philharmonic Debut for a Tribute to L.I." *New York Times,* 22 March 1998, section 14LI, 15.

26.   Program notes from world premiere of *Prout's Neck,* Rochester Philharmonic Orchestra, Thursday, 28 October 1993.

27.   William Howe Downes, *The Life and Works of Winslow Homer* (Boston and New York: Houghton Mifflin, 1911), 119. Quoted in Patricia Junker, "Expressions of Art and Life in 'The Artist's Studio in Afternoon Fog,'" in *Winslow Homer in the 1890s: Prout's Neck Observed* (New York: Hudson Hills Press, 1990), 53.

28.   Junker, "Expressions of Art," 39–40. Junker explains: "By 1880 four express trains passed daily between Portland and Boston, in addition to the frequent local trains between Portland and Kennebunk. For travelers, another pleasant way to make the journey to southern Maine was via the inexpensive overnight steamer of the Boston and Portland line; from Portland, steamer passengers could catch a local train and be at Prout's Neck or nearby Old Orchard 'in time for early breakfast.'" Junker quotes from John Staples Locke, *Shores of Saco Bay: A Historical Guide to Biddeford Pool, Old Orchard Beach, Pine Point, Prout's Neck* (Boston: J. S. Locke, 1880), 88–89.

29.   Building their own homes also meant they did not have to socialize with anyone they didn't care to.

30.   For an extended discussion of the Homers' purchase and development of land at Prout's Neck, see Junker, "Expressions of Art," 40–53.

31.   Ibid., 53.

32.   Stevens added a second-story covered balcony that wrapped around two sides of the simple structure, thereby affording Homer the opportunity to scan the shore and waters and bring nature within his studio. For a discussion of the possible religious connotations of the studio architecture, see Junker, "Expressions of Art," 44–46.

33.   Ibid., 37–38. The trend continues to this day for artists of all types, as the final chapter on composer Steve Reich makes clear.

34.   Composer's program notes, Rockford Symphony Orchestra, 26 January 2002.

35.   Ibid.

36.   Most of Homer's paintings are of approximately this size. Dimension alone is one characteristic that distinguishes his works from the panoramic works of Church and Bierstadt, whose canvases often encompass many feet in either direction.

37.   Composer's program notes, Rockford Symphony Orchestra, 26 January 2002.

38.   In the composer's words: "'The Artist's Studio in Afternoon Fog' . . . is one of the two paintings to which I allude. This superb masterpiece of a sustained mood influenced the final third of my orchestral piece." The rest of the piece draws upon the other inspirational painting, *Right and Left,* which was Homer's penultimate work, done after he had suffered a stroke. Perna explains: "This painting depicts two ducks which were shot and are in stages of death: one is dead and is falling backwards, while the other has the look on its face that having been shot, it will fall forward, dead when it hits the water. This is somewhat more literally depicted within the structure of the music. I also thought that these two ducks had to have been shot by someone (perhaps hunters). There is some reference possibly alluding to this in the music." Composer's program notes, Rockford Symphony Orchestra, 26 January 2002.

39.   Perna uses this adverb numerous times: in measures 17, 39, 59, and 107, among other places.

40. See measure 53 for the "bird-like" piccolo, and measures 81 through 93 for Perna's more literal depiction of ducks being shot out of the air.

41. The larger piece actually traverses a much-expanded dynamic range, from triple *piano* to triple *forte*, with the loudest music occurring where Perna depicts the birds being shot and careening to their deaths. His own instructions to instrumentalists to "shriek" (measure 85) and "explode" (measure 90), along with all-involving descending glissandi, make a literal reading of this inspiration not inappropriate. Even with this more dramatic interlude, the predominant and lingering effect of the work is subdued containment.

42. For a particularly Debussyian moment, see measures 22–29. As has been discussed, the middle section is more narrative in nature.

43. Burghardt, "Philharmonic Debut," 15.

44. Ibid. Additional remarks in brackets come from notes to the score. See Dana Paul Perna, *Three Places on Long Island* (Pernaskopy Music, 1998), 1. Notes by Allen Jenkins, 1997.

45. Walt Whitman referred to Long Island as "fish-shape Paumanok" in his 1860 poem "Starting from Fish-Shape Paumanok, Where I Was Born." That poem achieved its final form in 1881. Paumanok was the name given to the island by its original Indian inhabitants. See Whitman, *Complete Poetry and Collected Prose*, 176.

46. Whitman refers to Paumanok many times in his poetry and prose. An 1865 poem begins, "From Paumanok starting I fly like a Bird." Whitman, *Complete Poetry and Selected Prose*, 420. Perna's version of the Whitman line is reminiscent of Charles Ives's many references to poems by Emerson and Thoreau, in which Ives caught the meaning of the words if not their exact articulation.

47. Perna, *Three Places*, notes to the score.

48. Burghardt quoting Perna in "Philharmonic Debut" 15.

49. "Majestic and commanding" are Perna's instructions to the instrumentalists. See Whitman, "The Mystic Trumpeter," *Complete Poetry and Collected Prose*, 579–580, stanza 1.

50. See "Beat! beat! drums!—blow! bugles! blow!" as another example of a poem that uses these martial instruments as a recurring image. Whitman, *Complete Poetry and Collected Prose*, 419–420.

51. Whitman, "The Mystic Trumpeter," stanza 8, line 65.

52. In a personal interview with the composer, 24 July 1999, Perna explained: "I am creating, not as someone being nationalistic."

53. Perhaps no other White House child would enjoy such adoration until "John John" Kennedy. He too died young and in a plane crash, but without the glory of going down in war.

54. Edward J. Renehan Jr., *The Lion's Pride: Theodore Roosevelt and His Family, in Peace and War* (New York: Oxford University Press, 1998), 5–6.

55. Andrew Carroll, *War Letters: Extraordinary Correspondence from American Wars* (New York: Scribner, 2001), 146–147. President Roosevelt wrote these lines in a letter to Mrs. Harvey L. Freeland dated 14 August 1918, exactly one month after Quentin's death.

56. This is the first movement of Ives's *Three Places in New England*. For two studies of this work, see Denise Von Glahn Cooney, "New Sources for 'The St. Gaudens' in Boston

Common (Colonel Robert Gould Shaw and His Colored Regiment),'" *Musical Quarterly* 81, no. 1 (spring 1997): 13–50; and Denise Von Glahn, "The Musical Monument of Charles Ives," in *Hope and Glory: Essays on the Legacy of the 54th Massachusetts Regiment,* ed. Martin H. Blatt, Thomas J. Brown, and Donald Yacovone (Amherst: University of Massachusetts Press, 2000).

57. Ives used a similar distant taps to close his chamber piece and song "The Pond," also known as "Remembrance."

58. The composer is quoted by Burghardt, "Philharmonic Debut," 15.

59. See "Elegy," measures 82–86; and "Evocation," measures 183–193.

60. See "Fanfare," measures 40–45; "Elegy," measures 76–78; and "Evocation," measures 129–132 in the piccolo for the morphing melody. The first two appearances of this melodic fragment consist of a descending minor third, rising minor second, descending minor third, rising major second, and descending major third, although the final descending interval does not appear in the second movement's version. They are distinguished from each other by key only. In "Evocation" the pattern becomes: descending tritone, rising major third, descending major sixth, rising tritone, descending major third. (These intervals are described in their simplest form. The opening descending tritone is actually written as a diminished fifth.) It is perhaps noteworthy that Perna instructs the soloist to play the melody in "Evocation" "with sweetness." Historically, tritones are intervals to be avoided; they have been dubbed "the devil in music." Given Perna's remarks about this movement, we can conclude that the composer hears something else in this interval.

61. This is the first stanza of Whitman's fifteen-line poem. The last suggests the sense of limitlessness that one can feel while looking out onto the ocean from Montauk Point: "Then we burst forth, we float,/In Time and Space, O Soul, prepared for them,/Equal, equipt at least, (O joy! O fruit of all!) them to fulfil,/O Soul." See Whitman, *Complete Poetry and Collected Prose,* 558.

62. I am extremely grateful to Ellen Taaffe Zwilich for hours of conversation about this piece, and about many other issues related to music and its place in America. The sensitivity that Zwilich exhibits to musical nuance is matched by an equal sensitivity to verbal nuance. She is a thoughtful spokesperson for her art.

63. W. J. Beal Botanical Garden, visitor's brochure (East Lansing, Mich.: University Publications).

64. Ibid.

65. The economic plants collection contains plants that are useful to humans—medicinal, aromatic, and fiber plants, as well as wild and cultivated varieties of vegetables, for example. See the garden brochure.

66. Personal interview with the composer, 25 October 2001.

67. Elaine M. Chittenden, "Endangered and Threatened Plants in Michigan" (East Lansing, Mich.: W. J. Beal Botanical Garden, Michigan State University, 1996).

68. Personal interview with the composer, 25 October 2001.

69. Thoreau, *Walden,* 238–239.

70. Henry David Thoreau, *Faith in a Seed: The Dispersion of Seeds and Other Late Natural History Writings* (Washington, D.C.: Island Press, 1993), 131.

71. Novak, *Nature and Culture,* 102, 104.

72.   Henry David Thoreau, *Selected Journals of Henry David Thoreau,* ed. Carl Bode (New York: Signet, 1967), 220–221. Quoted in Novak, *Nature and Culture,* 113.

73.   In a paper that the distinguished historian Joyce Appleby read before the American Historical Association on 9 January 1997, she observed that in the nineteenth century "most American history was compensatory, giving to the people an account that justified the country's egregious differences." Appleby concluded, "American history turned the nation's deficits into assets." This paper, "The Power of History," later appeared in the *American Historical Review* 103, no. 1 (February 1998). See page 13 for specific remarks.

74.   The capital letters are Stravinsky's and appear opposite the first page of music. See Igor Stravinsky, *Symphony of Psalms for Mixed Chorus and Orchestra* (London: Boosey and Hawkes, 1948).

75.   Zwilich explained that she had not thought of the Michigan State University gardens as an exhibit until she saw them. After viewing them, she "wanted to celebrate the gardens." Personal interview with the composer, 25 October 2001.

76.   Ibid.

77.   See measures 34 through 54 of the score. Ellen Taaffe Zwilich, Symphony No. 4, *"The Gardens,"* for Orchestra, with Mixed Chorus and Children's Chorus (Bryn Mawr, Pa.: Theodore Presser Company, 2000).

78.   See liner notes by Ellen Taaffe Zwilich, Symphony No. 4, Koch International Classics, 2000, CD 3-74877-2 HI.

79.   From the opening of the symphony to the close of the second movement, Zwilich begins her traverse through the A-minor triad that will outline the largest harmonic motion of the work.

80.   Zwilich, liner notes to Koch CD 3-74877-2 HI.

81.   Ibid. Avoiding literal depictions is an ongoing concern of many contemporary composers. In this study, the same sentiment has been articulated by composers as varied as Varèse, Perna, and Zwilich, and it will be repeated by Reich.

82.   See measures 58, 122, and 151 of the score.

83.   See starting at measure 105 of the score.

84.   See measures 219–222 of the score.

85.   See measures 242–243 of the score.

86.   See measures 105–112; 175–188.

87.   At this point Zwilich has completed her traverse of the A minor triad. She will work her way back to A by the close of the piece.

88.   This melody recalls the *Dies Irae,* a sequence from the medieval Requiem Mass (the Mass for the Dead). Throughout Western music history it has been borrowed by composers, including Berlioz, Liszt, Saint-Saëns, and Rachmaninoff, for various symbolic purposes. Whether Zwilich consciously intended to model her melody on this famous earlier one is not central to this discussion. The suggestion of the ancient melody brings with it its initial context and the weight of its subsequent uses. It may be that the greater prominence of bells in the third movement, and their associations with churches and religion, underscores the similarities of Zwilich's melody and the *Dies Irae* at this point in the symphony.

89.   See Zwilich, liner notes to Koch CD 3-74887-2 HI.

90. Ibid.

91. Isaiah 11:6.

92. Personal interview with the composer, 25 October 2001.

93. Stephanie Ross, *What Gardens Mean* (Chicago: University of Chicago Press, 1998), xi–xii.

94. Personal interview with the composer, 25 October 2001.

95. Ross, *What Gardens Mean,* xi.

96. Laura C. Martin, *Gardens of the Heartland* (New York: Abbeville Press, 1996), 60–61. Emphasis mine.

97. Ross, *What Gardens Mean,* 24.

98. Ibid., 11, 14.

99. Ibid., 11. Ross's discussion continues for more than two hundred pages. The above condensation does not pretend to offer a complete representation of her finely shaded argument, but selects only those points that have bearing on the present study. Among the topics that the current study does not address are the challenge of much modern art, which, Ross points out, "fails to fit any of the theories just mentioned," and current theories of reception and perception, which take the "art" out of the object and locate it in the observer. Ross discusses these ideas and more.

NOTES TO CHAPTER SIX

1. And perhaps with its mass culture: MacDonald's arches in Russia, Starbucks in London, Disneyland in Tokyo, its popular music everywhere. This is not to say that iconic "places" are not still identified with America. The destruction of the World Trade Center and bombing of the Pentagon on 11 September 2001 testify to the symbolic importance of specific places, although now the iconic places are often man-made structures.

2. William Carlos Williams, *I Wanted to Write a Poem: The Autobiography of the Works of a Poet* (New York: New Directions, 1978), 73. Elsewhere in this same volume, Williams addressed the issue of American language even more specifically: "From the beginning I knew that the American language must shape the pattern; later I rejected the word language and spoke of the American idiom—this was a better word than language, less academic, more identified with speech" (65).

3. During a phone interview with Steve Reich on 5 June 2002, the composer observed that Williams's "localness is his universality," a sentiment similar to that which has been expressed regarding Charles Ives, another American who drew upon vernacular culture.

4. For a lengthy discussion of what Reich means by this term, see his essay "Music and Language" (1996), reprinted in Reich, *Writings on Music, 1965–2000* (New York: Oxford University Press, 2002), 193–201. He quotes extensively from the Hungarian composers Janáček and Bartók, whose music reflects the cadences of their native language. This concept was first articulated by Leoš Janáček in 1918.

5. Reich explains that his interest in African music developed as a result of studying with William Austin at Cornell, followed by further work of his own. In 1962 Gunther Schuller recommended that the young composer consult A. M. Jones's book *Studies in African Music,* originally published in 1949 as part of the Occasional Papers of the Rhodes-Livingstone Museum Series. It was reprinted in 1958 under the expanded title *African Music*

in Northern Rhodesia and Some Other Places (preface by J. Desmond Clark, director, Rhodes-Livingstone Museum; no location or publisher given). Although only eighty pages in length, this book contains chapters on African singing, the creation of African songs, drumming, musical instruments, the social background of Barotse music, and two critical essays, "African Drumming" and "The Study of African Musical Rhythms." Even a cursory survey of the book reveals how confirming and inspiring this volume must have been for the young composer, who had heard much African music but not studied its construction. Numerous examples of multiple, relatively simple, simultaneous, staggered "crossing" rhythms call to mind Reich's phase pieces. As Reich later explained in an interview: "Bear in mind that before I went to Africa [in 1970] I'd done *Piano Phase,* all of the tape pieces, *Violin Phase, Phase Patterns* (which is *Drumming* on the keyboard), *Four Organs,* polyrhythmic pieces in 12/8, everything. All the new information came from the Jones book." Even as Jones distinguishes African rhythm from jazz, in which style he says "the essence of syncopation is to throw emphasis on the main beats" (Jones, *African Music,* 22), Reich asserts, "I never would have become as interested in African music if I hadn't been an American and raised on jazz." See William Duckworth, *Talking Music* (New York: Schirmer Books, 1995), 304–305.

6. These two works are exemplars of Reich's ideas concerning American speech melody, as well as his position on civil rights issues.

7. Edward Strickland, *Minimalism: Origins* (Bloomington: Indiana University Press, 1993), 226.

8. These trains rides took place in 1937–40. As Reich observed in a phone interview, 5 June 2002: "The words 'New York' and 'Los Angeles' keep cropping up in *Different Trains,* especially at the beginning and ending of the piece. Place plays a role. But it isn't really central to the work."

9. Reich, phone interview, 5 June 2002.

10. By extension, Reich uses only instruments he can find in his local environs, hence no African drums or bells. In an interview with Edward Strickland, he made this very clear: "If it isn't on 48th Street, the hell with it! That's my attitude." Reich also eschews ensembles that fuse an exotic instrument from another culture within an otherwise Western setting: "They try to adapt the *sounds* rather than the structures of an alien culture, which is really the most superficial aspect of its music—the sitar-in-the-rock-band phenomenon—though the composers I'm thinking of are anything but superficial themselves." See Edward Strickland, *American Composers: Dialogues on Contemporary Music* (Bloomington: Indiana University Press, 1991), 42–43. In addition to philosophical objections, this position has practical ramifications as well. When writing a work as conservative as his *Vermont Counterpoint,* Reich included a part for alto flute in his score, knowing that most flutists had one in their possession. He did not include a bass flute because most flutists do not.

11. Reich, phone interview, 5 June 2002.

12. Reich, *Writings on Music,* 127.

13. Ibid., 128.

14. Reich, phone interview, 5 June 2002. The emphasis is Reich's.

15. Reich has since spent long periods in the deserts of the Middle East while working on *The Cave* (1993), a documentary video-music theater work in three acts, co-created with Beryl Korot.

16. Reich, phone interview, 5 June 2002.

17. Reich's aversion to traditional formal structures and the genres they spawn grows out of his adherence to strict processes, which do not conform to the harmonic behaviors required by those forms. In his texted pieces, language dictates the micro and macro shapes of the works.

18. Reich welcomes this kind of performance, especially as it relates to *New York Counterpoint*. As a real fan of the clarinet sound, he believes that a fully live performance allows for a greater "clarinet-ness" to emerge. Reich generally prefers acoustic sound over taped or electronic music. Reich, phone interview, 5 June 2002.

19. In addition to *Vermont Counterpoint* (1982) and *New York Counterpoint* (1985), Reich has written *Electric Counterpoint* (1987) for the guitarist Pat Metheny, and he has plans to write *Cello Counterpoint* for Maya Beiser.

20. Reich, phone interview, 5 June 2002.

21. See composer's program notes, *Vermont Counterpoint* (London: Hendon Music, Boosey and Hawkes, 1982), unnumbered page.

22. A version of this piece, titled *Tokyo/Vermont Counterpoint*, which Mika Yoshida arranged for electronically sampled (MIDI) marimbas, bears no resemblance at all to the softer, gentler flute work. As Reich explained, "The Japanese have a proclivity for very sharp, percussive sound. I call this arrangement *Vermont Counterpoint Goes South*." Reich, phone interview 5 June 2002.

23. Reich, phone interview, 5 June 2002.

24. Ibid.

25. Ibid.

26. Reich himself used the word "love" to describe his feelings about the clarinet sound. Reich, phone interview, 5 June 2002.

27. Ibid.

28. K. Robert Schwarz, liner notes, Steve Reich, *Bang on a Can, New York Counterpoint, Eight Lines, Four Ogans,* Nonesuch 79481–2. Schwarz adds, "Its tricky, pervasive syncopations are indebted to jazz, and Reich admits that, while writing the piece, he could not banish thoughts of Benny Goodman and earlier jazz."

29. Reich explained: "When I close my eyes, it's black. I don't have imagery when I close my eyes" (phone interview, 5 June 2002). In another instance, however, he described a *vision* he had "where light became a metaphor for harmony, for tonality. . . . I used to get a vision of a kind of barge of light, floating down a river in very dark surroundings, in complete darkness. . . . And it sails, in my mind, like a ship of light down an endlessly dark corridor, preserving itself as long as it can" (Reich, *Writings on Music,* 131). Distinctions between images and visions may involve degrees of difference between more purely visual manifestations and intellectual constructs.

30. Reich, phone interview, 5 June 2002.

31. For a discussion of the French influence in Reich's music, see William Duckworth's conversation with the composer as transcribed in *Talking Music,* 314.

32. In the first movement, "Fast," the pulsing chord is all that is heard for the first minute and a half of the piece. It returns intermittently for the last minute and a half of the five-minute movement as well. In the second movement, "Slow," a similar pulsing

chord enters approximately 1:12 into the two-minute, forty-four second piece, and then drops out for the last time around 2:29.

33.   This flexibility has an analogue in William Carlos Williams's idiomatic poetry. The writer referred to the elastic quality of American syllable lengths that colored vernacular speech patterns as the "flexible foot." It would seem that Reich heard a similar quality in American jazz and commandeered it for his piece. Many African rhythms use a 12/8 meter, which is discussed as such in the A. M. Jones book, *African Music.*

34.   Reich, *Writings on Music,* 130.

35.   The piece uses twenty-seven vocalists and up to eighty-nine instrumentalists. For a complete listing of the performing forces and their placement on stage, see Steve Reich, *The Desert Music* (London: Boosey and Hawkes), 1984, front matter.

36.   Williams, *I Wanted to Write a Poem,* 29.

37.   Ibid., 88. Emphasis is Williams's. When discussing an early collection, *Sour Grapes,* Williams explained, "To me, at that time, a poem was an image, *the picture* was the important thing," 35. Emphasis mine.

38.   The book of the prophet Isaiah is especially rich in references to the desert, which is portrayed as a potentially dangerous place that can be transformed by faith into "the garden of the Lord." Isaiah 51:3. The last line of the same verse reads, "joy and gladness shall be found therein, thanksgiving, and the voice of melody."

39.   Reich, *Writings on Music,* 217.

40.   William Carlos Williams, *Selected Poems,* ed. Charles Tomlinson (New York: New Directions, 1985), 204–205.

41.   Ibid., 205.

42.   The entire text is sung twice in the second movement and once in the fourth.

43.   Reich, *The Desert Music,* unnumbered page.

44.   Ibid., 205. Williams was always striving for the most efficient expression, and hence eliminating repetitions. It seems that he would have distinguished his own vernacular-based poetry from music, especially Reich's repetitive music. Perhaps he did not hear the American vernacular as particularly musical in the traditional sense of the word. In describing his work *The Complete Collected Poems of William Carlos Williams, 1906–1938* (Norfolk, Conn.: New Directions, 1938), Williams recalled: "I remembered writing several poems as quatrains at first, then in the normal process of concentrating the poem, getting ride of redundancies in the line—and in the attempt to make it go faster—the quatrain changed into a three line stanza, or a five line stanza became a quatrain" (*I Wanted to Write a Poem,* 66).

45.   William Carlos Williams, *Asphodel, That Greeny Flower, and Other Love Poems* (New York: New Directions, 1994), 37, 40.

46.   Ibid., 40.

47.   Reich, *Writings on Music.* An earlier book, *Writings about Music* (Halifax: Press of Nova Scotia College of Art and Design), appeared in 1974. The new volume includes what appeared there and more. See also *Steve Reich: The Desert Music,* Nonesuch Digital 79101-2.

48.   Reich, *Writings on Music,* 121.

49.   Ibid.

50. Ibid., 128.

51. Ibid., 124. Perhaps Reich, like a modern Isaiah, believes that joy, gladness, thanksgiving, and "the voice of melody" reside within the desert, if we don't destroy ourselves first. See Isaiah 51:3.

52. Reich's debt to Stravinsky is audible in these tight, percussive, piano clusters.

53. Reich, *Writings on Music,* 128. In the score Reich instructs the singers: "'De De' is pronounced like the English 'be,' as in 'to *be* or not to *be.*'" See Reich, *The Desert Music,* 2. His inclusion of the Shakespearean quote itself seems to speak to the essential issue that he raises in the piece: whether humanity will continue to exist.

54. The third movement contains its own archlike three-part form within the larger five-movement piece, thus creating a symmetrical shape within a larger one. This movement is longer than any of the others, close to eighteen and a half minutes. The first and second movements require approximately fifteen minutes total, as do the fourth and fifth, creating another symmetrical aspect of the piece. Tempi of movements are symmetrical as well: the first movement is fast; the second moderate; the third slow-moderate-slow; the fourth moderate; the fifth fast. Familiar with Bartók's music, Reich was keenly aware of that composer's use of five-part arch form.

55. Reich quoted in Strickland, *American Composers,* 49.

56. Reich, *The Desert Music,* 187. Reich explained that his inspiration for using the siren sound came from a real fire siren he heard during the summer of 1983 at his Vermont home. He immediately knew this was the effect he needed.

57. Reich, *Writings on Music,* 124.

58. Orwell's novel about a totalitarian government controlling all aspects of people's lives and thoughts was published in 1949. Its prescient, fictional description of a world run rampant with "doublespeak" and "newspeak" is nightmarishly real in 2003.

59. The melodic fragment is initially raised a half-step but returns to its original pitch content at rehearsal 318.

60. An example of the scoring of Reich's luminescent sound can be found at rehearsal 366. He achieved similar effects in 1981 in his first work to set text, *Tehillim.*

61. Beryl Korot is a documentary video artist, weaver, and writer. She has been Steve Reich's wife since 1976. They have a son, Ezra, born in 1978. Reich is especially satisfied with *Different Trains,* referring to it as "one of the best pieces I've ever done in my life." Reich, phone interview, 5 June 2002.

62. Percussion include two vibraphones, cymbals, snare drum, and two bass drums, one high and one low.

63. Reich, phone interview, 5 June 2002. Reich lived four blocks from the World Trade Center, which was bombed for the first time in 1993. Nine years later the effects of that event and the more cataclysmic 2001 attacks weigh heavily on the composer's mind: "I'm still sitting here wondering if the Muslim Fundamentalist terrorists who've threatened to put an atom bomb in New York are going to succeed or not. It's a clear and present danger."

64. The recorded voices become part of the sampled sounds that are retrieved at the sampler. The absence of taped music allows for a more spontaneous performance, and hence a potentially more intimate one.

65. In this regard, it is not unlike Copland's opening of *Quiet City.*

66. Introductory music returns at the end of the first movement to frame that movement, although the frame remains open. Like the meters themselves, the first movement will elide directly into the second. All movements move attacca one to the next.

67. Reich, liner notes to *Steve Reich, City Life, Proverb,* Nonesuch CD 79430-2.

68. Reich, phone interview, 5 June 2002.

69. Reich, liner notes to *Steve Reich, City Life, Proverb,* Nonesuch CD 79430-2. These four dominant-function chords can be heard for the first time in the second movement at measures 213, 239, 252, and 271.

70. Ibid.

NOTES TO CONCLUSIONS: WHERE WE ARE

1. J. Hector St. John de Crèvecoeur, *Lettres d'un cultivateur américain,* 2 vols. (Paris: Cuchet, 1784).

2. Thomas Philbrick has observed that late-eighteenth-century attitudes were "transforming farming from folk art into a technology." See Philbrick, *St. John de Crèvecoeur,* 56.

3. See ibid., 95, for a discussion of the folk legends upon which Crèvecoeur draws.

4. For a discussion of the extent of Crèvecoeur's debt to Raynal, see ibid., 44–45, 67–70, and especially 94–95. As Philbrick shows, Thomas-François-Guillaume Raynal's book *A Philosophical and Political History of the British Settlements and Trade in North America* (Edinburgh: C. Denovan, 1779) provided a close model for Crèvecoeur in content and style.

5. J. Hector St. John de Crèvecoeur, *Letters from an American Farmer,* ed. Susan Manning (Oxford: Oxford University Press, 1997), viii.

6. Ibid., 25, 27.

7. Quoted in Upton's *Anthony Philip Heinrich,* 50.

8. Crèvecoeur, *Letters,* 45, 48.

9. Ibid., 187.

10. Philbrick observes, "The natural world which the book has pictured, a world which begins as a peaceable kingdom . . . ends as a jungle of hostility" (*St. John de Crèvecoeur,* 105).

11. It is doubtful whether Crèvecoeur's/Farmer James's observations were understood by many at the time to be much more than they purported to be. Regardless of their documentary or artistic merits, they remain the emotionally charged reactions of a Franco-American, British-loyalist farmer caught in the crossfire of the American Revolution.

12. Crèvecoeur, *Letters,* xxxvi.

SELECT BIBLIOGRAPHY

Adamson, Jeremy Elwell. "Nature's Grandest Scene in Art." In *Niagara: Two Centuries of Changing Attitudes, 1697–1901,* ed. Jeremy Adamson Edwell. Washington, D.C.: Corcoran Gallery of Art, 1985.

Allen, Frederick Lewis. *Only Yesterday: An Informal History of the 1920s.* New York: John Wiley and Sons, 1997.

Anderson, Jervis. *This Was Harlem: A Cultural Portrait, 1900–1950.* New York: Farrar, Straus and Giroux, 1982.

Appleby, Joyce. "The Power of History." *American Historical Review* 103, no. 1 (February 1998).

Arvey, Verna. *In One Lifetime.* Fayetteville: University of Arkansas Press, 1984.

———. *Studies of Contemporary American Composers: William Grant Still.* New York: J. Fischer and Bro., 1939.

Barg, Lisa. "Black Voices/White Sounds: Race and Representation in Virgil Thomson's *Four Saints in Three Acts.*" *American Music* 18, no. 2 (summer 2000): 121–161.

Beadle and Adams Dime Novel Digitization Project. A Project of the Northern Illinois University Libraries, DeKalb, Ill. http://www.niulib.niu.edu/badndp (4 April 2003).

Beckerman, Michael. "The Dance of Pau-Puk-Keewis, the Song of Chibiabos, and the Story of Iagoo: Reflections on Dvořák's 'New World' Scherzo." In *Dvořák in America, 1892–1895,* ed. John C. Tibbetts. Portland, Oreg.: Amadeus Press, 1993.

Bellamann, Henry. "Charles Ives: The Man and His Music." *Musical Quarterly* 19 (1933): 45–58.

Bernard, Jonathan. *The Music of Edgard Varèse.* New Haven: Yale University Press, 1987.

Biancolli, Louis. *The Concert Companion: A Comprehensive Guide to Symphonic Music.* New York and London: McGraw-Hill, 1947.

Blaugrund, Annette. *The Tenth Street Studio Building: Artist Entrepeneurs from the Hudson River School to the American Impressionists.* Southampton, N.Y.: Parrish Art Museum, 1997.

Bode, Carl, in collaboration with Malcom Cowley, eds. *The Portable Emerson.* New York: Viking Press, 1981.

Bremer, Fredericka. *The Homes of the New World.* 2 vols. London: Hall, Virtue, 1853.

Bristow, George Frederick. Sketches to *Niagara: Symphony for Grand Orchestra and Chorus.* New York: New York Public Library, Microfilms ZZ2935, reels 1–3.

Brodhead, Thomas M. "Ives's Celestial Railroad and His Fourth Symphony." *American Music* 12, no. 4 (winter 1994): 389–424.

Broyles, Michael. *Mavericks and Other Traditions in American Music.* New Haven: Yale University Press, forthcoming.

———. *"Music of the Highest Class": Elitism and Populism in Antebellum Boston.* New Haven: Yale University Press, 1992.

Bryant, William Cullen, ed. *Picturesque America; or, The Land We Live In. A Delineation by Pen and Pencil of the Mountains, Rivers, Lakes, Forests, Water-falls, Shores, Canons, Valleys, Cities, and Other Picturesque Features of Our Country. With Illustrations on Steel and Wood by Eminent American Artists.* 2 vols New York: D. Appleton, 1874.

Burghardt, Linda F. "Philharmonic Debut for a Tribute to L.I." *New York Times,* 22 March 1998, section 14LI, 15.

Burkholder, J. Peter. *All Made of Tunes: Charles Ives and the Uses of Musical Borrowing.* New Haven: Yale University Press, 1995.

———. *Charles Ives: The Ideas Behind the Music.* New Haven: Yale University Press, 1985.

———, ed. *Charles Ives and His World.* Princeton: Princeton University Press, 1996.

Cage, John. *Silence: Lectures and Writings by John Cage.* Middletown, Conn.: Wesleyan University Press, 1961.

Carroll, Andrew. *War Letters: Extraordinary Correspondence from American Wars.* New York: Scribner, 2001.

Carter, Elliott. "France-America Ltd." Trans. by Jonathan Bernard. In *Composers on Modern Musical Culture: An Anthology of Readings on Twentieth-Century Music.* New York: Schirmer Books, 1999.

Casey, Edward S. *The Fate of Place: A Philosophical History.* Berkeley and Los Angeles: University of California Press, 1998.

———. *Representing Place: Landscape Paintings and Maps.* Minneapolis: University of Minnesota Press, 2002.

Champlain, Samuel de. *Voyages.* Trans. Charles Pomeroy Otis. Boston, 1880; reprint, New York: Burt Franklin, 1966.

Chase, Gilbert. *America's Music: From the Pilgrims to the Present.* Rev. 3d ed. Urbana: University of Illinois Press, 1987.

Chittenden, Elaine M. "Endangered and Threatened Plants in Michigan." East Lansing, Mich.: W.J. Beal Botanical Garden, Michigan State University, 1996.

Chmaj, Betty E. "Father Heinrich as Kindred Spirit: Or How the Log-House Composer of Kentucky Became the Beethoven of America." *American Studies* 24, no. 2 (fall 1983): 35–57.

Church, F. E. *F. E. Church's Painting of Nature's Grandest Scene; The Great Fall, Niagara. Painted by F. E. Church.* New York: Williams, Stevens, Williams and Co., 1857.

Clurman, Harold. *The Fervent Years: The Story of the Group Theatre and the Thirties.* New York: Alfred A. Knopf, 1945.

Collier, James Lincoln. *Duke Ellington.* New York: Oxford University Press, 1987.

Conzen, Michael P., ed. *The Making of the American Landscape.* New York and London: Routledge, 1994.

Copland, Aaron. *Music for the Theatre: Suite in Five Parts for Small Orchestra.* New York: Boosey and Hawkes, 1960.

———. "One Hundred and Fourteen Songs." *Modern Music* 11, no. 2 (January–February 1934).

———. *Quiet City.* New York: Hawkes and Son, 1941.

Copland, Aaron, and Vivian Perlis. *Copland: 1900 through 1942.* New York: St. Martin's/ Marek, 1984.

———. *Copland: Since 1943.* New York: St. Martin's Press, 1990.

Crèvecoeur, J. Hector St. John de. *Letters from an American Farmer,* ed. Susan Manning. Oxford: Oxford University Press, 1997.

Culbertson, Evelyn David. *He Heard America Singing: Arthur Farwell, Composer and Crusading Music Educator.* Metuchen, N.J.: Scarecrow, 1992.

Danly, Susan, and Leo Marx, eds. *The Railroad in American Art: Representations of Technological Change.* Cambridge: MIT Press, 1988.

de Kooning, Elaine. *The Spirit of Abstract Expressionism: Selected Writings*. New York: George Braziller, 1994.

———. "Subject: What, How, or Who?" *Art News*, April 1955, 61–62.

Dewey, Frederick. "Cimarron Jack, the King-Pin of Rifle-Shots; Or, The Phantom Tracker, a Tale of the Land of Silence." Beadle's Half-Dime Library, 24 July 1883. (Florida State University Strozier Library, Microfilm 8509, reel 60:58).

Donovan, Frank P., Jr., *The Railroad in Literature: A Brief Survey of Railroad Fiction, Poetry, Songs, Biography, Essays, Travel and Drama in the English Language, Particularly Emphasizing Its Place in American Literature*. Boston: Railway and Locomotive Historical Society, 1940.

Dow, Charles Mason, LL.D. *Anthology and Bibliography of Niagara Falls*. Albany: State of New York, 1921.

Downes, William Howe. *The Life and Works of Winslow Homer*. Boston and New York: Houghton Mifflin, 1911.

Driscoll, John. *All That Is Glorious around Us: Paintings from the Hudson River School*. Ithaca, N.Y.: Cornell University Press, 1997.

Du Bois, W. E. B. *The Souls of Black Folk*. 1903; reprint, New York: Penguin, 1995.

Duckworth, William. *Talking Music*. New York: Schirmer Books, 1995.

Dwight, John Sullivan. *Dwight's Journal of Music*. New York: Johnson Reprint, 1968.

"Edna Ferber, Novelist, 82, Dies." *New York Times*, 17 April 1968.

Egan, Timothy. "As Others Abandon Plains, Indians and Bison Come Back." *New York Times*, 27 May 2001, 1.

Ellington, Edward Kennedy. *Harlem*. Arranged by Luther Henderson and Maurice Peress. New York: G. Schirmer Rental Library (copyist's manuscript).

———. *Music Is My Mistress*. Garden City, N.Y.: Doubleday, 1973.

Emerson, Ralph Waldo. *Ralph Waldo Emerson: Essays and Lectures*. New York: Literary Classics of the United States, 1983.

Farr, Cheryl Leas. *Frommer's 2000 New York City*. New York: Macmillan, 1999.

Farrington, James. "Ferde Grofé: An Investigation into His Musical Activities and Works." Master's thesis, Florida State University, 1985.

Farwell, Arthur. "Roy Harris." *Musical Quarterly* 18 (1932): 18–32.

Feder, Stuart. "Charles Ives and Henry David Thoreau: 'A Transcendental Tune of Concord.'" In *Ives Studies*, ed. Philip Lambert. New York: Cambridge University Press, 1997.

———. "Thoreau Was Somewhere Near: The Ives-Thoreau Connection." In *Thoreau's World and Ours*, ed. Edmund A. Schofield and Robert C. Baron. Golden, Colo.: North American Press, 1993.

Feld, Steven, and Keith H. Basso, eds. *Senses of Place*. Santa Fe, N.Mex.: School of American Research Press, distributed by the University of Washington Press, Seattle, 1996.

Ferber, Edna. *Cimarron*. New York: Doubleday, 1931.

Flexner, Thomas. *That Wilder Image: The Painting of America's Native School, from Thomas Cole to Winslow Homer*. Boston: Little, Brown, 1962.

Fry, William Henry. *Niagara Symphony*. Philadelphia Free Library, unpublished score.

Green, Constance McLaughlin. *Washington: Capital City, 1879–1950*. Princeton: Princeton University Press, 1963.

Grofé, Ferde. *Grand Canyon Suite*. New York: Robbins Music Corporation, 1943.

———. *Mississippi Suite*. New York: Leo Feist, 1926.

————. *Niagara Falls Suite.* New York: Robbins Music Corporation, 1961.

————. Interview by anonymous interviewer. Tape 114, Ferde Grofé Tape Archive, Florida State University, Allen Music Library.

————. Interview by anonymous interviewer, 14 October 1966, Laguna Beach, Calif. Tape 95, Ferde Grofé Tape Archive, Florida State University, Allen Music Library.

————. Interview by Joe O'Brien, 27 July 1940, New York World's Fair. Tape 55, Ferde Grofé Tape Archive, Florida State University, Allen Music Library.

————. Interview by Bruce Wendell, 7 July 1957, Beverly Hills, Calif. Tape 72, Ferde Grofé Tape Archive, Florida State University, Allen Music Library.

"Grofé's America." *Time* 24, no. 3 (1 February 1937): 38.

Guernsey, A. H. "Niagara." *Harper's Monthly,* August 1853, 289–305.

Haas, Robert Bartlett, ed. *William Grant Still and the Fusion of Cultures in American Music.* Los Angeles: Black Sparrow Press, 1972.

Harris, Roy. *Cimarron: Symphonic Overture.* New York: Mills Music, 1941.

————. *Concerto for Piano and Strings; Elegy and Dance; Cimarron: Symphonic Overture; Toccata, Chorale and Fantasy: For Organ, Brass and Timpani.* SRV 347SD Bay Cities BCD-1002 Stereo Classical.

————. "Folksong—American Big Business." *Modern Music* 18, no. 1 (November–December 1940): 8–11.

Haugen, Einar, and Camilla Cai. *Ole Bull: Norway's Romantic Musician and Cosmopolitan Patriot.* Madison: University of Wisconsin Press, 1993.

Heinrich, Anthony Philip. *The War of the Elements and the Thundering of Niagara: Capriccio Grande for a Full Orchestra.* Ed. Andrew Stiller. Philadelphia: Kallisti Music Press, 1994.

Heller, Adele, and Lois Rudnick, eds. *1915 the Cultural Moment: The New Politics, the New Woman, the New Psychology, the New Art, and the New Theatre in America.* New Brunswick, N.J.: Rutgers University Press, 1991.

Helmholtz, Hermann. *On the Sensations of Tone as a Physiological Basis for the Theory of Music.* Trans. Alexander John Ellis. London: Longmans, Green, 1875.

Hentoff, Nat, and Nat Shapiro, eds. *Hear Me Talkin' to Ya: The Story of Jazz as Told by the Men Who Made It.* London: Peter Davies, 1955. Reprint, New York: Dover Publications, 1966.

Herbert, Robert L. *Modern Artists on Art: Ten Unabridged Essays.* Englewood Cliffs, N.J.: Prentice-Hall, 1964.

Hitchcock, H. Wiley. *Music in the United States: A Historical Introduction.* 3d ed. Englewood Cliffs, N.J.: Prentice-Hall, 1988.

Horan, James D. *Across the Cimarron: The Adventures of "Cimarron" George Bolds, Last of the Frontiersmen.* New York: Crown Books, 1956.

Horowitz, Joseph. *Wagner Nights.* Berkeley and Los Angeles: University of California Press, 1994.

Howard, John Tasker. *Our American Music: Three Hundred Years of It.* New York: Thomas Y. Crowell, 1931.

————. *Our Contemporary Composers: American Music in the Twentieth Century.* New York: Thomas Y. Crowell, 1941.

Howells, William Dean. *The Niagara Book.* New York: Doubleday, Page, 1901.

Hughes, Langston. *The Collected Poems of Langston Hughes.* Ed. Arnold Rampersad and David Roessel. New York: Alfred A. Knopf, 1994.

Hughes, Robert. *American Visions: The Epic History of Art in America.* New York: Alfred A. Knopf, 1997.

Ives, Charles E. *Memos.* Ed. John Kirkpatrick. New York: W. W. Norton, 1972.

———. *A New England Symphony: Three Places in New England.* Ed. James B. Sinclair. Bryn Mawr, Pa.: Mercury Music Corporation, 1976.

———. *114 Songs.* Self-published in Redding, Conn., 1922. Reprint, New York: Peer International, Associated Music Publishers, and Theodore Presser, 1975.

———. *Orchestral Set No. 2.* Ed. James B. Sinclair. New York: Peer Music, 2001.

———. *Symphony No. 4.* New York: Associated Music Publishers, 1965.

James, Henry. *Portraits of Places.* Boston: James R. Osgood, 1884.

Janick, Herbert. "'Connecticut' the Suburban State." *Connecticut Humanities Council News* (fall 1993): 7.

Johnson, Frederick H. *A Guide for Every Visitor to Niagara Falls.* Rochester, N.Y.: D. M. Dewey, 1852.

Johnson, Kirk. "Town Immortalized by Art Is Divided over Industry." *New York Times,* 30 June 2001.

Johnson, Robert Underwood. *Songs of Liberty, and Other Poems.* New York: Century, 1897.

Jones, A. M. *African Music in Northern Rhodesia and Some Other Places,* preface by J. Desmond Clark, director, Rhodes Livingstone Museum, 1958. No location or publisher is given.

Junker, Patricia. "Expressions of Art and Life in 'The Artist's Studio in an Afternoon Fog.'" In *Winslow Homer in the 1890s: Prout's Neck Observed.* New York: Hudson Mills Press, 1990.

Kammen, Michael. *American Culture, American Tastes: Social Change in the Twentieth Century.* New York: Alfred A. Knopf, 1999.

Kandinsky, Wassily. "Reminiscences/Three Pictures." Reprinted in *Kandinsky: Complete Writings on Art, 1901–1921,* vol. 1, ed. Kenneth C. Lindsay and Peter Vergo. Boston: G. K. Hall, 1982.

Katz, Bernard, ed. *The Social Implications of Early Negro Music in the United States.* New York: Arno Press and the New York Times, 1969.

Lambert, Eddie. *Duke Ellington: A Listener's Guide.* Metuchen, N.J.: Scarecrow Press, 1999.

Lawrence, Vera Brodsky. *Strong on Music: The New York Music Scene in the Days of George Templeton Strong, 1836–1875,* vol. 1, *Resonances.* New York: Oxford University Press, 1988.

———. *Strong on Music: The New York Music Scene in the Days of George Templeton Strong, 1836–1875,* vol. 2, *Reverberations, 1850–1856.* Chicago and London: University of Chicago Press, 1995.

Levy, Beth E. "'The White Hope of American Music': Or, How Roy Harris Became Western." *American Music* 19, no. 2 (summer 2001): 131–167.

Lipman, Samuel. "Copland as American Composer." *Commentary* 61 (1976): 70–74.

Locke, Alain. *The New Negro: An Interpretation.* New York: A. and C. Boni, 1925.

Locke, John Staples. *Shores of Saco Bay: A Historical Guide to Biddeford Pool, Old Orchard Beach, Pine Point, Prout's Neck.* Boston: J. S. Locke, 1880.

Lowens, Irving. *Music and Musicians in Early America.* New York: W. W. Norton, 1964.

Martin, Laura C. *Gardens of the Heartland.* New York: Abbeville Press, 1996.

Martin, Linton. "Catcalls Greet Orchestra Work." *Philadelphia Inquirer,* 10 April 1926, 10.

Marx, Leo. *The Machine in the Garden: Technology and the Pastoral Ideal in America.* New York: Oxford University Press, 1964.

Mattis, Olivia. "Edgard Varèse and the Visual Arts." Ph.D. dissertation, Stanford University, 1992.

McFarland, Horace J. "Shall We Make a Coal-Pile of Niagara?" *Ladies' Home Journal* 23 (October 1906): 39.

Mellers, Wilfrid. *Music in a New Found Land: Themes and Developments in the History of American Music*. New York: Oxford University Press, 1987.

Meredith, Sarah. "Twentieth-Century Music in the Fourth and Fifth Grade Textbooks of Silver Burdett, 1960–1990." Unpublished paper, Florida State University, December 2001.

Metzer, David Joel. "The Ascendency of Musical Modernism in New York City, 1915–1929." Ph.D. dissertation, Yale University, 1993.

Miller, Perry. *The Life of the Mind in America, from the Revolution to the Civil War*. New York: Harcourt, Brace and World, 1965.

———. *Nature's Nation*. Cambridge: Harvard University Press, 1967.

———. "The Shaping of the American Character." *New England Quarterly* 28, no. 4 (December 1955): 435–454.

———, ed. *The Transcendentalists: An Anthology*. Cambridge: Harvard University Press, 1950.

Mills, Stephen F. *The American Landscape*. Edinburgh: Keele University Press, 1997.

Milner, Clyde A., II, ed. *A New Significance: Re-envisioning the History of the American West*. New York: Oxford University Press, 1996.

Möllhausen, Heinrich. *Diary of a Journey from the Mississippi to the Coasts of the Pacific*. 1858; reprint, 2 vols., New York and London: Johnson Reprint Company, 1969.

Moore, Laura. "Bombastic Bamboolas and Boston Brahmans: L. M. Gottschalk and J. S. Dwight and Their Viewpoints on American Music." Master's thesis, Florida State University, 2000.

Morgan, Robert. "Spatial Form in Ives." In *An Ives Celebration*, ed. H. Wiley Hitchcock and Vivian Perlis. Urbana: University of Illinois Press, 1977.

Murchison, Gayle Minetta. "Nationalism in William Grant Still and Aaron Copland between the Wars: Style and Ideology." Ph.D. dissertation, Yale University, 1998.

Nash, Roderick. *Wilderness and the American Mind*. New Haven: Yale University Press, 1967.

Nicholson, Stuart. *Reminiscing in Tempo: A Portrait of Duke Ellington*. Boston: Northeastern University Press, 1999.

Noble, Louis Legrand. *The Life and Works of Thomas Cole*. Ed. Elliot S. Vesell. Hensonville, N.Y.: Black Dome Press, 1997.

Novak, Barbara. *American Painting of the Nineteenth Century: Realism, Idealism, and the American Experience*, 2d ed. Boulder, Colo.: Westview Press, 1979.

———. *Nature and Culture: American Landscape and Painting, 1825–1875*. New York: Oxford University Press, 1995.

Nye, David E. *American Technological Sublime*. Cambridge: MIT Press, 1994.

Oja, Carol J. "The Copland-Sessions Concerts and Their Reception in the Contemporary Press." *Musical Quarterly* 65 (1979): 212–229.

———. "Creating a God: The Reception of Edgard Varèse." Paper presented at the Modernist Studies Association conference, Pennsylvania State University, October 1999.

———. *Making Music Modern*. New York: Oxford University Press, 2000.

Olmsted, Frederick Law. "Notes by Mr. Olmsted." In *Special Report of the Commissioners of the New York State Survey of 1879*. Albany, N.Y.: C. Van Benthuysen, 1880.

Osborn, John W. "The Brand Burners of Cimarron." Beadle's Dime-Store Novels. New York: Beadle and Adams, 1897. (Florida State University Strozier Library, Microfilm 8509, reel 43:31.)

Ouellette, Fernand. *Edgard Varèse.* Trans. Derek Coltman. New York: Orion Press, 1968.

Perkins, Francis D. "Grofé Presents Modern Music in Pool Benefit." *New York Herald Tribune,* 20 January 1937, 12.

Perlis, Vivian. *Charles Ives Remembered: An Oral History.* New Haven: Yale University Press, 1974.

Perna, Dana Paul. *Three Places on Long Island.* New York: Pernaskopy Music, 1998.

Philbrick, Thomas. *St. John de Crèvecoeur.* New York: Twayne Publishers, 1970.

Pierson, William H., Jr. *American Buildings and Their Architects: The Colonial and Neo-Classical Styles.* Garden City, N.Y.: Anchor Press/Doubleday, 1976.

Plumb, Stephen W. *The Streets Where They Lived: A Walking Guide to the Residences of Famous New Yorkers.* St. Paul, Minn.: Marlor Press, 1989.

Pollack, Howard. *Aaron Copland: The Life and Works of an Uncommon Man.* New York: Henry Holt, 1999.

———. "Samuel Barber, Jean Sibelius, and the Making of an American Romantic." *Musical Quarterly* 84, no. 2 (summer 2000): 175–205.

Reich, Steve. *City Life.* London: Hendon Music, Boosey and Hawkes, 1995.

———. *City Life.* New York: Nonesuch CD 79430-2, 1996.

———. *The Desert Music.* London: Boosey and Hawkes, 1984.

———. *New York Counterpoint.* London: Hendon Music, Boosey and Hawkes, 1985.

———. *Vermont Counterpoint.* London: Hendon Music, Boosey and Hawkes, 1982.

———. *Writings on Music, 1965–2000.* New York: Oxford University Press, 2002.

Reis, Claire R. *Composers, Conductors, and Critics.* New York: Oxford University Press, 1955.

Renehan, Edward J., Jr. *The Lion's Pride: Theodore Roosevelt and His Family in Peace and War.* New York: Oxford University Press, 1998.

Reynolds, David S. *Walt Whitman's America: A Cultural Biography.* New York: Vintage Books, 1996.

Ricciotti, Dominic. "City Railways/Modernist Visions." In *The Railroad in American Art: Representations of Technological Change,* ed. Susan Danly and Leo Marx. Cambridge: MIT Press, 1988.

Robertson, James Oliver. *American Myth, American Reality.* New York: Hill and Wang, 1980.

Robinson, Joyce Henri. "'Hi Honey, I'm Home': Weary (Neurasthenic) Businessmen and the Formulation of a Serenely Modern Aesthetic." In *Not at Home: The Suppression of Domesticity in Modern Art and Architecture,* ed. Christopher Reed. London: Thames and Hudson, 1996.

Rogers, Delmer Dalzell. "Nineteenth-Century Music in New York City as Reflected in the Career of George Frederick Bristow." Ph.D. dissertation, University of Michigan, 1967.

Rosenfeld, Paul. *An Hour with American Music.* Philadelphia and London: J. B. Lippincott, 1929.

Ross, Stephanie. *What Gardens Mean.* Chicago: University of Chicago Press, 1998.

Rubinfien, Leo. "The Poetry of Plain Seeing." *Art in America* (December 2000): 74–85, 132–133, 135.

Sadie, Stanley, ed. *The New Grove Dictionary of Music and Musicians.* New York: Grove's Dictionaries of Music, 2001.

Salter, Sumner. "Early Encouragements to American Composers." *Musical Quarterly* 18 (1932): 84–105.

Schama, Simon. *Landscape and Memory.* New York: Vintage Books, 1995.

Schofield, Edmund A., and Robert C. Baron, eds. *Thoreau's World and Ours.* Golden, Colo.: North American Press, 1993.

Schuller, Gunther. *The History of Jazz,* vol. 1, *Early Jazz: Its Roots and Musical Development.* New York: Oxford University Press, 1968.

Schwartz, Elliott, and Barney Childs, eds. *Contemporary Composers on Contemporary Music.* New York: Da Capo Press, 1998.

Schwarz, K. Robert. Liner notes, *Steve Reich, Bang on a Can, New York Counterpoint, Eight Lines, Four Organs.* 1997. Nonesuch 79481-2.

Shaw, Irwin. *Quiet City.* Boston University, Mugar Memorial Library, Special Collections.

Shirley, Wayne. "Central Avenue and Lenox Avenue." Paper presented at conference "A Tribute to William Grant Still," Flagstaff, Arizona, 26 June 1998.

Sinclair, James B. *A Descriptive Catalogue of the Music of Charles Ives.* New Haven: Yale University Press, 1999.

Slonimsky, Nicolas. *Music Since 1900,* 4th ed. New York: Scribner's Sons, 1971.

Smith, Catherine Parsons, ed. *William Grant Still: A Study in Contradictions.* Berkeley and Los Angeles: University of California Press, 2000.

Smith, Henry Nash. *Virgin Land: The American West as Symbol and Myth.* Cambridge: Harvard University Press, 1950.

Smith, Wendy. *Real Life Drama: The Group Theatre and America, 1931–1940.* New York: Alfred A. Knopf, 1990.

Spencer, Jon Michael, ed. *The William Grant Still Reader: Essays on American Music.* Durham, N.C.: Duke University Press, 1992.

Starer, Robert. *Continuo: A Life in Music.* New York: Random House, 1987.

———. *Hudson Valley Suite.* New York: Belwin-Mills, 1983.

Starr, Larry. *A Union of Diversities.* New York: Schirmer Books, 1992.

———. "The Voice of Solitary Contemplation: Copland's *Music for the Theatre* Viewed as a Journey of Self-Discovery." *American Music* 20, no. 3 (fall 2002): 297–315.

Stehman, Dan. *Roy Harris: A Bio-Bibliography.* Westport, Conn: Greenwood Press, 1991.

Stern, Phillip Van Doren, ed. *The Annotated Walden.* New York: Clarkson N. Potter, 1970.

Stewart, Rex. *Jazz Masters of the Thirties.* 1972; reprint, New York: Da Capo, 1982.

Still, Judith Anne, ed. *William Grant Still: An Oral History.* Flagstaff, Ariz.: Master-Player Library, 1998.

Still, Judith Anne, Michael J. Dabrishus, and Carolyn J. Quin. *William Grant Still: A Bio-Bibliography.* Westport, Conn.: Greenwood Press, 1996.

Stratemann, Klaus. *Duke Ellington Day by Day and Film by Film.* Copenhagen, Denmark: JazzMedia, 1992.

Stravinsky, Igor. *Symphony of Psalms for Mixed Chorus and Orchestra.* London: Boosey and Hawkes, 1948.

Strickland, Edward. *American Composers: Dialogues on Contemporary Music.* Bloomington: Indiana University Press, 1991.

———. *Minimalism: Origins.* Bloomington: Indiana University Press, 1993.

Swafford, Jan. *Charles Ives: A Life with Music.* New York: W. W. Norton, 1996

Tawa, Nicholas E. *American Composers and Their Public: A Critical Look.* Metuchen, N.J.: Scarecrow Press, 1995.

———. *From Psalm to Symphony: A History of Music in New England.* Boston: Northeastern University Press, 2001.

———. *High-Minded and Low-Down: Music in the Lives of Americans, 1800–1861.* Boston: Northeastern University Press, 2000.

Taylor, Edward T. *Father Taylor, the Sailor Preacher. Incidents and Anecdotes of Rev. Edward T. Taylor, for Over Forty Years Pastor of the Seaman's Bethel, Boston.* Boston: B. B. Russell, 1872.

Taylor, J. Hillary. "Our Musical Condition." *Negro Musical Journal* 1, no. 7 (March, 1903): 137.

Thayer, Eugene. "The Music of Niagara." *Scribner's Magazine,* February 1881, 583–586.

Thomson, Virgil. *A Virgil Thomson Reader.* New York: E. P. Dutton, 1981.

Thoreau, Henry David. *Faith in a Seed: The Dispersion of Seeds and Other Late Natural History Writings.* Washington, D.C.: Island Press, 1993.

———. *Selected Journals of Henry David Thoreau.* Ed. Carl Bode. New York: Signet, 1967.

———. *Walden.* Ed. J. Lyndon Shanley, introduction by Joyce Carol Oates. Princeton: Princeton University Press, 1971.

Timreck, T. W. *Charles Ives: A Good Dissonance Like a Man.* New York: Metropolitan Museum of Art Home Video Collection, Home Vision 412-9055, 1977.

Tucker, Mark. *Ellington: The Early Years.* Urbana and Chicago: University of Illinois Press, 1995.

Turner, Frederick Jackson. *Rereading Frederick Jackson Turner: The Significance of the Frontier in American History, and Other Essays.* Commentary by John Mack Faragher. New York: Henry Holt, 1994.

Upton, William Treat. *Anthony Phillip Heinrich: A Nineteenth-Century Composer in America.* 1939; reprint, New York: AMS Press, 1967.

———. *William Henry Fry: American Journalist and Composer-Critic.* New York: Crowell, 1954.

Varèse, Edgard. *Amériques.* Rev. and ed. Chou Wen-Chung. New York: Colfranc Music Publishing, 1973.

Varèse, Louise. *A Looking Glass Diary,* vol. 1, *1883–1928.* New York: W. W. Norton, 1972.

Von Glahn, Denise. "Charles Ives, Cowboys, and Indians: Aspects of 'The Other Side of Pioneering.'" *American Music* 19, no. 3 (fall 2001): 291–314.

———. "The Musical Monument of Charles Ives." In *Hope and Glory: Essays on the Legacy of the 54th Massachusetts Regiment,* ed. Martin H. Blatt, Thomas J. Brown, and Donald Yacovone. Amherst: University of Massachusetts Press, 2001.

——— [Cooney]. "New Sources for 'The St. Gaudens' in Boston Common (Colonel Robert Gould Shaw and His Colored Regiment)." *Musical Quarterly* 81, no. 1 (spring 1997): 13–50.

——— [Cooney]. "Reconciliations: Time, Space, and the American Place in the Music of Charles Ives." Ph.D. dissertation, University of Washington, 1995.

——— [Cooney]. "A Sense of Place: Charles Ives and 'Putnam's Camp, Redding, Connecticut.'" *American Music* 14, no. 3 (fall 1996): 276–312.

Whitman, Walt. *Complete Poetry and Collected Prose.* New York: Literary Classics of the United States, 1982.

———. *Poetry and Prose.* New York: Literary Classics of the United States, 1982.

Williams, William Carlos. *Asphodel, That Greeny Flower, and Other Love Poems.* New York: New Directions, 1994.

———. *I Wanted to Write a Poem: The Autobiography of the Works of a Poet.* New York: New Directions, 1978.

———. *Selected Poems.* Ed. Charles Tomlinson. New York: New Directions, 1985.

Worster, Donald. *Under Western Skies: Nature and History in the American West.* New York: Oxford University Press, 1992.

Yeiser, Frederick. "Blue Grass." *Cincinnati Enquirer,* 22 March 1936.

Zeaman, John. "Birth of the Box-Office Blockbuster." Bergen County *Record,* 5 February 1999.

Zwilich, Ellen Taaffe. *Symphony No. 4 ("The Gardens") for Orchestra, with Mixed Chorus and Children's Chorus.* Bryn Mawr, Pa.: Theodore Presser, 2000.

———. *Symphony No. 4 ("The Gardens") for Orchestra, with Mixed Chorus and Children's Chorus.* Composer's liner notes Koch International Classics CD 3-74877-2 HL.

INDEX